The Linux+™ Cram Sheet

This Cram Sheet contains the distilled key facts about the CompTIA Linux+ exam. Review this information last thing before entering the test room, paying special attention to those areas where you feel you need the most review. You can transfer any of the facts onto a blank piece of paper before beginning the exam.

PLANNING THE IMPLEMENTATION

1. There are several important Linux services:
   - *Apache*—Provides a Web server for users on a LAN or the Internet.
   - *Squid*—Allows proxy or caching service for users on a LAN.
   - *BIND*—Creates a database of domain names and IP addresses. Also known as DNS or a nameserver.
   - *Firewall*—Regulates traffic to and from a network, with utilities such as **ipchains** or **iptables**. (Can also act as a proxy service.)
   - *Sendmail*—Creates a mail server.
   - *NFS*—Network File System. For communication between Unix-based computers, including Linux.
   - *NIS*—Network Information System. Configures a common database of usernames and passwords on a LAN.
   - *Samba*—Sets up communication between Linux and Microsoft operating systems. Also known as the Common Internet File System (CIFS).
2. A caching service fulfills requests for Web pages, etc., that would otherwise have to be transmitted to the Internet.
3. A proxy service represents other computers on a LAN on the Internet.
4. All you need for Linux is a 386 CPU and a floppy drive. For some services, such as a router, a gateway, or an X Window terminal, no hard drive is required.

5. Kernels are numbered in *major.minor.patch* format.
6. While **iptables** was developed for kernel 2.4, **ipchains** is still in common use.

INSTALLATION REQUIREMENTS

7. Network installation of multiple computers normally requires NFS.
8. The log file most closely related to installation is /var/log/messages.
9. Try critical applications on test computers first.
10. Files with the .tgz or .tar.gz extensions are compressed archives.
11. To archive and compress files in the */example* directory, use **tar -xvf** */example* and **gzip example.tar**. Alternatively, **tar -xzvf** */example* also archives and compresses.
12. As **root**, you can install, upgrade, or uninstall a **rpm** package as follows:
    - *Install*—**rpm -i** *package*.**rpm**
    - *Upgrade*—**rpm -U** *package*.**rpm**
    - *Uninstall*—**rpm -e** *package*
13. The most common partition scheme includes a root (/) and a swap partition. A swap file can be substituted for a swap partition. Other partitions are commonly used /boot, /home, and /var.
14. X Window installation requires a practical minimum 32MB of RAM.
15. KDE/GNOME can be installed on a terminal; all you need is a video controller. A hard drive is not required.

86. Stop a running daemon such as **httpd** with **kill 'cat /var/run/httpd.pid'**, or substitute the actual PID. **kill -1 *PID*** or **kill -HUP *PID*** restarts a process. **kill -9 *PID*** stops a process immediately, leaving temporary files behind.

87. Stop a running process with the **killall *processname*** command.

88. Program priorities range from −20 (highest) to 19 (lowest). Start *program1* with a high priority with a command like **nice -n -10 *program1***. Raise the priority of a currently running program with a command like **renice -10 *program1***.

89. Several **shutdown** commands are available. **shutdown -h +15** halts Linux in 15 minutes. **shutdown -r now** reboots Linux immediately. Related commands include **halt**, **reboot**, and **poweroff**.

90. The PC reset button is the absolute last resort. Data in RAM that you thought you saved is lost. Hard drive inodes can be misaligned, which can damage more data.

91. If you forget the **root** password, start single user mode. Then reset the **root** password with the **passwd** command.

92. If you see only LI where you should see LILO boot:, the secondary boot loader (/boot/boot.b) may be missing.

93. To restore LILO, boot Linux with a rescue disk, then run **/sbin/lilo**.

94. To bypass a graphical login, use the **Ctrl+Alt+F1** command for a command-line login.

HARDWARE CONFIGURATION

95. If your computer beeps more than once and does not boot when powered on, you may have a CPU or RAM problem.

96. Overclocked CPUs can lead to excessive heat and intermittent crashes.

97. Detected hardware is listed in the /proc directory; e.g., detected CPU information is stored in /proc/cpuinfo.

98. If the floppy indicator light stays on and the drive does not work, the controller cable is probably installed upside down.

99. IDE devices are based on a standard known as ATA or ATAPI.

100. Avoid installing a hard drive and CD drive on the same IDE controller. When the CD drive is in use,

hard drive data transfer speed may be limited.

101. CMOS settings determine where the computer looks first for an operating system.

102. Reserve legacy hardware channels in CMOS.

103. A dead computer battery can erase CMOS settings and the BIOS password.

104. **append** can be used to set the IRQ, I/O, or DMA of a device in /etc/lilo.conf.

105. Regular SCSI connectors have 50-pins; Wide SCSI connectors have 68-pins.

106. A SCSI terminator is required at the end of a daisy-chain of SCSI devices.

107. Memorize the following COM port information:
    - COM1, IRQ4, I/O 03f8
    - COM2, IRQ3, I/O 02f8
    - COM3, IRQ4, I/O 03e8
    - COM4, IRQ3, I/O 02e8

108. Memorize this printer port information: LPT1=IRQ7; LPT2=IRQ5.

109. Current print cables accommodate bidirectional communication. They conform to EPP (enhanced parallel port) or ECP (enhanced capabilities port) standards.

110. BNC connectors are used for Ethernet Thinnet networks; RJ-45 connectors are used for Ethernet twisted-pair networks.

111. MAC addresses are also known as *hardware addresses*, which are in hexadecimal notation and look like 00-11-c5-65-3e-d5.

112. **arp** associates network card hardware (MAC) and IP addresses (IPv4 or IPv6).

113. Many software and PCI modems are "winmodems," which are difficult and sometimes impossible to configure in Linux.

114. Reserve the IRQs, I/Os, and DMAs required for legacy hardware in CMOS, to prevent their use by plug-and-play hardware.

115. Linux kernel 2.4 *partially* supports "hot-swap" requirements of PCMCIA, USB, and IEEE 1394 devices. Occasionally, a reboot may help detect a newer device.

116. If loadable modules are enabled, the associated driver might be installed or removed automatically while Linux is running. Alternatively, use **modprobe**, **insmod**, or **rmmod**.

CORIOLIS™
Certification Insider Press

16. There are several key Linux configuration files:
    - */etc/inittab*—Run levels, login screen, reboot modes
    - */etc/fstab*—Default mounts for each partition
    - */etc/lilo.conf*—The Linux Loader (LILO)
    - */etc/syslog.conf*—Organizes Linux configuration files
    - */etc/httpd/httpd.conf*—Apache configuration
    - *~/.bashrc, /etc/profile*—bash configuration files
    - */etc/services*—TCP/IP port numbers
    - */etc/inetd.conf or /etc/xinetd.d*—Allows TCP/IP services
    - */etc/crontab*—**crond** daemon configuration

17. In /etc/inittab, to change the login screen, change *x* in the **id:*x*:initdefault** line. Typically, *x*=3 sets up a command-line login; *x*=5 sets up a GUI login.

18. Apache Web server configuration files are located in the directory defined by the **DocumentRoot** variable, as configured in httpd.conf.

19. The **tcp_wrappers** package is required for regulating traffic through a firewall using the /etc/hosts.allow and the /etc/hosts.deny files.

20. /etc/hosts.allow and /etc/hosts.deny contain IP address filtering information; e.g., **192.168.0.0** in /etc/hosts.allow permits messages from computers with that network IP address. **ALL:ALL** in /etc/hosts.deny stops all traffic.

21. IPv4 addresses include 32 bits; IPv6 addresses include 128 bits.

22. To use a DHCP server on a remote network, the BOOTP protocol is required.

23. Test a DHCP server with **/sbin/dhcpcd -r**. On Red Hat Linux, use **/sbin/pump -r**. The command should be part of the **/sbin/ifup** script.

24. **nslookup** can test a DNS server.

25. **pppd** is most closely associated with a modem connection.

26. **ypbind** ensures that NIS clients are bound to a NIS server.

27. Volumes formatted to the ext2 and ReiserFS file systems are resizeable.

28. There are several basic Linux newsreaders, including **tin** and **trn**.

29. **xf86config** can configure the X Window through /etc/X11/XF86Config. Related tools include **XFree86 -configure**, **SuperProbe**, and **XF86Setup**. **XFree86** can be found in the /usr/X11R6/bin directory.

30. The Red Hat X Window configuration tool is **Xconfigurator**.

31. After you add a user with **useradd**, you still need to assign a password.

32. New users get default files from the /etc/skel directory.

33. If you know the **root** password, run **root** commands with **su -c "*command*"**.

34. If you're authorized in /etc/sudoers, run **root** commands with **sudo *command***.

35. Know the types of files associated with the following directories:
    - */*—The top level directory
    - */bin*—Basic command-line utilities
    - */boot*—Boot files
    - */dev*—Device drivers
    - */etc*—Basic configuration files
    - */proc*—Current processes and resource allocations
    - */sbin*—System administrative commands
    - */var*—Log files and print spools

36. The dot (.) represents the current directory. The double-dot (..) represents the parent of the current directory.

37. To supersede a setting in /etc/fstab, specify the file system; e.g., **mount -t vfat /dev/fd0 /mnt/floppy**.

38. Know basic commands:
    - *copying, moving, removing, and linking a file*—**cp, mv, rm, ln**
    - *creating and deleting a directory*—**mkdir, rmdir**
    - *listing files*—**ls**
    - *identifying and changing directories*—**pwd, cd**

39. Use **ln** to point to the active version of an application.

40. **man -k *topic1*** returns a list of commands with "topic1" in its man page title.

41. Use the absolute path when using **tar** to back up key directories.

42. If you use the relative path when using **tar** for backups, navigate to the same directory to restore files to the original locations.

43. Direct data in a file as standard input to a program with ***program* < *data***.

44. Direct the standard output from a command to a file; e.g.: **ls > *file***.

45. Combine redirection arrows and pipes. For example:
    - **program1 < *data* | program2**—*data* is processed by program1; the result is standard input to program2.

- **program3 < *data* > output**—*data* is processed by program3; the result is standard input to the output file.

46. The ampersand (**&**) at the end of a command runs that command in the background; the bash shell then takes you to another prompt.

47. **root** can use the **init 1** command to start single user mode. Alternatively, reboot Linux and type **linux single** at the LILO boot: prompt.

48. You can add short user login messages to /etc/motd.

SYSTEM MAINTENANCE

49. The best documentation is kept in a local, readily available physical file.

50. Memorize the fields in an /etc/crontab entry. From left to right: minute, hour, day, month, day of week.

51. **logrotate** can be used to rotate and/or delete logs periodically; usually documented in /etc/crontab.

52. Find the differences between two text files with **diff**.

53. Find text strings in a file with **grep** *"string" filename*.

54. **grep** is commonly used as a *filter* for a long list of data.

55. **dmesg** lists detected hardware.

56. Watch for files owned by **root** on each individual user's directory. If the SUID or SGID bit is set on any of these files, a cracker can access it from any account.

57. Memorize /etc/passwd entries. From left to right: username, password, UID, GID, user information, home directory, default shell.

58. Deactivate an account by replacing the password entry in /etc/passwd with an asterisk (*).

59. Use **groupadd** to add a new group. Open /etc/group to add more members.

60. Each /etc/group entry includes from left to right: group name, group password, GID, and the usernames of all members of the group.

61. **pwconv** and **grpconv** convert /etc/passwd and /etc/group to Shadow Password Suite files /etc/shadow and /etc/gshadow. **pwunconv**, **grpunconv** reverse the process.

62. New file default permissions are based on **umask**. For example, if **umask**=023, the default permissions for newly created files are 754 (=777−023), which corresponds to **rwx** permissions for the owner, **rx** permissions for the group, and **r** permission for other users.

63. **chmod u+s** *program* activates the SUID bit for full access for all users.

64. **chmod g+s** *program* activates the SGID bit for access equal to the group owner.

65. When you set the immutable flag with **chattr +i** *file*, even **root** can't delete it.

66. Use **15G** to get to line 15. Alternatively, **G** goes to the last line of the file.

67. To run a shell command in **vi**, type **:!**, followed by the actual command.

68. In **vi**, display line numbers with **:set nu**.

69. Any user can use **ls ~** to list the files in her home directory.

70. **fsck** can fix misaligned inodes.

71. **resize2fs** can resize partitions formatted to ext2.

72. Unused TCP/IP port numbers in /etc/services can be reassigned to other services such as HTTP, FTP, or POP.

73. **ifconfig**, **ifup**, and **ifdown** activates and deactivates network interfaces. For example, **ifconfig eth0 up** activates network card eth0.

74. **ifconfig eth0 irq 12 io_addr 0x300** assigns IRQ 12 and I/O 0x300 to eth0.

75. **ifconfig eth1 10.11.12.14 netmask 255.0.0.0** assigns the given IP address and network mask.

TROUBLESHOOTING

76. Commands such as **ATDT** (ATtention, Dial Touch-tone) and **ATDP** (ATtention, Dial Pulse) check connections in modem utilities such as **minicom**.

77. Radius servers are modem authentication servers that verify usernames and passwords. Reboot Radius if you have authentication problems.

78. One Denial of Service (DoS) attack includes a script that calls but does not complete the connection. The resulting traffic keeps the Web server so busy that regular users can't connect.

79. On **telnet**, **TERM=vt100** sets terminal emulation to a system suitable for a remote connection.

80. For network problems, check physical connections first. Then use **ping** and **traceroute** to check the logical connections.

81. If Web access works and mail does not (or vice versa), check allowed services on the firewall, the proxy server, and /etc/inetd.conf or /etc/xinetd.d.

82. **route -n** and **netstat -n** returns a routing table with IP addresses. Since this does not require access to a DNS server, it does not load the network.

83. Modify routing tables with the **route** (not the **netstat**) command.

84. An **rpm** "Permission denied" error message may be caused by trying to run **rpm** as a regular (not **root**) user.

85. Use **ps aux** to find a process's PID and %CPU usage.

Linux+™

Michael Jang

Linux+™ Exam Cram

Copyright ©2002 The Coriolis Group. All rights reserved.

Limits of Liability and Disclaimer of Warranty

The author and publisher of this book have used their best efforts in preparing the book and the programs contained in it. These efforts include the development, research, and testing of the theories and programs to determine their effectiveness. The author and publisher make no warranty of any kind, expressed or implied, with regard to these programs or the documentation contained in this book.

The author and publisher shall not be liable in the event of incidental or consequential damages in connection with, or arising out of, the furnishing, performance, or use of the programs, associated instructions, and/or claims of productivity gains.

Trademarks

Trademarked names appear throughout this book. Rather than list the names and entities that own the trademarks or insert a trademark symbol with each mention of the trademarked name, the publisher states that it is using the names for editorial purposes only and to the benefit of the trademark owner, with no intention of infringing upon that trademark.

The Coriolis Group, LLC
14455 N. Hayden Road
Suite 220
Scottsdale, Arizona 85260

(480)483-0192
FAX (480)483-0193
www.coriolis.com

Library of Congress Cataloging-in-Publication Data
Jang, Michael H.
    Linux+ / by Michael Jang.
      p. cm. -- (Exam cram)
    ISBN 1-58880-194-2
    1. Linux. 2. Operating systems (Computers) I. Title. II. Series.

QA76.76.O63 J37   2001
005.4'32--dc21

                       2001053647
                       CIP

QA76.76
.063
J37
2002

Printed in the United States of America
10 9 8 7 6 5 4 3 2 1

1 1588801942

CORIOLIS™

President and CEO
Roland Elgey

Publisher
Al Valvano

Associate Publisher
Katherine R. Hartlove

Acquisitions Editor
Sharon Linsenbach

Product Marketing Manager
Jeff Johnson

Project Editor
Sally M. Scott

Technical Reviewer
Elizabeth Zinkann

Production Coordinator
Todd Halvorsen

Cover Designer
Laura Wellander

The Coriolis Group, LLC • 14455 North Hayden Road, Suite 220 • Scottsdale, Arizona 85260

A Note from Coriolis

Our goal has always been to provide you with the best study tools on the planet to help you achieve your certification in record time. Time is so valuable these days that none of us can afford to waste a second of it, especially when it comes to exam preparation.

Over the past few years, we've created an extensive line of *Exam Cram* and *Exam Prep* study guides, practice exams, and interactive training. To help you study even better, we have now created an e-learning and certification destination called **ExamCram.com**. (You can access the site at **www.examcram.com**.) Now, with every study product you purchase from us, you'll be connected to a large community of people like yourself who are actively studying for their certifications, developing their careers, seeking advice, and sharing their insights and stories.

We believe that the future is all about collaborative learning. Our **ExamCram.com** destination is our approach to creating a highly interactive, easily accessible collaborative environment, where you can take practice exams and discuss your experiences with others, sign up for features like "Questions of the Day," plan your certifications using our interactive planners, create your own personal study pages, and keep up with all of the latest study tips and techniques.

We hope that whatever study products you purchase from us—*Exam Cram* or *Exam Prep* study guides, *Personal Trainers, Personal Test Centers*, or one of our interactive Web courses—will make your studying fun and productive. Our commitment is to build the kind of learning tools that will allow you to study the way you want to, whenever you want to.

Visit ExamCram.com now to enhance your study program.

Help us continue to provide the very best certification study materials possible. Write us or email us at **learn@examcram.com** and let us know how our study products have helped you study. Tell us about new features that you'd like us to add. Send us a story about how we've helped you. We're listening!

Good luck with your certification exam and your career. Thank you for allowing us to help you achieve your goals.

ExamCram.com Connects You to the Ultimate Study Center!

Look for these related products from The Coriolis Group:

Linux Core Kernel Commentary, 2nd Edition
by Scott Maxwell

Open Source Development with CVS, 2nd Edition
by Moshe Bar and Karl Fogel

Server+ Exam Prep
by Drew Bird and Mike Harwood

A+ Practice Tests Exam Cram, Second Edition
by Mike Pastore

Also recently published by Coriolis Certification Insider Press:

MCSE ISA Server 2000 Exam Cram
by Diana Bartley and Gregory Smith

Oracle 8i DBA: Performance Tuning Exam Cram
by Zulfiqer Habeeb

CISSP Exam Cram
by Mandy Andress

CCSA Exam Cram
by Tony Piltzecker

Server+ Exam Cram
by Deborah Haralson and Jeff Haralson

Remember the victims of September 11, 2001.
In these difficult times, if we are tempted to sacrifice our civil liberties,
we should remember the words used by Benjamin Franklin in 1759:

"They that can give up essential liberty
to obtain a little temporary safety
deserve neither liberty nor safety."

About the Author

Michael Jang (LCP, MCSE) is currently a full-time writer on Linux and Microsoft operating systems. His experience with computers goes back to the days of jumbled punch cards. His recent work includes *Sair Linux/GNU Installation and Configuration Exam Cram* (Coriolis, 2001); *Mastering Linux, Second Edition* (Sybex, 2001); and *Linux Networking Clearly Explained* (Morgan-Kaufmann, 2001). Michael has also written *Windows 98 Exam Prep* (Coriolis, 1999) as well as *A Guide to Microsoft Windows 98* (Course Technology, 1998). In addition, he has served as Technical Editor for several Microsoft Help Desk books, including Windows NT Workstation 4, Windows 98, and Office 2000.

In his previous life as a Boeing Engineer, Michael worked on a variety of jobs, including working as a project manager for the first FAA type certified In-Seat Video systems.

Acknowledgments

Many dedicated people helped create this book. Sharon Linsenbach, Acquisitions Editor, moved quickly to organize a fabulous team. Elizabeth Zinkann, Technical Editor, made sure everything worked. With her years of Unix experience, she helped make this book useful for the widest possible audience. Sally Scott, Project Editor, gave me all the time that I needed to get the book right, while keeping production on schedule. I'd also like to thank Gene Redding, Copyeditor, for his exacting grammatical standards. I'd also like to express my appreciation to Todd Halvorsen, Production Coordinator; Laura Wellander, Cover Designer; and Jeff Johnson, Product Marketing Manager, for putting everything together.

The tragedies of September 11, 2001, happened while this book was in progress. Everyone on the team did a marvelous job to make sure everything kept moving despite our sorrow.

Thank you, Nancy, for all your love and support. And thanks to the bears from Momma Bears' Bears, who surround me and make my workspace much more pleasant.

Finally, thanks to the Linux community of developers, who, with their selfless devotion to better software, are proving that a community can compete effectively with a monopoly.

—*Michael Jang*

Contents at a Glance

Table of Contents

Chapter 6
Package Installation and Configuration 105

Chapter 13
Linux Maintenance 267

Introduction

Welcome to *Linux+ Exam Cram!* The purpose of this book is to get you ready to take—and pass—the CompTIA Linux+ certification exam. In the following pages, I've outlined the CompTIA Linux+ certification in general, and I talk about how this *Exam Cram* can optimize your knowledge of Linux and help you focus on critical exam topics.

This book is aimed strictly at exam preparation and review. It will *not* teach you everything you need to know about a topic. Instead, it will present and dissect the question topics that you're probably going to see on the exam. I've drawn on material from CompTIA's own listing of requirements, from preparation guides for similar exams, and from the exams themselves. My aim is to bring together as much information as possible about the Linux+ certification exam.

My explicit purpose in writing this book is to stuff as many facts and technical answers about Linux as possible into your brain before you begin the test. The Linux+ exam makes a basic assumption that you already have a *solid* background of experience with Linux and PC hardware. On the other hand, I think that Linux is changing so fast that no one can be a total expert. I believe this book is the most up-to-date analysis of the Linux+ exam on the market.

Depending on your experience with PCs, I recommend that you begin your studies with some classroom training or that you visit the CompTIA Web site (**www.comptia.org**) for a definition of what it means to be Linux+ certified. I *strongly* recommend that you install, configure, and generally "fool around" with the Linux operating system environment that you'll be tested on. Nothing beats hands-on experience and familiarity when it comes to understanding the questions you're likely to encounter. Book learning is essential, but hands-on experience is the best teacher of all!

 While there are several dozen Linux distributions available, the Linux+ exam has a slight bias towards the Red Hat and allied distributions such as Mandrake. Several exam topics such as **rpm** package management, system administration tools, and rescue disk creation require knowledge of Red Hat tools and methods.

Perhaps a quick way for you to decide where you stand in relation to the current certification process is to turn to the end of the book and examine the Sample Test (Chapter 15). This is a highly accurate representation of both the test format and the types of questions you will encounter.

The New Linux+ Certification Program

The Linux+ Certification Program was started in September 2001 as a distribution-neutral certification program for Linux users with six months of experience. On their Web site (**www.comptia.org**), CompTIA has stated that Linux+ certification is suitable for the following types of job roles:

➤ Entry-level helpdesk

➤ Technical sales/marketing

➤ Entry-level service technician

➤ Technical writers

➤ Resellers

➤ Application developers

➤ Application customer service representatives

Linux+ Exam Scoring

There are 95 questions on the CompTIA Linux+ exam. All questions are multiple-choice, with one correct answer. Grading is based on the first 94 questions. You need to answer at least 69 percent of the questions correctly to pass; this translates to 65 correct questions. On the CompTIA scale, this corresponds to a passing score of 655 on a scale of 100 to 900.

 The 95th question asks you to give CompTIA permission to use your name, if you pass, in their database of certified professionals. You may decline to give CompTIA this permission, or you may choose not to answer the question. It does not affect your score.

Taking a Certification Exam

Unfortunately, testing isn't free. You'll be charged between $140 and $200 for each test you take, whether you pass or fail. The price you pay depends on whether you're a member of CompTIA and whether you're taking the exam in the United States. If you fail, you can pay to take the test again immediately; if you fail a second (or greater) time, you need to wait 30 days between exams. Since you're taking the time to prepare, however, think positively. You've selected the best Linux+ test preparation book on the market.

The U.S. and Canadian tests are administered by Prometric/Thomson Learning (formally known as Sylvan Prometric) and VUE. Prometric can be reached in the United States and Canada at 1-800-895-3926 or **www.2test.com**. VUE can be reached at 1-952-995-8800 or **www.vue.com**.

To schedule an exam, you must call at least one day in advance. To cancel or reschedule an exam, you should call at least one business day before the scheduled test time, or you may be charged. The actual rules vary by testing service and local testing center. When calling either service, please have the following information ready for the sales representative who handles your call:

➤ Your name, organization, and mailing address.

➤ Your ID for Prometric/Thomson Learning or VUE. While this is normally a U.S. Social Security Number, you can request a different number.

➤ The name and number of the exam(s) you wish to take (Linux+, exam number XK0-001).

➤ A method of payment.

The most convenient payment method is to provide a valid credit card number with sufficient available credit. Otherwise, payments by check, money order, or purchase order (PO) must be *received* before a test can be scheduled. If you choose one of these latter methods, ask your sales representative for more details.

Keep in mind that if you choose to pay for your exam by a method that involves the postal service and banking system (i.e., check, PO, and so on), you'll have to call to schedule your exam much earlier than one day in advance.

Arriving at the Exam Site

On the day of your exam, try to arrive at least 15 minutes before the scheduled time slot. You must bring *two* forms of identification, one of which *must* be a photo ID. Both forms of ID *must* include your signature. Typically, a driver's license and credit card are valid forms of identification. Insurance cards, birth certificates, state ID cards, employee identification cards, or any other legal identification can often also be used. An American Social Security card is usually *not* an acceptable form of ID. If you're not sure whether your identification is acceptable, or if you have a question on any other security procedure, call the test site where you're scheduling your exam.

You will be given a user ID code as an identification number for your test, which you enter into the computer at the time you begin your exam(s). The exam is fully computer based, and it is all multiple choice. While ordinarily your ID number is the same as your Social Security number, you may be able to request a different number when you register with Prometric/Thomson Learning or VUE. Your ID number will be used to track your session.

The Linux+ exam includes a two-hour time limit. If you plan to bring food or coffee into the exam room, call ahead. Each testing center has its own security regulations. Some centers even inspect the contents of your pockets. You might have to leave food, coffee, and/or personal items such as backpacks or purses outside the testing room or the testing center.

In the Exam Room

All exams are completely closed-book. In fact, you will normally not be permitted to take anything with you into the testing area other than a blank sheet of paper and a pencil provided by the exam proctors. We suggest that you *immediately write down the most critical information* about the test you're taking on the blank sheet of paper you're given. *Exam Cram* books provide a brief reference that lists essential information from the book in distilled form. This reference is The Cram Sheet, a tear-out card located in the front of the book. You need to master this information (by brute force, if necessary) so you can dump the information out of your head onto a blank sheet of paper before answering any exam questions. You need to remember the information only long enough to write it down when you walk into the test room. (You're required to turn in this sheet at the end of the exam.) You might even want to look at The Cram Sheet in the car or in the lobby of the testing center just before you walk in to take the exam.

Each question offers you an opportunity to mark that question for review. We strongly suggest that you mark any questions about which you have any shade of doubt. Each exam gives you an ample amount of time to complete the questions; by marking questions for review, you can go back without the pressure of worrying whether you'll have time to complete the whole exam.

How long you take to answer each question is not factored into scoring your test. Your answers can be changed at any time before you terminate the session, and the review option is not tracked for scoring. Many terms and words are easy to mix up, so take the time to review your work.

When you complete the exam, the software will tell you whether you've passed or failed. Even if you fail, I suggest that you ask for (and keep) a detailed report. You can use the report to help you prepare for another go-round, if necessary. As stated earlier, if you do not pass a CompTIA exam the first time, you can retake it at any time. If you do not pass a CompTIA exam a second time, you must wait 30 days before you can retake that exam. If you pass a CompTIA exam, you can retake it one year later. If you need to retake an exam, you must call one of the testing services, schedule a new test date, and pay another fee (about $190) per exam.

Certification

When you've passed the Linux+ exam, you will be Linux+ certified for life. It's a good idea to save the test results you are given at the conclusion of the test, because they are your immediate proof. Official certification normally takes anywhere from four to six weeks, so don't expect to get your credentials overnight. When the package arrives, it will include a Welcome Kit, an ID card, and a certificate (suitable for framing).

As an official recognition of hard work and broad-based knowledge, Linux+ certification is also a badge of honor. Many organizations view certification as a necessary foundation for a career in the information technology (IT) industry.

How to Prepare for an Exam

Preparing for any Linux exam requires that you obtain and study materials designed to provide comprehensive information about the specific exam for which you are preparing. The following list of materials will help you study and prepare:

➤ Online documentation found on the CompTIA Web site.

➤ The Linux Documentation Project (online resource found at **www.linuxdoc.org**)

You'll find that this book will complement your studying and preparation for the exam, either on your own or with the aid of the previously mentioned study programs. In the section that follows, I'll explain how this book works and why this book counts as a member of the required and recommended materials list.

In the past, candidates have used many individual reference books that, taken together, cover most of the required material on the exam. A good professional should always have a solid reference library as a matter of course. See the "Need to Know More?" sections at the end of each chapter for my lists of recommended references.

In addition, you'll probably find any or all of the following materials useful in your quest for Linux+ expertise:

➤ *Study guides*—The Coriolis Group certification series includes the following:

   ➤ *The Exam Cram series*—These books give you information about the material you need to know to pass the tests.

➤ *The Exam Prep series*—These books provide a greater level of detail than the *Exam Cram* books and are designed to teach you everything you need to know from an exam perspective. Each book comes with a CD that contains interactive practice exams in a variety of testing formats.

Together, the two series make a perfect pair.

➤ *Multimedia*—These Coriolis Group materials are designed to support learners of all types—whether you learn best by reading or doing:

➤ *The Exam Cram Personal Trainer*—Offers a unique, personalized self-paced training course based on the exam.

➤ *The Exam Cram Personal Test Center*—Features multiple test options that simulate the actual exam, including Fixed-Length, Random, Review, and Test All. Explanations of correct and incorrect answers reinforce concepts learned.

About This Book

Each *Exam Cram* chapter follows a regular structure, along with graphical cues about especially important or useful material. The structure of a typical chapter includes:

➤ *Opening hotlists*—Each chapter begins with lists of the terms you'll need to understand and the concepts you'll need to master before you can be fully conversant with the chapter's subject matter. We follow the hotlists with a few introductory paragraphs to set the stage for the rest of the chapter.

➤ *Topical coverage*—After the opening hotlists, each chapter covers a series of topics related to the chapter's subject title. Throughout these sections, I highlight topics or concepts likely to appear on the exam by using a special Exam Alert layout that looks like this:

 This is what an Exam Alert looks like. An Exam Alert stresses concepts, terms, software, or activities that will most likely appear in one or more certification exam questions. For that reason, I think any information found offset in Exam Alert format is worthy of unusual attentiveness on your part.

Even if material isn't flagged as an Exam Alert, *all* the content in this book is associated in some way to something test related. The book is focused on high-speed test preparation; you'll find that what appears in the meat of each chapter is critical knowledge.

➤ *Notes*—Notes throughout the text dip into nearly every aspect of working with and configuring Linux. Where a body of knowledge is far deeper than the scope of the book, I use Notes to indicate areas of concern or specialty training.

Note: Cramming for an exam will get you through a test, but it won't make you a competent IT professional. Although you can memorize just the facts you need to become certified, your daily work in the IT field will rapidly put you in water over your head if you don't know the underlying principles of computers.

➤ *Tips*—I provide tips that will help you build a solid foundation of knowledge. Although the information may not be on the exam, it is highly relevant and will help you become a better test-taker.

 This is how tips are formatted. Here's an example of a tip: While there are a number of solid GUI administrative tools available for Linux, most Linux administrators rely on the command-line interface to manage their systems.

➤ *Practice questions*—This section presents a series of mock test questions and explanations of both correct and incorrect answers. Each chapter has a number of practice questions that highlight the areas I found to be most important on the exam.

➤ *Details and resources*—Every chapter ends with a section titled "Need to Know More?" This section provides direct pointers to resources that offer further details on the chapter's subject matter. In addition, this section tries to rate the quality and thoroughness of each topic's coverage. If you find a resource you like in this collection, use it, but don't feel compelled to use all these resources. On the other hand, I recommend only resources that I have used on a regular basis, so none of the recommendations will be a waste of your time or money.

The bulk of the book follows this chapter structure, but there are a few other elements that I would like to point out:

➤ *Sample Test and Answer Key*—A close approximation of the Linux+ exam is found in Chapter 15. Chapter 16 presents the answers to the sample test, as well as explanations of the correct and incorrect answers.

➤ *Glossary*—An extensive glossary of terms and acronyms.

➤ *The Cram Sheet*—A tear-out card inside the front cover of this *Exam Cram* book, this is a valuable tool that represents a condensed and compiled collection of facts and numbers that I think you should memorize before taking the test.

Using This Book

If you're preparing for the Linux+ certification exam for the first time, I've structured the topics in this book to build upon one another. Therefore, the topics covered in later chapters will make more sense after you've read earlier chapters. In my opinion, many computer manuals and reference books are essentially a list of facts. Rather than simply list raw facts about each topic on the exam, I've tried to paint an integrated landscape in your imagination, where each topic and exam fact takes on a landmark status.

I suggest you read this book from front to back for your initial test preparation. You won't be wasting your time, because everything I've written pertains to the exam. If you need to brush up on a topic or you have to bone up for a second try, use the index or Table of Contents to go straight to the topics and questions you need to study. After taking the tests, I think you'll find this book useful as a tightly focused reference and an essential foundation of Linux knowledge.

I've tried to create a real-world tool that you can use to prepare for and pass the Linux+ exam. I am definitely interested in any feedback you would care to share about the book, especially if you have ideas about how I can improve it for future test-takers.

I would like to know if you found this book to be helpful in your preparation efforts. I'd also like to know how you felt about your chances of passing the exam *before* you read the book and then *after* you read the book. Of course, I'd love to hear that you passed the exam; even if you just want to share your triumph, I'd be happy to hear from you.

Send your questions or comments to Coriolis at **learn@examcram.com**. Please remember to include the title of the book in your message. Also, be sure to check out the Web pages at **www.examcram.com**, where you'll find information updates, commentary, and certification information.

Thanks for choosing Coriolis as your personal trainers, and enjoy the book!

Self-Assessment

I'm including a Self-Assessment in this *Exam Cram* book to help you evaluate your readiness to tackle the CompTIA Linux+ certification. Before you tackle this Self-Assessment, however, let's talk about concerns you may face when pursuing the Linux+ certification and what an ideal candidate might look like.

CompTIA Linux Certified Professionals in the Real World

In the next section, I describe an ideal Linux+–certified candidate. Many people may see these tests as a great starting point for gaining the basic Linux knowledge that can be used for advanced Linux skills and certifications such as those from Sair, LPI (Linux Professional Institute), and Red Hat.

Many people are already certified, so it's obviously an attainable goal. You can get all the real-world motivation you need from knowing that many others have gone before, so you'll be able to follow in their footsteps. If you're willing to tackle the process seriously and do what it takes to obtain the necessary experience and knowledge, you can pass the Linux+ exam. In fact, *Exam Crams*, and the companion *Exam Preps*, are designed to make it as easy as possible for you to prepare for certification exams. But prepare you must!

The same, of course, is true for other related certifications, including the following:

➤ CompTIA's A+ certification is the nationally recognized credential for hardware technicians in the computer industry, and the A+ hardware exam is the basis for a surprising number of questions on the Linux+ exam. More information on the A+ hardware exam is available at **www.comptia.org**.

➤ Sair GNU/Linux's certifications include some of the major mid-level Linux certifications in the industry, for users with at least two years of experience. More information on Sair's exams is available at **www.linuxcertification.org**.

➤ LPI's certifications include the other major mid-level Linux certifications in the industry, also for users with at least two years of experience. More information on LPI's exams is available at **www.lpi.org**.

➤ The Red Hat Certified Engineer is perhaps the elite certification in Linux, as it consists of mostly practical hands-on problem solving exercises, with a minimum of multiple-choice questions. The ability to pass this exam is associated with users with several years of experience. More information on Red Hat's exams is available at **www.redhat.com**.

The Ideal Linux+ Candidate

Just to give you some idea of what an ideal Linux+ candidate is like, the following are some relevant statistics about the background and experience such an individual might have. Don't worry if you don't meet these qualifications—this is a far from ideal world, and where you fall short is simply where you'll have more work to do.

➤ Academic or professional training in network theory, concepts, and operations. This training includes everything from networking hardware and software to the Linux operating system, services, and applications.

➤ Six months or more of professional networking experience, including experience with Ethernet, modems, and other networking media. This experience should include installation, configuration, upgrading, and troubleshooting.

➤ Six months or more in a networked environment with hands-on experience with Linux. An understanding of hardware at the CompTIA A+ level and multiple Linux distributions is helpful.

➤ Familiarity with the basics of key Linux-based TCP/IP-based services, including Apache, DHCP, DNS, FTP, Samba, Squid, NFS, and firewalls.

CompTIA implicitly acknowledges that many candidates who take the Linux+ exam may not (yet) be qualified Linux system administrators. The list of potential job roles, listed on the CompTIA Web site as of this writing, include the following:

➤ Entry-level helpdesk

➤ Technical sales/marketing

➤ Entry-level service technician

➤ Technical writers

➤ Resellers

➤ Application developers

➤ Application customer service representatives

With the possible exception of application developers, many qualified people in each of these fields are not Linux gurus; if you feel you are not such an expert, don't let that discourage you from taking this exam.

Put Yourself to the Test

The following series of questions and observations is designed to help you figure out how much work you must do to pursue the Linux+ certification and what kinds of resources you may consult on your quest. Be absolutely honest in your answers; otherwise, you'll end up wasting money on exams you're not yet ready to take. There are no right or wrong answers, only steps along the path to certification. Only you can decide where you really belong in the broad spectrum of aspiring candidates.

Two things should be clear from the outset, however:

➤ Even a modest background in Linux or Unix will be helpful.

➤ Hands-on experience with Linux or another Unix-based operating system is an essential ingredient of certification success.

Educational Background

1. Have you ever taken any computer-related classes? [Yes or No]

   If Yes, proceed to Question 2; if No, proceed to Question 4.

2. Have you taken any classes on computer operating systems? [Yes or No]

   If Yes, you'll probably be able to handle commands and hardware configuration. If you're rusty, brush up on basic Linux concepts, especially commands, configuration files, hardware configuration methods, and general computer security topics.

   If No, consider some basic reading in this area. I strongly recommend a good general book on Unix, such as *Unix Made Easy*, by John Muster (Osborne/McGraw-Hill, 1996, ISBN 0-07882-173-8). If this title doesn't appeal to you, check out reviews of other, similar titles at your favorite online bookstore.

3. Have you taken any networking concepts or technologies classes? [Yes or No]

   If Yes, you'll probably be able to handle Linux's networking terminology, concepts, and technologies (brace yourself for frequent departures from normal usage). If you're rusty, brush up on basic networking concepts and terminology, especially networking media, transmission types, and networking technologies such as Ethernet and WAN links.

If No, you might want to read one or two books in this topic area. The two best books that I know of are *Computer Networks, 3rd Edition*, by Andrew S. Tanenbaum (Prentice-Hall, 1996, ISBN 0-13349-945-6), and *Linux Network Administrator's Guide*, by Olaf Kirch and Terry Dawson (O'Reilly and Associates, 2000, ISBN 1-56592-400-2).

Skip to the next section, "Hands-on Experience."

4. Have you done any reading on Linux operating systems or networks? [Yes or No]

   If Yes, review the requirements stated in the first paragraphs after Questions 2 and 3. If you meet those requirements, move on to the next section, "Hands-on Experience."

   If No, get a copy of Linux. Install it on your computer. Read the documentation that comes with your copy of Linux or that is available online at the Web site associated with the distribution. More information on available Linux distributions is available in Chapter 1.

Hands-on Experience

The most important key to success on all the CompTIA tests is hands-on experience, especially with basic computer hardware, as well as with Linux. If I leave you with only one lesson after you take this Self-Assessment, it should be that there's no substitute for time spent installing, configuring, and using Linux and its components, upon which you'll be tested repeatedly and in depth.

Before you even think about taking any exam, make sure you've spent enough time with the related hardware and software to understand how it may be installed and configured, how to maintain such an installation, and how to troubleshoot when things go wrong. This will help you in the exam, and in real life.

Testing Your Exam-Readiness

Whether you attend a formal class on a specific topic to get ready for an exam, or you use written materials to study on your own, some preparation for the Linux+ certification exams is essential. In the United States, each attempt to take the exam costs $190. The price varies depending on the country in which you take the exam and whether you're a member of CompTIA. In addition, volume discounts are available. At these prices—pass or fail—you want to do everything you can to pass on your first try. That's where studying comes in.

For any given subject, consider taking a class if you've tackled self-study materials, taken the test, and failed anyway. The opportunity to interact with an instructor and fellow students can make all the difference in the world, if you can afford that privilege. For information about CompTIA classes, visit the CompTIA Web site at **www.comptia.org** (follow the Certification link to find training).

If you can't afford to take a class, visit the Web page anyway because it also includes a detailed breakdown of the objectives for the Linux+ certification exam. This will serve as a good roadmap for your studies. Even if you can't afford to spend much, you should still invest in some low-cost practice exams from commercial vendors (in addition to the practice exam at the end of this book), because they can help you assess your readiness to pass a test better than any other tool. The CompTIA Web site lists sources for additional study material.

5. Have you taken a practice exam on Linux+? [Yes or No]

If Yes, and you scored 75 percent or better, you're probably ready to tackle the real thing. If your score isn't above that crucial threshold, keep at it until you break that barrier.

If No, obtain all the free and low-budget practice tests you can find and get to work. Keep at it until you can break the passing threshold comfortably.

 When it comes to assessing your test readiness, there's no better way than to take a good-quality practice exam and pass with a score of 75 percent or better. When I prepare myself, I shoot for 80-plus percent, just to leave room for the "weirdness factor" that sometimes shows up on exams.

One last note: I can't stress enough the importance of hands-on experience in the context of the Linux+ certification exam. As you review the material for that exam, you'll realize that hands-on experience with basic Linux commands, utilities, daemons, applications, and PC hardware is invaluable.

Onward, through the Fog!

Once you've assessed your readiness, undertaken the right background studies, obtained the hands-on experience that will help you understand the products and technologies at work, and reviewed the many sources of information to help you prepare for a test, you'll be ready to take a round of practice tests. When your scores come back positive enough to get you through the exam, you're ready to go after the real thing. If you follow this assessment regime, you'll know what you need to study, as well as when you're ready to make a test date through Prometric/ Thomson Learning or VUE. Good luck!

Linux+ Certification Tests

Terms you'll need to understand:

✓ Exhibit

✓ Careful reading

✓ Strategy

✓ Exam domains

✓ Command-line interface

✓ Linux distributions

✓ Linux+ exam domains

Concepts you'll need to master:

✓ Preparing to take a certification exam

✓ Budgeting your time

✓ Marking for review

✓ Using one question to figure out another question

✓ Analyzing responses logically

✓ Guessing (as a last resort)

✓ Understanding the coverage of the Linux+ exam

As experiences go, test-taking isn't something most people anticipate eagerly, no matter how well they're prepared. In most cases, familiarity reduces exam anxiety. In other words, you probably wouldn't be as nervous if you had to take a second CompTIA Linux+ certification exam as you will be taking your first one. I've taken a lot of exams, and this book is partly about helping you to reduce your test-taking anxiety. This chapter explains what you can expect to see in the exam room itself.

Whether it's your first exam or your tenth, understanding the exam particulars (how much time to spend on questions, the setting you'll be in, and so on) and the testing software will help you concentrate on the material rather than on the environment. Likewise, mastering a few basic test-taking skills should help you recognize—and perhaps even outfox—some of the tricks and "gotchas" you're bound to find in CompTIA Linux+ exam questions.

While the CompTIA Linux+ exam is focused on relative newcomers to Linux— people with six months of experience—I expect that many more experienced users will also take this exam and (I hope) read this book as part of their preparation. Even if you're familiar with other *Exam Cram* books, there are some basic surprises in the CompTIA Linux+ exam that I cover later in this chapter.

The Test Site

When you arrive at your scheduled testing center, you'll be required to sign in with a test coordinator. He or she will ask you to produce two forms of identification, one of which must be a photo ID. After you've signed in and your time slot arrives, you'll be asked to deposit any books, bags, or other items you brought with you, and then you'll be escorted into a closed room.

Typically, the testing room will be furnished with anywhere from one to six computers. Each workstation will be separated from the others by dividers designed to keep you from seeing what's happening on someone else's computer.

When you sign in with the exam administrators, you'll generally be furnished with a pen or pencil and a blank sheet of paper—or, in some cases, an erasable plastic sheet and an erasable felt-tip pen. You're allowed to write down any information you want on both sides of this sheet. As I mentioned in the Introduction, you should memorize as much of the material that appears on the Cram Sheet (inside the front cover of this book) as you can and then write down that information on the blank sheet as soon as you are seated in front of the computer. You can refer to your rendition of the Cram Sheet anytime you like during the test, but you'll have to surrender the sheet when you leave the room.

Most exam rooms feature a wall with a large picture window. This is to permit the test coordinator to monitor the room and to observe anything out of the ordinary that might go on, and also to prevent test-takers from talking to one another. The exam coordinator will have preloaded the Linux+ certification test, and you'll be permitted to start as soon as you're seated in front of the computer.

All Linux+ certification exams are designed to be taken within a 120-minute period, and there's a countdown timer on the screen showing you the time remaining. In my opinion, the amount of time is fair and generous, and it offers ample time for reviewing your responses. Just in case, however, plan your time before entering the exam room. You may want to budget time for:

➤ Recording key points from the Cram Sheet on your blank sheet of paper.

➤ Reading through every question.

➤ Answering every question.

➤ Reviewing your answers.

➤ Taking short breaks.

These are just suggestions, though. What you do depends on the rules of the test facility, your needs, and your experience. If you have doubts on the rules of the test facility, call ahead!

Linux+ certification exams are computer generated and use a multiple-choice format. Although this may sound easy, the questions are constructed to check your mastery of basic facts and figures, as well as to test your ability to evaluate one or more sets of circumstances or requirements.

You might be asked to select the best or most effective solution to a problem from a range of choices, all of which technically are correct. You might be asked to select the best choice from a graphic image. All in all, it's quite an adventure, and it involves real thinking. This book shows you what to expect and how to deal with the problems, puzzles, and predicaments you're likely to find on the test.

The sample test in Chapter 15 is as close an approximation of the Linux+ exam as is allowed. You can find detailed answers to these questions in Chapter 16.

In the final analysis, knowledge breeds confidence, and confidence breeds success. If you study the materials in this book carefully, review the practice questions at the end of each chapter, and take the sample test in Chapter 15, you should be aware of all the areas where additional studying is required.

Test Layout and Design

As mentioned earlier, the questions on Linux+ exams are multiple choice. Some questions will provide the information in paragraph format, and others will provide an exhibit (line drawing) and ask you to identify specific components. *Paying careful attention* is the key to success!

Each question stands alone in a windowed page. The text of the question appears near the top of the screen, and the response choices are listed below the question. Each response appears next to a typical Windows radio button, and clicking on the appropriate circle turns it black. You can change your selection at any time from within the question window. The time you take to respond and the number of times you change a response are not factored into the scoring process. Along the top of the screen is the countdown timer. If there is an exhibit for the question, you'll see an Exhibit button at the bottom of the screen. Other buttons at the bottom of the screen allow you to move to the previous or the next question.

Review Responses

When you complete the last question of the exam and press the Next button, you will find that a final screen will offer you the option to review your responses and any questions that you specifically marked for review. A listing of all of the question numbers, along with your chosen response letter, shows on the screen, and the marked questions have a graphic indicator. Unanswered questions are highlighted in yellow. When you select a marked question and choose Review, the software displays the selected question.

When you review a question, you'll see a window displaying the original question and your response. You can use the window to change or verify your answer. When you're satisfied with your response, you can unmark the question by clicking on the Mark For Review checkbox, or you can proceed to the next review question. At the bottom of the screen, you'll see a Review Next button, which will take you to your next marked question (bypassing unmarked questions). The number of questions you choose to review is not factored into the scoring process.

Take Your Test Seriously

The most important advice I can give you about taking any test is this: *Read each question carefully*! Some questions are deliberately ambiguous, offering several responses that could be correct, depending on your reading of the question. Other questions use terminology in very precise ways. I use exam alerts and tips throughout this book to point out where you might run into these types of questions.

I've taken numerous practice and real tests, and in nearly every case I've missed at least one question because I didn't read it closely or carefully enough. For example, the use of the word *requires* commonly causes test-takers to answer incorrectly. Consider the following sample question.

Sample Question 1

Which of the following requires its own partition?

○ a. /boot

○ b. /root

○ c. swap space

○ d. /

The correct answer is d. Only the root (/) directory requires its own partition. Although it is a common practice to mount the /boot directory on its own partition, it is not a requirement. Therefore, answer a is not correct. The /root directory is a subdirectory of the root (/) directory. As there is no requirement to mount this directory on its own partition, answer b is also not correct. Although it is standard to mount swap space on its own partition, this is also not a requirement to install Linux. Therefore, answer c is also not correct.

Here are some suggestions for dealing with the tendency to select an answer too quickly:

➤ Read every word in the question! If you find yourself jumping ahead impatiently, go back and start over.

➤ Schedule your exam on a day when you don't have a lot of other appointments and errands. This should help you feel a little more relaxed.

➤ As you read, try to rephrase the question in your own terms.

➤ When returning to a question after your initial read-through, reread every word again—otherwise, you might fall into a rut. Sometimes, seeing a question fresh after turning your attention elsewhere enables you to catch something you missed earlier. This is where the review option comes in handy.

➤ If you return to a question more than twice, try to explain to yourself what you don't understand about the question, why the answers don't appear to make sense, or what appears to be missing. If you ponder the subject for a while, your subconscious might provide the details you're looking for, or you might notice a "trick" that will point to the right answer.

Finally, try to deal with each question by thinking through what you know about the Linux operating system and computer hardware. By reviewing what you know (and what you've written down on your Cram Sheet), you'll often recall or understand concepts sufficiently to determine the correct answer.

Question-Handling Strategies

Based on the tests I've taken, I've noticed a couple of interesting trends in exam question responses. Usually, some responses will be obviously incorrect, and two of the remaining answers will be plausible. Remember that only one response can be correct. If the answer leaps out at you, reread the question to look for a trick—just in case.

Unfamiliar Terms

My best advice regarding guessing is to rely on your intuition. None of the exam topics should come as a surprise to you if you've read this book and taken the sample test. If you see a response that's totally unfamiliar, chances are good that it's a made-up word. Recognizing unfamiliar terms can help narrow down the possible correct answers for a question. For example, the following sample question shows how you can use the process of eliminating unfamiliar terms to arrive at the correct answer.

Sample Question 2

Which of the following packages is most closely associated with the Linux graphical user interface?

○ a. LinuxWest

○ b. CarsonJ

○ c. X Window

○ d. GeorgeB

The correct answer is c. If you've used the Linux graphical user interface, chances are that you've at least heard of the *X Window* before, thereby enabling you to take an educated guess at this question.

Last-Minute Guesses

As you work your way through the test, the traditional exam format indicates the number of questions completed and questions outstanding. Budget your time. Make sure that you've completed one-fourth of the questions a quarter of the way through the test period. Check again three quarters of the way through. If you're not finished with the test at the five-minute mark, use the last five minutes to *guess* your way through the remaining questions.

Guesses are more valuable than blank answers, because blanks are *always* wrong. A guess has a 25 percent (one in four) chance of being right. If you don't have a clue regarding the remaining questions, pick answers at random, or choose all a's, b's, and so on. The important thing is to submit a test for scoring that has *an answer for every question.*

Linux+ Exam Surprises

The Linux+ exam doesn't just cover Linux. And while it is officially "distribution neutral," some parts of the Linux+ exam criteria explicitly point to tools available only in Red Hat Linux and allied *distributions.* As you study for the exam, remember the seven domains, as shown in Table 1.1.

The last domain, "Identify, Install, and Maintain System Hardware," includes objectives that are quite similar to the CompTIA A+ exam. While you need to know the Linux tools associated with this domain, some of what you will see on the exam requires a detailed knowledge of personal computer hardware, independent of Linux.

 Expect a significant number of A+–style questions on PC hardware that are unrelated to Linux.

This book covers every objective on the CompTIA Linux+ exam. For example, the details that you need to know about personal computer hardware are covered in Chapters 3 and 9. While you will not see copies of actual exam questions in this book, you will learn just what you need to know for the Linux+ exam.

For those of you who are using some of the newest Linux distributions, one more issue is the Linux+ exam coverage of the older Linux boot loader, known as LILO.

Table 1.1 Linux+ exam domains.	
Domain	**Percentage of Exam**
Planning the Implementation	4%
Installation	12%
Configuration	15%
Administration	18%
System Maintenance	14%
Troubleshooting	18%
Identify, Install, and Maintain System Hardware	19%

If you have Red Hat Linux 7.2 (or later) and Linux-Mandrake 8.0 (or later), you may have the GRand Unified Boot loader (GRUB) installed in place of LILO. As of this writing, the Linux+ exam does not cover GRUB.

If this is your situation and Linux is the only operating system on your computer, install the latest LILO **rpm** package, then use the **/sbin/lilo** command to install the Linux loader in place of GRUB. For general information on these techniques, refer to Chapters 6 and 14. For details or guidance on other situations, consult the documentation for your specific Linux distribution.

Different Types of Users

The CompTIA Linux+ exam is targeted at Linux users with six months of experience. If you fit into this target group, there are some differences between Linux and other operating systems that you're just beginning to understand.

For Relative Newcomers

Perhaps the biggest difference for newcomers to Linux is the focus on the command-line interface. While there are graphical Linux tools that are comparable to a "control panel" or a "management console," most Linux administrators work from the command-line interface. While a command-line prompt

```
mj@linux:~>
```

may seem limiting to users of other operating systems, it actually provides more options than are available in the typical graphical tool.

Since Linux is administered from the command line, there are no clear differences among commands, utilities, programs, scripts, or even applications. Many Linux commands are in fact executable scripts of other Linux commands. Many of these commands are also utilities, based on how they configure hardware or software. Many of these commands start programs or applications where you can use—surprise!—other commands at a command-line interface.

For Linux Veterans

If you are a Linux user with more experience, you already know all of this information. When you read through this book, remember that the purpose of the *Exam Cram* series is to provide just the information that you need for the specific exam.

To help newer users understand the basic concepts, there are a number of "oversimplifications" in this book. These oversimplifications are intended to help the less-experienced reader grasp the concepts quickly, and hopefully will keep you, the Linux veteran, from overthinking when taking the exam.

All *Exam Cram* books include a "Need to Know More?" section at the end of every substantive chapter. These sections include books and online resources where all readers can get more information on the topics discussed in the chapter.

Which Linux?

When you read this book, it helps to have Linux installed on a computer. This will allow you to test each command as you read this book. There are several dozen "flavors" of Linux, known as *distributions*. Each distribution includes the same basic software. The Linux distribution that you install is up to you.

 A Linux distribution is an integrated set of software packages, including the kernel. Many distributions such as Red Hat Linux include a customized installation program. Several Linux distributions are listed in the "Need to Know More?" section at the end of this chapter.

While there are a few commands and concepts in the Linux+ exam objectives that are specific to Red Hat Linux, they are few and far between and well defined in this book. Several distributions are based on Red Hat Linux and include the same special commands. But if you already have another Linux distribution installed on a computer, that should be good enough. If you're installing Linux for the first time, you can explore some of the available distributions through the **www.linux.com** Web site, available as of this writing at **www.linux.com/learn/getlinux**.

Many Linux distributions are available in computer stores. These boxed sets generally include books that can help you install Linux on your computer. If you are already familiar with installing Linux, you can purchase the CDs for many distributions inexpensively ($2 to $10) from online shops such as **www.cheapbytes.com** or **www.linuxmall.com**. Alternatively, if you have a faster Internet connection, you can download the applicable CDs, each of which includes more than 600MB of files, from the Web site associated with each Linux distribution.

Additional Resources

By far, the best source of information about Linux+ certification tests comes from CompTIA. Because products and technologies—and the tests that go with them—change frequently, the best resource for obtaining exam-related information is the Internet. If you haven't already visited the CompTIA Web site, do so at **www.comptia.org**.

There's *always* a way to find what you want on the Web, if you're willing to invest some time and energy. As long as you can get to the CompTIA site (and I'm pretty sure that it will stay at **www.comptia.org** for a long while yet), you have a good jump on finding what you need.

Need to Know More?

Visit **www.caldera.com**, the Web site for Caldera Systems, whose focus is on the business market. The Caldera Web site provides Hardware Compatibility Lists (HCLs) and a knowledge base as well as downloads of Caldera's latest version of Linux. Caldera uses the Red Hat style **rpm** package system.

Explore the Web site for Debian GNU/Linux at **www.debian.org**. This may be the most popular Linux distribution for Linux developers. Creators of Debian are primarily volunteers. You can also download Debian GNU/Linux from this site. Debian uses the **dpkg** system, which is different from the Red Hat style **rpm** system covered on the Linux+ exam.

Investigate the Web site for the Linux Documentation Project at **www.linuxdoc.org**, which is the central repository for Linux manuals, HOWTOs, and a number of other book-length documents. If you're installing Linux for the first time, review the Hardware-HOWTO at **www.linuxdoc.org/HOWTO/Hardware-HOWTO/index.html**.

Examine the Web site for the Linux Hardware Database at **lhd.datapower.com**, which provides a searchable database of hardware components that can be installed on a Linux computer.

Review a wide range of available Linux distributions at the Tucows Linux Web site at **www.hkt.linuxberg.com/distribution.html**. Several dozen Linux distributions are available, including many in languages other than English.

Visit **www.linux-mandrake.com**, the Web site for Linux-Mandrake, created by MandrakeSoft. Its version of Linux builds on Red Hat Linux and has a number of additional graphical and other installation tools. You can download its version of Linux from this Web site. If you use Linux Mandrake version 8.x or later, consult the documentation for instructions on how to install the Linux loader, also known as LILO. Linux-Mandrake uses the Red Hat style **rpm** package system.

Although the Linux+ exam is nominally distribution neutral, it explicitly covers a number of commands and tools available only on Red Hat Linux (and allied distributions). Visit **www.redhat.com**, the Web site for Red Hat, Inc. Red Hat's Web site offers Hardware Compatibility

Lists (HCLs) and a knowledge base as well as downloads of its latest version of Linux. If you use Red Hat Linux 7.2 or later, consult the documentation for instructions on how to install the Linux loader (LILO).

 Check out the Web site for the Slackware Linux Project at **www.slackware.com**. Its standard version of Linux along with its compact ZipSlack packages are available on this Web site. Slackware is affiliated with Walnut Creek CD-ROM and BDSi, who work with a different Unix derivative known as the Berkeley Software Distribution. Slackware uses its own package system, which is different from the Red Hat style **rpm** system covered on the Linux+ exam.

 Visit **www.suse.com**, the Web site for S.u.S.E. GmBH, the best selling Linux distribution in Europe. The S.u.S.E. Web site offers Hardware Compatibility Lists (HCLs) and a knowledge base, as well as downloads of its latest version of Linux. S.u.S.E. uses the Red Hat style **rpm** package system.

 Explore the Web site for Turbolinux at **www.turbolinux.com**, the best-selling Linux distribution in Asia. The Turbolinux Web site allows you to install its distribution by downloading its files to a hard drive or by using boot disks to start a Linux connection to its FTP server. Turbolinux uses the Red Hat style **rpm** package system.

 Browse the Web site for Xandros Linux, previously known Corel Linux, at **www.xandros.com**. Xandros Linux focuses on the desktop market. A download of its latest version of Linux is also available from this Web site. The original Corel version of Linux is built upon the Debian distribution. Xandros uses the Debian **dpkg** system, which is different from the Red Hat style **rpm** system covered on the Linux+ exam.

Linux Software Planning

Terms you'll need to understand:

✓ Source code

✓ GNU

✓ TCP/IP

✓ Services

✓ Apache

✓ Cache

✓ Squid

✓ BIND

✓ **ipchains**, **iptables**

✓ Samba

✓ Sendmail

✓ Distribution

✓ Patch

✓ Hardware Compatibility List (HCL)

✓ Upgrade

✓ Binary

✓ Kernel

✓ General Public License (GPL)

Techniques you'll need to master:

✓ Understanding the background behind Linux

✓ Describing the services that you can use with Linux

✓ Explaining the resources needed to work with Linux

✓ Comprehending the versatility of Linux solutions

✓ Understanding the reasons for patching or upgrading the Linux kernel

✓ Working with the best practices for documentation

Linux is a versatile operating system. It is installed in everything from high-end servers to handheld devices and cellular telephones. You can find the same basic Linux kernel in all of these devices, but you won't see exactly the same Linux configuration in a server and a telephone.

As a Linux administrator, you need to understand what Linux can do so that you can customize the software you install with Linux. Although this chapter won't teach you how to install Linux on a telephone, it will help you learn enough about various Linux services to know what to install on different types of server or workstation computers.

Customer Needs

Linux is cheap. Linux is reliable. Linux is customizable. Linux is supported by a world of developers. No other operating system has all of these advantages, yet most of the computing world uses other operating systems.

Linux also has a number of disadvantages, however. Some of these disadvantages are real; others are a matter of perception. As a Linux administrator, you may at some point recommend Linux to your managers or customers. When you do so, you need to be able to explain three things: why Linux (and not some other operating system), what you can use Linux for, and what resources are required to install and maintain Linux.

Why Linux

Linux was developed as a clone of the Unix operating system. To understand the mania and strengths associated with Linux, you need to understand the development of Unix.

Unix was developed in 1969 by Bell Labs, which was then the research arm of the American Telephone and Telegraph Company (AT&T). At that time, AT&T was a regulated monopoly and was prohibited from selling software. Therefore, AT&T kept the license for Unix and, for a nominal fee, distributed it with the programming instructions, or *source code*, to universities. It was a license without a warranty. This release technique is now known as *open source*.

When the U.S. government settled its antitrust suit against AT&T in 1982, one of the conditions allowed AT&T to get into the computer business. AT&T soon started selling Unix for profit, without the source code, with all of the standard protections associated with a copyright.

In response, Richard Stallman started the Free Software Foundation (FSF) in 1984 to develop an alternative to Unix. He wanted an operating system with all of the functionality of Unix; to get around AT&T's copyrights, however, he needed to develop this alternative without reference to Unix's source code. This type of software is sometimes known as a *clone*. By 1991, the FSF had developed clones for all the major components of Unix except the kernel. When complete, this operating system would be known as GNU, short for "GNU's Not Unix." Later in this chapter you'll learn about the license he used to protect the developments of the FSF.

Note: As strange as it sounds, GNU really does stand for "GNU's Not Unix." Linux is filled with many of these recursive acronyms. It is almost like a game to Linux developers, intended perhaps as a jab at the normal way of doing things.

In 1991, Linus Torvalds wanted a free operating system that would work with his 386 Personal Computer. He developed what became known as the Linux kernel and incorporated much of the work of the FSF to create a relatively complete operating system that soon became known as Linux. Because it is a combined work, the FSF believes that the Linux operating system is more properly known as GNU/Linux.

Basic Capabilities

To understand what Linux can do also requires a history lesson. In the 1970s, the U.S. Department of Defense wanted to develop a communications network that could survive a nuclear war. This required a network with multiple routes and a network language in which messages could take advantage of those different routes from the source to the destination. This redundant network was the precursor of the Internet.

Most of this work was done at the same U.S. universities where Unix was popular. The computer scientists needed a common language to support this network communication. The language they developed became known as the TCP/IP protocol suite. (TCP/IP is an acronym for two protocols, Transmission Control Protocol and Internet Protocol.) Because TCP/IP was developed on Unix, Linux as a Unix clone carries all of Unix's advantages as an operating system for the Internet.

To support Internet communication, a number of *services* were developed between the 1970s and 1990s, including the following:

➤ *Web service*—Apache

➤ *Proxy and caching service*—Squid

➤ *Domain Name Service*—BIND

➤ *Firewall utilities*—**ipchains, iptables**

➤ *Email*—Sendmail

➤ *Communications with Windows and IBM computers*—Samba

Remember the function of each of the major Linux services. For example, know that if you want to set up an email server, you need to install the Sendmail service.

More information on each of these services is available later in this chapter. With the help of these services, a Linux computer can be configured with several other functions:

➤ *File server*—A centralized location for sharing files.

➤ *Application server*—A centralized location from which users can call up different applications, such as word processors and spreadsheets.

➤ *Print server*—A computer connected to a printer that serves all connected computers on a network.

➤ *Router*—A computer that serves as a junction between two networks, such as a local area network (LAN) and the Internet.

Required Resources

Two levels of resources are required to support Linux: hardware and support. The hardware depends on the Linux distribution. Mainstream distributions are available for everything from 386 PCs with just a floppy drive to complex computers with several central processing units (CPUs). The support required is different from a "conventional" operating system because Linux does not come with a warranty. In addition, the availability of the source code encourages users to make their own changes.

There is a freedom associated with Linux that is based on minimal cost and on access to the complete source code. With freedom comes responsibility, however. If your Linux installation fails, Microsoft is not there to give you support. You can either purchase support from a vendor such as Linuxcare or you can provide the support yourself, which means you need people who know how to maintain Linux.

Major Linux Services

If you have the resources, you can set up Linux for any or all of the previously listed services and more. Linux can function for just one purpose, such as a Web server, or it can function as a fully featured server and workstation, with all of the capabilities of the most advanced operating systems. What you do with Linux depends in part on the hardware you have at your disposal. To understand what you can do, you need to know about each of the major services in more detail.

Service Options

The Unix services previously discussed were developed between the 1970s and the 1990s to support Internet communication. As a Unix clone, Linux runs all of these services. As Linux grew in the late 1990s, many of these services were developed specifically for Linux. To see how these services fit together requires one more history lesson.

Perhaps the key development in Unix/Linux services came from the European Particle Physics Laboratory (which goes by its French acronym, CERN) and the National Center for Supercomputing Applications (NCSA) around 1990.

In 1989, thousands of universities, governments, and companies were on the Internet. At CERN, Tim Berners-Lee created a proposal to use hypertext to help preserve knowledge on interconnected networks. In 1990, Berners-Lee created the first Web browser to use these hypertext links. This eventually became the Hypertext Transfer Protocol (HTTP), which was the start of the World Wide Web.

This work continued at NCSA, where a graduate student named Marc Andreesen developed the first commercially available Web browser, known as Mosaic. The first commercial Web servers were also developed at NCSA.

Note: Andreesen eventually left NCSA to become one of the founders of Netscape.

When development on the NCSA server stalled in the mid-1990s, a group of Webmasters came together by email to coordinate their changes, or *patches*, to the NCSA Web server. Their development of "a patchy server," or Apache for short, was first released in April 1995. Apache is by far the most popular Web server on the Internet today.

To support this communication, they needed a service that would translate domain names, such as **Coriolis.com**, to the IP addresses such as 192.168.0.63 used in computer communication. Because names like **Coriolis.com** and **mommabears.com** are known as *domain names*, this service became known as the Domain Name Service, or DNS.

 Keep in mind that the Domain Name Service (DNS) is known in Linux as a nameserver, using the Berkeley Internet Name Domain (BIND).

As the World Wide Web developed, IP addresses became scarce. Linux administrators often had only one real IP address available for their LANs. They needed a computer that could be used to represent the other computers on a LAN. This is also known as a *proxy*. In addition, Webmasters noticed that certain Web sites were used more often than others. To reduce the amount of traffic on the Internet, proxy servers were developed with a storehouse, or *cache* of recently viewed Web pages. The proxy and caching server most associated with Linux is known as Squid.

Note: IP addresses will be discussed in more detail in Chapter 4.

As the Web developed further, security became an issue. One of the major ways to protect a network from outside attack is known as a *firewall*. A firewall can block unauthorized access using various network filters. Linux includes the services of three different firewall tools: **ipfwadm, ipchains,** and **iptables. ipfwadm** is now obsolete; the other firewall tools are discussed in more detail later in this book. Although the ipchains firewall is still common today, iptables is eventually expected to take over as the latest Linux kernel, version 2.4.x, comes into common use.

 Even though the **iptables** firewall was developed specifically for the newest kernel, version 2.4.x, remember that the **ipchains** tool is still in common use for this kernel.

As all of these systems developed around Unix and Linux, there were other developments in the world of computing, centered primarily around two companies: IBM and Microsoft. Both companies developed their own version of networking based on the Server Message Block (SMB) set of protocols. SaMBa (or Samba) was developed to allow Unix and Linux to communicate with the various IBM and Microsoft operating systems.

 Samba is also known as the Common Internet File System, or CIFS— something to keep in mind.

Finally, there is the specter of email. Sendmail was developed in the 1980s as a service to send and receive email.

To summarize, the following key services can be installed on Linux:

➤ *Apache*—The most popular Web service for the Internet.

➤ *Squid*—The service that caches commonly used Web pages to minimize the load on the Internet.

➤ *BIND*—The Berkeley Internet Name Domain service translates domain names such as **Coriolis.com** to the IP address that computers connected to a network use for communication. BIND is also known as a nameserver or a Domain Name Service (DNS).

➤ *ipchains*—A major firewall tool, developed for the Linux kernel version 2.2.x. It is still in common use with the Linux kernel version 2.4.x.

➤ *iptables*—A major firewall tool, developed for the Linux kernel version 2.4.x.

➤ *Sendmail*—A mail server service.

➤ *Samba*—A service that allows communication between computers that run the Unix and Linux operating systems and those that run operating systems developed by Microsoft and IBM.

 Know each of the following services and what they do when installed on Linux: Apache, Squid, BIND, **ipchains**, **iptables**, Samba, and Sendmail. Based on a requirement, such as a Web server, know that you can install Apache to meet this requirement. While you do not have to know the details of how to install each of these services, you will need to know some of the basics of configuration, especially Apache, as discussed in later chapters.

Designated Hitter

As with Linux, all of the services listed earlier are downloadable without a fee. All of these services can be run on Linux. Linux can be run on just about any computer with at least the power of a 386 PC. With the right services, you can use Linux on older computers for specific purposes or to fill a specific role, similar to the designated hitter role in baseball. For example, Linux has been configured in the following ways on older computers:

➤ *Firewall/router*—An older computer used as a junction between your network and the Internet requires only a 386 computer with a floppy disk installation of Linux with the ipchains or iptables utilities to protect your network. You don't even need a hard drive.

➤ *Print server*—An older computer can be set up easily as a Linux print server in a central location, away from any specific desk or workstation.

➤ *DNS server*—An older computer with appropriate network connections and just a bit of memory can serve as an effective BIND or nameserver.

➤ *Diskless workstations*—An older computer without a hard disk can be used as a specialized Linux terminal; with enough RAM, such a terminal can be set up with a graphical user interface.

These are just a few uses for older computers with Linux. Of course, if you want to use the full power of a Linux-based PC as a workstation, you'll want the most advanced PC that you can afford, which brings us to the question of the Linux compatibility of your hardware.

Hardware Compatibility

The vast majority of hardware is compatible with Linux, but there are a few problem areas. The newest hardware often does not come with Linux drivers. Fortunately, the ingenuity of Linux developers usually makes it possible to run almost all of the newest hardware just a few weeks after release.

If you have any doubts about your own hardware, the first step is to review the Linux Hardware Compatibility List (HCL), available online at **www.linuxdoc.org/ HOWTO/Hardware-HOWTO/index.html**. If you don't see your hardware on this list, all is not lost.

Some hardware manufacturers provide their own drivers for Linux. If you don't see support for your hardware in Hardware-HOWTO or your distribution's Web site, check your hardware manufacturer's Web site. You might be pleasantly surprised. If all else fails, review the information provided throughout this book for more information on hardware configuration in Linux.

Selecting a Distribution

Your choice of a Linux distribution depends in part on three factors: your hardware, the amount of work you're willing to do to maintain the distribution, and the availability of the distribution.

It Depends

The distribution you select depends on your hardware. For example, if you have a simple 386 PC with just a few megabytes of memory, you can still have a useful Linux computer. All you need is a floppy drive and the distribution from the Linux Router Project. You don't even need a hard drive. When you start the computer, Linux boots from the regular 1.44MB floppy drive. As a router, it also loads a firewall tool such as ipchains or iptables.

If you have a 386 or 486 PC with just a bit more memory (16MB), you can have a fully functional Linux computer. Many later Linux distributions run well on these computers as long as you don't use the X Window, which is the Linux graphical user interface (GUI). Even though all you would have is the command line, the best Linux administrators believe that you can do more (compared to the GUI) at the command-line interface (CLI). Most of the Linux+ exam is based on understanding the CLI.

*Note: An older computer such as a 386 PC with a small hard drive is commonly set up as a BIND server, also known as a DNS or a nameserver. A BIND server translates domain names such as **Coriolis.com** to IP addresses such as 192.168.12.66.*

Finally, if you have the latest hardware, you can go for the full package from one of the regular Linux distributions. A distribution is a compilation of Linux and related packages, often configured with a branded installation utility. Some of the major names in Linux distributions include Red Hat, S.u.S.E., Mandrake, Debian, TurboLinux, Caldera, Corel, Slackware, and Storm. Depending on what you install, some require a few hundred megabytes to a few gigabytes. Most distributions handle more hardware than you see in the standard Linux Hardware Compatibility Lists. If you're considering several distributions and have hardware issues, look at the Web sites for individual HCLs. However, there are other issues besides hardware.

Binaries vs. Source Code

When you choose a distribution, you also need to know how you're going to maintain that distribution. In other words, when you install or upgrade software, do you use binaries or compile from source code?

If you compile your own source code, you're starting with the basic programming instructions. If you have improvements to make to the software, you can make the changes yourself. You don't have to wait for Microsoft or any other software company to make changes and hope that it comes close to your needs.

Note: The latest source code is usually collected in tape archive files, or .tar for short.

Alternatively, if you rely on *binaries*, you're using installation files that have already been compiled from source code. And you're relying on the experience of Linux developers who are working with the same software in the field and who are often trying to meet the same needs.

There are two major types of Linux binaries. The first is rpm, based on the Red Hat Package Manager, which is in common use on Red Hat, S.u.S.E., Mandrake, and Caldera. The second is deb, which was first used for the Debian distribution. It's also used on Corel and Storm Linux. The primary binary addressed in this book is the rpm.

If you use a distribution that relies on binaries, you can still install new services from source code. The drawback is that binaries and source code often install their files in different directories.

Availability

Availability is a two-part question: the availability of a Linux distribution and the availability of the packages to install or upgrade software for that distribution. Most—but not all—distributions are available for free download from the Internet, per the GNU General Public License (GPL). Generally, you can download a CD's worth of files, record that information on an actual CD, and then use the CD to install Linux. However, that is 650MB of information per CD, which can take several days to download over a regular 56Kbps telephone modem connection.

You can purchase the distribution from the manufacturer for a standard price of about $30. Alternatively, most distributions are available for around $5 from groups such as CheapBytes (**www.cheapbytes.com**) or LinuxMall (**www.linuxmall.com**). This is just a bit more than the cost of downloading and recording the distribution on CDs.

Packages such as Apache, Squid, ipchains, and Sendmail are available in several different formats. They are generally included with the CDs for many Linux distributions. They can be downloaded (with source code) from the Internet home pages associated with each package. Binaries such as rpms are often available from the Internet home page for your Linux distribution and in central repositories. A common central repository for Linux packages is **www.rpmfind.net.**

Linux Is Just the Kernel

Stallman's Free Software Foundation developed most of what we know as the Linux operating system. Torvalds developed the kernel. In other words, Linux is just the kernel. But what is a kernel?

A *kernel* is the part of an operating system that translates commands from programs or utilities for use by your hardware. The Linux kernel communicates with hardware through dedicated device drivers. For example, when your computer communicates with your CD-ROM drive, a specific kernel driver sends messages to and from that drive.

Many Kernel Numbers

The Linux kernel that you see includes a label such as 2.4.22. This is a version number in a specific format, *major.minor.patch*. In this case, the first number (*major*—2) refers to the second major release of the Linux kernel. The second number (*minor*—4) refers to the fourth minor release of the specified major kernel. The final number (*patch*—22) refers to the twenty-second patch to the specified minor release of the kernel.

The second (minor) number is significant in another way. It tells you whether or not that Linux kernel is in beta test or in a production release. Odd numbers correspond to test or beta kernels that are not suitable for computers being used in a production environment. Even numbers correspond to production-quality kernels.

In practice, changes to the minor number of a kernel are significant. For example, dynamic loading of kernel drivers as *modules* was introduced in Linux kernel version 2.4.

Note: A driver is the part of the kernel that allows Linux to communicate with your hardware. Some drivers are integrated directly into the kernel; others are loaded as modules after Linux boots on your computer.

Improvements in Kernel 2.4

Naturally, Linux kernel 2.4 supports the latest in processor hardware, including the latest 64-bit CPUs. The Compaq Alpha and Sun Sparc 64-bit chips were already supported in later versions of kernel 2.2; kernel 2.4 is ready to support the Intel Itanium series 64-bit processors when released.

Kernel 2.4 also includes improvements in the way it recognizes the latest plug-and-play devices, from older internal ISA devices to the latest in USB and IEEE 1394 devices (also known as *FireWire* or *i.LINK*).

 Be sure to remember that Linux with kernel 2.4 supports the "hot-swap" configuration of most USB and IEEE 1394 devices without rebooting.

Another key change that started with kernel 2.4.1 is the use of journaling file systems. Generally, they are more efficient on a system with mostly very small and very large files. When disk checks are required, these systems are much faster. Two of the journaling file systems that can now be used with Linux—ReiserFS and ext3—will be covered in Chapter 5.

These are just a few of the changes made for Linux kernel 2.4. One more change that's relevant to the Linux+ exam is the use of dynamic modules, which are most suitable for hot-swappable devices that conform to USB, IEEE 1394, and PCMCIA or PC Card standards (these last two are synonymous). Linux kernel 2.4 supports dynamic modules. When this includes support for your dynamic device, you can install and remove it while your computer is on. Installing the device causes Linux to install the relevant modules. Removing the device causes Linux to remove the relevant modules. However, Linux support for these types of devices (or PCMCIA cards) is not complete.

 Know that if module support for your PCMCIA hardware is compiled into a Linux 2.4 kernel, you can install or remove that component while your computer is on. The associated driver, if available, is automatically loaded or unloaded, as required.

Remember that Linux kernel support is not complete for all USB, IEEE 1394, or PCMCIA devices. For this reason, you'll sometimes have to reboot to get Linux to recognize the hot-swap hardware that you just installed, even if the driver is readily available.

Recompiling, Patching, and Upgrading

For the Linux+ exam, you need to know when to recompile, patch, or install a new kernel. You do not need to know the actual process. Those of you who have been wrestling with recompiling kernels along with patches and upgrades can take a step back.

Sometimes, your current kernel is good enough. If it includes the features that you need, such as support for a driver or a USB component, all you may need to do is recompile the kernel. When you recompile, you get a chance to review all of the options associated with that kernel. If you need a new option such as a driver, you can turn on that option during the process.

At other times, your current Linux kernel may not be good enough. There are four major reasons to change the kernel:

➤ You want to take advantage of a new driver because you've checked your current kernel and found that it cannot be recompiled to support the hardware you need.

➤ You want to incorporate a "bug fix," a flaw in the kernel. You know that the problem affects the way you use Linux.

➤ You want to take advantage of a new feature. For example, if you have Linux kernel 2.4.0 and want to take advantage of the journaling file system known as ReiserFS, you need to patch or upgrade to Linux kernel 2.4.1.

➤ You want to address a security issue. You've read about the problem and know that it affects you.

Whether you patch or reinstall depends on the difference between the kernel that you have and the kernel that you want. For example, suppose you're using Linux kernel 2.4.0 and want to use ReiserFS. You've read that you need kernel 2.4.1 for this purpose. In that case, you can apply the kernel 2.4.1 patch to upgrade your kernel.

Alternatively, if you have Linux kernel 2.2.16 and want to install kernel 2.4.1, there is no patch available. Your only option is to install a new kernel. A kernel can be several dozen megabytes in size, so this can be a fairly time-intensive process.

Keeping Track

When you keep records in Linux, you want to record every significant item related to your computer, as well as how it may be connected or networked with other computers. You also want to keep track of the different licenses that you use because not all software used on Linux is covered under the General Public License (GPL).

GNU and Other Linux Licenses

Several major licenses are associated with Linux software. Most prominent are the GPL and various software licenses approved by the Open Source Initiative (OSI).

Stallman developed the GPL to give GNU and Linux software the advantages that were once available with Unix. Three basic principles are associated with the GPL:

➤ All GPL software must make a complete copy of the source code freely available. The code or programming instructions must include clear documentation.

➤ Any software added to the GPL software must also include clear documentation. If there is interaction between the two software packages, the package as a whole must be distributed under the GPL.

➤ GPL software comes without a warranty.

Legal interpretations of the actual license are covered under various copyright laws, which are beyond the scope of this book. You can find a copy of the GPL in the Appendix.

Eric Raymond created the rival OSI in part to set criteria to define open source software. There are numerous disagreements between the OSI and the FSF that often become emotional. One example of the difference is that OSI-approved licenses allow changes only through software patches. The detailed differences are beyond the scope of the Linux+ exam.

Four other major types of license are associated with software that you can use with Linux:

➤ *Freeware*—As strange as it may sound, freeware licenses are generally more restrictive than the GPL or any open source license. Freeware licenses generally do not allow you to modify the software.

➤ *Shareware*—This is generally more restrictive than freeware. Anyone who uses a copy of shareware for longer than a set period of time is required to pay a fee.

➤ *Artistic license*—This allows the original copyright holder to have control of any modifications that other developers make public. It is similar but not identical to the GPL.

➤ *Closed source*—Any software for which the source code is not generally available to the public.

This is only a small portion of the actual licenses associated with software used on Linux. Again, legal interpretation of those licenses is beyond the scope of this book. A more comprehensive list is currently available on the FSF Web site, at **www.fsf.org/philosophy/license-list.html.**

Documentation Practices

If you ever have a problem with your Linux computer, you want a record of the hardware and software that you currently have installed. You also want a record of problems that you may have had with your computer and network.

There is no one set of "best practices" for documenting what you do with a Linux computer. Some simply suggest that you document everything, which isn't very helpful. A few documentation practices are important:

➤ Document your hardware configuration. Even perfectly configured hardware can fail on occasion. A documented hardware configuration is important to installing Linux, as you will see in Chapter 3.

➤ Document your software configuration. As discussed in later chapters, the key to Linux software configuration rests in the configuration files, especially in the /etc directory as discussed in Chapter 6. Any changes to these files should be documented, since they are critical to the smooth operation of your system.

➤ Keep your documentation readily available. Any information technology discipline is a time-sensitive business. If you do not have documentation readily available onsite, there will be unnecessary delays when you have a problem.

 The key fact to remember is that the best documentation is kept in a local, readily available physical file. Any documentation that you keep on a computer may get lost whenever you have a problem with your computer.

Practice Questions

Question 1

> If you want to install Linux on a computer as a dedicated proxy server, which of the following services do you need?
>
> ○ a. BIND
>
> ○ b. Squid
>
> ○ c. Samba
>
> ○ d. Sendmail

Answer b is correct. Squid is the name of the Linux proxy server, which also caches Internet Web pages on the local computer for service to the local network. BIND (the Berkeley Internet Name Domain) translates domain names such as **Coriolis.com** to IP addresses. Therefore, answer a is incorrect. Samba is the service that enables Unix/Linux computers to communicate with computers that are running Microsoft or IBM operating systems. Therefore, answer c is incorrect. Sendmail is the service that sends and receives email. Therefore, answer d is incorrect.

Question 2

> If you want to install Linux on a computer as a dedicated file and Web server on a network with computers that have Microsoft Windows installed, which of the following services do you need?
>
> ○ a. Fileservice and Samba
>
> ○ b. Apache and Sendmail
>
> ○ c. Samba and **ipchains**
>
> ○ d. Apache and Samba

Answer d is correct. Apache is the Web server most closely associated with Linux. Samba is the service that allows Unix/Linux computers to communicate with other computers that are running the Microsoft Windows operating system. Since there is no Fileservice service in Linux, answer a is incorrect. Sendmail is a service for sending and receiving email on a local network. Therefore, answer b is incorrect. And finally, **ipchains** is a utility commonly used as a firewall. Therefore, answer c is incorrect.

Question 3

> Which of the following is another name for Samba?
>
> ○ a. Common Internet File System
>
> ○ b. Nameserver
>
> ○ c. Windows Networking
>
> ○ d. Peer-to-Peer Networking

Answer a is correct. The Common Internet File System (CIFS) is another name for Samba. Since nameserver is another name for BIND, answer b is incorrect. Although Samba is a way for Unix/Linux computers to network with Microsoft Windows computers, Samba isn't the only means of Windows networking. Therefore, answer c is incorrect. Peer-to-peer networking is a type of networking in which no one server governs logins or authentication. Because this is independent of Samba, answer d is also incorrect.

Question 4

> Suppose you have an older personal computer with a 386 CPU. Although the 1.44MB floppy drive and network cards on this computer still work, the hard drive does not. What hardware do you need to add in order to install Linux on this computer?
>
> ○ a. An upgraded CPU
>
> ○ b. A new hard drive of at least 100MB capacity
>
> ○ c. Apache
>
> ○ d. Nothing

Answer d is correct. You can install a simple distribution of Linux from a 1.44MB floppy disk, based on the work of the Linux Router Project. The router that is created can serve as the junction between your network and another network such as the Internet. Since the Linux Router Project distribution doesn't require an upgraded CPU or a hard drive, answers a and b are incorrect. Since Apache is a type of software service and not a type of hardware, answer c is also incorrect.

Question 5

What is the difference between **iptables** and **ipchains**?

○ a. The **iptables** utility can be used with all Linux distributions; **ipchains** is a tool found exclusively on Red Hat Linux.

○ b. The **ipchains** utility is associated with Linux kernel 2.2.x; **iptables** is associated with Linux kernel 2.4.x. You can't use **ipchains** on any system with Linux kernel 2.4.x.

○ c. The **ipchains** utility is associated with Linux kernel 2.2.x; **iptables** is associated with Linux kernel 2.4.x. You can't use **iptables** on any system with Linux kernel 2.2.x.

○ d. The **iptables** utility is associated with Linux kernel 2.2.x; **ipchains** is associated with Linux kernel 2.4.x. You can't use **iptables** on any system with Linux kernel 2.2.x.

Answer c is correct. The **ipchains** utility was developed for Linux kernel 2.2.x, and can still be used on systems on which kernel 2.4.x is installed. The **iptables** utility was developed for Linux kernel 2.4.x. Because **iptables** cannot be used on distributions with Linux kernel 2.2.x and **ipchains** can be found on a variety of Linux distributions, answer a is incorrect. Because you can use **ipchains** on Linux distributions with kernel 2.4.x, answer b is also incorrect. Since the **iptables** utility is not associated with Linux kernel 2.2.x, answer d is also incorrect.

Question 6

You're in the process of checking your computer for hardware compatibility with Debian Linux. Which of the following resources would you use? [Check all correct answers]

❑ a. **www.redhat.com**

❑ b. The Linux Hardware Compatibility List at **www.hardware-compatibility.com**

❑ c. **www.debian.org**

❑ d. Web sites of the manufacturers of your hardware

Answers c and d are correct. A Hardware Compatibility List is usually available on the Web site associated with a specific distribution. Some hardware manufacturers also list drivers or some other help to make their equipment work with Linux. Since you wouldn't expect the Red Hat Linux Web site to have a correct Hardware Compatibility List for the Debian distribution, answer a is incorrect.

Since there is no **www.hardware-compatibilty.com** (at least as of this writing), answer b is incorrect.

Question 7

> You have a USB camera that doesn't work with your current Linux kernel 2.2.16. You know that there are downloadable drivers available for your camera. Camera drivers are also a part of Linux kernel 2.4.6, but they need to be activated as loadable modules. Which of the following actions will enable your USB camera to be hot-swappable; that is, installable without rebooting your computer?
>
> ○ a. Download the driver from the manufacturer's Web site. Make sure the camera driver is activated as a loadable module.
>
> ○ b. Upgrade your kernel to version 2.4.6. Make sure loadable modules are not active for the camera driver.
>
> ○ c. Upgrade your kernel to version 2.4.6. Make sure loadable modules are active for the camera driver.
>
> ○ d. Upgrade your kernel to version 2.4.6. Download the driver from the manufacturer's Web site.

Answer c is correct. The question states that the right driver is available in Linux kernel 2.4.6. Modules can be dynamically loaded when made active in Linux kernel 2.4.x. Since the current Linux kernel as stated in the question is version 2.2.16, the camera driver cannot be loaded dynamically based on answer a. That answer is therefore incorrect. Unless the right loadable modules are active, an upgrade to Linux kernel 2.4.x won't matter. Therefore, answer b is incorrect. As stated in the question, the driver is already available as part of Linux kernel 2.4.6; therefore, downloading the driver is not necessary, and answer d is incorrect.

Question 8

> Assume you have a Linux computer in a locked room. Where is the best place to keep documentation on the hardware and software configuration of that computer?
>
> ○ a. In a filing cabinet at a remote site
>
> ○ b. On a file on your computer
>
> ○ c. On a file on a nearby computer
>
> ○ d. In a filing cabinet near the computer

Answer d is correct. If the Linux computer provides critical services, you want configuration information as close to the computer as possible. Since answer a does not meet this criterion, it is incorrect. If you have a failure on your computer, you won't be able to access its files. Therefore, answer b is incorrect. If you have a systemic failure of several computers in the same room, from a power surge for example, files on a nearby computer may not be available either. Therefore, answer c is incorrect.

Question 9

If you want to install the ReiserFS file system on your computer, which of the following might you have to do?

○ a. Upgrade your current Linux file system from ext2 to ext3.

○ b. Install Linux kernel 2.4.0 or higher.

○ c. Install Linux kernel 2.4.1 or higher.

○ d. Start with a new installation of the latest version of Linux.

Answer c is correct. Support for the ReiserFS file system was incorporated into Linux kernel version 2.4.1. Because ext2 and ext3 are entirely different file systems from ReiserFS, answer a is incorrect. Because support for ReiserFS is not included in Linux kernel 2.4.0, answer b is also not correct. Although answer d could work, this is more trouble than it's worth (and it would destroy the data currently loaded on your computer). Therefore, answer d is also incorrect.

Question 10

Which of the following statements is not a characteristic of the GPL?

○ a. If you plan to develop a new program that interacts closely with a current program covered under the GPL, the entire package when released must also be covered under the GPL.

○ b. If you plan to develop a new program that interacts closely with a current program covered under the GPL, you do not need to release the source code for your new program.

○ c. The source code associated with GPL software must include clear documentation.

○ d. You do not need to provide a warranty with GPL software.

Answer b is correct. If you develop a new program that interacts closely with a program covered under the GNU General Public License (GPL), you need to release the source code for your new program. Since answers a, c, and d are all characteristics associated with the GPL, these answers are all incorrect.

Need to Know More?

 Torvalds, Linus, and David Diamond. *Just for Fun, The Story of an Accidental Revolutionary.* New York, NY: HarperCollins, 2001. ISBN 0-06662-072-4. A slightly irreverent autobiography by the developer of Linux that also provides valuable technical insights into the key developments associated with Linux.

 Explore the Web site for the Free Software Foundation (FSF), the governing body for the GNU project, at **www.fsf.org**. This site includes a history of the FSF as well as excellent descriptions of free and open source software.

 For the latest developments on the Linux kernel, explore the Linux kernel archives at **www.kernel.org**. You can download the latest kernel and appropriate patches and review changes dynamically as the Linux kernel continues to develop.

 Perhaps the best place to understand open source software is at the Web site for the Open Source Initiative at **www.opensource.org**.

 Some of the key documents behind Linux can be found on the Web site of the Linux Documentation Project. These include the Hardware-HOWTO (**www.linuxdoc.org/HOWTO/Hardware-HOWTO**), which includes a basic Linux Hardware Compatibility List, and the Kernel-HOWTO (**www.linuxdoc.org/HOWTO/Kernel-HOWTO**), which describes installation requirements and instructions for recompiling, patching, and upgrading kernels.

 One amazing Linux distribution can be downloaded from the Web site for the Linux Router Project at **www.linuxrouter.org**. You can download this distribution onto one single 1.44MB floppy disk.

Linux Hardware Planning

Terms you'll need to understand:

✓ Power-On Self Test (POST)

✓ BIOS

✓ CMOS

✓ ATAPI, IDE

✓ SCSI

✓ PCI

✓ ISA

✓ USB, IEEE 1394

✓ PCMCIA

✓ IRQ, DMA, I/O

✓ PS/2, COM, LPT

✓ Hardware Compatibility List (HCL)

Techniques you'll need to master:

✓ Understanding the boot process

✓ Defining the differences between BIOS and CMOS

✓ Associating internal PC cables with floppy, IDE, and SCSI drives

✓ Remembering the IRQ and I/O addresses associated with the first four COM ports

✓ Memorizing the IRQ associated with the first two LPT ports

✓ Understanding the priorities associated with SCSI numbers

✓ Remembering typical IRQ assignments for various devices

Although it has no prerequisites, the Linux+ exam is perhaps the most advanced in a sequence of CompTIA exams. The Linux Professional Institute (LPI) at **www.lpi.org** has suggested that beginning candidates may take various certification exams in the following sequence:

➤ CompTIA's A+ Exam

➤ CompTIA's Network+ Exam

➤ CompTIA's Linux+ Exam

➤ LPI's LPIC 1a Exam

An alternative at the same level as LPI is the Sair Linux and GNU Certification and its Linux Certified Administrator exams. More information on these exams is available online at **www.linuxcertification.org**.

The first exam in this sequence is A+, which is in part an exam on personal computer (PC) hardware. In the belief that all systems administrators should have some knowledge of hardware, CompTIA has included the essence of some of its A+ hardware objectives on the Linux+ exam.

 Although six months of experience with Linux is recommended, there are no prerequisites for the Linux+ exam. At the same time, however, experience with the topics covered in the CompTIA A+ and Network+ exams can be helpful.

In other words, you'll need to know some of the basics of installing, configuring, and troubleshooting computer hardware, independent of what you know about Linux.

Physical Hardware

When you turn on your personal computer, it goes through a series of tests. First, the power-on self test (POST) makes sure your computer can communicate with your CPU and RAM. Next, the BIOS (or the basic input/output system) detects and configures some basic components, including ATAPI hard drives. While Linux loads from a hard drive, it begins to detect and configure your other peripherals: some installed on PCI and ISA cards, others external to your computer.

This section should be a review to those of you who are familiar with hardware, especially in the context of CompTIA's A+ hardware exam.

Power-On Self Test (POST)

When you turn on your computer, your CPU and RAM have nothing in memory. They look to your BIOS for help. The first thing that a BIOS does on a PC is the POST. This checks the most important hardware on your motherboard. If everything checks out OK, the BIOS sends one beep through your computer's speaker.

Note: Computer speakers are generally installed inside your computer's case and are different from any speakers that may be connected through a sound card.

Note: If you do not hear any beeps when you first start (or cold boot) your computer, your computer's speaker is probably not connected to the motherboard.

If you hear more than one beep, you could have a variety of problems with your hardware.

Assume you have a working system. If you upgrade your CPU or RAM, the POST can tell you if the new hardware is good or has been installed correctly. If there is a problem, you'll hear more than one beep, and the boot process will stop.

 Remember that when you install a new CPU or RAM, and your computer beeps more than once and does not boot, the most likely cause is a problem with your new hardware such as improper installation.

BIOS on CMOS

After the power-on self test (POST), the next step for your computer is to read information on the BIOS. A BIOS includes routines to configure your clock, keyboard, display and disk drives. Sometimes the BIOS also may configure peripherals.

A PC's BIOS includes a configuration menu, accessible after a successful POST. Typically, you can access this menu by pressing the Ctrl, Esc, Del, F1, or F2 key just after POST. If none of these options work, consult the documentation for your PC.

 If you have one or more SCSI hard drives, you may also need access to your SCSI BIOS, which may be accessible with a command such as Ctrl+A. If this doesn't work, consult the documentation for the SCSI controller.

The settings associated with the BIOS configuration menu are stored in CMOS, which is short for complementary metal oxide semiconductor. CMOS stores basic information that changes on your computer, such as the time, the type and speed of the CPU, the amount of random access memory (RAM), and the parameters for your hard drives. Most BIOS menus allow you to password protect your CMOS settings. This information is stored in memory powered by a small battery, even when your computer is shut down or disconnected.

If the battery fails inside your computer, CMOS settings are normally lost, including any password protection. Because the BIOS menu is stored on a read-only memory (ROM) chip that does not depend on power, the basic menu is still there.

 If the battery fails inside your computer, CMOS settings are usually lost. When you replace the battery, you need to use the BIOS menu to restore your CMOS settings.

 If you set a password for your CMOS and then lose that password, you can start fresh. Remove your computer's battery. (Typically, the battery should be left out for a few minutes.) When you replace the battery and return to the BIOS configuration menu, there should be no password. (If this doesn't work, consult the documentation for the computer motherboard. One alternative, if available, is a Clear CMOS jumper.) You can then restore your CMOS settings.

After the BIOS configures your computer, it looks for something to boot. Generally, it looks first to your floppy, then your hard drive. Assuming that you don't have a disk in your floppy drive, the BIOS starts the first operating system that it sees on your hard drive. Most hard drives conform to one of two specifications: IDE (Integrated Drive Electronics) or SCSI (Small Computer Systems Interface).

If you have IDE and or SCSI hard drives, most BIOS systems allow you to configure whichever drive boots first. If you have a SCSI hard drive, you'll also need to configure the SCSI BIOS. Remember, the settings for your computer's BIOS are saved in CMOS.

 Keep in mind that the CMOS settings in your regular and SCSI BIOS menus determine where your computer looks first for an operating system. If you have multiple SCSI or IDE hard drives, the proper CMOS settings can determine the hard drive your computer uses to load an operating system.

Floppy Drives

Floppy drives have their own channel, cable, and connection to your motherboard. Floppy controller cables have 34 wires and 3 connectors. One connector is attached to the motherboard; the other two are reserved for floppy drives. In the

Linux world, the first two floppy drives are known as fd0 and fd1. In the Microsoft world, this corresponds loosely to the A:\ and B:\ drives.

Floppy controller cables are flat ribbon cables. Unlike other controller ribbon cables, many floppy cables do not have a "notch" to ensure proper installation. Thus, it is easy to install the floppy ribbon cable upside down accidentally. To install a floppy cable properly, you may need to make sure that the right cable matches the right wire. Floppy ribbon cables either have a number or are colored red next to the first wire to help guide the installation process.

 Remember that if your floppy drive does not work and the floppy indicator light is constantly on, the floppy controller cable is probably installed upside down.

IDE Drives

Most hard drives and CD drives built today are IDE drives, which conform to ATAPI (or the AT attachment packet interface). IDE drives are connected to ATAPI controllers with a 40-pin ribbon cable.

The standard PC includes two ATAPI controllers, generally known as the primary and secondary controllers. You can attach each controller to two different IDE drives. On each controller, there is a master drive and a slave drive.

 Keep in mind that IDE hard drives and CD drives conform to ATAPI standards, also known as ATA standards.

In Linux, each position corresponds to a different designator, as shown in Table 3.1. Even though the designator starts with "hd," this applies to any CD drives that may be installed. For example, if you have a CD drive attached as the master on the secondary controller, it is designated as *hdc* in Linux.

The optimal ATAPI configuration includes only one hard drive and one CD drive (or similar optical disk). The hard drive is installed as the master on the

Table 3.1 Linux designators for ATAPI drives.		
Controller	**Position**	**Linux Designator**
Primary	Master	hda
Primary	Slave	hdb
Secondary	Master	hdc
Secondary	Slave	hdd

primary controller (hda), and the CD drive is installed as the master on the secondary controller (hdc). Because each controller has a separate channel to your motherboard, your computer could read data from both your hard drive and CD drive simultaneously.

 If possible, avoid installing a hard drive and a CD drive on the same controller. PC data transfer to and from an ATAPI CD drive is generally much slower than to and from a modern hard drive. When the CD drive is in use, the speed at which your computer reads and writes to your hard drive would be limited to the data transfer speed of the CD drive.

SCSI Drives

Many computers, especially servers, have SCSI drives. They can be installed inside or outside your PC (internal or external). A wide variety of SCSI standards and connectors exist; these will be covered briefly in this section.

SCSI standards can be divided into three different categories: SCSI-1, SCSI-2, and SCSI-3. All SCSI devices are controlled by a host adapter. SCSI devices are connected in series; the last device in the series has a *terminator*, which identifies the end of the chain of devices.

SCSI devices can be controlled by an 8-bit or 16-bit bus. SCSI devices that use 16-bit buses are sometimes known as "Wide SCSI." Because 8-bit buses are associated with 50-pin cables, and 16-bit (Wide) buses are associated with 68-pin cables.

Note: A bus connects different components on a circuit board. For example, an 8-bit bus enables simultaneous data transfer through eight connected wires.

The following sections are a brief overview of the different SCSI standards.

SCSI-1

The first SCSI standard, SCSI-1, was released in 1986. With an 8-bit controlling bus, it allows data transfer at a maximum of 5MBps. The standard is now obsolete, but any SCSI-1 equipment you may have can be installed with SCSI-2 host adapters.

SCSI-1 is associated with three types of cables, each with 50 wires:

➤ Internal SCSI cables are ribbon cables similar to internal floppy and hard drive cables. Internal SCSI cables have two rows of 25 pins or sockets each.

➤ External "D-Shell" cables have connectors with 50 pins or sockets, depending on the interface.

➤ Centronics cables include two rows of flat contacts, 25 pins on each side.

SCSI-2

The second SCSI standard, SCSI-2, was released in 1994. Like SCSI-1, this standard also uses 50 wires on each cable. There are two variations on SCSI-2. Fast SCSI allows data transfer to the 8-bit bus at 10MBps. Wide SCSI includes a 16-bit controlling bus and has 68 wires on each cable. Fast Wide SCSI combines both advances for a maximum data transfer speed of 20 Mbps.

 Be sure you know how to associate a picture of a 50-wire connector with a regular (not Wide or Ultra Wide) SCSI interface, as shown in Figure 3.1.

SCSI-3

Many different SCSI-3 standards exist. Most important in SCSI-3 is the introduction of higher speeds of 20MBps through 160MBps. Some SCSI-3 standards are known as Ultra SCSI. One prominent SCSI-3 standard that uses a 16-bit bus is known as Ultra Wide SCSI. This standard allows data transfer at up to 40MBps. Another prominent SCSI-3 standard is known as Ultra2 Wide SCSI, which also uses a 16-bit bus but allows data transfer at up to 80MBps.

 68-wire SCSI cables are associated with 16-bit buses.

A number of variations on this theme, such as Ultra2 SCSI and Ultra3 SCSI, also manage data at the faster SCSI-3 speeds.

SCSI Device Setup

You can install an SCSI card in most PCs. Every SCSI device has two connectors and is connected to this card in a daisy-chain fashion.

For example, assume you have two SCSI devices, B and C. You can use one SCSI cable to connect the card to device B. A second SCSI cable can link device B's other connector to device C. If you have no more SCSI devices to connect, add a *terminator* to the open connector on device C.

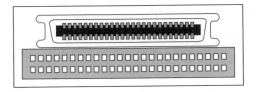

Figure 3.1   The ends of standard SCSI cables.

Keep in mind the fact that a terminator is required at the end of a daisy chain of SCSI devices.

ISA, PCI, and AGP

Hard drives aren't the only peripherals installed inside your computer. Common options include sound cards, modems, network adapters, and video cards. Each of these is installed in slots, as defined by one of three basic standards: ISA, PCI, and AGP.

The old standard for peripheral cards is based on the Industry Standard Architecture (ISA) specification. The bus that connects ISA cards runs at 8.33MHz, which seems fairly slow when compared to the typical speed of a CPU. ISA cards are generally *legacy* equipment, which means that they are no longer in production and are falling into disuse. Many newer computers don't even have a slot available for ISA cards.

The Peripheral Component Interconnect (PCI) specification defines a type of card that does not have to communicate directly with the CPU. In fact, using direct memory access (DMA) channels, PCI cards can communicate directly with other parts of your computer. PCI cards are connected to the PCI bus, which can run at 33MHz.

A common option for video cards is the Accelerated Graphics Port (AGP) standard. AGP video cards have the same access to your computer as RAM memory. Modern computers often include one dedicated AGP slot. One common option on PCs is shared memory, in which some of your RAM is used to boost the performance of your video card. AGP cards can run at 66MHz and higher.

Figure 3.2 places these cards in the context of basic PC components.

Hot-Swappable Hardware

Most peripherals aren't hot swappable; in other words, you shouldn't install or remove them while your computer is on. If you open your computer case and try to install an internal modem, chances are good that you will destroy a number of circuits in your computer.

External components such as a keyboard, mouse, and printer are generally different. If you attach or remove them from your computer, there is no permanent damage. If you were to replace one printer with another, however, the new printer probably wouldn't work.

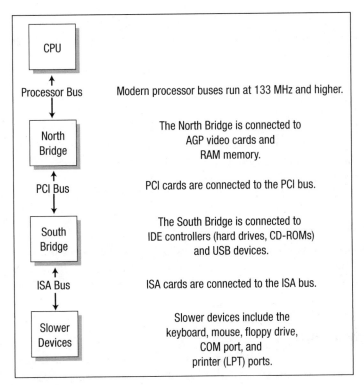

Figure 3.2   Basic PC architecture.

Three categories of hardware can be installed or removed while your computer is on. This is also known as *hot swapping*. The categories of hot-swappable equipment are USB, IEEE 1394, and PCMCIA. Your operating system should detect the device and install the appropriate driver without rebooting your computer. The following sections provide a brief overview of each of these categories.

USB

The Universal Serial Bus (USB) was first developed in 1996. Although developers have been slowly incorporating USB support into the Linux kernel, USB hot swapping was not fully supported until the development of Linux kernel 2.4, released at the beginning of 2001. USB supports communication at 1.5MBps, which is 12Mbps.

Note: Remember, there are 8 bits in a byte, so 12 megabits per second (Mbps) is the same as 1.5 megabytes per second (MBps). (12Mbps = 1.5MBps × [8 bits/Byte])

Computers with USB support include a *root hub*. Other hubs can be attached to the root hub. With a series of hubs, theoretically you can attach up to 127 devices to a USB-enabled computer.

You can install USB devices while your computer is on. USB capable operating systems, including Linux, should then detect and install the appropriate driver for that device.

IEEE 1394

IEEE 1394 is a standard from the Institute for Electrical and Electronics Engineers. Sometimes known as *FireWire* or *iLINK*, IEEE 1394 shares some characteristics with USB. Like USB, IEEE 1394 devices are hot swappable. Designed primarily for video applications, different IEEE 1394 devices can transfer data at 100Mbps (12.5MBps), 200Mbps (25MBps), and 400Mbps (50MBps).

PCMCIA

Laptop computers generally include one or more slots for installing devices that are about the size of a credit card. PCMCIA cards (from the Personal Computer Memory Card International Association) are also known as PC Cards. PCMCIA cards were the first hot-swappable cards. They were supported in the Linux kernel starting with version 2.2.

Mobile Hardware

Not all USB, IEEE 1394, or PCMCIA devices are truly hot swappable in Linux. In other words, when you install or remove one of these devices, your operating system may not recognize it and cannot install it unless you reboot your computer.

The same situation holds true for mobile hardware. To save space, some laptop computers are configured to enable you to exchange components such as floppy and CD-ROM drives in the same location.

Unless explicitly allowed in your computer's documentation, don't hot swap components such as a floppy, CD-ROM, or especially a laptop battery. Any electrical charge transmitted during this process could easily damage circuits on your computer's motherboard.

After you exchange a floppy and a CD-ROM on a laptop, your operating system should recognize what you just installed. If this does not happen, you may have to reboot your computer to get your operating system to recognize your change in hardware.

If you hot swap mobile components on a laptop, such as a CD-ROM and a floppy drive, and your computer doesn't recognize what you just installed, you may have to reboot your computer.

Other Peripherals

The remaining peripherals are external. You can attach them to one of the ports on the back of a standard PC. On today's computers, peripherals are attached to three different types of ports:

➤ *PS/2*—Keyboards and mice are often connected to PS/2 ports.

➤ *COM*—COM, which is short for serial communications port, is a typical connection for most modems and older mice. Most computers can have two physical serial interfaces.

➤ *LPT*—Printers are most commonly attached to LPT ports. Current printer cable standards accommodate bidirectional communication. The standards are EPP (enhanced parallel port) and ECP (enhanced capabilities port).

Remember that the two printer cable standards that accommodate bidirectional communication are EPP and ECP.

None of these ports are absolutely required; there are USB alternatives for each of the listed devices.

Channels, Ports, and Addresses

One major problem when configuring devices on a PC is conflict. If two or more devices use the same channel, they are in conflict. Unless there is a way for these devices to share the same channel, the result is that neither device works.

PC channels fall into a number of categories, including interrupt requests (IRQ), input/output (I/O) addresses, direct memory addresses (DMA), communication ports (COM), and printer ports (LPT).

Interrupt Requests

An IRQ allows a device to send a request to your CPU for service.

CPUs are busy. When you type something, you don't want to wait for your CPU to be free before what you type is shown on your screen. Thus, your keyboard sends an IRQ to your CPU, asking for service.

Sixteen IRQs are available on most modern PCs, numbered from 0 through 15. In this case, lower numbers have higher priorities. Table 3.2 lists all 16 IRQs and their typical assignments.

Note: On most Linux distributions, currently allocated IRQs are listed in the /proc/interrupts file.

Table 3.2	Typical IRQ assignments.
IRQ	**Device**
0	System timer
1	Keyboard
2	Cascade from IRQs 8 through 15
3	COM2 or COM4
4	COM1 or COM3
5	Some sound cards or LPT2 (second printer port)
6	Floppy disk controller
7	LPT1 (first printer port)
8	Realtime clock (in CMOS)
9	Varies
10	Varies
11	Varies
12	PS/2 mouse
13	Math coprocessor
14	Primary ATAPI controller
15	Secondary ATAPI controller

Generally, only IRQs 0, 1, 2, 8, and 13 are fixed. The other IRQs can be re-assigned to a different device if you haven't installed the associated hardware. For example, IRQ 12 is typically reserved for a PS/2 mouse. If you don't have a PS/2 mouse on your computer, IRQ 12 can be assigned to something else.

In most cases, devices that try to use the same IRQ won't work. But there are exceptions, including some hard drive and USB controllers.

Input/Output Addresses

Every device on your PC requires a few bytes of RAM located at one or more input/output (I/O) addresses. Information stored in these addresses is exchanged with the rest of the computer.

I/O addresses are typically shown in hexadecimal notation in two formats. For example, the I/O address associated with COM1 may be listed as 03f8 or 0x3f8.

Hexadecimal notation uses base-16. By comparison, we use digits, or base-10. Our numbers are 0, 1, 2, 3, 4, 5, 6, 7, 8, and 9; base-16 numbers are 0, 1, 2, 3, 4, 5, 6, 7, 8, 9, a, b, c, d, e, and f. For example, the range of I/O addresses associated with your keyboard may be 0060-006f.

The only I/O addresses that you'll need to know are associated with the four COM ports (COM1, COM2, COM3, and COM4) and the two LPT ports (LPT1 and LPT2).

Note: On most Linux distributions, currently assigned I/O addresses are listed in the /proc/ioports file.

Direct Memory Address Channels

Direct memory address (DMA) channels are used primarily to transfer information directly to and from memory. Most PCs have eight DMA channels. DMA channels are typically used by sound cards, floppy drives, and tape drives.

Note: On most Linux distributions, currently assigned DMA addresses are listed in the /proc/dma file.

COM Ports

COM ports are also known as serial ports. Most PCs can be set up with two physical serial port interfaces. Each of these interfaces can be assigned to one of two COM ports. Each COM port is associated with a specific IRQ and I/O address, as shown in Table 3.3.

 Memorize the IRQ and I/O address associated with the first four COM ports.

Some devices use port number COM5 or higher. Although Linux device drivers are available for such ports, their associated IRQs and I/O addresses are arbitrary and therefore can interfere with another device using a different COM port.

The most common users of COM ports are serial mice and modems. Even internal modems require a COM port.

Table 3.3	COM ports, IRQs, and I/O addresses.		
Port	Serial Interface	IRQ	I/O Address
COM1	Serial Port 1	4	03f8
COM2	Serial Port 2	3	02f8
COM3	Serial Port 1	4	03e8
COM4	Serial Port 2	3	02e8

Printer (LPT) Ports

Most PCs are set up with one physical printer port. You can get an adapter to set up a second physical printer port if you want. Printer ports are known as LPT, out of respect for the original type of printer (a line print terminal). For the Linux+ exam, you should know the two major LPT ports and their associated IRQ channels, as shown in Table 3.4.

 Be sure to memorize the IRQs associated with LPT1 and LPT2.

SCSI Numbers

Depending on whether you have an 8-bit or 16-bit SCSI bus, you can have 8 or 16 SCSI devices on your computer. Each of these devices is associated with an identification number from 0 through 7 (regular SCSI) or 0 through 15 (Wide SCSI). The number assigned to a device determines the priority that it has in accessing the SCSI bus.

The highest-priority device number, 7, is reserved for the SCSI controller, sometimes known as the *host adapter*.

 Do not assign SCSI device number 7 to any SCSI device. This number is reserved for your SCSI host adapter.

SCSI numbers are in the following order of priority, from highest to lowest: 7, 6, 5, 4, 3, 2, 1, 0, 15, 14, 13, 12, 11, 10, 9, 8.

Linux Hardware Support

As suggested in Chapter 2, not all hardware works with Linux. Since most computers still use Microsoft Windows, most hardware manufacturers develop a driver for that set of operating systems first. The situation is improving, however. Independent developers are constantly developing drivers for new and "incompatible"

Table 3.4 Printer ports, IRQs, and I/O addresses.		
Port	IRQ	I/O Address
LPT1	7	0378
LPT2	5	0278

hardware. Methods are available to configure many problem components. Plus, more manufacturers are releasing Linux drivers when they release new hardware.

In most cases, you can install Linux without concern for the hardware currently on your computer. As a Linux administrator, however, you need to be sure. Before installing Linux, you should identify the hardware that you have, cross-check that hardware against existing Hardware Compatibility Lists, and collect any drivers that may not be included in your selected Linux distribution.

Needed Hardware

One good practice is to document all of the hardware installed on your computer. At a minimum, the key components you should document are the CPU, amount of RAM, video (or graphics) cards, monitor capabilities, network cards, modems, printers, hard drive positions (as discussed in the IDE Drives section), and ID numbers for any SCSI devices.

If you have Microsoft Windows installed, you could also record the IRQ, I/O, DMA, and COM ports associated with each device. This could be useful if you run into a configuration problem after installing Linux. Chapter 6 includes one example of how you can use this information to configure a troublesome network card.

Linux Hardware Compatibility Lists

As discussed in Chapter 2, the Linux Hardware Compatibility List (HCL) is available online at **www.linuxdoc.org/HOWTO/Hardware-HOWTO/ index.html**. As you review this document, each of your devices will fall into one of three categories:

➤ It's on the HCL.

➤ It's on the list of Linux Incompatible Hardware, as defined at the end of the HCL. As of this writing, this list includes modems and printers, because of their dependence on Microsoft Windows.

➤ It fits in neither category, in which case review the HCL associated with your distribution. If available, this can generally be found on your distribution's Web site.

Collecting Drivers

If your hardware can't even be found in your distribution's HCL, as described in the previous section, check your manufacturer's Web site. A number of hardware manufacturers include Linux drivers for their devices for download, sometimes with instructions.

Video Basics

The Linux graphical user interface (GUI) is based on XFree86, which is the open source version of the X Window software first produced for Unix.

XFree86 software can accommodate just about any video card in one way or another. XFree86 includes drivers for hundreds of different video cards, as listed at **www.xfree86.org**. If your video card is not included in any of the XFree86 lists, you probably can configure it based on the amount of video memory on your card and the capability of your monitor.

Practice Questions

Question 1

> You've had your computer for several years. The clock inside your computer
> seems to be slow. You remove the battery from inside your computer and
> then realize you don't have the replacement battery with you. When you
> finally replace the battery the next day, which of the following settings will
> you probably have to reconfigure?
>
> ○ a. operating system
>
> ○ b. CMOS
>
> ○ c. active partition
>
> ○ d. BIOS

Answer b is correct. The CMOS settings are preserved by power from the battery in your computer. Therefore, if the battery is disconnected, CMOS settings are lost. Since the operating system is generally on your hard drive, its integrity does not relate to the battery inside your computer. Therefore, answer a is incorrect. The active partition is the logical area of a hard disk that boots on a specific hard drive. The integrity of that partition also is not related to the battery inside your computer. Therefore, answer c is incorrect. Since the BIOS menu itself is stored in ROM, it does not depend on power from the computer battery. Therefore, answer d is also incorrect.

Question 2

> You have a computer with an IDE hard drive connected as the master on the primary controller. A CD-ROM is also connected as the master drive on the secondary controller. You install a CD writer on the slave position of the primary controller. After installation, you notice that it takes a lot longer to load programs. Which of the following statements best describes the problem?
>
> ○ a. The two CDs share the same resources, which leads to conflicts between these two devices.
>
> ○ b. With the new CD in place, the CD-ROM interferes with the hard drive. Hard drive transfer speeds are often limited to the speed of the CD-ROM.
>
> ○ c. With the new CD in place, it begins to interfere with the hard drive. Hard drive transfer speeds are often limited to the speed of the CD writer.
>
> ○ d. You need to reboot your computer. After it reboots, the plug-and-play characteristics of each device will override any conflicts that may currently exist between either CD and the hard drive.

Answer c is correct. A CD and a hard drive that is connected to the same controller can adversely affect transfer speed to and from the hard drive. Even if there were device conflicts between the two CDs, that would not affect transfer speed to the hard drive. Therefore, answer a is incorrect. Since the CD-ROM is connected to a different controller than the hard drive, it does not affect the transfer speed to or from that hard drive. Therefore, answer b is incorrect. Rebooting your computer does not change the connection of both the hard drive and CD writer to the same primary controller. Therefore, answer d is incorrect.

Question 3

> Your modem isn't working. You believe that the root cause is an IRQ or I/O conflict between that modem and another device. The modem was working before, and you haven't added any new hardware. You suspect that another administrator accidentally changed the IRQ or I/O associated with COM4, the previously assigned port for that modem. What are the standard IRQ and I/O addresses associated with COM4?
>
> ○ a. IRQ 4, I/O 02e8
>
> ○ b. IRQ 3, I/O 02f8
>
> ○ c. IRQ 4, I/O 03e8
>
> ○ d. IRQ 3, I/O 02e8

Answer d is correct. IRQ 3 and I/O 02e8 correspond to COM4. If you see a similar question on the Linux+ exam, remember that COM1 and COM3 always correspond to IRQ 4, and COM2 and COM4 always correspond to IRQ 3. Also, the f in the I/O memory address correspond to COM1 or COM2, and the e corresponds to COM3 or COM4.

Question 4

Which of the following types of devices can you install without rebooting your computer? [Check all correct answers]

❏ a. USB

❏ b. IEEE 1394

❏ c. Printers

❏ d. Laptop computer floppy drives

Answers a and b are correct. Devices that conform to the USB and IEEE 1394 standards are designed to be hot swappable; in other words, if you install them while your computer is on, your operating system should recognize these devices and install the appropriate drivers automatically. Although you can physically connect a printer to your computer, only a few printers conform to USB standards. Whether your operating system is Linux or Microsoft Windows, it won't recognize the installation of most printers, nor will it install the appropriate drivers, at least without a reboot. (The more knowledgeable among you may note that Linux won't even recognize most printers while booting up.) Therefore, answer c is incorrect. If you have a laptop computer floppy drive, you shouldn't install it in your computer unless explicitly allowed by your laptop's documentation. Even if it is allowed, you still may have to reboot to get your operating system to recognize that drive. Therefore, answer d is also incorrect.

Question 5

You have a SCSI and an IDE hard drive. Each contains an operating system. You want to boot your computer with the operating system located on the SCSI drive. Which of the following actions is most appropriate?

- ○ a. Reconfigure the settings saved in your BIOS to recognize the SCSI drive, and make sure that it looks to this drive first in the boot order settings.

- ○ b. Reconfigure the settings saved in your CMOS to ignore your IDE hard drive completely. You'll still be able to access data on that drive when your SCSI drive boots.

- ○ c. Transfer the data you need to the SCSI drive, and then remove your IDE hard drive from your computer.

- ○ d. Reconfigure the settings saved in your CMOS to recognize the SCSI drive, and make sure that it looks to this drive first in the boot order settings.

Answer d is correct. When you start your computer, the settings for your hard drives and boot order are saved in your CMOS. Since the BIOS is just a menu that by itself doesn't include hard drive settings, answer a is incorrect. Although answer b would work, it means that you wouldn't be able to access the data on your IDE drive. Therefore, answer b is incorrect. Although answer c would work, it means that you wouldn't be able to take advantage of the storage space on your IDE drive. Therefore, answer c is also incorrect.

Question 6

You have a printer, a keyboard, a serial mouse, and a network card attached to your computer. You install an internal modem. After you reboot, assume Linux detects and installs the right drivers for the modem. When you try to connect to your ISP, you don't hear any sounds, and your computer does not connect. Furthermore, the behavior of your mouse seems erratic. Which of the following statements is the most likely cause of your problem?

- ○ a. You can't have both a network card and a modem on a Linux computer, because they try to use the same IRQ or I/O address.

- ○ b. Your modem and mouse are trying to use the same IRQ.

- ○ c. Two different devices are trying to use the same COM port.

- ○ d. Two different devices are trying to use the same LPT port.

Answer b is correct. The question notes problems with both the modem and the mouse. This is one possible result when both devices try to use the same interrupt request (IRQ). Network cards and modems are common on the same computer in Linux as well as in Windows. Neither device has a dedicated IRQ or input/output (I/O) address. The plug-and-play characteristics generally help these devices avoid conflicts. Therefore, answer a is incorrect. Although answer c would cause the problem noted in the question, it isn't necessarily a true statement. For example, the serial mouse could use COM1 while the modem is using COM3. But COM1 and COM3 both use IRQ 4. Therefore, answer c is incorrect. Because LPT ports are generally used for printers, answer d is also incorrect.

Question 7

You have seven SCSI devices installed in series to your computer. Your computer is configured to a regular (not Wide) SCSI-2 protocol. You've read that it can handle eight devices. You see that ID number 7 is still free. How can you install that eighth device?

- ○ a. Configure the new device with a SCSI ID of 7, and attach it at the end of the series of SCSI devices.
- ○ b. Replace an existing SCSI device, and use that device's SCSI ID number for your new device.
- ○ c. Reconfigure SCSI in your BIOS menu to handle additional devices.
- ○ d. Attach the new SCSI device to an IEEE 1394 port.

Answer b is correct. While Wide SCSI protocols are associated with 16 bits, which allow for 16 devices, regular SCSI protocols are 8-bit, which allows for 8 devices. For this question, one SCSI device has to be dedicated to the SCSI host adapter or controller. Therefore, your SCSI is at capacity, and you cannot just attach it to the end of the series of SCSI devices. In addition, SCSI ID 7 is the highest priority and can be assigned only to the host adapter. Therefore, answer a is incorrect. No BIOS menu currently allows you to add more than the maximum number of devices to a SCSI host adapter. Therefore, answer c is incorrect. Although IEEE 1394 is actually one of the later SCSI standards, no regular SCSI device can be connected to an IEEE 1394 port. Therefore, answer d is also incorrect.

Question 8

> Which of the following statements best describes the characteristics of a regular internal SCSI cable connector?
>
> ○ a. Two rows, 25 pins on each row
>
> ○ b. Five rows, 10 sockets on each row
>
> ○ c. Two rows, 34 pins on each row
>
> ○ d. Two rows, 50 pins on each row

Answer a is correct. A regular (not Wide) SCSI cable includes 50 wires. SCSI cables are narrow ribbon cables. Two rows of 25 pins each is the only one that fits this description and is characteristic of an actual regular SCSI connector. Because SCSI cables are supposed to be thin, answer b is incorrect. Answer c corresponds to a Wide SCSI cable, which has 68 wires. Therefore, answer c is incorrect. There are no SCSI cables with 100 pins; therefore, answer d is also incorrect.

Question 9

> You have just installed a new hard drive on your computer. Chances are good that your BIOS detects it when you boot your computer. You want to check your CMOS settings in your BIOS menu, just to be sure. When you start the BIOS menu, you realize that you forgot the CMOS password. What is the easiest way to reset your password?
>
> ○ a. Boot your computer to an MS-DOS floppy disk, and use the **fdisk /CMOS** command.
>
> ○ b. Open up your computer, then remove and replace your RAM.
>
> ○ c. Boot your computer to Linux, and use the **fdisk /CMOS** command.
>
> ○ d. Open up your computer and remove your computer's battery. Wait a few minutes, then replace it.

Answer d is correct. Like other CMOS settings, a CMOS password is stored in memory that is kept alive by the internal computer battery. If you remove this battery, CMOS settings, including the password, are reset to the BIOS defaults. (Sometimes you need to wait more than a few minutes before replacing the battery for this to work.) There is an **fdisk** command in both Microsoft Windows and in Linux, but there is no such thing as an **fdisk /CMOS** command in either operating system. Therefore, answers a and c are both incorrect. Since CMOS settings are not stored in your random access memory (RAM), answer b is also incorrect.

Question 10

> Which of the following is the typical IRQ assigned to the primary ATAPI controller?
>
> ○ a. 2
>
> ○ b. 5
>
> ○ c. 7
>
> ○ d. 14

Answer d is correct. IRQ 14 is typically reserved for the primary ATAPI hard disk controller. Because IRQ 2 is reserved for communications (cascade) from IRQs 8 through 15, answer a is not correct. Because IRQ 5 is typically used by sound cards or a second printer port, answer b is not correct. Because IRQ 7 is typically used as the first printer port, answer c is also incorrect.

Need to Know More?

 Gilster, Ron. *PC Technician Black Book.* Scottsdale, AZ: The Coriolis Group, 2001. ISBN 1-57610-808-2. An excellent problem solving reference for various components in a personal computer.

 Jones, James G., and Craig Landes. *A+ Exam Cram, 2nd Edition.* Scottsdale, AZ: The Coriolis Group, 2001. ISBN 1-57610-695-0. Since about 20 percent of the content of the Linux+ exam is based on hardware, there are a number of questions on the Linux+ exam that are similar to those on the A+ hardware exam.

 Reeves, Scott, Kalinda Reeves, Stephen Weese, and Christopher S. Geyer. *A+ Exam Prep, 3rd Edition.* Scottsdale, AZ: The Coriolis Group, 2001. ISBN 1-57610-699-3. Another good reference for A+ hardware style questions.

 Thompson, Robert Bruce. *PC Hardware in a Nutshell.* Sebastopol, CA: O'Reilly and Associates, Inc., 2001. ISBN 1-56592-599-8. An excellent general book on personal computer hardware.

 One great source for details on PC hardware is Charles Kozierok's PC Guide, available online at **www.pcguide.com**.

 A comprehensive source for general definitions on Personal Computers and software is Webopedia, available online at **www.webopedia.com**. Even though it is not the most complete source for definitions related to Linux, it is still quite helpful for understanding the basics (and a lot of the details) of PC hardware.

Basic Configuration

Terms you'll need to understand:

✓ Partition

✓ Volume

✓ Filesystem Hierarchy Standard (FHS)

✓ Local area network (LAN)

✓ Wide area network (WAN)

✓ Modem, Network Interface Card (NIC)

✓ Ethernet, Token Ring

✓ BNC, RJ-45

✓ Hub, Router, Gateway

✓ IP address

✓ Network address, network mask

✓ Hardware address, MAC address

✓ **tcp_wrappers**

✓ /etc/hosts.allow, /etc/hosts.deny

✓ **arp**, **nslookup**

✓ Dynamic Host Configuration Protocol (DHCP), **pump**

✓ Domain Name Service (DNS), nameserver, BIND

Techniques you'll need to master:

✓ Understanding appropriate Linux partition configurations

✓ Comprehending the basics of the Filesystem Hierarchy Standard

✓ Matching administrative commands to the appropriate directory

✓ Describing a local area network (LAN)

✓ Describing the three different types of relationships on a network

✓ Listing basic hardware required for a network

✓ Explaining the basics of TCP/IP on a LAN

✓ Understanding the key IP addresses of a LAN

✓ Describing the key commands for network configuration

This chapter addresses some basics of Linux configuration on a hard drive and on a network. Before you install Linux, you need to configure different partitions on a hard drive. Several viable ways exist for preparing your hard drive for Linux.

Next, this chapter covers some of the fundamentals of Linux networking using TCP/IP. From the hardware required to set up a network, you'll also examine options for Ethernet networking. Finally, you'll look at the types of addresses you need and the Linux services required to manage these addresses as well as access to the Internet.

Drives, Partitions, and Volumes

Partitions in Linux are somewhat different from partitions in Microsoft Windows. There are no C:\, D:\, or E:\ drives in Linux. You can assign a specific directory to a Linux partition, however.

The following sections examine the types of partitions you can create on a hard drive. Then you'll examine the types of directories that are available, as governed by the Filesystem Hierarchy Standard (FHS). That will give you the knowledge you need to set up the right number of partitions for your Linux directories.

Definitions

For those of you who are familiar with Microsoft Windows, drives, partitions, and volumes are somewhat different in Linux. Drives such as C:\, D:\, and E:\ on Microsoft Windows computers are installed on partitions. In contrast, the only real "Linux drives" are physical hard drives. In Linux, directories are directly installed (or "mounted") on partitions. These concepts are not as difficult as they look, as you will see in the following sections.

Partitions

In Chapter 3, you read about changing CMOS settings on your BIOS to point to a specific hard drive. After the CMOS identifies a hard drive, your computer looks for the Master Boot Record (MBR) on that drive. The MBR identifies the partitions on your drive, including the "active partition" that contains the boot files for your operating system.

Linux allows for three different types of partitions:

➤ *Primary partition*—You can create up to four different primary partitions on a hard drive. The primary partition that you set as active can include a boot loader such as Partition Magic, System Commander, the Windows NT/2000 boot loader, or the Linux Loader (LILO).

➤ *Extended partition*—If you need more partitions, one primary partition can be converted into an extended partition. The extended partition then can be further subdivided into logical partitions.

➤ *Logical partition*—An extended partition can be subdivided into as many logical partitions as you need. In the Microsoft world, these are known as *logical drives*.

Volumes

A volume is a fixed amount of space on one or more hard drives. It can include one or more partitions. When you mount a Linux directory, you can assign it to a specific partition or set it up in a volume that takes in more than one partition.

There are a number of different examples of a volume. If you mount the Linux root directory on a primary partition, that is a volume. If you then mount your home directory on a logical partition, that is a separate volume. Any swap space that you set up on a partition is also a volume. Volumes can be contained in one or more partitions even if this requires two or more separate hard drives. Thus, if you have a large Linux directory that takes up more space than any individual hard drive, you can still mount it on a volume.

Hard Disk Names

Based on your knowledge of partitions and volumes, along with what you learned about hard drive assignments in Chapter 3, you are now ready to examine the Linux names for different partitions. The rules in this section also apply to CD drives that are attached to the same ATAPI and SCSI interfaces.

The naming convention is fairly straightforward. The first two letters of the name depend on the drive attachment interface. For example, if you have a drive attached to an ATAPI interface, the letters are *hd* (short for hard drive). If you have a drive attached to a SCSI interface, the letters are *sd* (short for SCSI drive).

The third letter depends on the relative position of the drive. If the drive is attached at the master on the ATAPI primary controller, that letter is *a*. A drive attached as the slave on the primary controller is *b*. Similar criteria govern drives on the ATAPI secondary controller (*c* and *d*), as well as drives attached to SCSI interfaces.

If the drive is a hard drive, there is a fourth character. The four primary partitions are designated as numbers 1, 2, 3, and 4. If you use an extended partition, it is a substitute for a primary partition and is designated as number 4. The first logical partition is designated as number 5, even if you use only one primary partition. Some examples of how this works are shown in Table 4.1.

Table 4.1	Typical partition names.
Name	**Description**
hda2	The second primary partition of a master hard disk on the primary ATAPI controller.
sdc5	The first logical partition on the third SCSI hard disk.
hdd7	The third logical partition on the slave hard disk on the secondary ATAPI controller.
sda3	The third primary partition on the first SCSI hard disk.
hdc	Since there is no number, this name refers to a CD drive attached as the master on the secondary ATAPI controller.
sdb	Since there is no number, this name refers to a CD drive attached to the second position on a SCSI interface.

Filesystem Hierarchy Standard

When you install Linux, you can mount all of the Linux directories on a single partition. You can also set up just about any Linux directory as a volume by mounting it on a separate partition.

Separate partitions limit risks to your system. For example, Web servers such as Apache can accumulate log files that are hundreds of megabytes in size. This could easily crowd out all free space on your hard drive. Your users could no longer save files, there would be no room for Linux to prepare print jobs, and the result could be chaos. Alternatively, if you mounted the right directory on a separate partition, your users could still work and save files even if the partition with the log files was full.

Before you can select partitions for your Linux system, you first need to know about the options in Linux directories. Most distributions divide their files into directories according to the Filesystem Hierarchy Standard (FHS), as shown in Table 4.2.

Not all directories are formally required by the official Filesystem Hierarchy Standard. For more information, see **www.pathname.com/fhs**.

Be sure to know these Linux volumes, especially those that normally contain commands. Be able to associate a directory with a specific type of command. For example, most system administration commands are in the /sbin directory, and most basic command-line utilities are in the /bin directory.

Standard Partition Schemes

You now know that there is a variety of ways to set up partitions in Linux. To help guide your efforts, there are a few standard partition schemes.

Table 4.2	Linux Filesystem Hierarchy Standard directories.
Directory	**Description**
/	The root directory. All other directories are below the root directory in the filesystem hierarchy. In other words, they are "subdirectories." Any other directory not mounted on a separate partition is automatically part of the root directory volume.
/bin	Contains basic command-line utilities. You should not configure this directory in a separate partition. If you do, you wouldn't be able to access these utilities with a recovery disk.
/boot	Includes the commands and files required for Linux to boot on your computer, such as LILO and the Linux kernel. If you have a larger drive (over 8GB), it is generally a good idea to mount /boot on a separate partition. This helps to ensure that your Linux boot files remain accessible when you start your computer. A /boot partition typically does not have to be larger than 10MB.
/dev	Lists available device drivers. For example, if you mount a floppy drive, you might mount /dev/fd0 onto a directory such as /mnt/floppy. You should not mount this directory in a separate partition.
/etc	Contains basic Linux configuration files, including those related to passwords, daemons such as Apache and Samba, and the X Window.
/home	Includes home directories for all but the **root** user. If you mount this directory on a separate partition, leave enough room for each of your users to add files.
/lib	Lists program libraries needed by a number of different applications as well as the Linux kernel. You should not mount this directory in a separate partition.
/mnt	Contains the mount point of removable media, such as floppy (/mnt/floppy) and CD-ROM (/mnt/cdrom) drives. It is not used by all Linux distributions; for example, on S.u.S.E. Linux, floppy and CD-ROM drives are normally mounted on preconfigured /floppy and /cdrom directories.
/opt	Standard location for applications such as Sun StarOffice, Corel WordPerfect, or VistaSource Anyware Office.
/proc	Includes all kernel-related processes that are currently running. Some of the files in this directory list current resource allocations; for example, /proc/interrupts lists currently allocated interrupt request (IRQ) ports.
/root	The home directory for the **root** user. The /root directory is a subdirectory of the root (/) directory. Do not mount this directory separately.
/sbin	Contains many system administration commands. Do not mount this directory separately.
/tmp	Dedicated storage location for temporary files. Also a good place to download files. Some Linux installations are configured to empty this directory periodically.
/usr	Includes small programs and data available to all users. Contains many subdirectories.
/var	Contains variable data, including log files and print spools. On Linux servers, this directory is frequently mounted on a separate partition.

If a directory such as /boot is mounted on a single partition, that partition becomes known as the /boot partition.

First, the minimum number of partitions that you need for Linux is one. If you set up a primary partition, you can mount the root directory (/) on it. You do not even need a swap partition; it is possible to set up a swap file, similar to most Microsoft Windows operating systems. This is generally not a recommended configuration for Linux, however.

Note: Swap files or swap partitions act as overflow space from your RAM. If you don't have enough RAM for the programs you're using, less-used data is temporarily transferred to this overflow space.

A more typical configuration involves two partitions: one for the root directory, the other as a swap partition. This is a common configuration for computers with smaller hard drives.

A common configuration for larger hard drives includes three partitions. The root (/) and /boot directories, as well as swap, are mounted on separate partitions. This is the default setup for several Linux distributions, including Red Hat Linux 7.1. The /boot directory is commonly mounted on its own partition because many Linux installations cannot start if the files in the /boot directory are stored above hard drive cylinder 1024.

*Note: Hard drives are physically divided into cylinders. There is no fixed size for a cylinder; however, with the advent of larger hard drives, it is easier to install /boot accidentally in a cylinder above 1024. This should not be an issue if you have the latest BIOS with LBA32 addressing (check your BIOS menu) and a version of LILO above 21.3. On several distributions (Red Hat, Caldera, S.u.S.E., among others), you can check the version of LILO on your Linux computer with the **rpm -q lilo** command. The **rpm** command will be covered in Chapter 6.*

Other configurations may be appropriate if you're installing different Linux directories on different physical hard drives. Review Table 4.3 for a short list of possible Linux partition configurations.

Table 4.3	Potential Linux partition configurations.
Mounted Directories	**Explanation**
/	If just the root directory is used, you'll need a dedicated swap file.
/, swap	Typical configuration for a computer with one smaller hard drive.
/, /boot, swap	Typical configuration for a computer with a larger hard drive. Default configuration for Red Hat Linux 7.1 installation.
/, /boot, /var, swap	Possible configuration where log file size, such as from a Web server, is an issue. This can prevent "runaway" log files from crowding out all free space on your Linux computer.

The listed directories (as well as the swap partition) can be mounted on any primary or logical partition.

 Understand at least the first two Linux partition schemes—the one that uses just the root (/) directory, as well as the one with the root (/) directory and a dedicated swap partition.

File Systems

File systems are different from the Filesystem Hierarchy Standard. They are the way a partition is formatted. Microsoft Windows partitions are typically formatted to the VFAT, FAT32, or NTFS file system. In contrast, Linux partitions are typically formatted to the ext2, ext3, swap, ReiserFS, or XFS file system. Chapter 5 addresses some of these optional formats, as well as the associated tools.

Network Fundamentals

Linux networking is a rich and complex topic that could cover several large books. For the Linux+ exam, you just need to know a few network fundamentals, which include the basics on how a network really works, some of the required hardware, a basic understanding of some TCP/IP protocols, and a few of the commands needed to administer this kind of network.

Note: This chapter provides just enough of a brief overview of networking and TCP/IP on Linux for the Linux+ exam. There are a number of "oversimplifications" in this chapter that allow less-experienced readers to grasp the fundamentals quickly. If you want to set up a Linux network, consult some of the books and Web sites listed in the "Need to Know More?" section at the end of this chapter.

The Fundamentals of a Network

If you have two or more computers that communicate with each other, you have a network. It doesn't matter if you're using just a couple of telephone modems or even a serial cable. As long as you have two or more computers that are exchanging data, you have a network.

If the interconnected computers are relatively close to each other, such as in an office or a building, those computers are a local area network (LAN). It is a common practice to connect LANs together. Two or more interconnected LANs are an internet. Geographically distant but interconnected LANs are often known as a wide area network (WAN). The biggest WAN is the Internet.

Note: An intranet is two or more interconnected networks within a single office or organization.

There are three ways to describe relationships between computers on a network:

➤ *Client/server*—The most common relationship, where client computers with their own independent CPUs and hard drives get services such as files, print access, and Web pages from one or more server computers.

➤ *Master/slave*—Where computers with little or no independent processing power get access through a master computer. The slave computer, which may not even have a hard drive, can't boot an operating system independently of the master computer. Slave computers are sometimes known as terminals or diskless workstations.

➤ *Peer-to-peer*—All computers on this type of LAN can be used as workstations. While some peer-to-peer computers may act as servers in a minor capacity, such as for printers, they are still available as workstations for individual users.

The most common network in Linux is a client/server network. All of the relationships in this book are based on assigning client and server roles to various computers on a LAN.

Basic Hardware Configurations

A number of basic hardware components are associated with a network. This section addresses some of the fundamental components of a LAN, from what you see in your computer through the interconnection hardware.

To communicate with a network, you need a modem or a network interface card (NIC). When you connect to an Internet service provider (ISP) through a modem, your computer becomes part of its network. Unfortunately, such connections are limited to 56Kbps. For faster networks, a NIC is generally required.

Perhaps the major network in use today is Ethernet. This standard has come to dominate network configurations because of its relative simplicity and ease of configuration. There are several variations of Ethernet in terms of configuration and speed. Like any network, Ethernet hardware components can be divided into three categories: NICs, cables, and interconnections.

The network that you configure also depends on speed. Ethernet is currently available at three levels: 10Mbps, 100Mbps, and 1000Mbps. These networks are sometimes known as Ethernet, Fast Ethernet, and Gigabit Ethernet, respectively.

Note: Ethernet is a trade name. The formal specification for a 10Mbps Ethernet network is IEEE 802.3.

One alternative to Ethernet is known as *Token Ring*. This was once a common networking option at 10Mbps. It is more efficient because only the computer with the "token" can send messages. It is more resilient, since wiring is configured in a "ring," which allows some communication to continue if there is a break in the wire. A Token Ring style network is available at 100Mbps, but no current serious Token Ring network is under development at gigabit (1000Mbps) speeds.

Network Interface Cards (NIC)

To communicate with a network, your computer needs a card that translates a network language such as Ethernet to data that it can use. NICs serve this purpose. When you select a NIC, you need to take three factors into account: the interface to your computer, the interface to the rest of the network, and the type of network.

A NIC can be internal or external to your computer. Internal network cards are available for both PCI and ISA slots. External network cards attach to an interface such as a USB port.

The NIC you use also depends on the network interface. As discussed in the following section, Ethernet interfaces generally look like oversized telephone jacks or cable TV connectors. NICs are available with both types of interfaces and more.

Cables and Connectors

Three types of cables are most commonly associated with Ethernet: Thinnet, Thicknet, and twisted-pair. Each cable is associated with a specific type of connector. Basic characteristics are shown in Table 4.4.

Examples of Thinnet BNC and twisted-pair RJ-45 connectors are shown in Figure 4.1. As you can see, Thinnet connectors are round and slightly wider than

Table 4.4	Ethernet cable characterisitics.
Cable Type	**Characteristics**
Thinnet	Sometimes known as 10Base2, based on a data capacity of 10Mbps and a distance limit of 200 meters. Similar to the cables associated with TV service, Thinnet is characterized by the use of BNCs (British Naval Connectors) to attach its cables to each other and to computer network cards. Hubs are not used.
Thicknet	Sometimes known as 10Base5, based on a data capacity of 10Mbps and a distance limit of 500 meters. As the name suggests, Thicknet requires thicker cables. Hubs are not used.
Twisted-pair	Sometimes known as 10BaseT, based on a data capacity of 10Mbps. The maximum length of a twisted-pair cable is 100 meters. Twisted-pair Ethernet cables have RJ-45 connectors, which look like oversized telephone jacks. The difference is that there are eight wires in an Ethernet cable and thus eight wires on the connector. Twisted-pair cables connect NICs to hubs at the center of the LAN.

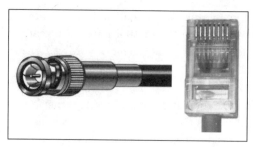

Figure 4.1 BNC and RJ-45 connectors.

their cables, and RJ-45 connectors are rectangular and snap into place just like a typical telephone jack.

 Know that a BNC connector attaches cables on an Ethernet Thinnet network, and an RJ-45 connector attaches wiring on a twisted-pair network.

Interconnections

After you've selected network cards and cables, the next step is to connect it all together. If you're using Thinnet or Thicknet cables, you don't need anything else; all computers on a LAN are connected to the same cable. If you're using a network based on twisted-pair, you need a *hub*. All the computers on your LAN are connected to that hub.

Traffic on a larger LAN is often regulated by a device known as a *bridge* or a *switch*. Traffic between LANs is generally regulated by devices known as *routers* or *gateways*.

Note: This is just the briefest overview of the ways computers and networks are interconnected. Many other variations are available for cable interconnections that are beyond what you need for the Linux+ exam.

The Language of the Internet

Most networks today use TCP/IP, which is also the way computers communicate with each other over the Internet. TCP/IP is a set of protocols, each of which includes rules that govern computer communication.

Near the top of the TCP/IP protocol stack is the domain. When you install Linux, most installation programs ask for your domain name, such as **ruleslinux.now**. The domain name you use should be unique to your LAN.

If you don't intend to give public Internet addresses to computers on your LAN, you can set the domain name of your choice. In that case, you don't need (and probably do not want) a domain name that ends in something like **.com**.

Next in line is the hostname. Every computer on a TCP/IP network needs a hostname, such as **mylaptop**. Every hostname on a TCP/IP network is associated with an IP address. Combining the hostname with the domain creates a fully qualified domain name (FQDN) such as **mylaptop.ruleslinux.now**.

Note: If your computer connects directly to the Internet, your ISP may assign you a domain name and hostname, especially if you have a higher-speed connection. You can still assign a different domain name and hostname for use within your LAN.

Databases of hostnames or FQDNs and their associated IP addresses can be stored locally in the Linux /etc/hosts file or remotely on a Domain Name Service (DNS) server.

DNS is short for Domain Name System or Domain Name Service. For the purpose of the Linux+ exam, these are the same thing.

What follows is the IP address, which consists of four numbers between 0 and 255, separated by dots. IP addresses are assigned to specific network cards.

Every network card ever built includes a unique hardware address such as 00-11-c5-66-3c-b2, which is in hexadecimal notation.

IP Addresses

On a TCP/IP network, every computer needs an IP address such as 123.234.156.218. You can find any computer on the Internet by its IP address. When you type in a name in a Web browser such as Netscape or Konqueror, a DNS or /etc/hosts file is used to translate that name into an IP address.

IP addresses range from 0.0.0.0 to 255.255.255.255. Most of these addresses are already assigned. If you want to set up your own network using private IP addresses, refer to the Linux Network Administrator's Guide Chapter 2, available online at **http://www.linuxdoc.org/LDP/nag2/x-087-2-issues.html**.

Your ISP can assign you a specific address. If one address is not enough, you can assign yourself one or more of the private IP addresses. If you have a lot of computers, you can automate the IP address-assignment process with a Dynamic Host

Configuration Protocol (DHCP) server. If you don't have enough IP addresses, DHCP can ration them for you. A DHCP server assigns an IP address when a computer wants to start communicating and "leases" IP addresses for a limited amount of time.

When you define a network, there are three key IP addresses:

➤ *Network address*—An address that is associated with a given LAN.

➤ *Network mask*—When combined with the network address, allows you to define the range of possible IP addresses on a specific LAN. Also known as a netmask.

➤ *Gateway address*—The address of a computer or router on a LAN that is also connected to another network such as the Internet.

The Linux+ exam assumes the use of IP version 4 (IPv4), which has been in use since the 1970s. There are 32 bits, or binary digits, in an IPv4 address. That makes for 2^{32}=4,294,967,296 different addresses. We are currently in transition to IP version 6 (IPv6). There are 128 bits in an IPv6 address. That makes for 2^{128} = 3.4 × 10^{38} addresses. IPv4 addresses will still work after the transition is complete.

 Remember that there are 32 bits in a regular IPv4 address, and 128 bits in an IPv6 address.

IP Address Security

If you're running a server for Web pages, files, or printers, you can stop traffic coming from a specific IP address. You can even use a network address and network mask to stop all traffic from a specific network. With more sophisticated tools, you can even restrict access from other computers, for example, to everything but your Web server. This allows you to run a Web site without fear that other computers will try to access your data in other ways.

The key to this control is the **tcp_wrappers** package, which allows you to restrict or filter incoming traffic by IP address through the /etc/hosts.allow and /etc/hosts.deny files.

 Associate **tcp_wrappers** with the /etc/hosts.allow and /etc/hosts.deny files. This is how inbound traffic is limited or otherwise regulated on a local area network.

Basic Communication

Communication between computers in some ways is similar to communication with a postal letter. In both cases, you need an origin and a destination address. While you use addresses such as **mylaptop.ruleslinux.now**, your computer uses addresses such as 00-11-c5-66-3c-b2.

A service such as DNS or /etc/hosts has already converted the server that you want, such as **myserver.ruleslinux.now**, to an IP address such as 192.168.11.142. After the message gets to that computer, the destination sends a message back with a hardware address such as 00-11-c5-66-3c-b2.

Note: Computer Network Interface Card (NIC) hardware addresses are typically shown in hexadecimal notation, which is base-16, as described in Chapter 3.

The two computers exchange Media Access Control (MAC) addresses. Only then can substantive communication begin between computers on a network.

Make a note of the fact that hardware addresses associated with a Network Interface Card are also known as MAC addresses.

Network Services

Linux is an operating system suited for networking. As you set up your Linux computer, a number of commands and services allow you to configure and test your system. Each computer carries a list of hardware addresses to ease communication within a LAN. When IP addresses are limited, larger LANs need DHCP servers to ration them. Although you can collect hostnames and IP addresses in a file, larger collections of domain names and IP addresses need a DNS server. The following sections explain these items, along with some associated commands.

The following sections assume that you have a running network on Linux. You can check this with the **/sbin/ifconfig** command, as shown in Figure 4.2. If you see an entry other than **lo** in the left column (for instance, **eth0**), your computer is properly configured for networking. Otherwise, you may need to first configure your network card, as discussed in Chapter 9.

Addresses on a Local Network

When computers talk on a network, it is from one network card to another, using their hardware addresses. As discussed earlier, in the sections that discuss the

```
[mj@laptop71 mj]$ /sbin/ifconfig
eth0       Link encap:Ethernet  HWaddr 00:60:08:8D:41:93
           inet addr:192.168.0.50  Bcast:192.168.0.255  Mask:255.255.255.0
           UP BROADCAST RUNNING MULTICAST  MTU:1500  Metric:1
           RX packets:3873 errors:0 dropped:0 overruns:0 frame:0
           TX packets:3795 errors:0 dropped:0 overruns:0 carrier:0
           collisions:0 txqueuelen:100
           Interrupt:3 Base address:0x300

lo         Link encap:Local Loopback
           inet addr:127.0.0.1  Mask:255.0.0.0
           UP LOOPBACK RUNNING  MTU:16436  Metric:1
           RX packets:6 errors:0 dropped:0 overruns:0 frame:0
           TX packets:6 errors:0 dropped:0 overruns:0 carrier:0
           collisions:0 txqueuelen:0

[mj@laptop71 mj]$ ▊
```

Figure 4.2   Checking the current network configuration.

language of the Internet and basic communication, IP addresses are used first. After contact is made, hardware addresses are exchanged, but this interchange takes time and uses the network. To avoid this process in the future, your computer could use a database of IP and hardware addresses. This is available in TCP/IP under the address resolution protocol (ARP).

One example of an ARP database is shown in Figure 4.3, which describes the hardware addresses on a small network with three computers.

 Know that the Linux **arp** command associates an IP address such as 192.168.0.166 with the hardware or MAC address of a computer's network card, such as 00:19:e2:34:2d:c6. The **arp** command can be used with IPv4 (32-bit) or IPv6 (128-bit) addresses.

DHCP and pump

The Dynamic Host Configuration Protocol (DHCP) allows a designated computer to assign IP addresses for a certain period of time on a LAN. Because that computer is serving IP addresses, it is a DHCP server.

Note: You don't need DHCP. In fact, you can assign IP addresses to specific computer network cards on a permanent basis.

DHCP servers can be located on your LAN, or they can be on a neighboring network remotely connected to your LAN. If the DHCP server is remote, the

```
[mj@laptop71 mj]$ /sbin/arp
Address                HWtype  HWaddress            Flags Mask        Iface
Experimental           ether   00:30:87:14:D4:6A    CM                eth0
192.168.0.184          ether   00:19:E2:34:2D:C6    CM                eth0
192.168.0.132          ether   00:14:B6:66:3C:B4    CM                eth0
[mj@laptop71 mj]$ ▊
```

Figure 4.3   An ARP database.

BOOTP protocol is required to allow that remote DHCP server to assign IP addresses to computers on your LAN.

Remember that if you're using a DHCP server on a remote network, you need to activate the BOOTP protocol to let that server assign IP addresses on your LAN.

In a client/server network, a DHCP server is not very helpful without DHCP clients. There are three major Linux DHCP client programs: **dhcpcd**, **pump**, and **dhclient**. Although the standard client is **dhcpcd**, the Red Hat Linux distribution uses **pump**. Although the Linux+ exam is distribution neutral, some of the objectives as of this writing explicitly cite utilities associated with Red Hat Linux.

A number of other Linux distributions, such as Linux-Mandrake, are based on Red Hat Linux. Therefore, if you see a reference to Red Hat, it is reasonable to assume that the reference applies to those other distributions.

The DHCP client that you use should become part of the **/sbin/ifup** script. This is an executable text file. In many cases, **/sbin/ifup** is already preconfigured to use **dhcpcd** or **pump**.

Keep in mind the fact that a DHCP client (**pump** or **dhcpcd**) should be part of the **/sbin/ifup** script. If you're using a distribution such as Red Hat Linux, you can test DHCP with the **/sbin/pump -r** command.

DNS and BIND

When you look for a Web page, your browser is sending a message to the appropriate Web server somewhere in the world. It finds that Web server based on its IP address. However, most users look for a Web page using a name such as **www.mommabears.com** instead of the IP address such as 192.168.1.66. The Domain Name Service (DNS) is a database of these names and their associated IP addresses.

The standard Linux implementation of DNS is known as the Berkeley Internet Name Domain (BIND). Although no individual DNS contains all of the Web page names and IP addresses on the Internet, there is a system by which DNS refers your request to another server with the IP address that you need.

In Linux, DNS and BIND are also known as *nameservers*. Every nameserver on a TCP/IP network also has its own IP address. On a Linux computer, these IP addresses are stored in the /etc/resolv.conf file. For example, if your ISP has a DNS server with an IP address of 10.121.33.53, you may see the following line in that file:

```
nameserver 10.121.33.53
```

You don't need to know how to set up a DNS server for the Linux+ exam, but you do need to know that you can test it with the **nslookup** command. This command can do the following:

➤ Test local DNS servers.

➤ Find the fully qualified domain name and IP address of the DNS server for another Web site.

➤ Test the remote DNS server of your choice.

 The **nslookup** command can be used to test the performance of local or remote DNS servers.

 If you have only a few computers on your LAN and don't connect to the Internet, you don't need a DNS server. All you need is an /etc/hosts file, which includes the hostname and IP address of each computer on your network. The drawback is that you need the identical file on each computer on your network. If you connect to the Internet, you need a DNS because you can't realistically store all Internet domain names and IP addresses in /etc/hosts.

Configuration Tools

Several distribution-specific configuration tools are available for network configuration and more. Two of the tools are addressed in the Linux+ exam criteria: Linuxconf and netconfig. Both are generally found on Red Hat Linux. Based on the release notes for Red Hat 7.1, Linuxconf may not be supported on Red Hat distributions in the future. In any case, exam questions on anything beyond the basic purpose of these tools seems unlikely. Examples of their network configuration options are shown in Figures 4.4 and 4.5.

Similar tools are available for many of the other major Linux distributions, including Caldera's Webmin, Corel's Control Center, and S.u.S.E.'s YaST.

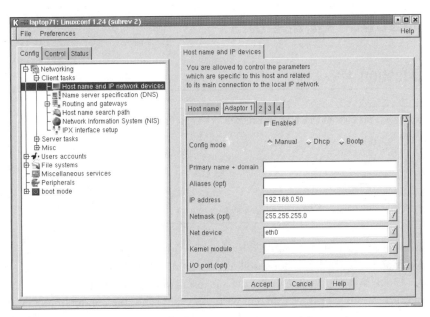

Figure 4.4   Linuxconf as a network configurator.

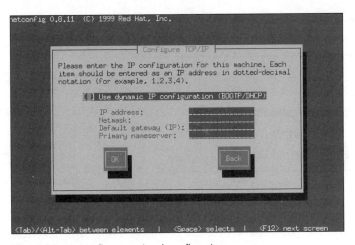

Figure 4.5   netconfig as a network configurator.

Practice Questions

Question 1

> What is the minimum number of partitions for a Linux installation?
>
> ○ a. One
>
> ○ b. Two
>
> ○ c. Three
>
> ○ d. It depends on the Linux distribution.

Answer a is correct. All you need is a **root** partition. Although a separate swap partition is standard, it is not absolutely required. You can configure swap space for Linux in a file. Although the default installation for different distributions may give you two or three different partitions, that is not the minimum requirement. Therefore, answers b, c, and d are incorrect.

Question 2

> What data is found in a swap partition?
>
> ○ a. Swap files
>
> ○ b. Programs not yet loaded from a hard drive
>
> ○ c. Data overflow from RAM
>
> ○ d. Data associated with currently running programs

Answer c is correct. Swap space, whether in file or partition form, is designed as temporary storage for less-used data that would otherwise occupy some of your RAM. Since swap files are stored on regular partitions, answer a is incorrect. Since programs not yet loaded from a hard drive haven't yet been loaded onto RAM, answer b is incorrect. Although some data from currently running programs may be stored on a swap partition, it is unlikely with a currently running program, unless you don't have enough RAM. Therefore, c is still the best available answer, and answer d is incorrect.

Question 3

Which of the following directories is at the highest level of the Filesystem Hierarchy Standard?

- ○ a. /root
- ○ b. /home
- ○ c. /boot
- ○ d. /

Answer d is correct. The root directory (/) is above all others based on the Filesystem Hierarchy Standard. This is different from the /root directory, which is the home directory for the **root** user and a subdirectory of root (/). Therefore, answer a is incorrect. Since the /home directory is the location for individual users' home directories and is a subdirectory of root (/), answer b is incorrect. Since the /boot directory is the location for the Linux boot files and is a subdirectory of root (/), answer c is also incorrect.

Question 4

Which of the following directories is the most appropriate location for system administration command utilities such as **arp** or **ifconfig**?

- ○ a. /bin
- ○ b. /sbin
- ○ c. /home
- ○ d. /etc

Answer b is correct. The /sbin directory is the location designated by the Filesystem Hierarchy Standard for most system administration commands. Since /bin typically contains regular command-line utilities, answer a is incorrect. Since /home contains the home directories of individual users, answer c is incorrect. Since /etc typically contains various configuration files, answer d is also incorrect.

Question 5

> When you search for a Web site, which of the following services can associate domain names with IP addresses?
>
> ○ a. DHCP
>
> ○ b. BIND
>
> ○ c. ARP
>
> ○ d. Apache

Answer b is correct. BIND is short for the Berkeley Internet Name Domain, which is an implementation of the Domain Name Service (DNS). DNS is the service that associates domain names such as **www.Coriolis.com** with IP addresses such as 10.10.10.10. Although the Dynamic Host Configuration Protocol (DHCP) is used to assign IP addresses to specific computers, it does not help you or your computer locate a specific Web site. Therefore, answer a is incorrect. ARP, the address resolution protocol, associates an IP address with the hardware address of a specific network interface card (NIC). Since this is unrelated to domain names, answer c is incorrect. Although Apache, as a Web server, is used to serve Web sites, it does not include a database of domain names and IP addresses. Therefore, answer d is also incorrect.

Question 6

> Which of the following is a client that you can use when working with DHCP?
>
> ○ a. BOOTP
>
> ○ b. ARP
>
> ○ c. nslookup
>
> ○ d. pump

Answer d is correct. One DHCP (Dynamic Host Configuration Protocol) client commonly used in Red Hat Linux is pump. Although BOOTP allows remote DHCP servers to assign IP addresses on a local area network (LAN), it is not a client to install on a client computer. Therefore, answer a is incorrect. Since the address resolution protocol (ARP) associates already-assigned IP addresses with network card hardware addresses, answer b is incorrect. Since nslookup tests DNS servers, which is a different service from DHCP, answer c is also incorrect.

Question 7

You're setting up an Ethernet network, using Thinnet. Which of the following hardware components will you have to use?

○ a. Hub

○ b. Router

○ c. BNC

○ d. Twisted-pair

Answer c is correct. BNC is a type of connecter used on a Thinnet Ethernet network to connect the cables from a network card to the cables of the rest of the network. Since a hub is not required on a Thinnet local area network (LAN) and is characteristic of a twisted-pair wiring-based network, answer a is incorrect. Although you could use a router to connect a Thinnet LAN to another network, you don't have to connect your network to any other network. Therefore, answer b is incorrect. Since cables are used on a Thinnet LAN and not telephone-style twisted-pair wires, answer d is also incorrect.

Question 8

Which of the following statements best describes the reasons for ARP?

○ a. When computers talk to each other, they use hostnames. ARP collects a database of hostnames on a local computer to minimize hostname search time before every message.

○ b. When computers talk to each other, they use IP addresses. ARP collects a database of hostnames and IP addresses on a local computer to minimize IP address search time before every message.

○ c. When computers talk to each other, they use MAC addresses. ARP collects a database of hostnames and MAC addresses on a remote computer to minimize MAC address search time before every message.

○ d. When computers talk to each other, they use hardware addresses. ARP collects a database of IP addresses and hardware addresses on a remote computer to minimize hardware address search time before every message.

Answer d is correct. Normally, before computers—or more specifically, their network cards—can talk to each other on a network, each needs to determine the other's hardware address. The address resolution protocol (ARP) collects a database of IP and MAC addresses, also known as hardware addresses, for specific network cards. Since computers use hardware addresses, not hostnames, to talk to each other, answer a is not correct. Although computers find each other with IP addresses, communication is by hardware address. Therefore, answer b is also not correct. Since ARP databases are kept on a local computer, answer c is also incorrect.

Question 9

You're trying to set up a new ISP for your network. The ISP has given you the IP addresses for its nameservers. Where on your computer would you store this information?

O a. /etc/hosts

O b. /etc/resolv.conf

O c. BIND

O d. DNS

Answer b is correct. The /etc/resolv.conf file is the standard location for nameservers, also known as BIND or DNS servers, for your network. Although you can store hostnames or domain names and IP addresses in an /etc/hosts file, you can't realistically store all domain names and IP addresses on the Internet in that file. Therefore, answer a is incorrect. BIND, the Berkeley Internet Name Domain, is the service used on Linux to implement DNS. However, it is not a file where you would locate the IP address of a DNS or a nameserver. Therefore, answer c is incorrect. Since DNS, the Domain Name Service, is not a file where you would locate a nameserver address, answer d is also incorrect. If you had a BIND or DNS server, you would store its address in the /etc/resolv.conf file as well.

Question 10

When you set up a DHCP server on a computer on a remote network with the BOOTP protocol, which of the following commands could you use to test the server?

O a. **/sbin/nslookup -r**

O b. **/sbin/pump -r**

O c. **/sbin/dhcp -r**

O d. **/sbin/bootp -r**

Answer b is correct. To implement the Dynamic Host Configuration Protocol (DHCP), you need a client and a server. The question sets up a DHCP server. The only command among the answers that is associated with a DHCP client (in this case for Red Hat Linux) is **pump**. Since **nslookup** tests a Domain Name Service (DNS) server, answer a is incorrect. Since there is no dhcp command (the other DHCP client is **dhcpcd**), answer c is incorrect. Although the DHCP server is set up on a computer on a remote network, no special command is required to test that server, and there is no bootp command. Therefore, answer d is also incorrect.

Need to Know More?

 Hunt, Craig. *Linux Network Servers*. Alameda, CA: Sybex, 1999. ISBN 0-78212-506-9. An excellent book that describes the details of how to set up network services, with many substantive examples.

 Pfaffenberger, Bryan, and Michael Jang. *Linux Networking Clearly Explained*. San Francisco, CA: Morgan-Kaufmann Publishers, 2001. ISBN 0-12533-171-1. An introductory guide to Linux networking.

 The Web site for the Linux Documentation Project (LDP) at **www.linuxdoc.org** is the central repository for Linux manuals, HOWTOs, and a number of other book-length documents. Important HOWTOs for this chapter include the DNS-HOWTO for setting up a DNS server, the DHCP Mini-HOWTO for setting up DHCP clients and servers, the Large Disk-HOWTO for setting up Linux on a large hard drive, and the Partition Mini-HOWTO for setting up hard disk partitions. Also important is the Network Administrator's Guide, which is available online through the LDP.

 Detailed information on the Filesystem Hierarchy Standard (FHS) is available online at **www.pathname.com/fhs/**.

Installation Process

Terms you'll need to understand:

✓ Installation sources
✓ Boot disk
✓ Network installation
✓ Kickstart
✓ Input devices
✓ **fdisk**, **fips**

✓ Linux Loader (LILO)
✓ ext2, ext3, ReiserFS, XFS
✓ Swap space
✓ Server installation, workstation installation
✓ Log files

Techniques you'll need to master:

✓ Describing alternate options for local installation
✓ Listing options for network installation
✓ Understanding basic tools required to install Linux on multiple computers
✓ Comprehending basic installation steps
✓ Describing common tools for preparing a hard drive

✓ Listing alternate file systems
✓ Understanding the requirements behind swap space
✓ Explaining general Linux installation options based on the role of the computer
✓ Documenting the installation through log files
✓ Explaining the need to test before installing Linux or a Linux application on a production computer

There are many different Linux distributions, most of which have their own unique installation programs. Despite the variations, all Linux installation programs share a number of tools.

You can install most distributions from local sources such as a CD-ROM or a hard drive. In addition, you can install most distributions simultaneously on multiple computers over a network. Most distributions also require some basic choices of input devices, hard drive partitions, partition formats, swap space, and more. You can customize an installation based on the desired functionality of the computer. When you're done, you can check on the success of your installation through various log files.

Installation Sources

Linux installation is very closely associated with a CD. You can purchase a Linux distribution CD, and in most cases you can also download the same information through the Internet. A number of books also include a "publisher's edition" of a Linux distribution, which may or may not include all of the packages of a regular purchased or downloaded CD.

Once you have the information on CD, you can start the installation process in one of several ways. You can boot your computer directly from the first Linux distribution CD, if allowed by your computer's BIOS. You might use a boot disk to use Linux distribution files that were copied to a hard drive. The CD or hard drive can be on your local computer or on a remote computer connected through a network. In fact, you can install Linux simultaneously from the same source on all computers on a network.

Installation by CD

Some Linux distributions include several gigabytes of files. Because DVDs and their associated drives are not yet common, the only convenient way to distribute that much data is through a CD.

Most Linux distribution CDs are bootable. In other words, if you can set your BIOS menu to boot from a CD, you can start a Linux installation program directly from that CD. Otherwise, it is relatively easy to create a Linux boot floppy that starts the installation program and then takes data directly from the CD.

Installation from the Hard Drive

You can copy the appropriate files from your Linux installation CD to your hard drive. In that case, start the installation program with a Linux boot floppy. When prompted, enter the partition and directory with your Linux installation files. The partition names that you might have to enter, such as hda3 or sdb2, are covered in Chapter 4.

Some Linux distributions, including Red Hat Linux, require that all data from a specific installation CD be copied to one single file, known as an ISO. For more information, see the Red Hat Installation Guide, described in the "Need to Know More?" section at the end of this chapter.

The Boot Disk

Boot disks come with most Linux distributions. If you purchase an "official copy," a 3.5-inch boot disk is probably included in the package. Alternatively, you may be able to create a boot disk from the first installation CD from your Linux distribution.

A number of different types of boot disks are available; all help you get to where the installation files are located. Some Linux distributions include special boot disks for older CD drives or those that can be connected through a PCMCIA card or even over a network. Sometimes, additional disks are available that include drivers for more specialized equipment.

The two major tools for creating a Linux boot disk are the **rawrite** and **dd** commands. The **rawrite** command works at the MS-DOS command line, and **dd** is a standard Linux command. An example of each command is:

```
D:\> rawrite \images\boot.img
$ dd if=/mnt/cdrom/images/bootnet.img of=/dev/fd0
```

These commands illustrate two ways to create a boot disk from a Linux CD-ROM. The Linux **dd** command is covered in more detail in Chapter 13.

Network Installation

You can install Linux through at least four different types of network connections: Network File System (NFS), Samba (SMB), File Transfer Protocol (FTP), or even a regular World Wide Web HTTP (Hypertext Transfer Protocol) connection. These are all network services, which in this case can allow you to use installation files from a remote computer that is connected through a network. The following is a brief explanation of each network service:

➤ *Network File System (NFS)*—The standard for communication between Unix/Linux computers. Generally used to share directories.

➤ *Samba (SMB)*—The heterogeneous standard that allows Unix/Linux computers to work on a network based on Microsoft and IBM standards. With Samba, you can mount a shared Microsoft directory in Linux or view a shared Linux directory in a Microsoft Windows Network Neighborhood.

➤ *File Transfer Protocol (FTP)*—The most common protocol for transferring files on the Internet. Most Linux distributions and software are downloadable from FTP servers.

➤ *Hypertext Transfer Protocol (HTTP)*—The standard that allows for links embedded in files to be viewed on a browser; more commonly known as the standard behind the World Wide Web.

If you want to install Linux over an Internet connection, make sure your connection is at least equivalent to a DSL or cable modem connection. If you try to install Linux over a regular telephone modem, the process could easily take several days. Any interruption in the telephone modem connection could make it necessary for you to start the installation process from scratch.

Network installations also require a boot disk—in this case, a boot disk that includes drivers for an attached network card. Depending on your distribution, these drivers are sometimes available on supplementary driver or module disks.

After your computer boots and sets up your network card, you need access data for the remote computer, such as hostname, domain name, or IP address. You also need the remote directory where the installation files are stored.

Network Interactions

At some point, you may be asked to install Linux on a large number of computers. When this happens, you want to be able to install Linux over a network; otherwise, the logistics of physically installing Linux on a large number of individual computers while users are not at work can be daunting. Besides, the PCs on many corporate networks may not even have a CD-ROM drive.

It is possible to install Linux on a large number of nearly identical computers simultaneously over a network. All you need to do is set up a server computer that can share a directory through the Network File System (NFS). When you copy the appropriate files from Linux distribution CDs to that directory, you can install Linux over a network. With the appropriate configuration file, such as one based on Red Hat's kickstart utility, you can install Linux simultaneously on a group of computers over your network.

Remember that to install Linux on multiple computers over a network, you need the Network File System (NFS) set up on the server with the Linux installation files from the Linux distribution CDs.

Common Steps

Although the installation program for most Linux distributions is proprietary, there are a number of common steps. Before you set up and install Linux on the desired partitions, you need to set up some basic parameters: the language, keyboard, mouse, and clock.

Languages

Most Linux installation programs can be set to a number of different languages. Unlike other operating systems, you don't need a country-specific CD if you have trouble with the English language. A number of different languages are integrated directly into the installation program associated with most Linux distributions; language selection is usually the first or second step in the installation process.

Input Devices

Linux classifies both keyboards and mice as input devices. Linux installation programs generally try to detect your keyboard and mouse. If detection is successful, you need only to confirm the selection.

Linux installation programs can accommodate a number of different languages, so these programs also can accommodate different keyboards associated with those languages. Although a mouse (or similar device) is not required in Linux, it is a useful convenience. The installation program associated with the latest Linux distributions can even detect most USB-attached keyboards and mice.

 The mouse installation step in many Linux distributions allows you to simulate a middle button if you have only a two-button mouse (with no wheel). The middle mouse button is typically associated with a useful menu in the Linux Graphical User Interface (GUI). Once configured, just press the left and right buttons simultaneously.

Clocks

Two decisions are related to the time you set on your computer. If you're running just Linux, set your system clock (in CMOS) to Greenwich Mean Time (GMT), which is sometimes listed by its French acronym, UTC. This helps synchronize your computer with those in other time zones, which can be useful if you're running a Web server with mirror sites in other locations.

If you're running Linux and another operating system such as Microsoft Windows, don't set your system clock to GMT/UTC. The other operating system won't be able to handle it. The drawback is that Linux won't adjust your clock for Daylight Savings Time.

Configuring the Hard Drive

Chapter 4 addressed many of the different partitions that you can set up on your hard drive and the directories that you can mount on each partition. A number of tools are available to configure the hard drive. If your configuration includes more than one operating system, you can also set up the Linux boot loader, known as LILO, to help you select the operating system that you want when your computer boots.

Hard Drive Configuration Tools

When you configure a hard drive, you'll probably want to create partitions. If you already have an operating system and a partition with sufficient empty space on your computer, you may also want to split partitions. The basic Linux tools in this area are **fdisk** and **fips** (short for First Interactive Partition Splitter). You can create or destroy partitions with **fdisk**, and split existing partitions nondestructively with **fips**.

Note: Although Linux fdisk is functionally similar to the MS-DOS tool of the same name, Linux fdisk is much more flexible. For example, instead of one primary partition, Linux fdisk can be used to create up to four primary partions. Linux fdisk can partition drives for MS-DOS, Microsoft Windows, IBM OS/2, and many more. MS-DOS fdisk has no such flexibility.

For example, if you have Microsoft Windows on your computer and a 15GB C: drive with 10GB of free space, you currently have one primary partition. You could back up the disk, destroy the partition with either version of **fdisk**, create the partitions you need, and restore the data to the hard drive, but that process can be painful. Alternatively, you could use **fips** to create a second partition from the available free space without destroying your existing partition. You could then use Linux **fdisk** to further subdivide that free space into the partitions you need.

The First Interactive Partition Splitter—**fips**—comes without a warranty. Use it at your own risk. Nevertheless, I've used it several dozen times without problems. If you want to use **fips**, read the documentation carefully. The **fips** Web site, with documentation, is listed in the "Need to Know More?" section at the end of this chapter. Remember, there is no guarantee that it will work for you.

Commercial third-party tools are also available for splitting and creating new partitions, including Partition Magic (**www.powerquest.com**) and System Commander (**www.v-com.com**).

Distribution Specific Tools

The **fdisk** and **fips** tools can be difficult to use. Many Linux distributions incorporate their own GUI-supported tools to configure and sometimes even split partitions, as described here and in Chapter 4. Examples include the following:

➤ *Disk Druid*—Red Hat Linux's powerful tool is a partition-management utility.

➤ *YaST*—S.u.S.E.'s "Yet another Setup Tool" includes partition-management tools.

➤ *Webmin*—Caldera's all-in-one configuration tool includes a browser-based partition-management utility.

The Linux Loader (LILO)

The Linux Loader (LILO) is a versatile tool for loading operating systems. You can set it to load Linux directly from the Master Boot Record of your hard drive. If you have another operating system with a boot loader, such as Windows NT/ 2000 (NTLDR), you can set it to load from a primary partition. If desired, you can even set up LILO on a floppy disk.

When LILO loads on your computer, you see the following prompt, usually just for a few seconds:

```
LILO boot:
```

*Note: Some distributions use a graphical adaptation of LILO. Most allow you to go into text mode with a command such as **CTRL + X**; this brings you to a LILO **Boot:** or equivalent prompt.*

If you press the Tab key, LILO lists the available operating systems. For example, if you've set LILO to boot either Linux or Microsoft Windows, you might see the following:

```
Linux    dos
boot:
```

In this case, you have two choices: you can type "linux" or "dos". After you press Enter, the operating system associated with your selection starts to boot.

Some of the newest Linux distributions use the Grand Unified Boot loader (GRUB) in place of LILO. The Linux+ exam does not cover GRUB. If you have GRUB and want to install LILO, consult your distribution's documentation for details.

Selecting a File System

It isn't enough to configure a partition. Before you can actually install files, you need to format the partitions that you need. In Microsoft Windows, you might format a partition to the VFAT, FAT32, or NTFS system. In Linux, you might format a partition to the ext2, ext3, ReiserFS, or XFS system.

Although ext2 is a traditional file system, ext3, ReiserFS, and XFS are known as *journaling file systems*. Journaling file systems constantly update data on the file structure. A disadvantage is that it takes time to constantly update the file structure, and this can reduce the performance of reading and writing to your hard drive. If you have a disk crash, however, location information on your files is readily available; the time required to check your disk for damage is therefore reduced to a minimum.

When you set up a file system on a partition, you don't have to format the whole partition. In that case, the volume is smaller than the partition.

ext2

The current Linux file system standard is known as the *second extended file system*, or ext2 for short. It was implemented starting with Linux kernel 2.2. The ext2 system allows files as large as 2GB. Believe it or not, that's already too small for some applications; for example, some log files associated with bigger Web servers are larger than 2GB.

After a disk crash, Linux automatically checks the integrity of a file system. On larger hard drives, this check could easily take over an hour, and your Linux computer could seem to be frozen. Inexperienced users have been known to cycle power on their computers during the disk check process, which can easily destroy the integrity of any data on the hard drive.

Remember that a volume formatted with the ext2 file system is resizable. If you did not format a whole partition to the ext2 file system, you can increase the size of the volume. But this is rare. Generally, you have to resize a partition to get more space.

ext3

One response to the problems associated with ext2 is the *third extended file system*, ext3 for short. Conceptually, it is the same as ext2, with a journal. Since journaling reduces the disk check time to a minimum after a crash, the associated risks are significantly reduced.

As of this writing, Red Hat has announced that its default file system will change to ext3, starting with Red Hat Linux 7.2. It is hoped that partitions will be easily convertible between ext2 and ext3.

ReiserFS

The Reiser file system (ReiserFS) is designed as a fast journaling file system, based on "balanced trees." It is more efficient if most of your files are very small (a few hundred bytes) or very large (a few megabytes or more). It is more efficient for smaller files because it can pack as many files as can fit in a disk block. In contrast, regular file systems handle no more than one file per block.

ReiserFS is somewhat available on systems with Linux kernel 2.4.2 and above. As of this writing, bugs in this file system were being addressed through Linux kernel 2.4.5. Despite these minor issues, some distributions now allow you to format individual partitions to ReiserFS.

XFS

XFS was originally developed by Silicon Graphics (SGI) as a journaling file system for SGI's IRIX operating system. Like Linux, IRIX is a clone of Unix, primarily for computers with 64-bit processors.

In mid-2001, SGI adapted, or *ported*, the XFS file system for Linux kernel 2.4. As a 64-bit file system, it definitely supports larger files. The file size limit in XFS is 8,192 petabytes. A petabyte is equal to approximately 1 million gigabytes. It will be some time before Web server log files exceed this limit!

Note: The standard file system in use today is 32 bits.

Other File Systems

A substantial number of other file systems are available for Linux. Some are illustrated in Figure 5.1. Some of these, such as NTFS, one of the standard file systems on Microsoft Windows NT and 2000, should only be set up as read-only; nevertheless, the list is impressive.

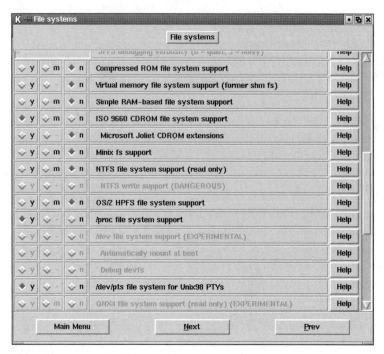

Figure 5.1 A partial list of alternative file systems.

Swap Space

Swap space is used to extend the amount of effective RAM on your computer. The amount of swap space that you need is a matter of some controversy. Since swap space is formatted somewhat differently from ext2, it is really a different file system.

Why Swap Space

Swap space is essentially an overflow cache for your RAM. Less-used data in your RAM is often transferred temporarily to a swap partition to leave some RAM free for other programs and data.

On a 32-bit computer, programs can address up to 4GB (2^{32}) of memory space. Unless you have 4GB of RAM, you probably need some swap space.

Swap Space Size

Depending on whom you believe, there are several guidelines for the right amount of swap space. You could configure your computer with the same amount of swap space as your RAM. Or it could be twice the amount of RAM. Or it could even be four times the amount of RAM.

An appropriate amount of swap space is not necessarily a function of RAM. Some distributions will automatically set up 64MB, 128MB, or 256MB of swap space, depending on whether you're configuring Linux as a workstation or a server.

Swap Space Management

Since the right amount of size for swap space is uncertain, you may need to increase it at some time.

Finding the right amount of space for your swap partition can be a trial-and-error process. For example, if you hear your hard drive churning because of constant data transfer between your RAM and hard drive, that is a sign you need more swap space.

Another way to see if you need more swap space is with the **top** command, which might give you the result shown in Figure 5.2.

Two key lines are shown near the top of the output, as follows:

```
Mem:     38120K av,  37340K used,    780K free
Swap:   133016K av,  16420K used, 116596K free
```

The **Mem:** line indicates the usage of your RAM. Although about 38MB of RAM is available, almost all of it is used. With this much use, overflow to swap space can be expected.

As you can see in the **Swap:** line, about 130MB of swap space is available, but just over 16MB is being used. This configuration has plenty of swap space available.

If the amount of swap space being used starts to approach what is available, you should increase the swap space on your system.

```
 6:32pm  up  2:59,  3 users,  load average: 0.51, 0.13, 0.04
60 processes: 58 sleeping, 2 running, 0 zombie, 0 stopped
CPU states: 10.4% user,  4.3% system,  0.0% nice, 85.2% idle
Mem:    38120K av,   37340K used,     780K free,       0K shrd,     292K buff
Swap:  133016K av,   16420K used,  116596K free                  13896K cached

  PID USER     PRI  NI   SIZE  RSS SHARE STAT %CPU %MEM   TIME COMMAND
 1229 mj        14   0   2840 2840  2248 S     5.5  7.4   0:00 screenshot
  960 root      17   0  15360  10M  1736 S     2.5 29.4  20:01 X
 1085 mj        16   0   2744 2060  1704 S     2.1  5.4   0:01 kdeinit
 1226 root      14   0   1016 1016   812 R     1.5  2.6   0:01 top
 1089 mj        12   0   4772 4180  3204 S     1.1 10.9   0:03 kdeinit
 1115 mj         9   0   4776 4340  3612 R     0.5 11.3   0:02 kdeinit
    4 root      10   0      0    0     0 SW    0.3  0.0   0:01 kswapd
  458 root      10   0    132   56    52 S     0.1  0.1   0:00 syslogd
 1084 mj         9   0   1948 1124   892 S     0.1  2.9   0:01 knotify
 1087 mj         9   0   3692 2948  2268 S     0.1  7.7   0:03 kdeinit
    1 root       8   0    104   60    60 S     0.0  0.1   0:03 init
    2 root       8   0      0    0     0 SW    0.0  0.0   0:00 keventd
    3 root       9   0      0    0     0 SW    0.0  0.0   0:00 kapm-idled
    5 root       9   0      0    0     0 SW    0.0  0.0   0:00 kreclaimd
    6 root       9   0      0    0     0 SW    0.0  0.0   0:00 bdflush
    7 root       9   0      0    0     0 SW    0.0  0.0   0:00 kupdated
    8 root      -1 -20      0    0     0 SW<   0.0  0.0   0:00 mdrecoveryd
  463 root       9   0    620    0     0 SW    0.0  0.0   0:00 klogd
  477 rpc        9   0     84    0     0 SW    0.0  0.0   0:00 portmap
  492 rpcuser    9   0    104    0     0 SW    0.0  0.0   0:00 rpc.statd
  553 root       8   0    156    0     0 SW    0.0  0.0   0:00 cardmgr
```

Figure 5.2 Output from the **top** command.

The Rest of the Story

After a file system is selected, the next step is to set up the actual installation. Whatever your distribution, Linux installation is based on a series of packages. Not only are there packages for individual programs, but there are also groups of packages that are often available by function, such as news servers or laptop add-ons. In other words, what you install of Linux depends on the role of your computer, as well as any specialized packages that you may need.

*Note: Although some distributions allow you to set up parameters such as IP addresses and firewalls, the only other required step is to assign a password to the **root** user.*

Basic Computer Role

Some Linux distributions allow you to set up base packages commensurate with the primary function of your computer. In other words, installation can depend on whether your computer should function as a workstation or as a server.

Note: Generally, you need to enter a Custom or Detailed package selection mode if you want to select different packages or package groups.

Package Selection

In most cases, even modern Linux workstations need a graphical user interface (GUI). A number of required and optional package groups are associated with the Linux GUI, including the following:

➤ *X Window*—The base package group for the GUI. This is the foundation group of packages required to make your computer work with a GUI. This requires a practical minimum of 32MB of RAM and a video controller.

 Know that the X Window requires a practical minimum of 32MB of RAM plus a video controller. If you're setting up the X Window on a terminal, you don't even need a hard drive.

➤ *KDE*—The K Desktop Environment is one of the two main available Linux desktops. It gives your GUI its look and feel.

➤ *GNOME*—The GNU Network Object Model Environment is the other major Linux desktop. It also gives your GUI its look and feel.

➤ *Multimedia*—Most Linux distributions include a multimedia package of sound, graphics, and video applications.

When experienced Linux administrators set up a server, they don't need the GUI. All Linux administrative tools are available at the command line.

Note: If you feel the need to administer Linux from the GUI, there are a number of good GUI Linux administration tools available. They do have some disadvantages, however. GUI tools are less flexible. Also, since they involve more code than corresponding command-line tools, they are more prone to error.

The essential packages for a server are those that you want to share with various workstations. Some of these packages have already been discussed, including Web servers (Apache), proxy servers (Squid), mail servers (Sendmail), Domain Name Service (BIND), and Microsoft Windows interoperability (Samba). These packages are commonly available in groups. Some other available packages include the following:

➤ *News*—A Linux server can be set up as a newsgroup server.

➤ *SQL*—The Structured Query Language is a key to databases. SQL is often integrated with Apache for more responsive Web sites.

➤ *Emacs*—This is a popular text editor. Remember, vi is the text editor of choice for the Linux+ exam.

➤ *Source code*—One of the provisions of the General Public License (GPL) requires easy access to the source code—the programming instructions. This is often made available in a separate package. If you have the skills to modify the source code, you can customize Linux packages to meet your needs.

Post-Installation Analysis

To paraphrase an old song about a restaurant in Berkeley, California: "You can have almost any log you want…in a Linux restaurant." The menu of available log files is impressive. You can set up logs by service or by the severity of the problem.

By reviewing the right log files, you can see what happened with an installation of Linux or many Linux applications. After you understand the success or failure of an installation, you can proceed to installing Linux or associated applications on production computers.

Log Files

You can use a system log file to diagnose a problem with installation, booting, specific services, and more. Logs can be further subdivided into eight categories, listed here in descending order of importance:

➤ emerg (emergency)

➤ alert

➤ crit (critical)

➤ err (error)

➤ warning

➤ notice

➤ info

➤ debug

Log files are organized as described in the Linux /etc/syslog.conf configuration file. One well-organized syslog.conf file is part of the Corel Linux distribution, shown in Figure 5.3. As you can see, messages are subdivided into categories such as auth (authentication—a.k.a. password security) and cron (scheduled jobs).

Be sure to remember that log files are organized in the /etc/syslog.conf file.

Installation Messages

After you install or boot Linux, there are two ways to check for the success or failure of the installation: the **dmesg** command and the /var/log/messages file.

Keep in mind the fact that the log file most closely related to installation and boot problems is /var/log/messages.

```
#    /etc/syslog.confConfiguration file for syslogd.
#
#                For more information see syslog.conf(5)
#                manpage.
#
# syslog.conf changed by Brian

# auth and authpriv are combined
authpriv, auth.=debug              /var/log/auth/auth.debug
authpriv, auth.=info               /var/log/auth/auth.info
authpriv, auth.=notice             /var/log/auth/auth.notice
authpriv, auth.=warning            /var/log/auth/auth.warning
authpriv, auth.=err                /var/log/auth/auth.err
authpriv, auth.=crit               /var/log/auth/auth.crit
authpriv, auth.=alert              /var/log/auth/auth.alert
authpriv, auth.=emerg              /var/log/auth/auth.emerg

cron.=debug                        /var/log/cron/cron.debug
cron.=info                         /var/log/cron/cron.info
cron.=notice                       /var/log/cron/cron.notice
cron.=warning                      /var/log/cron/cron.warning
cron.=err                          /var/log/cron/cron.err
cron.=crit                         /var/log/cron/cron.crit
cron.=alert                        /var/log/cron/cron.alert
cron.=emerg                        /var/log/cron/cron.emerg
```

Figure 5.3   An excerpt from a /etc/syslog.conf configuration file.

```
Freeing unused kernel memory: 112k freed
Adding Swap: 133048k swap-space (priority 42)
VFS: Disk change detected on device ide1(22,0)
ip_conntrack (512 buckets, 4096 max)
pcnet32_probe_pci: found device 0x001022,0x002000
PCI: Enabling device 00:10.0 (0001 -> 0003)
     ioaddr=0x001000  resource_flags=0x000101
eth0: PCnet/PCI II 79C970A at 0x1000, 00 50 56 a7 00 23
pcnet32: pcnet32_private lp=c3725000 lp_dma_addr=0x3725000 assigned IRQ 9.
pcnet32.c:v1.25kf 26.9.1999 tsbogend@alpha.franken.de
IPv6 v0.8 for NET4.0
IPv6 over IPv4 tunneling driver
eth0: duplicate address detected!
eth0: duplicate address detected!
eth0: duplicate address detected!
eth0: duplicate address detected!
apm: set display: Unrecognized device ID
apm: set display: Unrecognized device ID
isapnp: Scanning for PnP cards...
isapnp: No Plug & Play device found
isapnp: Scanning for PnP cards...
isapnp: No Plug & Play device found
Soundblaster audio driver Copyright (C) by Hannu Savolainen 1993-1996
sb: No ISAPnP cards found, trying standard ones...
sb: dsp reset failed█
ISO 9660 Extensions: Microsoft Joliet Level 3
ISO 9660 Extensions: RRIP_1991A
```

Figure 5.4   An excerpt from a **dmesg** command.

The **dmesg** command recounts the messages you may have seen on your screen the last time you booted Linux. In the excerpt shown in Figure 5.4, you can see that Linux successfully detected an Ethernet network card (**eth0**), but there is a problem with its IP address (**eth0: duplicate address detected!**). From the messages near the bottom of the screen, you might conclude that Linux successfully detected a sound card. The more experienced among you might notice a problem based on the **sb:** (short for Sound Blaster) messages.

 Many of the same messages from the **dmesg** command can also be found in a /var/log/boot.* file, where * varies by Linux distribution.

The problem is more clear when you review the associated excerpt from the /var/log/messages file. More than half the messages shown in Figure 5.5 are related to problems with the sound card.

Testing

Post-installation analysis is useful after installing Linux for the first time on a computer. It is also useful after installing a new application for the first time on a Linux computer. The productivity penalty associated with post-installation problems is usually high enough that testing is appropriate.

Especially in larger organizations, it's useful to have test computers that aren't used for anything critical to the organization. *Test computers* are typically isolated from the main network. In contrast, the computers used for the main work of the organization are sometimes known as *production computers*.

```
Jul 16 07:32:02 linux insmod: /lib/modules/2.4.4-4GB/kernel/drivers/sound/sb.o: in
smod char-major-14 failed
Jul 16 07:32:03 linux kernel: isapnp: Scanning for PnP cards...
Jul 16 07:32:03 linux kernel: isapnp: No Plug & Play device found
Jul 16 07:32:04 linux kernel: Soundblaster audio driver Copyright (C) by Hannu Sav
olainen 1993-1996
Jul 16 07:32:04 linux kernel: sb: No ISAPnP cards found, trying standard ones...
Jul 16 07:32:04 linux kernel: sb: dsp reset failed.
Jul 16 07:32:04 linux insmod: /lib/modules/2.4.4-4GB/kernel/drivers/sound/sb.o: in
it_module: No such device
Jul 16 07:32:04 linux insmod: Hint: insmod errors can be caused by incorrect modul
e parameters, including invalid IO or IRQ parameters
Jul 16 07:32:04 linux insmod: /lib/modules/2.4.4-4GB/kernel/drivers/sound/sb.o: in
smod char-major-14 failed
Jul 16 07:32:04 linux modprobe: modprobe: Can't locate module sound-slot-0
Jul 16 07:32:05 linux modprobe: modprobe: Can't locate module sound-slot-0
Jul 16 07:32:06 linux modprobe: modprobe: Can't locate module sound-service-0-3
Jul 16 07:32:06 linux modprobe: modprobe: Can't locate module sound-slot-0
Jul 16 07:32:06 linux modprobe: modprobe: Can't locate module sound-service-0-0
Jul 16 07:32:08 linux modprobe: modprobe: Can't locate module sound-service-0-0
Jul 16 07:32:08 linux modprobe: modprobe: Can't locate module sound-slot-0
Jul 16 07:32:09 linux modprobe: modprobe: Can't locate module sound-slot-0
Jul 16 07:32:09 linux modprobe: modprobe: Can't locate module sound-service-0-0
Jul 16 07:32:11 linux modprobe: modprobe: Can't locate module sound-service-0-0
Jul 16 07:32:11 linux modprobe: modprobe: Can't locate module sound-slot-1
Jul 16 07:32:12 linux modprobe: modprobe: Can't locate module sound-slot-1
Jul 16 07:32:12 linux modprobe: modprobe: Can't locate module sound-service-1-0
```

Figure 5.5 An excerpt from a /var/log/messages file.

Before you install Linux or any Linux application on a production computer, install it on a test computer first. Check the appropriate log files for post-installation messages. Test the new software in a production environment. When you're satisfied with the result, then install Linux or the Linux application on a production computer.

Before installing critical applications on a production computer, try it out on a test computer first.

Practice Questions

Question 1

> Which of the following can you use as a source when installing Linux on your computer? [Check all correct answers]
>
> ❑ a. Hard drive
>
> ❑ b. Remote CD-ROM
>
> ❑ c. Remote FTP server
>
> ❑ d. Local CD-ROM

Answers a, b, c, and d are all correct. The default way to install Linux is from a local CD-ROM. You can also copy a Linux installation CD to your hard drive and install Linux from there, usually with the help of a boot disk. If you have a network connection to another computer, you can install Linux from a remote CD-ROM. If you have a sufficiently fast network connection, such as cable modem or DSL service, you can also install Linux from a remote FTP server.

Question 2

> If you're installing Linux from files on several other computers on your network simultaneously, which of the following types of network services should you use?
>
> ○ a. Samba
>
> ○ b. NFS
>
> ○ c. FTP
>
> ○ d. **fdisk**

Answer b is correct. NFS, the Network File System, is the network service required to share files between Unix/Linux computers. It is also required if you're installing Linux on several computers on your network simultaneously. Although you can install Linux on a single computer using a Samba connection, this service won't work for installing Linux on multiple computers. Therefore, answer a is incorrect. The same is true for FTP; therefore, answer c is also incorrect. The **fdisk** utility creates and destroys partitions, but it does not install Linux on a computer. Therefore, answer d is also incorrect.

Question 3

> Which of the following file systems is resizable?
>
> ○ a. ext2
>
> ○ b. FAT32
>
> ○ c. ReiserFS
>
> ○ d. XFS

Answer a is correct. Of the available choices, only the second extended file system (ext2) is resizable. Remember, if you need more space on a partition, you'll need to increase the size of the partition. This is not an option if the formatted area already fills the partition.

Question 4

> Which of the following utilities can you use to create a new partition?
>
> ○ a. **/sbin/ifconfig**
>
> ○ b. **dmesg**
>
> ○ c. **fdisk**
>
> ○ d. **/sbin/lilo**

Answer c is correct. The **fdisk** command utility can be used to create new partitions. Although similar to the MS-DOS utility of the same name, Linux **fdisk** can be used to create up to four primary partitions. Since the **/sbin/ifconfig** command checks the current network configuration, it is not related to partitions; therefore, answer a is incorrect. The **dmesg** command reviews the messages produced during the Linux boot process and cannot be used to create partitions, so answer b is incorrect. The **lilo** command utility incorporates the Linux Loader into the hard disk Master Boot Record (MBR). While this may point to new partitions, it does not create new partitions. Therefore, answer d is also incorrect.

Question 5

> Which of the following statements is a characteristic of a journaling file system?
>
> ○ a. Because a journaling file system constantly updates data on the file structure, it is characterized by superior hard drive performance.
>
> ○ b. Because a journaling file system rarely updates data on the file structure, it is characterized by superior hard drive performance.
>
> ○ c. Because a journaling file system constantly updates data on the file structure, disk checks take very little time.
>
> ○ d. Because a journaling file system rarely updates data on the file structure, disk checks take very little time.

Answer c is correct. Most of the time spent in a file check for a traditional file system is in collecting data on the file structure. Since this data is readily available in a journaling file system, disk checks take very little time. Unfortunately, since constant updates to the file structure reduce disk performance, answer a is incorrect. Since journaling file systems constantly update file structure data, answers b and d are both incorrect.

Question 6

> If you want to find the kind of log file information from different categories and services logged on a Linux computer and their associated files, where would you look?
>
> ○ a. /etc/lilo.conf
>
> ○ b. /etc/syslog.conf
>
> ○ c. dmesg
>
> ○ d. /var/log/messages

Answer b is correct. /etc/syslog.conf is a configuration file of services, the types of messages that are logged, and the location of each associated log file. /etc/lilo.conf is the configuration file for the Linux Loader, which is unrelated to log file management, so answer a is incorrect. The **dmesg** command lists the messages that you see during Linux boot; that isn't even an official log file. Therefore, answer c is incorrect. Although the /var/log/messages file is a log of various Linux boot and startup messages, it is only one log file. Therefore, answer d is also incorrect.

Question 7

> If you suspect a problem during Linux boot or installation, in which of the following files would you look first for help?
>
> ○ a. kickstart
>
> ○ b. dmesg
>
> ○ c. /var/log/wtmp
>
> ○ d. /var/log/messages

Answer d is correct. The /var/log/messages file contains messages related to the Linux boot process. Since kickstart is a Red Hat utility for installing Linux on multiple computers, you might look to its configuration file for help once you have an idea about what is wrong. But you should look first to a log file on a computer on which you're installing Linux. Therefore, answer a is incorrect. Although the **dmesg** command lists some of the boot messages and can be useful, it is a command and not a log file. Therefore, answer b is incorrect. The /var/log/wtmp file is unrelated to the Linux boot process. In fact, it contains login records for users on your system. Therefore, answer c is also incorrect.

Question 8

> Your management has decided not to upgrade to Microsoft Office XP. They have authorized you to examine copies of various Linux office suites such as VistaSource's Anyware Office, Corel's WordPerfect, and Sun's StarOffice. You will select one suite for installation. Which of the following choices is the best way to approach this process?
>
> ○ a. Install each of these suites on computers in the management offices. You can have confidence in these Linux office suites and can immediately take credit for improved productivity.
>
> ○ b. Install each of these suites on a separate test computer in your office. Test each computer with demands consistent with those you may see in a production office. Install one of these suites on production computers only after testing is complete.
>
> ○ c. Install each of these suites on a single computer in your office. Test each suite with demands consistent with those you may see in a production office. Install one of these suites on production computers only after testing is complete.
>
> ○ d. Browse the newsgroups. Look for opinions on each of these office suites. Select the one with the most positive comments, and install it on your production computers.

Answer b is correct. It is best to check out new applications on test computers first. Any application may have unknown interactions with your hardware or operating system. Answer a is a recipe for problems; it is therefore incorrect. Because production computers will typically have only one office suite, it is best to install only one office suite per test computer. The extra load from multiple suites could otherwise lead you to install more RAM and/or hard disks than you actually need. Therefore, answer c is incorrect. Newsgroup users may not have the same hardware or software (or interests) as yours, so what you read on the newsgroups may not work for you. Therefore, answer d is also incorrect.

Question 9

Based on observation and the output from the **top** command, which of the following pieces of information tells you that swap space needs to be increased?

- ○ a. The amount of available memory nearly equals the amount of used memory.

- ○ b. The amount of available swap space nearly equals the amount of RAM.

- ○ c. You hear constant noise from your hard drive.

- ○ d. The CPU utilization level is near 100%.

Answer c is correct. Constant noise from a hard drive is a sign of constant exchange of data between RAM and a swap area. If almost all of the available memory (RAM) is used on your computer, you may need more RAM. However, that does not mean you need more swap space. Therefore, answer a is incorrect. While some criteria suggest that swap space should be double the amount of RAM (or more), that does not necessarily mean that your particular computer does not have enough swap space. Therefore, answer b is incorrect. Constant use of your CPU may mean that you need a faster processor or have a troublesome program, but that is not necessarily related to your level of swap space. Therefore, answer d is also incorrect.

Need to Know More?

 Jang, Michael. *SAIR Linux/GNU Installation and Configuration Exam Cram.* Scottsdale, AZ: The Coriolis Group, 2001. ISBN 1-57610-953-4. This review guide for the more advanced SAIR Linux/GNU exams includes more detailed information about the Linux installation process.

 Maginnis, Tobin. *SAIR Linux and GNU Certification, Level I: Installation and Configuration Exam Cram.* New York, NY: John Wiley & Sons, 2000. ISBN 0-47136-978-0. This review guide for the more advanced SAIR Linux/GNU exams also includes more detailed information about the Linux installation process.

 Volkerding, Patrick, Kevin Reichard, and Eric Foster-Johnson. *Linux Configuration & Installation.* Foster City, CA: Hungry Minds, 1998. ISBN 0-76457-005-6. This guide to Slackware Linux installation covers the details of Linux installation almost completely, since Slackware Linux does not include an all-in-one installation program.

 The home page for the First Interactive Partition Splitter (**fips**) at **www.igd.fhg.de/~aschaefe/fips/** includes free GPL-licensed software and a guide to splitting partitions without having to move any data. Because this is GPL software, it is available without a warranty; in other words, use it at your own risk.

 The Web site for the Linux Documentation Project (LDP) at **www.linuxdoc.org** is the central repository for Linux manuals, HOWTOs, and a number of other book-length documents. Important HOWTOs for this chapter include the Kickstart HOWTO for setting up an installation of multiple computers at **www.linuxdoc.org/HOWTO/KickStart-HOWTO.html**. Also important is the Network Administrator's Guide, also available online through the LDP at **www.linuxdoc.org/LDP/nag2/index.html**.

 The Red Hat Linux 7.1 Installation Guide, available online at **www.redhat.com/support/manuals/RHL-7.1-Manual/install-guide/**, is a good, detailed introduction to how to install Linux. Although the Linux+ exam is distribution neutral, about half of the Linux market as of this writing is covered by various Red Hat Linux distributions. Many of the questions on the Linux+ exam reflect a partial bias toward Red Hat commands and utilities.

6

Package Installation and Configuration

. . . .

Terms you'll need to understand:

✓ **tar**

✓ tar.gz, tgz

✓ **gzip, gunzip**

✓ rpm

✓ deb

✓ Patches

✓ Compiling

✓ Test computer

✓ lilo.conf

✓ fstab

✓ inittab

✓ Bourne Again Shell (bash)

✓ /etc/services

Techniques you'll need to master:

✓ Creating, extracting, and editing archives

✓ Extracting and querying rpm and deb packages

✓ Downloading packages and patches

✓ Installing applications after Linux is installed

✓ Describing key configuration files

✓ Accommodating different configuration options

✓ Identifying default configuration file directories

Installing Linux is just the first part of the job. Even if you selected the exact applications you need, more installation work is required. You may want to upgrade your applications. Your users may identify new applications they want.

Linux applications and software are configured into various packages. Some include source code and need to be compiled. Others are already in binary format and can be installed immediately.

Installation is not the end of the job, either. You also need to understand and work with different settings of key configuration files, associated with applications and the basic Linux operating system.

Managing a Group of Files

Packages are groups of files. In Linux, packages can be archived and then compressed, similarly to the zip utilities in Microsoft Windows. The **tar** command and related file formats are a recurring theme in the Linux+ exam objectives. You'll examine the **tar** command in detail, along with examples, in this and following sections.

Archiving by tar

The tape archive (**tar**) command is the traditional way to collect a group of files together for storage. It collects a series of files together into a single large file. As suggested by its name, backups used to be made primarily to tape drives. For example, if you wanted to collect all of the files in user **mj**'s home directory together, you could use the following command:

```
tar cvf mjbackup.tar /home/mj
```

First, review the format of a Linux command. The command is **tar**. The letters that follow a command are known as *switches*. Three switches are shown: c, v, and f. Most commands require a dash (-) before a switch; the **tar** command does not. The next name is a filename, mjbackup.tar. The command is applied to all of the files in the /home/mj directory.

It's important to use the absolute path, as indicated by the first slash. Otherwise, it is difficult to control where your files are restored. The format of this and other commands is addressed in more detail in Chapter 7.

Now examine the switches. The first switch creates (c) a backup and lists the name of every file being archived (v=verbose) in the file (f) named mjbackup.tar. The list is taken from the home directory of user **mj**, which is normally /home/mj. If there are subdirectories in the /home/mj directory, they are automatically saved in the same archive. You can now save the archive file to a backup area such as another volume or a tape drive.

It is a good practice to save your archives with a .tar extension. This can help others identify what you have saved as an archive.

It is easy to reverse this process. For example, if you need to restore the files to mj's home directory from mjbackup.tar, use the following command:

```
tar xkvf mjbackup.tar
```

This command restores the files previously archived. The first switch (**x**) extracts the files in the archive. The next switch (**k**) makes sure that files already in the /home/mj directory are not overwritten. Verbose mode (**v**) directs **tar** to scroll the file names across your screen as they are restored. The final switch, file (**f**), directs **tar** to do all of this from the mjbackup.tar file.

More switches for the **tar** command are shown in Table 6.1.

Unfortunately, a **tar** archive takes up more space when compared to all of the individual files put together. One common practice is to add the zip (**z**) switch, which allows you to compress file archives. If this is your preference, make sure to use the .tar.gz or .tgz extension to help others identify these files as compressed archives. For example, the following commands create and then restore a compressed archive from your /tmp directory:

```
tar czvf temporary.tar.gz /tmp
tar xzvf temporary.tar.gz
```

Table 6.1   Command switches for tar.

Switch	Purpose
c	Creates an archive.
d	Compares files between an archive and a current directory.
f	Uses the following file name for the archive.
k	Does not overwrite existing files.
r	Adds files to the end of an archive.
t	Lists files in a current archive.
v	Verbose option; lists all files going in or coming out of an archive.
x	Extracts files from an archive.
z	Compress files to or from an archive. Also known as zip.

Alternately, these next two commands create and then restore a compressed archive in the .tgz format:

```
tar czvf temporary.tgz /tmp
tar xzvf temporary.tgz
```

 Remember that files with the .tgz or .tar.gz extension are *compressed* archives.

Compressing a File

Separate Linux commands can compress and uncompress a file. These are the **gzip** and **gunzip** commands. The syntax of these commands is fairly simple; you can compress a file (or an archive) with the following command:

```
gzip myarchive.tar
```

Since **gzip** automatically adds a .gz extension to the end of a file, the output is a compressed file named myarchive.tar.gz. You can reverse the process with the **gunzip** command:

```
gunzip myarchive.tar.gz
```

You don't need **gunzip**, however, because you can also uncompress a file with the following command:

```
gzip -d myarchive.tar.gz
```

As discussed in the previous section, the zip (**z**) switch also allows the **tar** command to compress and uncompress a file.

 Be sure to know the commands required to archive and compress. Be able to use just the **tar** command or a combination of **tar** and **gzip** for the same purposes.

Installing Packages

One of the key skills for a Linux administrator is the ability to install and configure a package, such as an application, a service, or even a new Linux kernel. Since Linux is covered under the General Public License, downloaded packages usually include the source code. Thus, to install a package, you need to download, uncompress, unarchive, and then compile the code in the package. Depending on the package, this can be a difficult process.

Alternatively, many packages are precompiled into a binary format for easy installation. There are two major formats for binary packages: rpm and deb.

Installing a Regular Package

There are many sources for Linux packages. One useful example is the **efax** package, available online from **www.cce.com/efax**. At the time of this writing, the current version of this package is **efax-09.tar.gz**, which can be downloaded from a link at the bottom of the noted Web site.

*Note: The Linux **efax** package is unrelated to the applications associated with efax.com.*

Download this package to an appropriate location, such as the /tmp directory. Once you've downloaded this file, you can uncompress and unarchive with the following set of commands:

```
gunzip /tmp/efax-09.tar.gz
tar xvf /tmp/efax-09.tar
```

The **gunzip** command uncompresses the **efax** package; then the **tar** command unarchives the result. The **gunzip** command automatically removes the .gz extension from the downloaded file.

While **gzip** normally compresses a file, the -d switch reverses the effect and uncompresses a file, just like **gunzip**. The **tar** command unarchives the result in the same way:

```
gzip -d efax-09.tar.gz
tar xvf efax-09.tar
```

Alternatively, you can uncompress and unarchive in one command, just by adding the **z** switch to the **tar** command, as shown:

```
tar xzvf efax-09.tar.gz
```

Typically, uncompressed, unarchived packages are saved in a directory of the same or a similar name. In this case, if the package is downloaded to /tmp, the unarchived files are saved to the /tmp/efax-09 directory. Normally, such packages include README files with detailed installation instructions for compiling and installing the package. You could even review any INSTALL files in the package. If you understand the code, you can modify it to customize the configuration.

Binary Packages

Tape archive files are not just for archiving or backing up personal files. A large number of Linux packages and applications are made available in tar.gz format. But modifying and compiling packages can be a difficult process. Alternatives are available, based on the Red Hat Package Manager (rpm) and the Debian (deb) package systems.

The source code for these packages is already compiled into binary format with settings for a specific kind of installation. While this makes it more difficult to modify how a package is installed, most package distributors make the source code available. Nevertheless, one primary purpose of rpm and deb packages is to ease the effort required to install and upgrade a system.

Red Hat Package Manager

The Red Hat Package Manager may be the most popular way to distribute binary packages in Linux. The **rpm** system is a popular alternative for a number of Linux distributions, including Red Hat, Mandrake, S.u.S.E., Caldera, and more.

If you have one of these distributions, most of the installation process uses the **rpm** system. Before installing a new application, the first step is to see if you already have it installed. For example, if you want to check for the **efax** package described earlier, run the following command:

```
rpm -q efax
```

You'll see a message similar to this:

```
efax-0.9-8
```

which is the name of the package. Or you'll see this:

```
package efax is not installed
```

If you haven't installed this package before, it is fairly easy to do so. For example, if it's on your Linux installation CD, just mount it and install it. The default mount directory of a CD varies with distribution. Assuming that a Red Hat 7.1 CD is mounted on the /mnt/cdrom directory, the **efax** package could be installed with the following command:

```
rpm -i /mnt/cdrom/RedHat/RPMS/efax-0.9-8.i386.rpm
```

The actual directory and package vary by Linux distribution. Mounting and the associated **mount** commands are covered in more detail in Chapter 13.

Sometimes it's necessary to upgrade a package that is already installed. For example, if there is a new feature in **efax**, assume you download it to the /tmp directory, and the new version is efax-1.1-4. You could then upgrade it with the following command:

```
rpm -Uvh /tmp/efax-1.1-4.i386.rpm
```

This command upgrades (-**U**) a previous package. If there is no previous package, it installs it. As the package is installed, messages are verified (-**v**) and shown on the screen. As installation progresses, hash (**#**) marks (-**h**) are added on the screen.

If you're not sure if an application was previously installed, you can still use the **rpm -Uvh** command. If there is no package to upgrade, the new package is simply installed.

Know how to install, uninstall, or upgrade with the **rpm** command.

Only the **root** user or someone with **root** user privileges can run the **rpm** command. Otherwise, any attempt to use **rpm** leads to the following message:

```
error: cannot open Packages index using db3 - Permission denied (13)
error: cannot open Packages database in /var/lib/rpm
```

Remember that the **rpm** command can be run only by the **root** user or someone with **root** user privileges.

Finally, many Linux packages won't work without other packages. For example, you can't install some C language compilers without the right binary utility packages. In that case, you would see the following message:

```
failed dependencies
```

with a list of packages that need to be installed. In that case, you should install the other packages first. Some of the more important command switches for the **rpm** command are shown in Table 6.2.

Table 6.2	Red Hat Package Manager (rpm) command switches.
Switch	**Purpose**
-i	Installs a package.
-e	Removes a package.
-U	Upgrades a package.
-v	Verifies the files in a package.
-h	Displays a series of hash marks, or pound signs (#), as installation progresses.
--nodeps	Allows installation of a package without checking whether it depends on other packages. Generally not a recommended option for novice users.

Debian Package System

The other major package manager is based on the work of the volunteers behind the Debian Linux distribution. The Debian package system, deb, is used for binary packages on Debian, Corel, and Storm Linux.

The following are the basic Debian package (**dpkg**) commands required to install (-**i**) and remove a package (-**r**):

```
dpkg -i package-name.deb
dpkg -r package-name.deb
```

Application Management

Packages are just the basic building blocks. Users need applications to do their work. Most applications are available at least as a compressed archive, typically in either .tar.gz or .tgz files. Many applications are also made available as binary packages, typically in Red Hat Package Manager (**rpm**) format.

When an application from a binary package is being installed, the installation directories are predetermined. When installing an application from a compressed archive, however, you can usually customize installation parameters such as the directory.

One example is shown in Figure 6.1, which is an excerpt from the Makefile for the previously mentioned **efax** package. As you can see, you can modify the installation directory for executable files (BINDIR) as well as the man pages (MANDIR). The other lines in the Makefile show the files that are installed during each part of the process. Details of how to modify this and other scripts is beyond the scope of the Linux+ exam.

```
#
# Change the following to the destination directories for
# binaries and man pages. Probably /usr/bin and /usr/man on
# Linux, /usr/local/{bin,man} on other systems.

BINDIR=/usr/bin
MANDIR=/usr/man

.c.o:
        $(CC) $(CFLAGS) -c $<

all:    efax efix

efax:   efax.o efaxlib.o efaxio.o efaxos.o efaxmsg.o
        $(CC) -o efax $(LDFLAGS) efax.o efaxlib.o efaxio.o efaxos.o efaxmsg.o
        strip efax

efix:   efix.o efaxlib.o efaxmsg.o
        $(CC) -o efix $(LDFLAGS) efix.o efaxlib.o efaxmsg.o
        strip efix

install:
        cp fax efax efix $(BINDIR)
        cp fax.1 efax.1 efix.1 $(MANDIR)/man1

clean:
        rm -f efax efix efax.o efix.o efaxlib.o efaxio.o efaxos.o efaxmsg.o
```

Figure 6.1   A typical installation Makefile.

 When setting up an application from a .tar, tar.gz, or .tgz package, the files are unarchived into a subdirectory. Look at various text files in this subdirectory. Some provide detailed installation instructions. Others are scripts with names such as Makefile or INSTALL that illustrate precisely how the application is normally installed. If you understand the language of the script, you can customize them for your needs.

Installing and Removing

Installing applications is a straightforward process and was covered in the previous section, "Installing Packages." The default installation may not meet your needs, however. For example, some organizations want all applications installed in specific directories. Unless the rpm or deb package default installs the application in the desired directory, the only option is to install from a compressed archive. You can then modify the appropriate installation script as needed. Details of this process are beyond the scope of the Linux+ exam.

If you want to delete an application, some packages include removal scripts.

Testing

The right way to test an application is a matter for debate. The details often depend on the needs of your organization. Nevertheless, it is important to remember the following best practices for testing all applications:

➤ Test new applications on a test computer. Interactions with software and hardware are often difficult to predict. The problems may be harmful. To avoid problems for the business or organization, do not test new applications on a production computer.

➤ Use test procedures provided by the developers of the application. Although you should also test the new application based on production requirements, many developers have created test procedures that look for problems encountered by a variety of users.

➤ Check the Web site associated with the application if you encounter any problems. When other users have problems, they typically report them to the developers. Most developers report solutions on the application Web sites.

Key Configuration Files

After installation, there is configuration. Several key configuration files are associated with the Linux operating system. The /etc/lilo.conf file determines how Linux and other operating systems can be loaded onto a PC. Linux reads the /etc/fstab file to determine where to mount specific directories. Then it reads the /etc/inittab file to see how to start the operating system. When users log in, Linux starts a default command-line interface known as *bash*, or the Bourne Again SHell, with configuration files in the /etc and individual users' home directories. Finally, network communication is regulated by the /etc/services file.

With a few exceptions, key configuration files are normally stored in the /etc directory.

 Keep in mind that most key configuration files are located in the /etc directory.

Linux Loader (LILO)

As discussed in earlier chapters, the Linux loader (LILO) allows you to select an operating system when your computer boots. It also allows you to set hardware parameters when you load Linux. A typical LILO in an /etc/lilo.conf file is seen in Figure 6.2.

The **boot=/dev/hda** line tells the PC to look at a specific hard drive. As discussed in Chapter 4, this is an IDE device attached as the master drive on the primary ATAPI controller. The **message=/boot/message** line determines how Linux presents the **LILO Boot:** prompt discussed in Chapter 4. The **default=dos** line tells you that LILO starts the **other** operating system shown at the bottom of the file, by default, from partition **/dev/hda1**. The line **root=/dev/hda6** tells you that the Linux root directory is on the **hda6** partition.

```
boot=/dev/hda
map=/boot/map
install=/boot/boot.b
prompt
timeout=50
message=/boot/message
linear
default=dos

image=/boot/vmlinuz-2.4.2-2
        label=linux
        read-only
        root=/dev/hda6

other=/dev/hda1
        optional
        ▌label=dos
~
~
~
~
~
~
~
~
"/etc/lilo.conf" 17L, 215C
```

Figure 6.2   A typical LILO, in /etc/lilo.conf.

Note: The other lines in the /etc/lilo.conf file are beyond the scope of the Linux+ exam. For more information, see the books listed in the "Need to Know More?" section at the end of this chapter.

The two sections at the bottom of the /etc/lilo.conf file are known as *stanzas*, each of which specifies the settings associated with each operating system. One thing that you can add to a stanza is the **append** command, which tells Linux a bit more about your hardware.

For example, if Linux is having trouble detecting your Ethernet network card, you can tell it about its IRQ and I/O addresses by adding the following command:

```
append="ether=15,0x300,eth0"
```

This option tells Linux to assign IRQ 15 and the I/O address block starting with 0x300 to the first Ethernet card (eth0) on your system. The quotes define the information to be processed by the **append** command.

Alternatively, you could enter this information when your computer boots and you see the LILO **Boot:** prompt. Just enter the same information without the **append** command:

```
LILO Boot: linux ether=15,0x300,eth0
```

The "linux" is required to tell LILO which operating system to boot and should match a **label** entry in the /etc/lilo.conf file. The parameters for your first Ethernet card are entered immediately afterward.

On some distributions, there is a graphical boot loader screen, which should include instructions for going into "text mode" or accessing the LILO **Boot:** prompt. In Red Hat Linux, the command is **Ctrl+X**; the command may vary by distribution.

Remember that you can use the **append** command in the /etc/lilo.conf file to help Linux detect hardware.

fstab

The volumes configured during Linux installation—and a few more—are incorporated into the /etc/fstab file. This file determines what directories are mounted on their own partitions and the way they are mounted. A sample of this file is shown in Figure 6.3.

Important information is shown in the first four columns of the /etc/fstab file. The final two columns are included for reference:

➤ *Partition*—The first column shows the subject partition. For example, the partition shown in the first line of Figure 6.3 (**/dev/hda6**) corresponds to the second logical partition on the primary IDE hard disk on your computer. If this isn't clear, review Chapter 4.

➤ *Mount Point*—The second column lists the directory associated with the specified partition.

➤ *Format*—This column corresponds to the way each directory is mounted. Some of the options are listed in Table 6.3.

```
# (Partition)           (Mount Point)       (format)   (Mount Option)
#
/dev/hda6               /                   ext2       defaults          1 1
/dev/hda2  ▮            /boot               ext2       defaults          1 2
/dev/fd0                /mnt/floppy         vfat       noauto,owner      0 0
none                    /proc               proc       defaults          0 0
none                    /dev/pts            devpts     gid=5,mode=620    0 0
/dev/hda5               swap                swap       defaults          0 0
/dev/cdrom              /mnt/cdrom          iso9660    noauto,owner,ro   0 0
#
#
#
#
#
#
#
#
#
#
#
#
#
#
#
```

Figure 6.3 Typical mounts in /etc/fstab.

Table 6.3	Different formats in /etc/fstab.
Format	**Description**
ext2	Second extended file system (default Linux format).
swap	Linux swap file system.
vfat	Virtual File Allocation Table; both FAT16 and FAT32 can be mounted to the Linux vfat format.
iso9660	The standard file system for most CD drives.
proc	A virtual file system, not mounted on any partition, for current hardware and process information.
devpts	Another virtual file system, related to virtual consoles (covered in Chapter 11).
auto	Finds the file system by reading the first block in the given partition, based on the options in the /etc/filesystems file. Typical option for a floppy drive.

➤ *Mount Option*—The fourth column specifies the users who are allowed to mount and permissions such as **ro** (read-only) or **rw** (read-write).

➤ *Dump*—The fifth column specifies whether a file is written to cache (**1**) in RAM or directly to the filesystem (**0**).

➤ *Mount Order*—The final column tells Linux when to actually mount a directory. In Figure 6.3, the root directory (/) is the first one mounted, followed by /boot. Other directories can be mounted after users log into Linux.

Although the format listed in the /etc/fstab file is the default format, you can override it. For example, if an ext2 file system is set up on a writeable CD, the iso9660 format won't work for that CD. To supersede the default iso9660 format shown in Figure 6.3, mount the CD with the following command:

```
mount -t ext2 /dev/cdrom /mnt/cdrom
```

Depending on the distribution, the CD may be mounted normally on a different directory such as /cdrom or /cd. The **mount** command will be reviewed in more detail in Chapter 13.

 Remember how to supersede the file system settings in the /etc/fstab file when mounting a CD or a floppy drive.

inittab

When Linux starts, it boots a kernel, detects any new hardware, and then turns the computer over to the first program, known as init. The way init sets up the

```
# Author: Florian La Roche <florian@suse.de>, 1996
#
# This is the main configuration file of /etc/init, which
# is executed by the kernel on startup. It describes what
# scripts are used for the different run-levels.
#
# All scripts for runlevel changes are in /etc/init.d/ and the main
# file for changes is /etc/rc.config.
#
▐
# default runlevel
id:3:initdefault:

# check system on startup
# first script to be executed if not booting in emergency (-b) mode
si:I:bootwait:/etc/init.d/boot

# /etc/init.d/rc takes care of runlevel handling
#
# runlevel 0  is  System halt    (Do never use this for initdefault)
# runlevel 1  is  Single user mode
# runlevel 2  is  Local multiuser without remote network (e.g. NFS)
# runlevel 3  is  Full multiuser with network
# runlevel 4  is  Not used
# runlevel 5  is  Full multiuser with network and xdm
# runlevel 6  is  System reboot (Do never use this for initdefault)
#
                                                      15,0-1        7%
```

Figure 6.4 An excerpt from /etc/inittab.

look and feel of Linux is based on the /etc/inittab file. The key to this file is run levels, as shown in the excerpt in Figure 6.4.

There are generally seven run levels in Linux. As you can see, each run level has a different function. For most distributions, they correspond to the levels shown in Figure 6.4. The level that starts when you boot Linux is determined by the **id** command. For example, the following command in /etc/inittab—

```
id:3:initdefault
```

—leads Linux to start in run level 3, which starts full multiuser mode, and allows network connections.

Alternatively, if you configured or changed this line to the following:

```
id:5:initdefault
```

Linux would start in run level 5. This starts Linux in full multiuser mode, with networking, and xdm, which is the X Display Manager. In other words, users would see a graphical login screen when they wanted to use Linux.

Note: Some distributions use different run levels. For example, older versions of S.u.S.E. Linux included a run level S (instead of 1) for Single User Mode. Nevertheless, run level 0 always corresponds to "halt," and run level 6 always corresponds to "reboot" in all Linux distributions.

Remember that for many Linux distributions, you can set up a graphical login by changing the number in **id:3:initdefault** from 3 to 5. You can set up a command-line login by reversing the process. The actual numbers that you use vary by distribution; the /etc/inittab file on most Linux distributions includes comments that associate a specific level with a function such as Full Multiuser Mode with Networking or xdm.

bash

A shell is a user interface with a command line. In Linux, users log in at a text prompt like that shown in Figure 6.5. After the user logs in, he is taken to a shell. Then he can use the operating system by entering text commands at a command-line interface.

The default Linux shell is *bash* (the Bourne Again Shell). A number of other shells are available, including Korn, tcsh, csh, ash, and more. Each shell has advantages and disadvantages, but a discussion of these is beyond the scope of this book.

After the user logs in, Linux turns him over to his assigned shell. Some configuration is required for everything from the shell prompt to default file permissions to aliases for common commands. This configuration is defined in a number of files, including the .bashrc file in each user's home directory and /etc/profile for all users.

*Note: A period in front of a file hides it from normal commands. A tilde (~) defines a generic Linux home directory. Therefore, if a .bashrc file exists in a user's home directory, that user can edit his own .bashrc file with the **vi ~/.bashrc** command. The **vi** editor is discussed in Chapter 12, and the tilde (~) is discussed in Chapter 7.*

 Remember that the key configuration files for bash are ~/.bashrc and /etc/profile.

```
Welcome to SuSE Linux 7.2 (i386) - Kernel 2.4.4-4GB (tty2).

linux login: mj
Password:
Last login: Mon Jul 23 10:17:09 on tty1
Have a lot of fun...
mj@linux:~ > _
```

Figure 6.5 Logging into bash.

/etc/services

The /etc/services file defines the channels used by TCP/IP for communication.

There are 65,536 channels available in TCP/IP, from 0 through 65,535. These channels are known as *ports*. These ports can be divided into three categories:

➤ *Well-known ports*—Between 0 and 1,023. These ports are dedicated for more common types of communication, as shown in Table 6.4.

➤ *Registered ports*—Between 1,024 and 49,151. These ports may already be assigned for specific services such as caches, chat, and Internet telephones.

➤ *Private ports*—Between 49,152 and 65,535. These ports are unassigned by the Internet Assigned Numbers Authority (IANA) and are frequently used as optional channels for common services such as Web pages (HTTP). When a private port is used, the assigned service becomes more secure.

Note: Each assigned port is detailed by the Internet Assigned Numbers Authority (IANA). For more information, see the IANA Web site at www.iana.org.

Note: Please note that the /etc/services file does not use commas (or periods) to define port numbers equal to or above 1,000, but we've added them here to help with readability.

Anyone who has the right equipment and knows the ports on your system can monitor traffic to and from your network. Therefore, a configuration that uses well-known ports is not secure. One common practice is to reassign a port; for example, if you were to assign HTTP to port number 51,023, users could see your Web pages only if they knew to use that specific port. You can set HTTP to port 51,023 in the /etc/services file.

Note: Linux definitions don't always match those of the rest of the world. For example, hackers are good people who just want to make better software. On the other hand, crackers are people who try to break into software and networks for malicious purposes.

Table 6.4 Some well-known ports.	
Port Number	**Description**
21	FTP (File Transfer Protocol)
25	SMTP (Simple Message Transfer Protocol, for sending email)
42	DNS (Domain Name Service)
80	HTTP (Hypertext Transfer Protocol)
110	POP3 (Post Office Protocol, for receiving email)
443	HTTPS (Secure HTTP, commonly used for secure Web pages)

Keep in mind the fact that you can assign a registered or private port to another service such as HTTP, FTP, or POP. Just make sure you're not already using that port for another service.

Practice Questions

Question 1

> Which of the following conditions is required before successfully running the **rpm** command?
>
> ○ a. Make sure that all supporting packages have already been installed.
>
> ○ b. Log in as the **root** or super user.
>
> ○ c. Make sure that no older version of the same package is installed.
>
> ○ d. Download the applicable package in tar.gz format.

Answer b is correct. The **rpm** command works only for users with **root** or super user privileges. Since the --**nodeps** switch allows the installation of an **rpm** file without supporting packages, answer a is not correct. Since you can use **rpm** to upgrade older versions with the -**U** switch, answer c is not correct. Since the **rpm** command cannot be used on tar.gz packages, answer d is also incorrect.

Question 2

> Which of the following is the typical file extension for a group of files that has been archived and compressed?
>
> ○ a. .tar
>
> ○ b. .tgz
>
> ○ c. .gzip
>
> ○ d. .tar.zip

Answer b is correct. The .tgz file extension is typical for a file that has been archived and compressed. Since the .tar file extension is typical for a file that has been archived but not compressed, answer a is not correct. Although **gzip** is a standard Linux compression command, it does not collect files into an archive. Also, there is no standard .gzip file extension. Therefore, answer c is not correct. Although there is a standard .tar.gz extension for archived and compressed files, there is no standard .tar.zip extension. Therefore, answer d is also incorrect.

Question 3

Assume you're having problems with security for an internal Web site. If you wanted to change the port associated with your internal Web server, what file would you revise?

- ○ a. /etc/inittab
- ○ b. /etc/services
- ○ c. /etc/lilo.conf
- ○ d. /etc/fstab

Answer b is correct. The /etc/services configuration file determines the port associated with each service, including that associated with Web servers (HTTP). If you change the port number associated with HTTP in this file, that step provides an additional level of security for those who access your Web server. The /etc/inittab configuration file relates to the programs that start first when you start Linux. This is not related to the ports used by Web servers or any other network service. Therefore, answer a is incorrect. The /etc/lilo.conf configuration file relates to the Linux boot menu when you start your computer. Therefore, answer c is incorrect. The /etc/fstab configuration file relates to directories and their associated partitions. Since that does not control ports used by network services, answer d is also incorrect.

Question 4

One of the lines in your /etc/inittab file shows the following:

```
id:3:initdefault
```

How would you change this line to set up a console command-line login? Assume that this is a typical Linux distribution.

- ○ a. Change **3** to **5**.
- ○ b. Change **initdefault** to **consoledefault**.
- ○ c. Change **3** to **6**.
- ○ d. Nothing.

Answer d is correct. This question is related to Linux run levels. Although the run levels associated with a command line and a graphical login vary by distribution, they are most commonly 3 and 5, respectively. Since answer a would set up a graphical login, it is incorrect. The **initdefault** variable in /etc/inittab sets up the default run level when Linux starts. There is no **consoledefault** variable. Therefore, answer b is incorrect. Since run level 6 always starts the reboot process in Linux, answer c is also incorrect.

Question 5

> You've installed an older version of an application from an rpm package on some computers in the office. Which of the following commands could you use to install a newer version of the same application on all of your computers? Assume the newer version is also available in an rpm package.
>
> ○ a. **rpm -i packagename.rpm**
>
> ○ b. **rpm -ivh packagename.rpm**
>
> ○ c. **rpm -uvh packagename.rpm**
>
> ○ d. **rpm -U packagename.rpm**

Answer d is correct. The -U switch for the **rpm** command normally upgrades an older version of an existing package. If there is no older version, that command still installs the package. Since **rpm -i** doesn't work for upgrades, answer a is incorrect. Since the -v and -h switches do not help install a package, the problems associated with the -i switch still apply, so answer b is also incorrect. Linux is case sensitive; the -u switch does not upgrade a package. Therefore, answer c is also incorrect.

Question 6

> If you've downloaded an application package, **newapp.tar.gz**, to the /tmp directory, which of the following sets of commands unarchives and uncompresses this package?
>
> ○ a. **gzip -d /tmp/newapp.tar.gz; tar xf /tmp/newapp.tar**
>
> ○ b. **tar czvf /tmp/newapp.tar.gz**
>
> ○ c. **gunzip /tmp/newapp.tar.gz; tar cvf /tmp/newapp.tar**
>
> ○ d. **tar xvf /tmp/newapp.tar.gz**

Answer a is correct. The **gzip -d** command uncompresses and the **tar xf** command unarchives the specified files. Since the **tar czvf** command archives and compresses a file, it does not help with a file that is already archived and compressed. Therefore, answer b is incorrect. Since the **tar cvf** command archives a file, answer c is also incorrect. Since the **tar xvf** command doesn't uncompress the specified file, answer d is also incorrect.

Question 7

> Which of the following configuration files are typically associated with con-
> figuring the Bourne Again Shell for individual users' logins?
>
> ○ a. /etc/profile, /etc/bashrc
>
> ○ b. ~/.bashrc¡ ~/.bash_profile
>
> ○ c. ~/.bash_history, /etc/bashrc
>
> ○ d. ~/.bashrc, /etc/profile

Answer d is correct. The ~/.bashrc file is a hidden resource configuration (**rc**) file associated with the Bourne Again Shell (bash) in each user's home directory. The /etc/profile file configures bash defaults for all users on a global basis. Since each user has his own bashrc file, a global configuration file with this name is not required. Therefore, answer a is incorrect. Since not all Linux distributions have a bash_profile file in users' home directories, answer b is also incorrect. Since a bash_history file relates to previously used commands, it isn't used to configure bash for any user. Therefore, answer c is also incorrect.

Question 8

> You're installing a new application from an rpm package. When you try to
> install the application newapp.i386.rpm, it gives you an error message re-
> lated to "failed dependencies," which suggests that you need to first install
> some other rpm packages. The other packages are on a different CD, so you
> want to install the application first. Which of the following commands would
> install the application before you install the other packages?
>
> ○ a. **rpm -Uvh newapp.i386.rpm**
>
> ○ b. **rpm -i newapp.i386.rpm**
>
> ○ c. **rpm -U --nodeps newapp.i386.rpm**
>
> ○ d. **rpm -i --forcedeps newapp.i386.rpm**

Answer c is correct. The -U switch upgrades an existing application package. If there is no previous version of the application, the package is installed. The --**nodeps** switch installs a package even if other required packages ("dependencies") have not yet been installed. If you use the --**nodeps** switch, just be sure to install the other required packages as soon as possible. Although the **rpm -Uvh** command upgrades or installs a package, it won't work if there are dependencies. Therefore, answer a is incorrect. Although the **rpm -i** command installs a new package, it does not upgrade, and it won't work if there are dependencies. Therefore, answer b is also incorrect. Since there is no **--forcedeps** switch associated with the **rpm** command, answer d is also incorrect.

Question 9

You're having trouble making Linux detect your only Ethernet network card. When using the card on Microsoft Windows, it used IRQ 11 and I/O addresses starting with 0x320. What command would you put in the /etc/lilo.conf file if you wanted Linux to use this port and address?

○ a. **linux ether=11,0x320,eth0**

○ b. **ether=11,0x320,eth0**

○ c. **append=ether=11,0x320,eth0**

○ d. **append="ether=11,0x320,eth0"**

Answer d is correct. The **append** variable passes parameters such as IRQ ports and I/O addresses to Linux when it boots. Quotes are required to bracket what is processed by **append**. Although answer a would serve the same purpose at the LILO **boot:** prompt, it does not work in the /etc/lilo.conf file. Therefore, answer a is incorrect. Since the port and address information does not work without the **append** variable, answer b is also incorrect. Since answer c does not have quotes, it isn't clear what is being passed to the **append** variable. Therefore, answer c is also incorrect.

Question 10

When you get a new application, what steps should you take before installing it on a production computer?

○ a. Test the application on a test computer. Use test procedures developed inhouse. If you run into any problems, check the log files associated with your application.

○ b. Test the application on a production computer. Use test procedures created by the application developers. If you run into any problems, check the Web site associated with the application.

○ c. Test the application on a test computer. Use test procedures discussed on applicable newsgroups. If you run into any problems, check the newsgroups for a solution.

○ d. Test the application on a test computer. Use test procedures created by the application developers. If you run into any problems, check the Web site associated with the application.

Answer d is correct. Because of potential interactions unique to your computers, any new application should first be tried out on a test computer. While it's important to test the application to your organization's production requirements, it's also useful to use test procedures created by the application developers. In addition, developers often act as a central repository of solutions; if you run into problems, the Web site associated with the application is often the best source for solutions. Although log files can be useful for identifying problems, they may be difficult to find. Some applications may not even have log files. In any case, the Web site associated with the application would have appropriate tips and procedures. Therefore, answer a is incorrect. Since you should never test a new application on a production computer, answer b is incorrect. Since the quality of procedures and solutions on newsgroups is at best variable, answer c is also incorrect.

Need to Know More?

 Bailey, Ed. *Maximum RPM*. Indianapolis, IN: Sams, 1998. ISBN 0-67231-105-4. A definitive guide to the Red Hat Package Manager.

 Danesh, Arman, and Michael Jang. *Mastering Linux, Second Edition*. Alameda, CA: Sybex, 2001. ISBN 0-78212-915-3. A comprehensive book that includes detailed discussions on installing various .rpm and .tar.gz packages.

 LeBlanc, Dee-Ann. *General Linux I*. Scottsdale, AZ: The Coriolis Group, 2000. ISBN 1-57610-567-9. Chapter 2 includes a more detailed discussion of how to install an application package from a .tar.gz download. Although the run levels used by some distributions have changed, Chapter 4 includes a good description of the different run levels that are available and that are used by various Linux distributions.

 Stanfield, Vicki, and Roderick W. Smith. *Linux System Administration*. Alameda, CA: Sybex, 2001. ISBN 0-78212-735-5. A detailed system administration guide that includes detailed explanations of many Linux configuration files.

 Welsh, Matt, Matthias Kalle Dalheimer, and Lar Kaufman. *Running Linux, 3rd edition*. Sebastapol, CA: O'Reilly & Associates, 1999. ISBN 1-56592-469-X. Possibly the key resource book on the Linux operating system. Although much of the information in this book is based on older versions of Linux, the basic data is concise, well written, and applicable today.

 The official list and description of registered ports for TCP/IP communication is maintained by the Internet Assigned Numbers Authority at **www.iana.org**.

 The basic guide to the Red Hat Package Manager is available online from Red Hat at **rpm.redhat.com/RPM-HOWTO/index.html**.

Basics of the Shell

Terms you'll need to understand:

- ✓ Command-line interface
- ✓ Interactivity
- ✓ Command completion
- ✓ Absolute path
- ✓ Relative path
- ✓ $PATH
- ✓ Standard input
- ✓ Standard output
- ✓ Standard error
- ✓ Redirection
- ✓ Pipe
- ✓ **cd, ls**
- ✓ **cp, mv, rm, ln**
- ✓ **mkdir, rmdir**
- ✓ **man, info**

Techniques you'll need to master:

- ✓ Using the command-line interface
- ✓ Understanding interactivity
- ✓ Managing paths
- ✓ Combining commands
- ✓ Running programs in the background
- ✓ Using special shell characters
- ✓ Navigating the file system hierarchy
- ✓ Creating files and directories
- ✓ Getting command help

This chapter serves as an introduction to the shell, the command-line interface for Linux. Although several shells are available, the most common default shell is the Bourne Again SHell, also known as *bash*. This shell has commands, and it includes special characters that enable you to combine, redirect, or reconfigure those commands. There are several ways to get help on each command.

This is the first of several chapters in which we focus on the command line. While there are many good Linux graphical tools, the primary focus of the Linux+ exam (and of most Linux system administrators) is on command-line tools.

Shell Management

A shell is a user interface to control a computer operating system. The bash shell is a user interface to control Linux. You can use the commands associated with bash to manage files, run programs, and work with hardware through the Linux kernel. You can configure bash through the configuration files discussed in Chapter 6.

As a command-line user interface, bash responds to specific commands such as **mkdir, cd,** or **ls**. It also responds to programs or scripts that you or others create.

Linux is case sensitive. The **ls** command lists the files in the current directory, but **LS, Ls,** and **lS** are meaningless to any of the major Linux shells.

Two of the advantages of the bash shell are its capability to retain a history of previous commands and the ease with which it can help you complete a longer command. These characteristics are known as *interactivity* and *command completion*. On the other hand, one of the difficulties is the *path*, the way file locations are defined in Linux.

Interactivity

It is easy to interact with a history of Linux commands. Open up a command-line interface and type the **history** command. If you've used the command-line interface in the past, the result should be similar to what is shown in Figure 7.1. The list you see corresponds to the commands that you have run, in order.

There are several ways to repeat previously used commands. The simplest way is by using the up and down arrow keys on your keyboard. At a command-line interface prompt such as this:

```
[jd@linuxtest jd]$
```

press the up arrow on your keyboard. You'll see the last command that you used. Continue pressing the up arrow. You'll see previous commands that you used scrolling at the command-line interface prompt. You can reverse this process by pressing the down arrow key.

```
265  rpm -i /mnt/cdrom/RedHat/RPMS/elm-2.5.3-11.i386.rpm
266  rpm -i /mnt/cdrom/RedHat/RPMS/elm-2.5.3-11.i386.rpm
267  man rpm
268  su
269  cd ~
270  ls
271  ls test/
272  cp fig0602.tif test/Chapter\ 6/
273  su
274  ls -a
275  ls /etc/ba*
276  ls /etc/pr*
277  vi /etc/profile
278  vi /etc/bashrc
279  vi .bash_history
280  su
281  cat /etc/fstab
282  mount /dev/fd0 /mnt/floppy/
283  su
284  cat /etc/fstab
285  mdir a:
286  mount /dev/fd0 /mnt/floppy/
287  su
288  cd /tmp/
289  ls
290  su
291  history
[mj@laptop71 /tmp]$ █
```

Figure 7.1   The **history** command lists previously used commands.

Alternatively, if you know the first letter of a recently used command, the exclamation point (!) can help. For example, based on the history shown in Figure 7.1, if you type the **!m** command, bash runs the **mount /dev/fd0 /mnt/floppy** command. More letters can help. With the same history, the **!ma** command prompts bash to run the **man rpm** command.

Command Completion

The bash shell allows you to use the Tab key to complete a command. If you want to run the **SuperProbe** command, you don't need to type all 10 letters. In most distributions with this command, just type the following:

```
Su
```

When you press the Tab key, bash completes the command for you, as shown here:

```
SuperProbe
```

If the letters that you type correspond to the beginning of more than one command, you'll see a list. For example, in S.u.S.E. 7.2, you would see this:

```
SuSEwizard    SuperProbe
jd@linux:~ > Su
```

This lists the commands that start with Su and brings you back to the command prompt with what you originally typed. In this case, you could type the third letter ("S" or "p") associated with the command of your choice (either **SuSEwizard** or **SuperProbe**) and press the Tab key again. The S.u.S.E. Linux bash shell would then have enough information to complete the command.

Path Management

The next key to managing a shell is the path, which specifies the location of a file. There are absolute paths and relative paths. An absolute path describes the location of a file relative to the root (/) directory, and a relative path describes the location of a file relative to the current directory. The major Linux directories are part of the Filesystem Hierarchy Standard (FHS), discussed in Chapter 4.

When you log into Linux, the shell takes you to your home directory. Assume that your username is **mj**, which means that your home directory is /home/mj. If you wanted to review the files associated with the K Desktop Environment (KDE), one of the major Linux graphical user interfaces (GUIs), you could type the following command, which uses the absolute path shown here:

```
cd /home/mj/.kde
```

This uses the change directory command, **cd**, to change the current working directory from /home/mj to /home/mj/.kde. Since this command uses the full path of the desired directory (/home/mj/.kde), this is the absolute path. One advantage is that you can use this command in any Linux subdirectory and you would get the same result.

Alternatively, you could use the relative path. Since you're already in the /home/mj directory, all you need to do is type the following command:

```
cd .kde
```

The disadvantage of using the relative path is that in a different directory it leads to a different result.

Absolute and relative paths are important when archiving with the **tar** command, which was introduced in Chapter 6. For example, if you want to save the information in the home directory for user **mj**, you should use the following command:

```
tar czvf mjbackup.tar.gz /home/mj
```

Since this command uses the absolute path, the mjbackup.tar.gz file can be used to restore the home directory for user **mj** from any directory location.

 Remember to use the absolute path, especially when backing up the information in key directories. Otherwise, the results are more difficult to control when restoring backed-up files.

Absolute and relative paths are different from the **$PATH** variable, which defines directly accessible directories. For example, the **tar** command is in the /bin directory. If /bin were not in your **$PATH**, you would have to type **/bin/tar** to access that command. To find the directories in your **$PATH**, type the **echo $PATH** command.

Making bash Work for You

Linux shells, including bash, contain powerful tools. With a simple switch, you can redirect the output of one command as the input to a second command. It is easy to set up aliases for longer commands. Programs can be started and moved to the background, which easily allows you to run other commands simultaneously.

Linux commands are flexible. Different kinds of wildcard characters are available, that can represent multiple files. Three different kinds of quotation marks, discussed later in the "Shell Quotes" section, help manage the input to a command.

You can run two or more commands on a single command line. Just separate them with a semicolon (;). For example, the **ls; cd /tmp** command first lists the files in the current directory, and then changes the working directory to /tmp.

Standard Input, Standard Output, and Standard Error

There are three data streams in Linux: data goes in, data comes out, and errors are sent in a different direction. These streams are also known as *standard input*, *standard output*, and *standard error*.

Standard input (stdin) normally comes from the keyboard and is associated with a specific command. For example, with the **ls g*** command, the **g*** is the standard input to the **ls** command.

Standard output (stdout) is what comes out of a command. The files that scroll across the screen after you type the **ls** command are an example of standard output. By default, standard output is sent to your monitor.

If you do not see standard output, there may be a problem. For example, if you tried a nonexistent command such as **mike**, you would see an error message

```
bash: mike: command not found
```

This is an example of the third data stream, standard error (stderr).

Redirection

Standard output normally comes to the screen. You can redirect standard output with a single arrow (>). For example, if you want to place the file names in the current directory into a file named cur-dir, use the following command:

```
ls > cur-dir
```

If there already is a file named cur-dir, that information is overwritten. Alternatively, if you want to add the information to the end of the cur-dir file, run the following command, with the double-arrow (>>):

```
ls >> cur-dir
```

Standard input normally comes from the keyboard. You can redirect standard input to come from a file with the back arrow (<). For example, if there is a list of data in the mydata file, and you want the data to be processed by the program named goodvibrations in the current directory, use the following command:

```
./goodvibrations < mydata
```

The **./** processes commands in the current directory. Unless your current directory or a dot is part of the **$PATH**, the **./** is required.

This command directs each line in the mydata file for processing to the goodvibrations program.

Remember how to redirect standard input from a file to a program, such as with the **program1 < data** command, and how to redirect standard output to a file, such as with the **ls > data** command.

Standard error normally is also sent to the screen. You can redirect standard error. For example, if you want to collect errors in a file named baderrors, you could redirect the output from a program such as goodvibrations with the error arrow (**2>**):

```
./goodvibrations 2> baderrors
```

Pipes

Instead of directing standard output to a file, you can pipe it as standard input to another command. For example, if there is a lot of output from the goodvibrations program, you could redirect the output to a file and then review that file with the following two commands:

```
./goodvibrations > filereview
less filereview
```

The first command stores the output of the goodvibrations program in a file named filereview. The **less** command allows you to scroll up and down the filereview file with the Page Up and Page Down keys and the up and down arrows on a keyboard.

There is a simpler way. You don't need to create the filereview file. You could combine the two commands with a pipe (|):

```
./goodvibrations | less
```

The pipe is the double vertical line just above the backslash on the standard U.S. keyboard, directly above the standard Enter key.

You can use the pipe and the redirection arrow together. For example, if you had a lot of data from the mydata file and expected a lot of output, you could put all of this information together in one line:

```
./goodvibrations < mydata | less
```

This takes the data in the mydata file and processes it through the goodvibrations program. The output is piped to the **less** command, which allows you to scroll up and down a long list of output.

Be sure you know how to combine programs and files on a single line with redirection arrows and pipes. For example, in the hypothetical command **program1 < data | program2**, program1 takes information from the data file and sends the result as standard input to program2.

Command Multitasking

Just like any other modern operating system, Linux is multitasking; you can run multiple programs simultaneously. If you don't have additional terminals or virtual consoles available (discussed in Chapter 11), you can run programs simultaneously from a single command line. For example, if you wanted to run a program to process data from large 2GB Web server log files, that could take some time.

There are two ways to run a program in the background. Assume that the program you want to run is called logprocessor in the /home/mj directory. To run it in the background, use the following command:

```
/home/mj/logprocessor &
```

With the proper permissions, you can use the full directory path to run any program in any directory.

The ampersand (&) sends the process for executing the logprocessor program to the background, returning you to the command-line interface.

Alternatively, if you started this program and forgot the ampersand (&), there is another way to send the program execution process to the background. First press Ctrl+Z, which suspends the program that is currently running. Then use the following command:

```
bg
```

The Ctrl+Z key combination suspends the program that is currently running in the shell. The **bg** command then restarts the program and sends it to the background, returning you to the command-line interface. You can restore the program to the foreground with the **fg** command.

You should be sure to know that if you add the ampersand (&) at the end of a command, that command runs in the background, and the bash shell takes you to another command prompt.

Wildcards

Two special characters in the bash shell are variations on the Microsoft concept of wildcards. These characters are the asterisk (*) and the question mark (?). The asterisk represents zero or more letters and/or numbers. The question mark represents one alphanumeric character. For example, the following command would return a list of all files that end with the letter *y*:

```
ls *y
```

If you have a file named *y*, it would also be part of the list. Alternatively, the following command would return a list of all files with two alphanumeric characters that end with *y*:

```
ls ?y
```

Unlike the previous command, a file named y would not be a part of this list. More complex file searches are possible. For example, look at the following command:

```
ls ?on?
```

This would return files with names such as tone, bone, zonk, mona, and so on. It would not list filenames such as crayons, Anthony, Ono, or bon.

Limited wildcards are also available. You can use square brackets ([]) to define a group or a range of characters for different files. For example, to list the files in a directory between fig08-04.tif and fig08-09.tif, the following command defines a group of numbers:

```
ls fig08-0[456789].tif
```

Alternatively, the following command defines a range of numbers:

```
ls fig08-0[4-9].tif
```

The square brackets work in the same way for upper- or lowercase characters. For example, the following command searches for all files in the range from fig08-02a.tif to fig08-02g.tif:

```
ls fig08-02[a-g].tif
```

The following searches for all files in the range from fig08-03A.tif to fig08-03G.tif:

```
ls fig08-03[A-G].tif
```

Remember, because Linux is case sensitive, fig08-02a.tif is a different file from fig08-02A.tif.

Shell Quotes

Linux shells typically read a command one word at a time. For example, if you wanted to search for the text string "Michael Jang" in a file such as /etc/passwd, you might try the **grep** command, which is discussed in more detail in Chapter 8:

```
grep Michael Jang /etc/passwd
```

The result might be this:

```
grep: Jang: No such file or directory
/etc/passwd:mj:x:500:100:Michael Jang:/home/mj:/bin/bash
```

What happened is that **grep** first looked for the text string "Michael" in a file named Jang. Since there is no such file, **grep** returned the first message. Then it looked for the text string "Michael" in a file named /etc/passwd. That file is standard in all Linux distributions; in my case, there is a text string "Michael" in that file. The **grep** command then returns the full line from /etc/passwd that contains the given text string.

Quotation marks, or quotes, help define the standard input (stdin) to a shell command. For example, you can use quotes to use the **grep** command to search for a phrase or a group of words.

There are three types of quotes available in the bash shell: the single quote ('), the double quote ("), and the back quote (`).

The back quote key is found directly above the Tab key on a standard U.S. keyboard.

Each type of quote has a distinct effect on variables such as **$NAME** and commands such as **date**. Specifically:

➤ *Single quotes*—The shell does not process any variables or commands inside the quotes.

➤ *Double quotes*—The shell processes variables but does not process commands.

➤ *Back quotes*—The shell processes all variables inside the quotes, then tries to process every word inside the quotes as a command.

The Linux shell accommodates a number of variables that can be used in commands and scripts. To see the variables currently set on your Linux distribution, type the **env** command. To review an individual variable such as **HOSTNAME** requires a $ in front of the variable. For example, to check the current value of **HOSTNAME**, use the **echo $HOSTNAME** command.

The following examples illustrate the use of each type of quote. The **echo** command returns everything that follows as standard output. Assume that you've set **$NAME=Michael**. The **date** command returns the current date and time.

```
echo Welcome $NAME, the date is date
echo 'Welcome $NAME, the date is date'
echo "Welcome $NAME, the date is date"
echo "Welcome $NAME, the date is `date`"
```

Note the location and type of quotation mark associated with each command. These commands return the following, in order:

```
echo Welcome Michael, the date is date
echo Welcome $NAME, the date is date
echo Welcome Michael, the date is date
echo Welcome Michael, the date is Mon Jul 30 12:33:21 EDT 2001
```

The first command has no quotes. The shell translated the **$NAME** variable, but it did not run the **date** command. The result was sent as standard input to **echo**.

The second command uses single quotes. Neither the variable nor the command was processed before being sent as standard input to **echo**.

The third command uses double quotes. While the result was the same as with no quotes, you know from the first example in this section that double quotes are useful for commands such as **grep**. The following command would search for the text string "Michael Jang" without the aforementioned error:

```
grep "Michael Jang" /etc/passwd
```

The final command added back quotes around the **date** command, which runs the command, even within the double quotes. Then it sent the result to **echo**.

Navigational Commands

To navigate the various directories in the bash shell, you need to know what directory you're in, to know what files and subdirectories are present in the current directory, and to be able to move between directories. The **pwd** command lists the current directory. The **ls** command lists all files in a directory, including other directories. The **cd** command allows you to move between directories. The tilde (~) represents the home directory of each user.

pwd

Many Linux distributions don't identify the current directory in the prompt. The **pwd** command returns the absolute location of the current directory. For example, when user **mj** logs onto Linux, that user is taken to his home directory. In that case, the **pwd** command returns the following output:

```
/home/mj
```

This command is helpful when you use other commands, such as **cd**, discussed later in this section. For example, before you can use **cd** to change directories, you need to know what directory you're in.

ls

The **ls** command is similar to the MS-DOS **dir** command. It returns a listing of files in the current directory. The **ls** command is a lot more versatile, however. With the correct switch, it can distinguish between different types of files. It can list the permissions associated with each file, and it can check ownership. The result can be sorted in any number of ways. Some examples of this command are shown in Table 7.1.

Note: File ownership and permissions are covered in Chapter 11.

Note: Directories are included in all file lists. In Linux, a directory is just a special kind of file. A file is accessed anytime it is read, written to, or executed.

Table 7.1	ls commands.
Command	**Result**
ls	Lists all regular files in the current directory in alphabetical order. Does not list hidden files (which start with a period).
ls -a	Lists all files in the current directory, including hidden files.
ls -r	Lists all regular files in the current directory in reverse alphabetical order.
ls -F	Lists all files by type. The character at the end of each file indicates the file type. For example, a forward slash (/) represents a directory, an asterisk (*) is associated with an executable file, and an "at" (@) represents a linked file.
ls -l	Lists all regular files, including the file that represents the current directory (.) and the parent directory (..). Also lists the size, owner, and permissions associated with each file. The output is known as *long listing format*.
ls -t	Lists files by the date of the last change; most recent files are listed first.
ls -u	Lists files by the date of the last access; most recent files are listed first.

Keep in mind the fact that the dot (.) is often used to represent the current directory, and the double dot (..) is often used to represent the parent of the current directory.

cd

The change directory command in Linux is **cd**. If you're familiar with MS-DOS commands, you'll find that a number of commands in the bash shell seem familiar. Typical commands for **cd** are shown in Table 7.2.

The Tilde (~)

The tilde (~) is important in the bash shell. It represents the home directory of the user who is logged on. On most standard U.S. keyboards, you can find this character with the back quote, above the Tab key.

You can use the tilde with most bash shell commands. For example, any user can use **cd** ~ to get to his home directory. Alternatively, he can use the **ls** ~ command to list all of the files in his home directory. Table 7.3 lists other commands used with the tilde.

Table 7.2   cd commands.

Command	Result
cd ~	Moves to your home directory.
cd ..	Navigates up one directory level. For example, if you're currently in the /home/mj directory, this moves you to the /home directory.
cd ../..	Moves up two directory levels. For example, if you're currently in the /etc/rc.d/rc0.d directory, this takes you to the /etc directory.
cd /home/mj	Changes to the home directory of user **mj**.

Table 7.3   Commands with the tilde (~).

Command	Result
cd ~	Changes to your home directory.
cd ~/.kde	Changes to the .kde subdirectory of your home directory. For example, if your username is mj, this moves you to the /home/mj/.kde subdirectory.
ls ~	Lists files in your home directory.
tar czvf backup.tar.gz ~	Backs up all files in your home directory.
~/niceprogram	Runs the program named **niceprogram** in your home directory.

File Creation

It seems that everything in Linux is a file. Directories are special kinds of files. Hardware device drivers also are files. Even the nodes associated with Universal Serial Bus (USB) hardware are set up as files. Special files can be linked to others, such as the icons on a Linux Graphical User Interface desktop.

There is one set of commands to copy, move, and delete files; there is another set for creating and deleting directories. One other special command applies to creating linked files.

cp

The bash shell copy command is **cp**. The simplest use of this command is **cp** *file1* *file2*, where the contents of *file1* are copied and placed in destination *file2*. With the right switch, it can overwrite destination files without prompting and copy all files in a directory and its subdirectories. Some examples of how the **cp** command works are shown in Table 7.4.

mv

There is no rename command in Linux. To rename a file, you move it instead. The **mv** command changes the name and possibly the directory where a file is located. Unless you move the file to a different volume (discussed in Chapter 4), everything else about the file stays the same. Some examples of how the **mv** command works are shown in Table 7.5.

Table 7.4 cp commands.	
Command	**Result**
cp *file1* *file2*	Copies the contents of source *file1* to destination *file2*. The destination file gets a new creation date.
cp *file** *Dir1*	Copies all files with names that start with *file* to destination directory *Dir1*.
cp -f *file1* *file2*	If you already have a file named *file2*, this command overwrites its contents without prompting.
cp -i *file1* *file2*	If you already have a file named *file2*, this command prompts you for confirmation before overwriting this file.
cp -r *Dir1* *Dir2*	Copies the contents of the directory named *Dir1*, including subdirectories, to *Dir2*. If there are lower-level subdirectories under *Dir1*, their files and directories are also copied.
cp -u *file1* *file2*	If you already have a file named *file2*, and *file1* is newer, this command overwrites its contents without prompting.

Table 7.5 mv commands.	
Command	**Result**
mv *file1 file2*	Changes the name of a file from *file1* to *file2*.
mv *file* Dir1*	Moves all files with names that start with *file* to the *Dir1* directory.
mv -f *file1 file2*	Overwrites the contents of *file2* without prompting.
mv -i *file1 file2*	Prompts for confirmation before overwriting the contents of *file2*.

The **mv** command actually works like the **cp** command. The difference is that the original file is deleted.

rm

The Linux command to delete a file is **rm**. With the correct switches, this command can be used to delete files and directories. Several examples of the **rm** command are shown in Table 7.6.

*Note: Many Linux distributions set up aliases such as rm="rm –i". If you're using one of these distributions, the shell prompts you for confirmation before the subject file is deleted. To check your settings, type the **alias** command.*

Do not run the **rm** command as the **root** or superuser unless absolutely necessary. The consequences can be tragic. For example, if user **ab** has left your company, you may want to delete all the files in his home directory. The most direct way to do this is with the **rm -rf /home/ab** command. But you might make a mistake and enter a space between the first slash and home:

```
rm -rf / home/ab
```

Table 7.6 rm commands.	
Command	**Result**
rm *file1*	Deletes *file1*.
rm -d *Dir1*	Deletes *Dir1* without prompting for confirmation.
rm -i *file1*	Deletes *file1* after prompting for confirmation from the user.
rm -f *file2*	Deletes *file2* without prompting for confirmation, even if an alias of **rm='rm -i'** is set.
rm –r ***	Deletes files recursively; subdirectories (and their files) are deleted as well.

If you run this command as the **root** or superuser, this command would first delete all of the files and directories under the root (/) directory. That is every file and directory on your Linux system. Then it would try to delete all of the files in the home/ab subdirectory. You would have to reload all of your files from a backup. Without any files on your system, this would be difficult at best.

mkdir

Although a directory is just a special file in Linux, you need a special command to create a Linux directory: the **mkdir** command. This command can create directories anywhere in the Linux Filesystem Hierarchy, as discussed in Chapter 4. With the correct switch, you can even assign specific permissions to the new directory. Permissions are described in more detail in Chapter 11. Examples of the **mkdir** command are shown in Table 7.7.

Make sure you know that the **mkdir** command creates directories.

A common practice among Linux users is to capitalize the name of new subdirectories. This practice can make it easier to scan a file list for user-created directories.

rmdir

The **rmdir** command can delete only empty directories. The target directory can be anywhere in the Linux file system hierarchy. You can delete several levels of directories if the first one you delete empties the next directory. For example, assume there are no files in the /home/mj/Desktop directory, and no other files

Table 7.7 mkdir commands.	
Command	**Result**
mkdir -p /*Dir1*/*Dir2*	Creates directory /*Dir1*/*Dir2*. If *Dir1* doesn't already exist, the **-p** switch creates it as well. Both are subdirectories of the root directory.
mkdir -m 755 /home/mj/*Dir3*	Creates the /home/mj/*Dir3* directory. The permissions (**755**) are **rwx** for the owner and **r-x** for other members of the group and everyone else. Permissions are described in more detail in Chapter 11.

in the /home/mj directory. You could then delete both directories with the following command:

```
rmdir -p /home/mj/Desktop
```

As long as there are other existing subdirectories of /home, the /home directory would not be empty and therefore would not be deleted.

Note: As discussed earlier, the **rm** *command, with the right switch, can delete directories with files.*

ln

You can create one file as a link to another. Linked files are common in Linux. For example, many distributions link the /dev/modem file to an actual hardware device file for a modem, such as /dev/ttyS0. The /dev/modem file is easier to remember.

Another use for links is for applications with many versions. For example, assume you've finished testing Netscape version 6.1 on your test computers. Before you declare it ready for general use in your organization, you want a few selected users to try it out. You could set up the following commands for various versions of Netscape:

```
netscape47
netscape60
netscape61
```

You could then link an executable file named netscape to the version approved for use in your organization. For example, the command

```
ln /usr/bin/netscape /opt/bin/netscape47
```

would link a file that anyone could access (/usr/bin/netscape) to a specific version of Netscape (4.7) in a specific directory (/opt/bin). The /usr/bin directory is in the default **$PATH** for most Linux distributions. Alternatively, you could then link to a different version of Netscape on other selected computers.

 Remember that you can use a link to manage the default version of an application on specific Linux computers.

Command Help

Although the documentation on the Internet supporting Linux is extensive, there is also significant documentation that comes with your Linux distribution. One source of information for commands and many configuration files is their manuals, more commonly known as *man pages*. Access to these manuals is available through the **man** and **info** commands. Graphical versions of these pages are also available.

The first place for help with most commands is the --help switch. For example, if you want more information on the switches available with the **cat** command, type the following:

```
cat --help
```

man

Almost every Linux command and many Linux configuration files come with a man page. Each Linux manual includes a complete description of a command as well as a description of the use of each command switch. For example, if you want to review the manual associated with the **grep** command, type the following at a command-line interface:

```
man grep
```

The database of man pages in Linux is extensive; there are a number of ways to search through the database for the command you need. For example, if you want to review the Linux commands associated with the Apache Web server, type the following command:

```
man -k apache
```

A list of commands available in your Linux distribution scrolls on the screen. While the list you see may not cover all applicable commands, it does include all commands with your search term in the title of its manual pages.

Be familiar with using the **man -k** command to find a list of commands related to a desired topic. This is one of the few situations related to a Linux command in which the case of the search term does not matter.

In Linux, command manuals are more frequently known as *man pages*. Learn to use this term. If you ask for a command manual, it's likely that you'll get something else.

info

With the **info** command, there is a structured way to look through most available man pages. Try the **info** command. You should see output similar to the screen shown in Figure 7.2. The actual output varies somewhat by Linux distribution.

Navigate through the screen with the keyboard arrows. When you get to the command or category of your choice, press Enter. If appropriate, the **info** utility takes you to a set of subsidiary options. Repeat the process until you get the man page that you need. Unfortunately, the database of the **info** command does not include all available man pages.

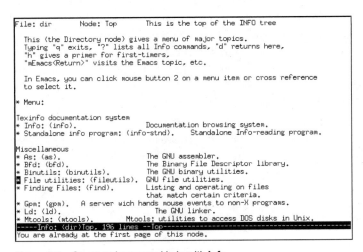

Figure 7.2   Structured command help with **info**.

Practice Questions

Question 1

Which of the following, when input at the command-line interface, starts the program or command in the background and gives you another command-line interface?

○ a. **ls**

○ b. *program1* **&**

○ c. **mkdir **

○ d. **bg**

Answer b is correct. The ampersand (&), when placed after the name of a command or program, allows that command or program to execute in the background and returns you to the command-line interface. The **ls** command is a regular command. Although it normally returns to the command-line interface fairly quickly, it does so only after scrolling through the list of files in the current directory. Therefore, answer a is incorrect. The backslash (\) is another special switch that tells the bash shell to ignore the next character, in this case the Enter key on your keyboard. The prompt you get is not the regular command-line interface; it is to complete the given command. Therefore, answer c is incorrect. The **bg** command can bring a currently paused program to the background, but it applies to a program that is already running. Therefore, answer d is also incorrect.

Question 2

Which of the following commands is the simplest way to review the output from a processed database? Assume that the data is in file /var/httpd/log/biglog and the processing program is /home/mj/cullit.

○ a. **/home/mj/cullit > /var/httpd/log/biglog I less**

○ b. **/home/mj/cullit I /var/httpd/log/biglog > less**

○ c. **/home/mj/cullit < /var/httpd/log/biglog I less**

○ d. **/home/mj/cullit I /var/httpd/log/biglog I less**

Answer c is correct. Since the data is in the /var/httpd/log/biglog file, it's appropriate to use it as standard input to the processing program. When the output is piped (|) to a utility such as **less**, you can use various navigation keys to scroll through the result. Since the /home/mj/cullit file is a program, it is not appropriate standard input for the /var/httpd/log/biglog data file. Instead, data is appropriate standard input for a program. Therefore, answer a is incorrect. In answer b, since there is no data for the /home/mj/cullit program to process, it is incorrect. Answer d is also incorrect for the same reason.

Question 3

Which of the following commands or sets of commands would you use if you wanted a list of commands related to Ethernet?

- a. **man -c Ethernet**
- b. **man -r eth0**
- c. **man Ethernet; man network; man arpwatch**
- d. **man -k ethernet**

Answer d is correct. The **man -k** command searches through the titles of each man page on your Linux system for a word—in this case, **ethernet**. Fortunately, the standard input to this command is not case sensitive, so it doesn't matter if you use **ethernet** or **Ethernet**. The -c switch reformats a man page. But that is not helpful, since there is no Ethernet man page. Therefore, answer a is incorrect. Since there is no -r switch associated with **man**, answer b is incorrect. The commands in answer c just give you the man pages for the specified commands. It does not search through any other man pages. Therefore, answer c is also incorrect.

Question 4

You're setting up a series of subdirectories for user **jd**, including travel, travel/Europe, and travel/Europe/France. These subdirectories start in user **jd**'s home directory. Assume none of these directories currently exists. Which of the following commands creates all of these directories most efficiently?

- a. **mkdir -p /travel/Europe/France**
- b. **mkdir -m /home/jd/travel/Europe; mkdir -m /home/jd/travel/France**
- c. **mkdir -p /home/jd/travel/Europe/France**
- d. **mkdir /home/jd/travel/; cd /home/jd/travel; mkdir -p Europe/France**

Answer c is correct. The -p switch allows the **mkdir** command to create subdirectories if they don't already exist. The home directory for **jd** is /home/jd. The requested directories are subdirectories of /home/jd. Answer c creates all of the requested subdirectories with a single command. Since the requested directories are supposed to be under **jd**'s home directory, answer a creates directories in the wrong location. Therefore, answer a is incorrect. Since the -m switch relates only to permissions of created directories, it does not allow you to create a series of subdirectories as with the -p switch. Therefore, answer b is also incorrect. Although answer d does create the requested subdirectories, it takes three different commands, which is less efficient than answer c. Therefore, answer d is also incorrect.

Question 5

Which of the following commands or command combinations allows you to scroll through the result without creating a new file? Assume that there are several hundred files in the current directory.

- ○ a. **ls -s**
- ○ b. **ls l less**
- ○ c. **ls > filelist; less filelist**
- ○ d. **ls > less**

Answer b is correct. The pipe (|) takes the output of the **ls** command, which is a list of files in the current directory. That output is redirected as standard input to the **less** command, which allows you to scroll through the result. The **ls -s** command includes the size of each file, which is unrelated to the object of the question. Therefore, answer a is incorrect. Although the **ls > filelist; less filelist** command accomplishes the same result as answer b, it does so by creating a file named filelist, which violates the conditions set in the question. Therefore, answer c is incorrect. The **ls > less** command creates a new file named less, which contains the contents of the current directory. Since that command by itself does not allow you to scroll through the result, answer d is also incorrect.

Question 6

> Which of the following commands uses the files in the current directory as standard input?
>
> ○ a. **echo ls**
>
> ○ b. **echo "ls"**
>
> ○ c. **echo 'ls'**
>
> ○ d. **echo `ls`**

Answer d is correct. Back quotes (``` `` ```) run the command enclosed between them. You can find the back quote above the Tab key on a standard U.S. keyboard. None of the other answers processes the **ls** command; they all return **ls** as standard output. Therefore, answers a, b, and c are incorrect.

Question 7

> As a Linux administrator, you have to work with different versions of major packages. Assume that you've installed WordPerfect for Linux versions 6, 7, and 8 on the Linux application server. The scripts that start each package are named WordPerfect6, WordPerfect7, and WordPerfect8, respectively. They are each located in the /opt directory. Which of the following commands would most help users access the preferred version, WordPerfect7? Assume all users have access to the /bin directory.
>
> ○ a. **ln /bin/WordPerfect7 /opt/bin/WordPerfect7**
>
> ○ b. **ln /bin/wp /opt/WordPerfect7**
>
> ○ c. **ln wp /opt/WordPerfect7**
>
> ○ d. **ln /opt/WordPerfect7 /bin/wp**

Answer b is correct. That command creates a file, /bin/wp, that is linked to the desired application. Since the WordPerfect7 script is in the /opt directory, answer a is incorrect. Besides, /bin/WordPerfect7 (including the uppercase characters) is not the easiest thing for users to remember. Since there is no information on the current directory, you don't know where you're creating the wp file. Therefore, you don't know if all users can access this file. Consequently, answer c is incorrect. The command in answer d has the options in the wrong order; therefore, answer d is also incorrect.

Question 8

> As a system administrator, you need to make frequent backups of your users' files. Most of these files are in their home directories. The backup for the **root** user was made from the root (/) directory with the **tar czvf ccfiles.tar.gz root** command. Which of the following commands restores **root** user files to the correct directory without overwriting those that still exist?
>
> ○ a. **cd /; tar czvf ccfiles.tar.gz**
>
> ○ b. **cd /; tar xzkf ccfiles.tar.gz**
>
> ○ c. **cd /root; tar xzvf ccfiles.tar.gz**
>
> ○ d. **cd /root; tar xkf ccfiles.tar.gz**

Answer b is correct. (Congratulations if you got this right! This can be a difficult question for newer Linux users, but it reflects the highest level of difficulty that you might see on the Linux+ exam.) The backup was made using the relative path. Therefore, it's necessary to use the same directory from which the backup was made, in this case, the root (/) directory. With the **tar** command, the x switch extracts, the z switch uncompresses, the k switch makes sure not to overwrite existing files, and the f switch points to the next item as the file to be extracted. The **tar czvf** command creates an archive; it does not restore files, so answer a is incorrect. Because the backup was made from the root (/) directory, restoring the backup from the **root** user's home directory (/root) would restore the applicable files to the /root/root directory. That is not the right directory, so answer c is incorrect. Answer d is incorrect for the same reason; also, the **tar** command does not include a z switch, which keeps it from uncompressing the ccfiles.tar.gz backup archive.

Need to Know More?

 Hughes, Phil. *Linux for Dummies Quick Reference.* Foster City, CA: IDG Books Worldwide, Inc., 1998. ISBN 0-76450-302-2. A quick reference book that serves as a handy guide for basic Linux options for most command-line interface commands.

 Muster, John. *Unix Made Easy.* Berkeley, CA: Osborne/McGraw-Hill, 1996. ISBN 0-07882-173-8. A solid textbook and reference guide for the command-line interface. Although this is a book on Unix, it is often used as a teaching text in conjunction with various Linux distributions.

 Pfaffenberger, Bryan. *Linux Command Instant Reference.* Alameda, CA: Sybex, 2000. ISBN 0-78212-748-7. A comprehensive guide to Linux commands, with switches and many examples. Commands are organized by function. Also includes a handy guide to several major text editors, including vi.

Commanding the Shell

Terms you'll need to understand:

✓ **file**

✓ **cat**

✓ **head**, **tail**

✓ **more**, **less**

✓ **diff**

✓ **grep**

✓ **find**, **locate**

✓ Process

✓ **ps**

✓ Process identifier (PID), parent process identifier (PPID)

✓ **kill**, **killall**

✓ **init**

✓ **lsof**

Techniques you'll need to master:

✓ Managing the file, inside and out

✓ Comparing different files

✓ Finding words within files

✓ Locating the files you need

✓ Breaking down the process

✓ Killing a process or a group of processes

✓ Starting and stopping processes

✓ Understanding the first process (init)

In Chapter 7 and in previous chapters, you learned some of the basics of Linux shells, specifically bash. In this chapter, you'll start making the bash shell work for you. Most Linux files—including many commands and utilities—are text files. Knowing how to read and manage different text files with bash commands is one of the key skills in Linux.

You'll start by identifying and reading files in different ways. Next, you'll start making a file work for you, based on its content and location. Finally, you'll learn about identifying, killing, and restarting the processes associated with different commands, utilities, and applications.

Managing the File

A number of different commands are associated with reading and managing files in the bash shell. These commands help you verify different types of files and allow you to read files from the top or even from the bottom. What you read can be limited to just a few lines or set up to scroll in different ways through the complete file.

Most important Linux files are text files. Many Linux file management commands are useful only on text files.

file

There are no standard file extensions in Linux. Commands don't end in .com, and applications don't end in .exe. Most text files don't bother with an extension, either. The **file** command helps you distinguish between file types in a directory. Take a look at a sample output from this command in Figure 8.1.

As you can see, the **file** command can distinguish between a number of different file types, even Microsoft Office documents. Note the sudoers file. Because user

```
[mj@laptop71 mj]$ file *
%:                      directory
Chapter 7.doc:          Microsoft Office Document
CompTIA-presentation.zip: Zip archive data, at least v2.0 to extract
core:                   ELF 32-bit LSB core file of 'kdeinit' (signal 11), Intel
 80386, version 1, from 'kdeinit'
Desktop:                directory
fig07-01.tif:           TIFF image data, little-endian
fig07-03.tif:           TIFF image data, little-endian
mail:                   ELF 32-bit LSB executable, Intel 80386, version 1, dynam
ically linked (uses shared libs), stripped
msg-dmesg:              ASCII English text
objectives.pdf:         PDF document, version 1.2
passwd:                 ASCII text
pcmcia:                 Bourne-Again shell script text executable
sudoers:                can't read `sudoers' (Permission denied).
temp.tgz:               gzip compressed data, deflated, last modified: Wed Jul 2
5 14:17:50 2001, os: Unix
test:                   directory
[mj@laptop71 mj]$ ▮
```

Figure 8.1 The **file** command defines file types.

mj doesn't have appropriate permissions, the **file** command can't even tell what kind of file that is. (It lists users with some form of **root** user privileges.)

cat

In Linux, you can use the **cat** (concatenate) command to scroll a file across the screen. You can use the **cat** command on any file for which you have the appropriate permissions. If you want to see the contents of the file named cradle in your current directory, type the following command:

```
cat cradle
```

Note: The corresponding MS-DOS command is type.

head and tail

Although **head** and **tail** are two separate commands, they are like two sides of the same coin. The **head** command returns the first 10 lines of a file, and the **tail** command returns the last 10 lines of a file. If you're not already familiar with this command, try it out:

```
head /etc/passwd
tail /etc/passwd
```

If you need just a bit more information about a file, you can regulate the number of output lines. For example, if you want to see the last 20 lines of the /etc/passwd file, use the following command:

```
tail -n20 /etc/passwd
```

*Note: In some Linux distributions, the **head** and **tail** commands won't work if there is a space between the "-n" and the number.*

/etc/passwd is a standard file on every Linux distribution. This file contains user ID numbers, group ID numbers, home directories, and default shells for every user on your Linux system. These issues are addressed in more detail in Chapter 11.

more and less

Although **more** and **less** are two separate but related commands, they are not exact opposites. Each command delivers text files as standard output, one screen (or page) at a time. Ironically, the **less** command is more versatile; unlike **more**, it allows scrolling up and down with the Page Up and Page Down keys on your keyboard.

Because they don't need to read in your whole file, these commands can open a file more quickly than a text editor such as **vi**. The **less** command allows you to use some vi commands to search through a file. The **vi** editor is covered in more detail in Chapter 12.

The **more** and **less** commands are often known as *pagers* because they allow a text file to be reviewed one page at a time.

Manipulating the File

A number of commands allow you to search through and search for different files. The **diff** command compares the contents of two files. The **grep** command searches for a text string within a file. The **find** and **locate** commands search for specific files.

diff

The **diff** command is relatively straightforward. It compares the contents of two different files. It is a relatively easy way to compare the contents of a current text file with a backup. For example, if you have a backup of the password file, it's easy to compare it to the contents of the current file. Assume the backup password file is named /etc/passwd.bak. You can then compare the two files with the following command:

```
diff /etc/passwd /etc/passwd.bak
```

Generally, these two files should differ only as a result of any recent additions or deletions of users. For example, if the standard output from this command is

```
26d25
< jkp:*:501:100:James Knox Polk:/home/jkp:/bin/bash
```

you know that you've recently added user **jkp** to your system. The left-facing arrow (<) points to the file with the additional information, in this case, /etc/passwd. The first line of output, "26d25", tells you that there are 26 lines in the /etc/passwd file and 25 lines in the /etc/passwd.bak file. This is the simplest output from two different files. More complex file differences are beyond the scope of the Linux+ exam.

Alternatively, if there is no standard output from the command, **diff** is telling you that there is no difference between the files.

 Remember that the **diff** command compares the contents of two different text files and returns output that lists the differences between the files.

grep

When you want to search through a text file, use the **grep** command. Web server administrators find **grep** useful when searching through the key Apache configuration file, httpd.conf. Assume this file is located in the /etc/httpd/conf directory. To search through this file for the directory assigned to the Apache variable known as **DocumentRoot**, you could use the following command:

```
grep DocumentRoot /etc/httpd/conf/httpd.conf
```

Depending on your distribution and configuration, you might see output such as the following:

```
# DocumentRoot: The directory out of which you will serve your
DocumentRoot "/usr/local/httpd/htdocs"
# This should be changed to whatever you set DocumentRoot to.
#     DocumentRoot /www/docs/host.some_domain.com
DocumentRoot "/usr/local/httpd/htdocs"
```

This output is a list of every line in one httpd.conf file with the text string "**DocumentRoot**", which is the root source directory for Web site files for an Apache Web server.

*Note: Apache and the **DocumentRoot** variable are covered in more detail in Chapter 10.*

With **grep**, you can also search for text strings. As discussed in Chapter 7, you can use **grep** with quotes to search for multiple words in a file. For example, if you want to search the /etc/passwd file for a user named "Michael Jang", use the following command:

```
grep "Michael Jang" /etc/passwd
```

 You ought to remember how to use **grep** to search for a word or a series of words in a file. Since **grep** returns the full line with the desired search term, it is known as a *filtering* command.

find

The **find** command looks through directories and subdirectories for a specific file. For example, to find the directory with the httpd.conf file, you can use the following command:

```
find / -name httpd.conf
```

This command searches through your Linux system starting with the root (/) directory. If the file isn't found there, it continues searching through all subdirectories. This search can take some time. For example, a search for the httpd.conf file on my laptop computer took nearly as much time as it did to write this paragraph.

Therefore, if you have more information on this file, you can start with a lower-level directory. Since you know that httpd.conf is a configuration file, one option is to start the search in the directory of configuration files: /etc. That leads to the following command:

```
find /etc -name httpd.conf
```

If you want to search for a series of files or you are not sure of the spelling of a file's name, you can use wildcards such as the asterisk (*) and question mark (?) in the search term. For example, if you wanted to search for a series of figures that you know start with "fig08", you could use the following command:

```
find / -name fig08*
```

locate

If the **find** command takes too long or you just can't remember the switches, an alternative is the **locate** command. Because this command searches through a database of files on your system, it finds the files you want much more quickly.

By default, most Linux distributions create this database once every 24 hours, typically in the middle of the night. Therefore, if you've created a file since the last database update, the **locate** command won't find that file.

Compared to **find,** the **locate** command works more like the **grep** command. It doesn't require wildcards; for example, if you were searching for all files with "fig08" in their names, all you would need is the following command:

```
locate fig08
```

The database search proceeds as if there were asterisks before and after the search term. It is functionally equivalent to the following **find** command:

```
find / -name *fig08*
```

Managing the Process

Everything that is running on a Linux system requires one or more processes. You can identify current processes on a current terminal with the **ps** command. Each process is associated with a process identifier. If the process won't stop, sometimes you need to use that identifier to kill a process with the **kill** or **killall** commands. All processes have a parent; the top of the parental process tree is known as **init**. Closely related to the process is the **lsof** (list open file) command.

Note: A Linux process is conceptually similar to a thread in Microsoft Windows. In other words, a Linux application often includes more than one process, each running independently.

ps

The **ps** command identifies currently running processes. Without switches, the **ps** command identifies the processes associated with your account, which usually includes the shell. The **ps aux** command shows everything running on your Linux system. It's impressive; with one application running, 63 processes are running on my Linux laptop computer as I write. An example of the output from **ps aux** is shown in Figure 8.2.

 Whenever there is more than one screen of output, including from the **ps aux** command, you want to be able to scroll up and down between screens. Combine the **ps aux** and the **less** commands with the pipe (|) by typing **ps aux | less**. You can then scroll up and down the output with the Page Up and Page Down keys on your keyboard.

Most of the columns in Figure 8.2 are significant. The following corresponds to the key columns identified atop the figure:

➤ USER—The owner of the specific process.

➤ PID—The process identifier. Every process has a PID.

```
USER       PID %CPU %MEM  VSZ  RSS TTY      STAT START   TIME COMMAND
root         1  0.0  0.1 1340   76 ?        S    Jul27   0:03 init [5]
root         2  0.0  0.0    0    0 ?        SW   Jul27   0:00 [keventd]
root         3  0.0  0.0    0    0 ?        SW   Jul27   0:00 [kapm-idled]
root         4  0.0  0.0    0    0 ?        SW   Jul27   0:08 [kswapd]
root         5  0.0  0.0    0    0 ?        SW   Jul27   0:00 [kreclaimd]
root         6  0.0  0.0    0    0 ?        SW   Jul27   0:00 [bdflush]
root         7  0.0  0.0    0    0 ?        SW   Jul27   0:00 [kupdated]
root         8  0.0  0.0    0    0 ?        SWK  Jul27   0:00 [mdrecoveryd]
root       457  0.0  0.4 1400  176 ?        S    Jul27   0:00 syslogd -m 0
root       462  0.0  0.0 1880    4 ?        S    Jul27   0:00 klogd -2
rpc        476  0.0  0.0 1484    4 ?        S    Jul27   0:00 portmap
rpcuser    491  0.0  0.0 1536    4 ?        S    Jul27   0:00 rpc.statd
root       552  0.0  0.0 1448    4 ?        S    Jul27   0:00 /sbin/cardmgr
root       627  0.0  0.0 1324    4 ?        S    Jul27   0:00 /usr/sbin/apmd -p
root       731  0.0  0.1 1452   44 ?        S    Jul27   0:00 /usr/sbin/automou
daemon     777  0.0  0.1 1372   48 ?        S    Jul27   0:00 /usr/sbin/atd
root       789  0.0  0.0 2560    4 ?        S    Jul27   0:01 /usr/sbin/sshd
root       809  0.0  0.0 2204    4 ?        S    Jul27   0:00 xinetd -stayalive
root       849  0.0  0.8 4972  340 ?        S    Jul27   0:00 sendmail: accepti
root       862  0.0  0.1 1368   56 ?        S    Jul27   0:00 gpm -t ps/2 -m /d
root       874  0.0  0.2 1524  108 ?        S    Jul27   0:00 crond
xfs        910  0.0  3.6 5200 1380 ?        S    Jul27   0:49 xfs -droppriv -da
root       945  0.0  0.0 1312    4 tty1     S    Jul27   0:00 /sbin/mingetty tt
root       946  0.0  0.0 2292    4 tty2     S    Jul27   0:00 login -- mj
root       947  0.0  0.0 1312    4 tty3     S    Jul27   0:00 /sbin/mingetty tt
root       948  0.0  0.0 1312    4 tty4     S    Jul27   0:00 /sbin/mingetty tt
:
```

Figure 8.2 *Currently running processes.*

➤ %CPU—The amount of CPU time in use by the process, as a percentage of total available CPU time. Unless a process is running, the percentage of CPU time taken by a specific process should be nearly zero.

➤ %MEM—The amount of RAM memory in use by the current process, as a percentage of total available RAM memory.

➤ TTY—Terminal. Linux operating systems today have multiple terminals. When you log in to a command-line interface, you're logging in to a terminal. If a process is associated with a terminal, the number such as **tty1** or **tty2** is shown in this column.

➤ STAT—Status. There are three possible status options for each process: running (**R**), sleeping (**S**), or swapped (**SW**) to the swap partition.

➤ TIME—The amount of time the associated process has run, in hour:minute format.

➤ COMMAND—The command associated with the particular process. All of the commands shown in Figure 8.2 are associated with booting and starting Linux.

 Be sure to remember how to find the **PID** (the process identifier) and the **%CPU** (the load on the CPU) associated with a particular program. You should consider killing any process that constantly uses a high **%CPU**.

Note: The name TTY is derived from TeleTYpe, which is an older computer terminal without a monitor; commands and output on a teletype were sent to what is essentially a networked typewriter.

A number of switches can be used with the **ps** command. A few are described in Table 8.1. Note that **ps** does not require a dash (-) before many of its switches.

Process Identifiers

The key to a process is its identifier, or PID. If you know a program's PID, you can usually kill that program. The associated commands, **kill** and **killall**, are covered in the following sections.

As noted earlier, just about every process has a parent. Sometimes you may have trouble killing a process, in which case you may be able to kill the parent of that process. The PID associated with the parent is the parent process identifier, or PPID. To find the PPID, run the **ps alx | less** command. One example of the result is shown in Figure 8.3.

Table 8.1   ps commands.

Command	Result
ps	Lists all processes associated with one particular terminal.
ps a	List all processes associated with a particular terminal, even if started by another user.
ps l	Lists all processes in long format. Includes key information such as PIDs (process identifiers) and PPIDs (parent process identifiers).
ps r	Lists all currently running processes. Does not include any processes that are swapped or sleeping.
ps u	Associates processes with a specific user. Processes are also listed with currently used percentage of CPU time. If a process is constantly using a significant amount of CPU time, either it is a resource-intensive program or it may just have locked up.
ps x	Includes processes not associated with a terminal. These processes are normally those associated with the startup of Linux.

*Switches can be combined. For example, the **ps aux** command shows every process currently running on your Linux system.*

```
  F   UID   PID  PPID PRI  NI   VSZ  RSS WCHAN  STAT TTY       TIME COMMAND
100    0     1     0   8   0  1340   76 do_sel S   ?        0:03 init [5]
040    0     2     1   8   0     0    0 contex SW  ?        0:00 [keventd]
040    0     3     1   9   0     0    0 apm_ma SW  ?        0:00 [kapm-idled
040    0     4     1   9   0     0    0 kswapd SW  ?        0:07 [kswapd]
040    0     5     1   9   0     0    0 krecla SW  ?        0:00 [kreclaimd]
040    0     6     1   9   0     0    0 bdflus SW  ?        0:00 [bdflush]
040    0     7     1   9   0     0    0 kupdat SW  ?        0:00 [kupdated]
040    0     8     1  -1 -20     0    0 md_thr SW< ?        0:00 [mdrecovery
040    0   457     1   9   0  1400  176 do_sel S   ?        0:00 syslogd -m
140    0   462     1   9   0  1880  180 do_sys S   ?        0:00 klogd -2
140   32   476     1   9   0  1484    0 do_pol SW  ?        0:00 portmap
140   29   491     1   9   0  1536    0 do_sel SW  ?        0:00 rpc.statd
140    0   552     1   8   0  1448    0 do_sel SW  ?        0:00 /sbin/cardm
140    0   627     1   8   0  1324    0 do_sel SW  ?        0:00 /usr/sbin/a
040    0   731     1   9   0  1452   44 pipe_w S   ?        0:00 /usr/sbin/a
040    2   777     1   9   0  1372    0 nanosl SW  ?        0:00 /usr/sbin/a
140    0   789     1   9   0  2560    0 do_sel SW  ?        0:01 /usr/sbin/s
040    0   809     1   9   0  2204    0 rt_sig SW  ?        0:00 xinetd -sta
140    0   849     1   9   0  4972  340 do_sel S   ?        0:00 sendmail: a
140    0   862     1   9   0  1368   56 nanosl S   ?        0:00 gpm -t ps/2
040    0   874     1   9   0  1524  108 nanosl S   ?        0:00 crond
140   43   910     1   9   0  5200 1552 do_sel S   ?        0:47 xfs -droppr
100    0   945     1   9   0  1312    0 read_c SW  tty1     0:00 /sbin/minge
100    0   946     1   9   0  2292    0 wait4  SW  tty2     0:00 login -- mj
100    0   947     1   9   0  1312    0 read_c SW  tty3     0:00 /sbin/minge
100    0   948     1   9   0  1312    0 read_c SW  tty4     0:00 /sbin/minge
:█
```

Figure 8.3   Processes with PPIDs.

There is also a back door to PIDs. When a process is started, its PID is sent as a file to a directory such as /var/run. The actual directory may vary by distribution. For example, if Apache is running on your computer, you can check this with the following command:

```
cat /var/run/httpd.pid
```

If Apache is running, this command typically returns a three- or four-digit number. This is the PID you can use to kill that process.

The program that runs the Apache Web server is httpd, short for Hypertext Transfer Protocol Daemon. A *daemon* is a process that runs in the background, waiting for input. It is commonly associated with services such as Apache that wait for users who want Web service.

kill

One of the reasons why Linux is popular among systems administrators is that it rarely crashes. There are reports of Web servers powered by Linux that have been running without a reboot for months (or more) at a time. One reason for this level of reliability is that system administrators can easily end most programs with the **kill** command. To use this command, you need the appropriate PID.

Linux applications at the graphical user interface (GUI) have been known to freeze at times. For example, if you were to have a problem with a Web browser, a few basic steps allow you to kill that application:

1. Open up a command-line interface. You can do this with a GUI command utility such as xterm, konsole, or gnome-terminal. Alternatively, start a new virtual console as discussed in Chapter 11.

2. Find the PID associated with the Web browser. For this example, assume the name of the Web browser command is **bingo**. Run the **ps ax | grep bingo** command. You should see output similar to this:

```
7790 pts/1   S      1:25 /usr/lib/bingo/bingo -session
7834 pts/1   S      0:00 grep bingo
```

3. The number in the far-left column associated with the browser is the PID, in this case, 7790. Run the **kill 7790** command.

4. If this doesn't work, you may need to kill the PPID (parent process identifier). To find this number, run the **ps axl | grep bingo** command. The number in the third column is the PID; the number in the fourth column is the PPID.

If you're trying to **kill** a daemon such as Apache (**httpd**), Samba (**smbd**), or advanced power management (**apmd**), there is a shortcut. You know that when these processes are running, their PIDs are available in a directory such as /var/run or /var/log. If you're not sure which directory they're in, use the **find** or **locate** command discussed earlier in this chapter.

You don't need the PID to kill some processes. As discussed in Chapter 7, back quotes process any command contained within before passing it along as standard input. In other words, a command such as the following:

```
kill `cat /var/log/httpd.pid`
```

can be divided into two steps. First the command inside the back quotes (`) is processed. The **cat** command reads the contents of the /var/log/httpd.pid file. As described in the previous section, that is the PID for Apache. Then the PID is passed as standard input to the **kill** command.

In other words, if you want to kill a daemon, you don't even need to use the **ps** command. You don't need to memorize the PID. All you need to know is how to feed the contents of the file with the PID to the **kill** command.

Know how to use a command such as **kill `cat /var/run/httpd.pid`** to kill a daemon. This assumes that /var/run contains the .pid files. Your Linux distribution may be different. Use the **locate** or **find** command to locate the proper directory.

killall

Another shortcut is the **killall** command. With **killall**, you don't need the PID, you just need to know the name of the process that you want to kill. Another advantage is that this command stops all processes with the given name. For example, when you run Apache, it starts not one but several different processes, each with its own identifier. This is shown in Figure 8.4, another excerpt from the output of a **ps ax** command.

By default, Apache runs multiple processes for multiple computers that try to connect to its Web pages. On an Apache server for a large installation, you might see hundreds (or more) Apache processes running simultaneously.

```
1202 ?        S        0:02 knotify
1203 ?        S        0:05 kdeinit: kwin
1205 ?        S        0:06 kdeinit: kdesktop
1207 ?        S        0:09 kdeinit: kicker
1213 ?        S        0:04 /usr/bin/autorun -l --interval=1000 --cdplayer=/usr/b
1218 ?        S        0:02 kdeinit: klipper -icon klipper -miniicon klipper
1219 ?        S        0:00 kdeinit: khotkeys
1221 ?        S        0:00 kdeinit: kwrited
1222 pts/0    S        0:00 /bin/cat
1306 ?        S        0:00 smbmount //Experimental/LinuxPlus test
7571 tty2     S        0:00 -bash
7605 tty5     S        0:00 -bash
7680 ?        S        0:03 kdeinit: konsole -icon konsole -miniicon konsole -cap
7681 pts/1    S        0:00 /bin/bash
7954 pts/1    S        0:00 su
7958 pts/1    S        0:00 bash
7978 ?        S        0:00 /usr/sbin/httpd
7979 ?        S        0:00 /usr/sbin/httpd
7980 ?        S        0:00 /usr/sbin/httpd
7981 ?        S        0:00 /usr/sbin/httpd
7982 ?        S        0:00 /usr/sbin/httpd
7983 ?        S        0:00 /usr/sbin/httpd
7984 ?        S        0:00 /usr/sbin/httpd
7985 ?        S        0:00 /usr/sbin/httpd
7986 ?        S        0:00 /usr/sbin/httpd
7988 pts/1    R        0:00 ps ax
7989 pts/1    D        0:00 less
(END)
```

Figure 8.4   Several Apache (httpd) processes run simultaneously.

The **killall** command simplifies the task of stopping all these processes. All you need is the following command:

```
killall httpd
```

 Be sure you know how to use the **killall** command. This command kills one or more running processes by name. It does not work with PIDs.

nice and renice

The **nice** and **renice** commands allow you to adjust the priorities of different processes. The priority of a program can range from –20 (highest) to 19 (lowest). Although this seems backwards, the **nice –n 19** *program1* command starts program 1 with the lowest possible priority. Alternatively, if you need to allocate more resources to a currently running job with a PID of 3242, the **renice –10 3242** command raises the priority of job 3242 up 10 notches.

Starting and Stopping

When you reconfigure a service such as Apache, DNS, or DHCP, one of the advantages of Linux is that you can implement configuration changes without restarting your computer. To get a service to read configuration changes, you need to stop and restart the service. Only when a Linux service restarts does it read in the changes you have made.

There are two basic approaches to stopping and starting a process associated with a service. One is to use the right **kill** command; the other is to use a special script designed to stop and restart the associated service, as allowed by several Linux distributions.

The **kill** command uses different signals. For example, some processes ignore the standard **kill** command. In that case (assume a PID of 456), try the following variation:

```
kill -9 456
```

The **-9** switch forces the specified process to stop completely. This is a last resort, since some applications leave temporary files that can fill up your partitions when killed in this way.

If you want to stop and restart a process, there is a different **kill** code for you: **-1**, also known as **-HUP** (short for *hang up*). For example, if you just reconfigured your DNS server and want to restart its process (assume a PID of 678), run the following command:

```
kill -HUP 678
```

The other way of stopping and restarting a service is available only on some Linux distributions. This method uses scripts for services such as Apache, NFS, and Sendmail in a directory such as /etc/rc.d/init.d. If you have such a directory of service scripts, you'll be able to start, stop, restart, reload, or status the service with a single command. For example, if you reconfigured Samba and want to restart this service from the noted directory, run the following command:

```
/etc/rc.d/init.d/smb restart
```

Look through these scripts on your Linux system. They are typically in text format. Even if you don't have experience with programming, back up the script and be willing to experiment. You might be surprised at what you can do.

Other useful command switches associated with these scripts are the following:

```
/etc/rc.d/init.d/smb stop
/etc/rc.d/init.d/smb start
/etc/rc.d/init.d/smb status
```

Each of these commands is self-explanatory; the **stop** switch halts a service, the **start** switch begins a service, and the **status** switch tells you if a service is currently running.

The First Process (init)

Now that you've seen the **ps** command, various PIDs, and PPIDs, you know a few things about Linux processes. Every process that you've seen has a parent. However, it all has to start somewhere. The starting point is more like the chicken and the egg, or in this case, the Linux kernel and init.

When you start Linux, the kernel loads and starts init. Then init starts and loads everything else, including the drivers from the kernel. The init program then mounts drive partitions, starts terminals, and opens up the command-line interface.

The init program works at several different run levels, numbered between 0 and 7. This was discussed in some detail in Chapter 6. To repeat, while the run levels shown in Table 8.2 do not apply in all cases, they work for the latest versions of the most common Linux distributions.

You can actually run **init** as a command at any time, if you're logged in with **root** user privileges. For example, the **init 6** command would automatically reboot Linux.

Table 8.2 Typical Linux run-level assignments.	
Run Level	**Assignment**
0	Halt
1	Single User Mode (some distributions assign this to run level S)
2	Multiuser, command-line interface, no networking
3	Multiuser, command-line interface, with networking
4	Not used (typically)
5	Graphical login (sometimes known as X11 or xdm)
6	Reboot

Except for 0 and 6, these run levels may vary by Linux distribution.

 Keep in mind the fact that the **root** user can use the **init 1** command to put most Linux computers into single user mode. The actual number or letter you use depends on the settings in the /etc/inittab file.

lsof

A process is anything that is running on your computer. Since everything on Linux is a file, most processes open up other files. The **lsof** command shows you the number of files opened by processes running on your computer. Depending on what you're running, it's not uncommon to have thousands of files open.

The value of **lsof** is as a troubleshooting tool, especially related to hardware. Each hardware component in Linux is related to a device file. For example, if you're having trouble with a modem, one thing to check is active serial ports. Try to start your modem. Run the following command to see what serial ports are open:

```
lsof /dev/ttyS*
```

Any response that you get is associated with hardware that would also open a Microsoft COM port. That is usually a serial mouse or a telephone modem.

Practice Questions

Question 1

> Which of the following services is associated with a PID of 1?
>
> ○ a. kernel
>
> ○ b. httpd
>
> ○ c. init
>
> ○ d. single user mode

Answer c is correct. The init process is the first process, the parent that is the origin of all other processes. When you run the **ps** command with appropriate switches, init is always associated with a process identifier, or PID, of 1. Although the Linux kernel starts init, init loads kernel drivers. Although the designation is somewhat arbitrary, init is the starting point—Linux's answer to the question of which came first: the chicken or the egg. Therefore, answer a is not correct. Since httpd is the daemon associated with the Apache Web server, it is not directly related to init; therefore, answer b is incorrect. While single user mode is most often associated with a run level of 1 in the /etc/inittab configuration file, it is also started by init. In fact, **root** users can start single user mode on most Linux distributions with the **init 1** command. The processes associated with single user mode get PIDs higher than 1. Therefore, answer d is also incorrect.

Question 2

> Which of the following commands can tell you if **rnixon** is a user on your Linux system?
>
> ○ a. **userreq rnixon /etc/passwd**
>
> ○ b. **lsof rnixon /etc/passwd**
>
> ○ c. **diff rnixon /etc/passwd**
>
> ○ d. **grep rnixon /etc/passwd**

Answer d is correct. The **grep** command uses the word that follows, in this case **rnixon**, as a search term in the file that follows. The /etc/passwd file contains all users on a Linux system. Since there is no **userreq** command in the bash shell, answer a is incorrect. Since the **lsof** command is used to list open files, it does not search through the /etc/passwd file for users. Therefore, answer b is incorrect.

Since the **diff** command compares the text of two different files, it cannot tell you if **rnixon** is a current user. Therefore, answer c is also incorrect.

Question 3

You just reconfigured the Linux mail service known as Sendmail. Based on the following output excerpt from the **ps aux** command, what command would you use to restart this service?

```
1389 ?        S      0:00 smbd -D
1394 ?        S      0:00 nmbd -D
1473 ?        S      0:00 sendmail: accepting
1479 pts/1    S    . 0:00 su
1483 pts/1    S      0:00 bash
```

○ a. **killall**

○ b. **kill -1 1473**

○ c. **killall sendmail**

○ d. **kill -HUP sendmail**

Answer b is correct. The **kill** command with the **-1** switch stops and restarts a service with the associated PID, the process identifier. Because the **killall** command doesn't work unless you specify a service to be killed, answer a is not correct. Although the **killall sendmail** command does kill this service, it does not restart it. Therefore, answer c is incorrect. Although the **kill -HUP** command is functionally equivalent to **kill -1**, the **kill** command works only with the PID and not the name associated with a particular service. Therefore, answer d is also incorrect.

Question 4

You have two configuration files for Apache: httpd.conf in the /etc/httpd/conf directory and httpd.bak in the /home/rn directory. The second file is a backup. What command would show you the changes made since the backup file was created?

○ a. **grep /home/rn/httpd.bak /etc/httpd/conf/httpd.conf**

○ b. **diff /etc/httpd/conf/httpd.bak /home/rn/httpd.conf**

○ c. **grep changes /etc/httpd/conf/httpd.conf**

○ d. **diff /home/rn/httpd.bak /etc/httpd/conf/httpd.conf**

Answer d is correct. The **diff** command compares two files, line by line. The differences are sent to the screen as standard output. Also, the backup file, httpd.bak, is in the /home/rn directory; the active configuration file, httpd.conf, is in the /etc/httpd/conf directory. Since **grep** uses the next word as a search term of the file that follows, it does not define the differences between two files. Therefore, answers a and c are both incorrect. Since answer b places each file in the wrong directory, that answer is also incorrect.

Question 5

The output from the **ps aux** command can be quite long. You want to isolate only those processes related to the Apache Web server, which uses httpd. Which of the following commands is best suited to that task?

○ a. **grep httpd < ps aux**

○ b. **ps aux I grep httpd**

○ c. **ps s httpd**

○ d. **ps aux I less**

Answer b is correct. The pipe (|) sends the output from the command to the left, in this case, **ps aux**, as standard input to the command to the right. Then **grep** can use **httpd** as a search term to isolate this service. The left-pointing arrow (<) takes the command or file to the right as standard input. Since there are no quotation marks, or quotes, **ps aux** is not processed before being sent as standard input to **grep httpd**. The result is that **grep** looks for a file named ps, doesn't find it, and returns an error. Therefore, answer a is incorrect. Since the **s** switch does not use **httpd** as a search term, answer c is incorrect. Although piping **ps aux** to the **less** command allows you to scroll through the result to search for httpd processes, it does not isolate those processes, as required by the question. Therefore, answer d is also incorrect.

Question 6

You've just reconfigured the Sendmail configuration file. Which of the following commands restarts the Sendmail service without using the process identifier? Assume .pid files are located in the /var/run directory.

○ a. **kill -HUP 'cat /var/run/sendmail.pid'**

○ b. **killall sendmail**

○ c. **kill -9 'cat /var/run/sendmail.pid'**

○ d. **kill sendmail**

Answer a is correct. The **kill** command with the -**HUP** switch restarts a process as long as it includes the right PID. The **cat** command lists the contents of the noted sendmail.pid file, which contains the right PID number. Since this command is enclosed in back quotes, it is processed before it is sent as standard input to the **kill** command. Since the **killall sendmail** command only stops and does not restart this service, answer b is incorrect. The **kill** command with the -9 switch kills a command without restarting. Also, although the command in quotes is correct, single quotes do not process this command. No number is sent to **kill**, so answer c is not correct and does not stop any process. Since the **kill** command requires a PID number to stop any program or process, answer d is also incorrect.

Question 7

Something is slowing down your system. Based on the figure below, which illustrates output from the **ps au** command, which process should you consider killing?

```
USER      PID %CPU %MEM   VSZ  RSS TTY     STAT START  TIME COMMAND
mj       1176  0.0  1.5  2504  580 pts/1   S    11:56  0:00 /bin/bash
mj       1249 20.5 10.2 24088 3912 pts/1   R    12:40  0:06 /usr/lib/netscape
mj       1273  0.0  0.0 17184    4 pts/1   S    12:40  0:00 (dns helper)
root     1479  0.0  2.6  2228 1004 pts/1   S    12:55  0:00 su
root     1483 53.2  3.7  2468 1416 pts/1   S    12:56  0:00 bash
root     1596 12.0  2.0  2612  768 pts/1   R    14:55  0:00 ps au
```

○ a. Netscape

○ b. The **root** user's bash shell

○ c. User **mj**'s bash shell

○ d. (dns helper)

Answer b is correct. The **%CPU** use of the bash shell, owned by the **root** user, is uncharacteristically high. Since its status is sleeping (**S**), there is no reason for bash to use significant CPU resources. Although Netscape is also using significant CPU resources, that process is running (**R**); that is not uncharacteristic of an application that is loading. Therefore, answer a is incorrect. Since the bash shell associated with user **mj** is not using any measurable CPU resources, it is not a problem. Therefore, answer c is incorrect. Since the dns helper process is not using any measurable CPU resources, answer d is also incorrect.

Question 8

You've just tried to kill the process associated with a new experimental application, bigprog. You've verified that the PID associated with the application is 1521. The PPID associated with bigprog is 784. Which of the following commands is most likely to stop bigprog?

○ a. **kill -HUP 784**

○ b. **kill -1 784**

○ c. **killall 1521**

○ d. **kill -9 1521**

Answer d is correct. When killing a process, the -9 switch is the last resort, since the process does not die gracefully and may leave unwanted elements such as temporary files. Since the **kill -HUP** command stops the process in the same way as the regular **kill** command, it may not work even though it's being applied to the PPID, the parent process identifier. Therefore, answer a is not correct. Since the -1 switch gives the **HUP** signal, answer b is also incorrect for the same reason as answer a. The **killall** command is intended only to provide a way to kill a process by name, not by PID. Since the signal doesn't change, it probably won't kill the stubborn process either. Therefore, answer c is also incorrect.

Question 9

Which of the following commands does not start the cron daemon, which is the utility that runs administrative commands on a schedule? Assume that the corresponding **crond** command is located in the /usr/sbin directory, and your Linux distribution includes start/stop/restart scripts in the /etc/rc.d/init.d directory.

○ a. **/usr/sbin/crond**

○ b. **/etc/rc.d/init.d/crond start**

○ c. **/etc/rc.d/init.d/crond restart**

○ d. **/etc/rc.d/init.d/crond status**

Answer d is correct. The **crond** script, with the **status** switch, does not start the cron daemon. Since there is a **crond** command available in the /usr/sbin directory, answer a is incorrect. Since there is a **crond** script available in the /etc/rc.d/init.d directory, and both switches (**start** and **restart**) start the daemon, answers b and c are both incorrect.

Need to Know More?

 LeBlanc, Dee-Ann. *General Linux I Exam Prep.* Scottsdale, AZ: The Coriolis Group, 2000. ISBN 1-57610-567-9. Chapter 1 includes an excellent description of the **kill** command and associated signals. This chapter also includes a number of exercises.

 Muster, John. *Unix Made Easy.* Berkeley, CA: Osborne/McGraw-Hill, 1996. ISBN 0-07882-173-8. A solid textbook and reference guide for the command-line interface. Although this is a book on Unix, it is often used as a teaching text in conjunction with various Linux distributions. It is most useful for file-manipulation commands such as **grep**.

 Pfaffenberger, Bryan. *Linux Command Instant Reference.* Alameda, CA: Sybex, 2000. ISBN 0-78212-748-7. A comprehensive guide to Linux commands, with switches and many examples. Commands are organized by function.

Configuring Hardware

Terms you'll need to understand:

✓ **dmesg**

✓ /proc

✓ Winmodem

✓ Apsfilter

✓ Legacy hardware

✓ Driver, module

✓ **ifconfig**, **ifup**

✓ **lsmod**

✓ **insmod**, **rmmod**

✓ **modprobe**

✓ Loadable modules

Techniques you'll need to master:

✓ Deciphering Linux hardware information

✓ Identifying hardware conflicts

✓ Understanding winmodem and printer configuration issues

✓ Working with legacy hardware

✓ Listing typical cable connector problems

✓ Using **ifconfig** to configure a network interface card (NIC)

✓ Loading, removing, and revising hardware modules

This chapter is, in many ways, a continuation of Chapter 3, which addressed the basics of hardware support in Linux. Now that you have a grasp of some of the key Linux files, directories, and commands, you have the tools to configure hardware the way you want on a Linux computer.

The process begins with the way Linux collects hardware information during boot and in a virtual directory. It continues with a discussion of a wide range of hardware issues. Special attention is given to network hardware configuration, because the Linux operating system is designed with networks in mind. Finally, you'll get a general lesson in installing and removing relevant Linux hardware modules.

Linux Collects Hardware Information

When the Linux operating system boots on a computer, it uses the information that it has on previously detected hardware. The latest Linux systems also detect most plug-and-play hardware during the startup process. There are two basic ways to identify the hardware that Linux installed during the boot process: the **dmesg** command and the files in the /proc directory.

dmesg

If you suspect a problem with your hardware, the first place to look is the startup messages. You can do this easily with the **dmesg** command. This command sends the main Linux boot messages to the screen. These messages normally include installed core hardware as well as critical services such as the internal computer clock, swap partition, and network protocols.

Note: In constrast, non-core hardware is generally external to your computer. This includes components such as local printers and USB devices.

Some of these messages are shown in Figure 9.1, which is an excerpt from the output from a **dmesg** command. As you can see, the list includes core hardware, such as one CPU (Initializing CPU#0), two IDE drives, three partitions, one floppy drive, a serial port, and a network card. If you add more of any of these devices, you can use the **dmesg** output to see if Linux has detected it.

 Remember that the **dmesg** command can help you find major hardware components detected by Linux. For example, if you have just installed another IDE hard drive or CPU, you should be able to find it listed in the output from the **dmesg** command.

 There is typically a lot of output from **dmesg**. It is easy to scroll through this output with the Page Up and Page Down keys on your keyboard. Just rerun this command with a pipe to the **less** command; in other words, type **dmesg I less**.

```
Linux version 2.4.4-4GB Fri May 18 14:11:12 GMT 2001
BIOS-provided physical RAM map:
 BIOS-e820: 0000000000000000 - 000000000009f000 (usable)
 BIOS-e820: 000000000009f000 - 00000000000a0000 (reserved)
Kernel command line: auto BOOT_IMAGE=linux ro root=303 BOOT_FILE=/boot/vmlinuz
Initializing CPU#0
Detected 560.967 MHz processor.
Console: colour VGA+ 80x25
VFS: Diskquotas version dquot_6.5.0 initialized
PCI: PCI BIOS revision 2.10 entry at 0xfd9de, last bus=0
Linux NET4.0 for Linux 2.4
apm: BIOS version 1.2 Flags 0x03 (Driver version 1.14)
ide: Assuming 33MHz system bus speed for PIO modes; override with idebus=xx
ide0 at 0x1f0-0x1f7,0x3f6 on irq 14
ide1 at 0x170-0x177,0x376 on irq 15
hda: 4095630 sectors (2097 MB) w/2KiB Cache, CHS=1015/64/63
hdc: ATAPI 1X CD-ROM drive, 32kB Cache
Partition check:
 hda: hda1 hda2 hda3
Floppy drive(s): fd0 is 1.44M
ttyS00 at 0x03f8 (irq = 4) is a 16550A
Real Time Clock Driver v1.10d
SCSI subsystem driver Revision: 1.00
IP Protocols: ICMP, UDP, TCP, IGMP
Adding Swap: 133048k swap-space (priority 42)
eth0: PCnet/PCI II 79C970A at 0x1000, 00 50 56 a7 00 23
pcnet32: pcnet32_private lp=c223d000 lp_dma_addr=0x223d000 assigned IRQ 9.
IPv6 v0.8 for NET4.0
```

Figure 9.1   Excerpts from **dmesg** output.

/proc files

When hardware is detected, the associated settings are relayed to the /proc directory. This is a *virtual directory*, which doesn't correspond to any physical drive or partition. An example file list from this directory is shown in Figure 9.2. About half of the files are numbers, which actually represent PIDs, the process identifiers discussed in Chapter 8. Most of the remaining files contain the settings associated with various hardware components; the more important files are covered here.

One important file in the /proc directory is cpuinfo, which lists the key characteristics of the CPUs detected by Linux. If you have more than one CPU or you have recently upgraded CPUs, check this file to make sure Linux detects your new hardware. The contents of a /proc/cpuinfo file are shown in Figure 9.3.

   Keep in mind that when you change or upgrade CPUs, it should be detected in the /proc/cpuinfo file. For example, if you install a second CPU and find only one CPU listed in /proc/cpuinfo, Linux didn't detect your second CPU.

```
[root@laptop71 /proc]# ls
1      1103  1266  2    7    962  cmdline      iomem    modules     tty
1071   1108  1278  3    778  963  cpuinfo      ioports  mounts      uptime
1073   1110  1279  4    793  964  devices      irq      net         version
1075   1111  1281  473  8    965  dma          kcore    partitions
1078   1112  1282  478  805  966  driver       kmsg     pci
1082   1136  1284  492  825  967  execdomains  ksyms
1090   1137  1344  5    865  975  fb           loadavg  slabinfo
1092   1232  1345  507  878  979  filesystems  locks    stat
1093   1236  1366  568  890  996  fs           mdstat   swaps
1095   1256  1370  6    926  apm  ide          meminfo  sys
1097   1265  1414  655  961  bus  interrupts   misc     sysvipc
[root@laptop71 /proc]# █
```

Figure 9.2   Files in the /proc directory.

```
[root@laptop71 /proc]# cat cpuinfo
processor       : 0
vendor_id       : GenuineIntel
cpu family      : 5
model           : 4
model name      : Pentium MMX
stepping        : 3
cpu MHz         : 199.311
fdiv_bug        : no
hlt_bug         : no
f00f_bug        : yes
coma_bug        : no
fpu             : yes
fpu_exception   : yes
cpuid level     : 1
wp              : yes
flags           : fpu vme de pse tsc msr mce cx8 mmx
bogomips        : 398.13

[root@laptop71 /proc]# █
```

Figure 9.3 Linux CPU information in the /proc/cpuinfo file.

The speed you see should approximately match the rated CPU of your system. The speed shown in Figure 9.3 is characteristic of a 200MHz CPU. If the speed shown in /proc/cpuinfo is higher than the rated speed, however, your CPU is *overclocked*.

Overclocking is generally not recommended. Since it takes more energy to make a CPU run faster, it creates extra heat. Unless there is sufficient cooling, the extra heat builds up in the CPU. If the CPU becomes too hot, it stops working, and your Linux system will crash. Since a CPU cools down after a crash, you should be able to boot your system again, at least until the CPU becomes too hot again. In other words, you end up with an intermittent crash.

 Remember that an overclocked CPU can lead to excessive heat and intermittent crashes of your computer.

Table 9.1 describes a few other important files in the /proc directory.

Common Hardware Issues

Now that you can search through the basic tools and files with detected hardware information, you're ready to tackle some basic Linux hardware issues. The most basic hardware problem is when two devices are trying to use the same IRQ port, I/O address, and/or DMA channel. There are special issues related to a number of other devices, including software modems, printers, and video adapters. One special problem for Linux administrators is legacy hardware that requires manual configuration.

Table 9.1 Some important /proc directory files.	
File	Description
cmdline	Specified location of the Linux kernel
cpuinfo	Detected characteristics of the CPU
dma	Assigned direct memory addresses
interrupts	Assigned Interrupt Request (IRQ) channels
ioports	Assigned I/O memory addresses
meminfo	Allocated RAM and swap space
modules	Installed driver modules
pci	Detected PCI devices
scsi	Detected SCSI devices by logical unit number (LUN)
version	Installed version of the Linux kernel

Conflicts

A hardware conflict occurs when two or more hardware devices try to use the same IRQ port, I/O address, and/or DMA channel. There are two basic scenarios in which you'll have a conflict.

The first scenario is based on a computer that was used for another operating system. When you install Linux on that computer, two hardware devices that formerly worked may have a conflict.

The other scenario is when you install a new component such as a modem or a sound card. The new component doesn't work. In addition, a previously installed hardware device no longer works.

In either case, you can use the appropriate file in the /proc directory to analyze the problem and then use that knowledge and experience to find a solution.

As described in Table 9.1, there are files that describe current IRQ, I/O, and DMA assignments. Sometimes these files identify the two devices using the same channel. At other times, both problem devices will be missing from the list.

Note: Only a few hardware devices use DMA channels, so DMA conflicts are rare.

When there are conflicts, the **append** variable can help. You can reassign the IRQ, I/O, and/or DMA for a specific device at the boot prompt or in the lilo.conf file. For details, refer to Chapter 6.

If you've used your configuration with another operating system and still have it available (in a *dual-boot* configuration, for instance), start that operating system.

Analyze the IRQ, I/O, and/or DMA used for the problem devices. The same IRQ, I/O, and DMA assignments used in other operating systems usually also work in Linux. Otherwise, some trial and error is required, based on the ports, channels, or addresses that currently are free.

A dual-boot configuration is a computer with two installed operating systems, such as Linux and Microsoft Windows. If you have a dual-boot, copy the hardware settings (IRQ, I/O, DMA) in Microsoft Windows. Use it as a guide to creating settings in Linux. This technique can help you address many hardware problems.

Winmodems

Just about every major class of hardware is compatible with Linux. One major exception is known as a *winmodem*. This is the name given to any modem that uses Microsoft Windows operating system library files. In contrast, the software required to operate a *hardware modem* is contained entirely within the physical modem. Linux has no problems with hardware modems.

Note: The only real modems are analog telephone modems. A modem translates the 1s and 0s of computer communication to the sound transmitted on telephone lines. Don't confuse this with the class of high-speed connections known as cable modems, satellite modems, or DSL modems. Those high-speed connections are more closely related to Ethernet adapters.

As of this writing, Microsoft does not share its source code under the General Public License (GPL). Therefore, Linux developers have had to use their own code to make a winmodem compatible with Linux. With the large number of winmodems on the market, some still don't work with Linux.

Since modems have been operating at a maximum speed of 56Kbps for years, Linux developers have had some time to adapt to most winmodems. A substantial number of winmodems work with Linux just as well as any hardware modem. Some of the remaining winmodems can be configured with a bit of help; the central source of information for these modems is the Linux winmodem support site at **www.linmodems.org**.

Remember that software modems and many internal PCI modems are winmodems. Because they were designed to use Microsoft Windows operating system libraries, they can be difficult to configure in Linux.

Printers

The other group of devices that has trouble with Linux is software printers. Just as with winmodems, these printers rely on Microsoft Windows operating system software to print text or graphics.

Because of the rapid evolution of printers over the past several years, not as much work has been done to make these printers compatible with Linux. In fact, many of these printers aren't even compatible with the latest Microsoft operating systems, such as Microsoft Windows 2000 or XP.

Printers are typically configured separately from other hardware components. Some Linux distributions include printer support in their "all-in-one" configuration utilities such as Linuxconf, Webmin, or YaST. One reliable third-party configuration utility uses the *magic filter* known as Apsfilter, available online at **www.apsfilter.org**.

Video Adapters

As discussed in Chapter 3, Linux can accommodate just about any video card. If it does not recognize the card, it can use a common video mode known as SVGA as a default. This assumes you've already created a basic configuration when installing Linux. Then the basic hardware issue is to maximize the resolution, within the limits of visual comfort.

Note: SVGA stands for Super Video Graphics Adapter, which is a video mode that just about any current video adapter with significant graphics capabilities can use.

After the hardware is recognized, adjustments for video adapters fall into the following three categories:

➤ *Resolution*—The number of dots sent to the screen or monitor, expressed in numbers such as 640×480, 800×600, 1024×768, or 1280×1024.

➤ *Color*—The number of colors used for each dot. Typically, this can range from 1 bit per pixel (bpp), which is black and white, to 32bpp, which is known as *true color.*

➤ *Refresh frequency*—The number of times data is sent to each horizontal line per second. Although it's helpful to set this as high as possible, do not exceed the capability of your monitor. In certain cases, it could irreparably damage your system.

Legacy Hardware

Sometimes older computer hardware is so reliable that it is still in service. Sometimes the resources may not be available for hardware upgrades. Whatever the reason, many computers are still in service that use *legacy hardware*. Although the term refers to any device that may be more than a couple of years old, it most commonly refers to hardware that does not conform to plug-and-play standards.

Sometimes you get lucky when configuring legacy hardware. Linux can recognize some legacy hardware devices and configure them without help. However, many legacy devices are hard-wired to use a specific IRQ, I/O, and/or DMA. While this is often adjustable through jumper plugs on the physical hardware, it may still require the use of a port, channel, or address that conflicts with the default configuration for an existing plug-and-play device.

In either case, the best option is to make provisions in your computer's CMOS settings. Depending on the BIOS menu, you may reserve a specific IRQ, I/O, and/or DMA setting for your legacy hardware. Alternatively, you may change a setting to make sure plug-and-play operating systems don't override legacy hardware settings. If all else fails, use the **append** variable as discussed in Chapter 6.

Know that when you use legacy hardware, it is best to reserve IRQ ports, I/O addresses, and DMA channels in your computer's CMOS. The plug-and-play configuration programs associated with Linux then cannot override the IRQs, I/Os, and DMAs that you need for your legacy hardware.

Cabling Errors

When troubleshooting computer problems, the most likely problem is the hardware. The first items to check with hardware are cables and connections. Are the cables good, and are the connections tight? If there is more than one connection of the same type, perhaps you've plugged in a cable in the wrong location. Common errors in this regard include the following:

➤ *Reversed cables*—Many SCSI, ATAPI, and floppy drive cable connectors are rectangular and connect two rows of wires. If there is no physical guide to ensure correct orientation, cable connectors can be easily installed upside-down. Just about every wire carries a specific kind of data. Upside-down connector installation means that the devices connected to those cables don't get the information or power that they need.

➤ *Misplaced cables*—When you have more than one of a specific type of connector, such as two serial ports, two printer ports, or several USB ports, it's easy to install a cable in the wrong location accidentally. This is even important for USB; once a USB device is installed, no other device can be plugged into the same location without reconfiguring the system.

➤ *Incorrect cables*—Sometimes more than one type of cable can fit in a specific location. For example, *crossover* network cables can be used in a network of two computers. However, these same crossover cables won't work when connecting a computer to a larger network through a hub.

RAM

The final common hardware issue is RAM, also known as random access memory, the main active memory in the PC. Although RAM has become a commodity, traded on world markets just like oil or wheat, not all RAM is alike. In fact, there are several different kinds of RAM hardware. Several types of RAM are physically compatible; accidental mixing of different kinds of RAM can damage your computer.

Two major types of RAM in use are as follows:

➤ *DIP*—Dual-inline packages. The first major type of RAM was organized into small packages with two rows of pins that attached to the PC motherboard. Closely related to SIP, or single-inline packages.

➤ *SIMM and DIMM*—Single and Dual Inline Memory Modules. This is the physical RAM standard of today. DIMMs look like SIMMs, except they have chips on both sides of the RAM package. While the first commercially available SIMMs processed memory at about 10MHz, current PC DIMMs process memory at 100MHz, 133MHz, and 200MHz.

Although you may not be able to find DIP RAM replacement parts, you can still find them on older computers. These "obsolete" computers are well suited as dedicated routers, DNS servers, DHCP servers, and more, as described in Chapter 2.

Another concern with older RAM was parity. The parity bit allows for error checking and correction (ECC) when processing data through RAM. While regular nonparity RAM included eight chips, parity RAM included nine chips. Sometimes parity RAM works on nonparity motherboards (the parity bit is ignored), but nonparity RAM does not work on motherboards that expect a parity bit.

 You need to remember that nonparity RAM does not work on motherboards that expect a parity bit.

Generally, you shouldn't mix RAM on a PC. Some motherboards can take only one type of RAM. Even if the RAM fits in the slot, be careful. At best, the wrong type of RAM won't work. At worst, it could destroy your motherboard or more.

Note: This list is definitely not comprehensive; for example, it does not address the differences between dynamic and static RAM (DRAM and SRAM), nor does it address video RAM.

Networks

The strength of Linux is in its networking capabilities. Your Linux computer can serve as the communications link with Microsoft Windows, Apple Macintosh, and many other types of computer operating systems. However, a network is only as good as each computer's connection to its network interface card (NIC). As discussed in previous sections, physical interfaces are important. However, command interfaces are important for configuration as well.

Note: Telephone modem configuration is addressed in Chapter 10.

Physical Connections

The basic rules for network configuration are the same as for any other device. The most likely problem is physical. Make sure the connections are solid. To check the NIC, use any available diagnostic tools.

Many NICs include a light that goes on if everything is properly connected. If the NIC is internal, look for the light on the back of your computer. If you've checked the connections and there is no light, it's time for some diagnostics.

Most NICs include a diagnostic disk. These disks are usually in MS-DOS format on a 3.5 inch floppy. You'll need to boot your computer in MS-DOS mode to make it work. If you don't have a diagnostic disk, one is usually downloadable from the NIC manufacturer's Web site.

Note: One good disk for booting a computer into MS-DOS mode is the Windows 98 boot disk. It is downloadable over the Internet from a number of sites. Find the one you like by running an Internet search with a term such as "Windows 98 boot disk" download.

If the NIC diagnostics tell you that everything should work, check for its IRQ, I/O, and/or a DMA. Some NICs have a default value that you can try with the **append** command described in Chapter 6. If you're not sure what IRQ, I/O, and/or DMA you should use, trial and error is an option. The **ifconfig** command allows you to test different IRQs, I/Os, and DMAs easily.

Remember that the **ifconfig** and **ifup** scripts are usually located in a directory such as /sbin, which is not part of **$PATH** for most users. In other words, you may need to use the full directory path to run each command, in this case, **/sbin/ifconfig** or **/sbin/ifup**.

Network Interface Card (NIC) Configuration Commands

The two key commands to help configure a NIC are **ifconfig** and **ifup**. In Chapter 4, you learned to use **ifconfig** to see if your network card is working. If it isn't working, the first thing to do is use one of these commands to try to turn on the NIC. If that doesn't work, you assign a different IRQ port and/or I/O address. Alternatively, you can see how it assigns an IP address and a network mask to a specific NIC.

Although the latest Linux distributions detect most NICs without a problem, configuration can be a bit more difficult with multiple NICs.

Activating a Network Interface

If **ifconfig** didn't see your NIC, the first step is to check the "on-off" switch. The following command is one way to try to activate the second Ethernet card on a computer:

```
ifconfig eth1 up
```

By default, the first Ethernet card on a computer is eth0, the second is eth1, and so on. Another command that can activate a network card is **ifup**:

```
ifup eth1
```

Sometimes you need to turn off a NIC. For example, assume you want to adjust current IRQ or I/O assignments, as discussed in the following section, but you find that those commands won't work if the NIC is active. You can use **ifconfig** or a related command known as **ifdown** to bring down a NIC:

```
ifconfig eth1 down
ifdown eth1
```

 Know how to use the **ifconfig**, **ifup**, and **ifdown** commands to activate or deactivate a network interface card (NIC).

ifconfig Hardware Configuration

As described in Chapter 4, the **ifconfig** command, used without switches, can detect active network interfaces. This same command can also set the IRQ port and I/O address for a NIC. For example, to set the second Ethernet NIC on your computer with an IRQ of 12 and an I/O of 0x300, run the following command:

```
ifconfig eth1 irq 12 io_addr 0x300
```

Now try the **ifconfig** command by itself again. If you see your second Ethernet card (eth1) listed, you were successful. You can now incorporate the result in the /etc/lilo.conf file with the **append** command, discussed in Chapter 6. Alternatively, you can try the **ifconfig** command again with other IRQs or I/Os.

Remember how to use the **ifconfig** command to assign an IRQ port and/or an I/O address to a specific network card.

ifconfig IP Address Configuration

Suppose you've done the work to set up IP addresses on a network. If you don't use DHCP to assign IP addresses, you're assigning them to individual computers yourself. Moreover, if you've set up a series of IP addresses, you should already have a network mask.

Note: Basic concepts such as IP addresses, network masks, and DHCP were covered in Chapter 4. If you need more information on how to really make these addresses work for you, see the "Need to Know More?" section at the end of that chapter.

Now you can assign the selected IP address and network mask to your NIC. Assume that the IP address is **10.168.0.36**, the network mask is **255.255.255.0**, and the NIC is the only Ethernet network card on your computer. Use the following command:

```
ifconfig eth0 10.168.0.36 netmask 255.255.255.0
```

To see whether your card has adapted this address and network mask, run the **ifconfig** command again, this time without switches.

It is important to know how to use the **ifconfig** command to assign IP addresses and network masks.

Hardware Drivers

Every hardware device needs a Linux driver. Some are integrated into the Linux kernel, while others are easily configurable as loadable modules. Hardware devices that rely on drivers already integrated into the kernel are set. The kernel is automatically loaded when you start Linux, so the associated drivers are loaded as well.

If all available drivers were part of the Linux kernel, however, it would grow to an unmanageable size. As discussed in Chapter 3, many drivers are set up as loadable modules. Ideally, the loadable module driver is installed when Linux detects your hardware device. This doesn't always work, however. Even when it works, you may want to use a different or updated driver.

Module Locations

Sometimes you'll need to load the driver for a hardware device yourself. The first place to look for a driver is within Linux. Most Linux distributions contain two directories with driver modules:

➤ */lib/modules/*a.b.c*/kernel/drivers*—Where a.b.c represents the version number of the currently installed Linux kernel.

➤ */usr/X11R6/lib/modules/drivers*—The special location for video or graphics card drivers.

If you need to update a driver, you'll probably download it from a location such as the Web site for your hardware manufacturer or Linux distribution. You can recognize most Linux driver modules because the file will include the .o extension.

lsmod

Before installing a new driver, you should check to see if it is already installed. The command that performs this task is **lsmod**. Run this command to review the currently loaded modules on your Linux system. Examine the following sample output:

```
Module            Size    Used by
nls_iso8859-1     2880    1      (autoclean)
smbfs             35696   1      (autoclean)
ide-cd            27104   0      (autoclean)
cdrom             27392   0      (autoclean) [ide-cd]
autofs            11136   1      (autoclean)
serial_cs         4912    0      (unused)
3c589_cs          8256    1
ds                7184    2      [serial_cs 3c589_cs]
i82365            13504   2
pcmcia_core       43456   0      [serial_cs 3c589_cs ds i82365]
ipchains          38944   0      (unused)
sb                7824    1
sb_lib            35760   0      [sb]
uart401           6608    0      [sb_lib]
sound             62112   1      [sb_lib uart401]
soundcore         4432    5      [sb_lib sound]
```

The first column (Module) includes a list of loaded modules. The next column (Size) lists the amount of memory used by each driver, in bytes. The Used by column lists the number of programs currently using that driver. The final column lists other modules that depend on that driver. These dependencies are similar to the dependent **rpm** packages discussed in Chapter 6. In this case, the **soundcore** module won't work unless the **sb_lib** and **sound** modules are also installed.

insmod

Sometimes the loadable modules feature fails to load the right module for a hardware device. Sometimes you may have downloaded the driver yourself. In either case, you need to use the **insmod** command to load the module. For example, if you just installed a D-Link DE-620 Ethernet pocket adapter on a computer with Linux kernel version 2.4.4-4, the following command loads the correct driver:

```
insmod /lib/modules/2.4.4-4/kernel/drivers/net/de620.o
```

Depending on the distribution, the directory path you use may be different. If you're installing a NIC, you can now use commands such as **ifconfig** to complete the configuration.

 If it doesn't work, one possible problem is the dependent modules discussed in the previous section. This can be addressed with the **modprobe** command.

modprobe

In the sample output shown earlier, in the column furthest to the right showing the **lsmod** output, some modules are shown to depend on others. The **modprobe** command is a slightly more powerful version of **insmod**, because it can install dependent modules automatically. The format of this command is essentially the same as **insmod**; both commands install the driver files with the .o extension as modules that allow the Linux kernel to communicate with specific hardware devices.

The **modprobe** command can also be used to remove modules; in either case, it takes the given driver and checks your computer to see if the associated hardware is installed. The driver module is then installed or removed to match your hardware.

If you've made a number of hardware changes, the **modprobe -r** command removes any other modules that may no longer be needed. For example, assume a setup based on the earlier output from the **lsmod** command. Assume that you've removed the soundcard. When you use **modprobe -r** to remove the **uart401**, **sound**, and **soundcard** modules, the **sb_lib** and then the **sb** modules are removed automatically. This is known as the *autoclean* process.

Be sure to know that the **modprobe** command can be used to install, delete, or autoclean the module associated with a hardware device.

Another problem is if the loadable module for the new hardware device is not enabled in the Linux kernel. If the **modprobe** command doesn't work, it may be necessary to recompile the kernel.

Remember that if you can't load a module for a hardware device that you just installed, you may need to enable loadable modules for that device by recompiling the Linux kernel.

The **insmod**, **modprobe**, and **rmmod** commands won't work unless you're in **root** user or superuser mode.

rmmod

It is easier to remove a module. Based on the output from **lsmod**, just remove it with the **rmmod** command. For example, the **3c589_cs** module is used by the 3Com Etherlink III network interface card (NIC). If you've upgraded to a different Ethernet NIC, you no longer need this module. You could then remove it with the following command:

```
rmmod 3c589_cs
```

If you try to remove a module that others depend on, the **rmmod** command won't work. For example, based on the **lsmod** output shown earlier, if you tried to remove the **sb** (sound blaster) module, you would get the following error message:

```
sb: Device or resource busy
```

This module is busy and cannot be removed because other modules depend on it. The dependent modules should be removed first.

Remembering Desired Modules

Once the modules are reconfigured the way you want, the next step is to make sure Linux remembers these modules the next time you reboot. Linux loads modules based on the contents of the /etc/modules.conf configuration file. You can edit this file, or you can use distribution-specific utilities such as Red Hat's Kudzu, Caldera's Webmin, and S.u.S.E.'s YaST.

Practice Questions

Question 1

Several months ago, you purchased a motherboard that allows you to use two CPUs. When you built your computer, you installed only one CPU. You installed Linux on this computer and have been running this operating system successfully since that time. You've just installed the second CPU. How can you confirm that Linux recognizes both CPUs? [Check all correct answers]

❑ a. Watch the boot messages as they scroll across your screen.

❑ b. Run the **dmesg I less** command. Review the messages for both CPUs.

❑ c. Run the **cpuinfo I less** command. Review the messages for both CPUs.

❑ d. Inspect the /proc/cpuinfo file to see if it contains parameters for both CPUs.

Answers a, b, and d are correct. For answer a, CPU detection is part of the process of booting the Linux operating system. Although the messages scroll so quickly that you may not be able to see the messages detecting both CPUs, the messages are there. For answer b, the **dmesg** command recounts the critical hardware messages during the boot process. Since CPUs are certainly critical hardware, they are listed in the output from **dmesg**. Although piping the output to **less** isn't absolutely necessary, it is a convenience that allows you to inspect a long list of output easily with the Page Up and Page Down keys on your keyboard. For answer d, the virtual /proc directory contains files for different kinds of hardware. The key file for detected CPUs is /proc/cpuinfo. Since there is no **cpuinfo** command, answer c is not correct.

Question 2

You've just purchased a new internal modem. The features of the modem, as listed on the box, include the fact that it is plug-and-play. It is also preconfigured to work with your operating system's libraries. After you install the modem, Linux doesn't detect it. Which of the following statements describes the most likely problem?

○ a.   You need to run **insmod** to make sure the modem is using the proper IRQ port and I/O address.

○ b.   You should have purchased an external modem, because Linux cannot detect internal modems.

○ c.   No modems are preconfigured to work with Linux operating system libraries. This modem is preconfigured to work with Microsoft Windows.

○ d.   There is an IRQ conflict between the modem and your serial mouse.

Answer c is correct. No modems are preconfigured to work with Linux operating system libraries. A modem that is "preconfigured" is probably a software modem, also known as a winmodem. Software modems are designed to use the Microsoft Windows operating system for part of their functionality. Since there are no Microsoft Windows operating system files that are part of Linux, winmodems may not work within Linux. Since this is a plug-and-play modem, you should not need to assign an IRQ port or I/O address. If you did, the appropriate command would be **ifconfig**. For both reasons, answer a is incorrect. Although external modems are easier to configure, there are many internal modems, including some winmodems, that work on Linux. Therefore, answer b is incorrect. Although an IRQ conflict between a modem and a serial mouse is quite possible, it should not happen with a plug-and-play modem. Therefore, answer d is also incorrect.

Question 3

Which of the following commands can be used to install or remove a hardware driver module?

○ a. **insmod**

○ b. **modprobe**

○ c. **rmmod**

○ d. **lsmod**

Answer b is correct. Since the **modprobe** command checks to see if the desired component is installed, it can be used to install or remove the associated driver module. Since the **insmod** command only installs driver modules, answer a is incorrect. Since the **rmmod** command only removes driver modules, answer c is incorrect. Since the **lsmod** command only lists currently installed driver modules, answer d is also incorrect.

Question 4

You've just taken a job as a Linux system administrator at a big company. They have a number of older computers with a mix of legacy and plug-and-play hardware. Your new boss wants you to install Linux on some of these computers so you can use them in light-duty applications such as DNS and print servers. You're having some trouble getting Linux to recognize the legacy hardware. Which of the following actions should you take?

○ a. Replace all of the legacy hardware.

○ b. Recommend the replacement of the older computers.

○ c. Uninstall the plug-and-play hardware. Replace with legacy hardware if available.

○ d. Use the diagnostic disk associated with each legacy component. Reserve the appropriate IRQ port, I/O address, and/or DMA channel in each computer's CMOS settings.

Answer d is correct. By definition, legacy hardware is not plug-and-play. Dedicated IRQ ports, I/O addresses, and possibly DMA channels are required to allow each legacy component to work in a plug-and-play environment. The appropriate reservations can usually be made in the CMOS settings of each computer's BIOS menu. Although replacing legacy hardware may work, it defeats the cost savings associated with using older hardware. Therefore, answer a is incorrect. Because replacing all of the older computers is a more expensive option, answer b is also incorrect. Replacing plug-and-play hardware with legacy components makes your job more difficult, since you'll then have to assign all of the IRQ ports, I/O addresses, and DMA channels yourself. Therefore, answer c is also incorrect.

Question 5

One of your customers tinkers a lot with his computer. He calls and tells you that since he installed some new components, the computer crashes intermittently. After the crash, he's always able to reboot and restart Linux. Which of the following statements describes the most likely cause of the problem?

○ a. Incompatible RAM

○ b. Overclocking on the CPU

○ c. A winmodem that Linux can't use

○ d. A bad BIOS

Answer b is correct. Overclocking on the CPU increases its speed, which produces more heat. If the CPU gets too hot, it stops working; Linux crashes without the CPU. Once the computer has crashed, the CPU cools down, so you're able to reboot almost immediately. Although incompatible RAM usually doesn't work, it usually leads to problems during the computer boot process. Therefore, answer a is incorrect. Although Linux has trouble with many winmodems, that usually doesn't cause a crash. Therefore, answer c is also incorrect. A bad BIOS may prevent booting of the computer, but it does not cause a crash after a computer boots up. Therefore, answer d is also incorrect.

Question 6

> Which of the following commands would you try to start your second Ethernet
> network card? The driver is de600.o. You also have the following excerpt
> from the **lsmod** command:
>
> ```
> serial_cs    4912    0    (unused)
> de600        8256    1
> ds           7184    2    [serial_cs de600]
> ```
>
> ○ a. **insmod /lib/modules/2.4.4-4/kernel/drivers/net/de600.o**
>
> ○ b. **/sbin/ifconfig eth2 up**
>
> ○ c. **/sbin/ifup eth2**
>
> ○ d. **/sbin/ifconfig eth1 up**

Answer d is correct. The first Ethernet card is designated as eth0, and the second
is designated as eth1. The **ifconfig** command allows a diversity of adjustments to
a network interface card (NIC), including activation with the **up** switch. Since
the excerpt from the **lsmod** command shows that the network card is already
installed, there is no need to install it again. Even after installation, configuration
and activation with commands such as **ifconfig** and **ifup** are required. Therefore,
answer a is incorrect. Since answers b and c activate the third Ethernet NIC
(eth2), these answers are also incorrect.

Question 7

> You're having trouble activating the second Ethernet NIC on your computer.
> Based on information in the appropriate /proc files, you know that IRQs 5,
> 11, and 12 and I/O addresses 0x300 and 0x330 are free. You're not sure
> which IRQ or I/O will work. You want to try each of these options using trial
> and error. Which of the following methods is the most appropriate way to
> start?
>
>
>
> ○ a. Run the **ifconfig eth1 irq 5 io_addr 0x300** command.
>
> ○ b. Add the **append="ether=5,0x300,eth1"** command to the /etc/
> lilo.conf file.
>
> ○ c. Run the **modprobe eth1** command.
>
> ○ d. When you boot your computer and see the **LILO boot:** prompt,
> type the **linux ether=5,0x300,eth1** command.

Answer a is correct. The **ifconfig** command can assign IRQ ports and I/O addresses to a specific Ethernet adapter. If what you assign does not work, you can run the **ifconfig** command again with a different IRQ port and I/O address without rebooting. Answer b is a valid way to assign IRQ 5 and I/O 0x300 to the second network card. Since you have to reboot Linux before any commands in the lilo.conf file takes effect, this answer leads to a more difficult process of trial and error. Therefore, answer b is incorrect. Since the **modprobe** command installs or removes driver modules, it is unrelated to assigning IRQ ports or I/O addresses. Therefore, answer c is incorrect. Answer d is a valid command, but since any command at the **LILO boot:** prompt is part of the Linux boot process, it is incorrect because it leads to a more difficult process of trial and error.

Question 8

> You've physically installed a new network device. You've tried loading the module for this device, but it doesn't load. You've verified that the module is the correct driver for the new network device. You've even tried installing a different network device, but that module won't load either. Which of the following statements is the best way to address this problem?
>
> ○ a. The driver doesn't work in Linux; you need to try to load a generic network module.
>
> ○ b. You need to turn off your computer, uninstall the device, reboot Linux, halt the computer, and then install the device again. Then you should be able to install the driver module.
>
> ○ c. You need to recompile the kernel to enable loadable modules.
>
> ○ d. You need to use the **modprobe** command to install the driver module.

Answer c is correct. If the module for a new hardware device isn't loadable with the standard commands, the most likely answer is that loadable modules are not enabled in the Linux kernel. While a generic network module might work if loadable modules are enabled, a generic module won't support all of the features of your new hardware device. Since you've also verified that you're using the correct driver, answer a is incorrect. Although answer b is a way to recheck driver installation for plug-and-play hardware for various Microsoft Windows operating systems, these steps should not be necessary in Linux. Therefore, answer b is incorrect. While the **modprobe** command is more efficient than **insmod** because it checks for dependent modules, it won't work if loadable modules aren't enabled. Therefore, answer d is also incorrect.

Question 9

You've just replaced all existing RAM with 256MB RAM chips on your computer. When you try to boot, you hear a series of beeps. Which of the following conditions would cause this problem?

- ○ a. The BIOS could not detect the new RAM.
- ○ b. The motherboard expects RAM with parity; you've installed new RAM that contains only eight chips.
- ○ c. Linux could not detect the new RAM.
- ○ d. You've installed more RAM than Linux can detect.

Answer b is correct. There are many different kinds of RAM for the PC. For example, if a motherboard expects RAM with parity, it expects RAM that contains nine chips, where the ninth chip accounts for the parity bit. While this also corresponds to a condition where the BIOS can't detect the new RAM, the root cause is the needs of the motherboard. Therefore, answer a is incorrect. Since the conditions in this question occur before Linux starts booting, whether or not Linux can detect the RAM is not an issue. Therefore, answers c and d are both incorrect.

Question 10

Which of the following directories contains current hardware information about your computer?

- ○ a. /lib/modules
- ○ b. /proc
- ○ c. /root
- ○ d. /mnt

Answer b is correct. The /proc directory is a virtual directory that contains information such as IRQ ports and I/O addresses for each detected device on your computer. Although the /lib/modules directory contains most of the hardware driver modules in Linux, it does not include hardware information such as IRQ ports or I/O addresses. Therefore, answer a is incorrect. Since the /root directory is the home directory for only the **root** user, it is unrelated to hardware information for all users. Therefore, answer c is also incorrect. The /mnt directory is the default directory for removable drives such as a floppy and a CD-ROM. Since this is unrelated to the /proc directory, answer d is also incorrect.

Need to Know More?

 Gilster, Ron. *PC Technician Black Book*. Scottsdale, AZ: The Coriolis Group, 2001. ISBN 1-57610-808-2. A comprehensive, generic problem-solving reference for various components in a personal computer. Although the focus of hardware installation is Microsoft Windows, it is still as comprehensive a PC hardware reference as I've ever seen.

 Thompson, Robert Bruce. *PC Hardware in a Nutshell*. Sebastopol, CA: O'Reilly and Associates, Inc., 2001. ISBN 1-56592-599-8. An excellent general book on personal computer hardware.

 One distribution-neutral tool for configuring printers is Apsfilter. Even though it is a menu-driven tool at the command-line interface, it is still fairly easy to use. You can download the package and review the documentation online at **www.apsfilter.org**.

 Because a large proportion of telephone modems sold today are winmodems, a lot of effort has been put into making each of these modems compatible with Linux. Most of this effort is documented at **www.linmodems.org**.

 Critical for understanding Linux hardware is the Linux Hardware Compatibility List, available online from the Linux Documentation Project at **www.linuxdoc.org/HOWTO/Hardware-HOWTO/index.html**.

 A comprehensive discussion of loadable modules is available online from the Linux Documentation Project at **www.linuxdoc.org/HOWTO/Module-HOWTO/index.html**. A similarly comprehensive discussion of how Plug-and-Play works on Linux is available from the same group at **www.linuxdoc.org/HOWTO/Plug-and-Play-HOWTO.html**.

Services and Configuration Options

Terms you'll need to understand:

- ✓ Dial-up
- ✓ **pppd**
- ✓ **kppp**, **rp3**
- ✓ **minicom**
- ✓ Samba, NFS
- ✓ Apache, Squid

- ✓ Remote access
- ✓ Radius
- ✓ Firewall
- ✓ **ipchains**, **iptables**
- ✓ Masquerading

Techniques you'll need to master:

- ✓ Listing the basic modem daemons
- ✓ Working with **minicom** to test modems
- ✓ Comprehending requirements behind NIS and Squid
- ✓ Setting up client connections to Samba and NFS shared directories

- ✓ Understanding basic parameters for Apache
- ✓ Listing the basic functions of Squid
- ✓ Allowing modem connections to your servers

Systems administrators cannot live by an operating system alone. Without applications, any operating system is just a toy. Applications such as Apache, Squid, NFS, and **minicom** are key to making Linux a productive operating system. With these applications, you can set up Web service for others, verify authorized users, and set up communications through modems.

This chapter is in part a more advanced look at configuration topics discussed in earlier chapters; these topics include individual services such as Apache and NFS, as well as modem configuration. More advanced topics include the Network Information System (NIS) and the Radius modem server.

Dial-Up Service

Although you might not see a telephone modem in large corporate networks, dial-up service is still the way most small businesses and consumers connect to the Internet. Like any other service, dial-up service requires its own Linux utilities. Although there are several good Linux graphical tools for modem connections, they are all based on command-line interface tools. When you don't have a graphical tool available, you need to know how to diagnose modem problems. One key Linux command-line modem diagnostic tool is **minicom**.

Note: As of this writing, only 10 percent of U.S. Internet connections use some form of high-speed (broadband) service such as cable modems, DSL, or satellite Internet. In other words, dial-up service is still a significant Linux configuration issue wherever you go.

Several Linux distributions make it easy to find the device associated with your modem. Type the **ls -l /dev/modem** command. In several Linux distributions, this device file is often linked to the actual device with your modem, such as /dev/ttyS0.

Key Utilities

Linux dial-up modem service requires a daemon and a number of utilities. As with any other form of Linux networking, the default protocol suite is TCP/IP. The protocol from TCP/IP most commonly associated with dial-up service is the Point-to-Point Protocol (PPP).

Even if you have TCP/IP installed on Linux, you also need the PPP daemon, known as **pppd**. It's usually located in the /usr/sbin directory. You can install it from the package manager supported by your Linux distribution such as **rpm** or deb. Alternatively, you can download and install the compressed archive from the official site at **ftp://cs.anu.edu.au/pub/software/ppp/**. Use the techniques discussed in Chapter 6 to install this .tar.gz package.

Several other important utilities are related to dial-up connections:

➤ *chat*—This utility allows Linux to communicate with a modem through the **pppd** daemon.

➤ *ppp-on*—This generic script can be easily modified for specific users, passwords, and Internet service providers (ISPs).

➤ *pap-secrets*—This file allows you to connect to servers that verify passwords with the password authentication protocol (PAP).

➤ *chap-secrets*—This file allows you to connect to servers that verify passwords with the challenge handshake authentication protocol (CHAP).

 | Remember that the Linux daemon associated with modem connections is **pppd**.

Graphical Tools

Two common tools for connecting to the Internet through the Linux GUI are **kppp** and **rp3**. Both offer a graphical frontend to the basic ppp utilities that Linux uses to connect to another computer or to the Internet through a modem. The **kppp** tool is associated with the KDE desktop, and the **rp3** tool is associated with the GNOME desktop. These tools are shown in Figures 10.1 and 10.2.

Both of these tools include terminal utilities that allow you to diagnose most modem problems. These tools share the same commands that you would use at a command-line interface.

minicom

One popular command-line tool for modem connections is **minicom**. You can start in a default configuration by running the **minicom -s** command as the **root** user. This starts the **minicom** configuration environment, shown in Figure 10.3.

Figure 10.1   The **kppp** tool for modem connections.

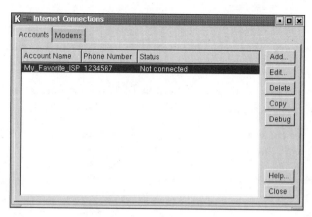

Figure 10.2 The **rp3** tool for modem connections.

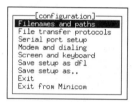

Figure 10.3 The **minicom** configuration menu.

To use **minicom**, you need to configure it through its Serial Port Setup menu. Depending on how Linux detected your modem, you may need to change the following settings from the Serial Port Setup menu:

➤ *Serial Device*—The device associated with your modem. If an **ls -1/dev/modem** command reveals a link to a device such as /dev/ttyS0, use /dev/modem. Otherwise some trial and error may be required with /dev/ttyS0 through /dev/ttyS3.

➤ *Bps/Par/Bits*—Data settings for your modem. The bits per second (Bps) data rate should be twice or even four times the speed of your modem, because modems compress data. Unless you have an older modem, the parity (Par) and stop bit (Bits) should match the default, 8N1.

Check your modem's documentation for any other settings such as bps or hardware flow control that you need to change.

Once configuration is complete, be sure to select *Save Setup As dfl*. To start troubleshooting your modem, select Exit (not Exit from Minicom). This initializes your modem and brings you to a main **minicom** screen, shown in Figure 10.4.

If you see "OK" in the **minicom** screen, it's ready. You can verify this by typing the AT command. It should return another OK.

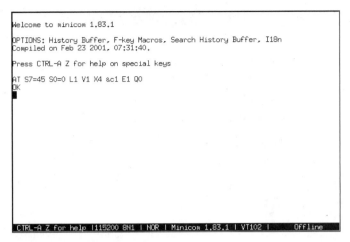

```
Welcome to minicom 1.83.1

OPTIONS: History Buffer, F-key Macros, Search History Buffer, I18n
Compiled on Feb 23 2001, 07:31:40.

Press CTRL-A Z for help on special keys

AT S7=45 S0=0 L1 V1 X4 &c1 E1 Q0
OK
```

```
CTRL-A Z for help |115200 8N1 | NOR | Minicom 1.83.1 | VT102 |      Offline
```

Figure 10.4   minicom is ready.

The most straightforward test is to try to dial your ISP. For example, if the number of your ISP is 5555-7777, type the following command:

ATDT55557777

If your modem speaker is enabled, you should hear a dial tone, followed by the beeps associated with touch-tone dialing. Ideally, your ISP will have a line free and can return a message such as this:

CONNECT 115200

Various **AT** commands can be used with other **pppd**-based utilities such as **rp3** and **kppp**. Other typical **AT** commands are shown in Table 10.1.

Keep in mind the fact that you can use the **ATDT** command to test your modem by calling a specific telephone number such as what you might use to connect to your ISP. You can do this with a command-line modem utility such as **minicom**.

You can find the assignments for a modem with the **setserial** command. For example, if your Linux distribution assigns the modem device file to /dev/modem, run the **setserial/dev/modem** command.

Table 10.1 Typical AT commands.	
Command	Description
AT	Attention
ATDT	Attention, use touch-tone dialing
ATDP	Attention, use pulse dialing
ATDT12345678	Call 12345678 using touch-tone dialing
ATDP98765432	Call 98765432 using pulse dialing
ATAO	Answer incoming modem call

Clients on a LAN

A client on a local area network (LAN) is typically a workstation. It stores shared data on servers usually connected to the same LAN. Within TCP/IP, there are two basic communication protocols for a Linux LAN: Samba and NFS. Samba is used to share directories in a mixed network of Linux and Microsoft Windows computers; NFS, the Network File System, is used to share files between Linux computers.

Note: For the purposes of setting up a LAN, Linux, Unix, and other Unix clones and derivatives (such as the Berkeley Standard Distribution [BSD] and Sun Solaris) are essentially equivalent operating systems. In other words, NFS can be used to share files between all of these systems.

In principle, a client with appropriate permissions can mount a directory from a remote server. You need an empty local directory to make this work, which is easy enough to create with the **mkdir** command, described in Chapter 7.

Samba

Sharing directories from a Samba server can be tricky. The details are beyond the scope of this book and the Linux+ exam. However, connecting to a shared Samba directory, also known as a *share*, is fairly easy. For example, if you're on a peer-to-peer network, you need only a password to connect to a Samba share. Assume there is a shared directory on another computer on the LAN. The name of the directory is Stuart, and the computer is named Lee. You want to mount it on the currently empty directory named /Jackson. You could then run the following command to connect to that share:

```
smbmount //Lee/Stuart /Jackson
```

Samba prompts you for the password for that share. Depending on permissions, you can then copy to or from that directory just as with any other directory on your system. You can unmount the shared Stuart directory from /Jackson easily with the **smbumount** command:

```
smbumount /Jackson
```

*Note: The spelling of "smbumount" may not be what you expect. In any case, there is no **smbunmount** command in Linux.*

Network File System (NFS)

Sharing directories from an NFS server can also be tricky. Fortunately, these details are also beyond the scope of this book and the Linux+ exam. Connecting to an NFS share is just as easy as connecting to a Samba share. Assume the same names apply from the example in the previous section. You could run the following command to connect to that share:

```
mount Lee:/Stuart /Jackson
```

Setting the right permissions requires additional work. The administrator of the Lee server could share the Stuart directory to allow any user to access it. That's often not desirable, however. The Network Information System (NIS) can help.

Network Information System (NIS)

The Network Information System (NIS) is designed as a central database for users and passwords on a network. You can have multiple servers with the password database. The other computers on an NIS network are clients.

With one database of users and passwords, you can have the same access to any computer on an NIS-enabled network. In other words, if you have access to the /etc directory on the local computer, you have access to the /etc directory on all other NIS-enabled computers on that network.

NIS server configuration is beyond the scope of this book and the Linux+ exam. The key daemon associated with an NIS client is **ypbind**, which binds NIS clients to NIS servers.

Note: A number of NIS-related daemons start with "yp" because this service was formally known as the "yellow pages." The name was changed for copyright reasons.

 Be sure to remember that the **ypbind** daemon ensures that NIS clients are properly connected to the NIS server on the LAN.

Client Applications

A number of applications allow client computers to connect to servers. Some clients such as Samba, NFS, FTP, and newsreaders operate at the command-line interface. The most prominent client applications are Web browsers such as Netscape, Opera, and Lynx.

Other common client applications include file managers and newsreaders. It's even possible to split the GUI into client and server components, which allows for networked graphical workstations without hard drives. A short list of typical Linux client applications is shown in Table 10.2.

 Remember the names and functions of some basic client applications, especially newsreaders.

Servers on a LAN

For every Linux client, there is a server. For example, the Samba and NFS clients need a server with a shared directory. Newsreaders such as **trn** need news servers. The Web browser needs a server such as Apache. Two of the more amazing Linux servers are Apache and Squid.

Apache

Apache serves Web pages. The configuration process on Apache is quite complex; the main configuration file, httpd.conf, would by itself take up several dozen pages in this book. The following parameters should be available in any Apache configuration file:

➤ *DocumentRoot*—Specifies the root directory for Apache HTML files. The files for the Web site should be in this directory or its subdirectories. Common locations for this directory are /home/httpd and /var/www.

Table 10.2	Typical Linux client applications.
Application	**Description**
Netscape	GUI Web browser
Opera	GUI Web browser
Lynx	Text Web browser
FTP	File transfer utility, suitable for uploads and downloads
tin	Threaded newsreader, common for newer users
trn	Threaded newsreader with different capabilities

➤ *Port*—Set to the channel associated with HTTP. As discussed in Chapter 6, these are configured in the /etc/services file. You can increase security on the Web server by changing the port here and in the /etc/services file. Your users just need to know the port number you select.

➤ *ServerName*—Set this to the name of your Web site. If you're setting up an Internet Web site, use the applicable domain name such as **mommabears.com**. On an intranet, set this to your computer's hostname.

➤ *ScriptAlias*—Specifies the directory with scripts that can customize the look and feel of the Web site for different users. The two major types of Web-related scripts are based on the Common Gateway Interface (CGI) and Active Server Pages (ASP).

Once properly configured, there should be a file such as index.html in the **DocumentRoot** directory. Then you can start Apache with the **/usr/sbin/httpd** command. If everything works, you should be able to open up an appropriate page in the local server by typing **localhost** in the browser's address or location text box. An example using the KDE Konqueror browser is shown in Figure 10.5. As shown in the figure, the **DocumentRoot** for Apache might be /home/httpd or /var/www, depending on the distribution.

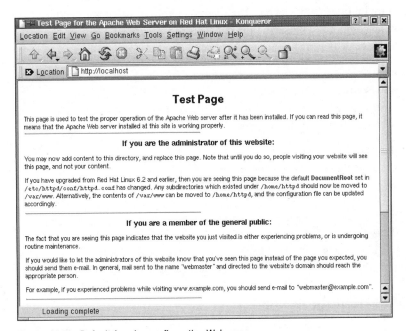

Figure 10.5 Default Apache configuration Web page.

Know that files for the Apache Web server are located in the directory specified by the **DocumentRoot** variable in the httpd.conf configuration file. Two common locations for **DocumentRoot** are /home/httpd and /var/www.

Squid

Squid serves two functions: as a proxy server and as a caching server. As a proxy server, it represents other computers on your LAN to external networks such as the Internet. As a caching server, it stores recent requests for service (and the responses) to and from your LAN. One appropriate place to install Squid is on a Linux computer that is also serving as a router, as the junction between your LAN and outside networks such as the Internet.

Normally, when you want to view a Web page, your browser sends the IP address assigned to your computer to the server that the Web page is on. If you request a Web page from behind a Squid server, Squid forwards the request with its own IP address. When the Web server returns the Web page to the router computer, Squid forwards the Web page to your computer.

As a caching server, Squid stores recently requested Web pages in its cache. If another user asks for the same Web page, Squid doesn't have to forward the request to the Internet. It can take the Web page from its cache and send it to the requesting computer. This saves time because the Web page is found on the LAN and the message doesn't have to be sent to the Internet.

Caching isn't always appropriate, however. For example, if you want a stock quote, you want realtime information, not old data from a cache. You can configure Squid to forward requests for realtime (or other) information automatically, even if a matching Web site is in its cache.

Proxy and caching services are not limited just to Web sites. Squid can be configured to fulfill these functions for any manner of requests to outside networks, including FTP, secure Web service (HTTPS), Gopher, newsreaders, and more.

 Remember that Squid can act as a proxy server and as a caching server. As a proxy server, it represents other computers on the LAN. As a caching server, it fulfills requests that would otherwise have to be transmitted to other networks such as the Internet.

Radius Remote Access

The earlier sections on modems were based on using a modem as a client to connect to a server such as that at an ISP, but modems can accept as well as receive connections. When a modem accepts a connection, it is acting as a server.

Dial-in service can help the small business that doesn't have a high-speed Internet connection. A small-business owner or employee can connect to the business LAN from a remote location such as his home. Dial-in service does not carry the security risks associated with a high-speed Internet connection. Since high-speed service is always on, crackers have more time to break into such a network.

Note: In the Linux world, crackers (not hackers) are people who try to break into computers and networks for malicious purposes.

Although you can set up Linux as a modem server by configuring various terminals, free modem servers are available, primarily FreeRADIUS and GNU Radius. Either option lets you set up and verify usernames and passwords for connecting users, also known as *authentication*.

 Be sure to remember that the primary way to set up remote access by modem is through a Radius server. Several types of Radius servers are available; all provide a way to set up usernames and passwords. In other words, they provide *authentication* services. More information on these servers is available from the Web sites listed in the Need to Know More? section at the end of this chapter.

Security

Security is an issue on any computer. If a computer has sensitive information, you may need to install it in a physically secure facility. If it is connected to any other computer, you need to be concerned about traffic coming in. If you have users who can get to outside networks such as the Internet, you need to be concerned about traffic going out. Firewalls can regulate network traffic in both directions.

Firewall Variations

Any LAN that is connected to the Internet needs a firewall. Ideally, that firewall should be located on a computer that serves as the only connection between your LAN and an outside network such as the Internet.

All computers on a TCP/IP network have an IP address. Both **ipchains** and **iptables**, introduced in Chapter 2, can regulate data transfer to or from a network. This is courtesy of the **tcp_wrappers** package, introduced in Chapter 4. The associated daemon, **tcpd**, monitors requests from other computers. Traffic can be blocked based on the following parameters (and more):

➤ *IP Address*—Regulates traffic according to the IP address of the source or destination computer.

➤ *Port*—Regulates traffic according to the port associated with the traffic. For more information, see the discussion of the /etc/services file in Chapter 6.

In principle, the best firewalls start by blocking all data in both directions. The first line in a /etc/hosts.deny file might be this:

```
ALL:ALL
```

Now that you have a solid firewall, you can set up rules to allow only certain types of network traffic through the firewall in the /etc/hosts.allow file. For example, the following line allows data transfer only to computers with the given network IP addresses:

```
127.0.0.0 192.168.0.0
```

The file with the **ipchains** and **iptables** rules should work in the same way—stop all traffic, then decide what you'll let in or out of your network.

Note: The files and utilities used to configure firewalls vary by Linux distribution.

Firewalls can also work as proxy servers; there are **ipchains** and **iptables** commands that allow the local computer to represent other computers on the LAN when communicating with other networks such as the Internet. This is known as *masquerading.*

 Know that when a firewall tool such as **ipchains** or **iptables** works as a proxy server, the proxy masquerades for all other computers on the LAN.

Denial of Service

Sometimes a cracker is not interested in getting information from you, but only in sabotage. Although you should be concerned about traffic such as computer viruses and Trojan horses, that is beyond the scope of the Linux+ exam. One other major form of sabotage is known as *Denial of Service* (DoS), which loads your network with large or repetitive messages to the exclusion of all other business.

Unfortunately, DoS attacks are easy. They are common attacks by less-experienced users who just want to "make their mark." When successful, they can prevent real users from accessing your Web sites. The most common DoS attack is based on **ping**, which checks for a valid connection path between two computers. If you have a connection to the Internet, try this command from the command-line interface:

```
ping somewebsite
```

Where *somewebsite* is the Web site of your choice. When you **ping** a Web site, that site responds to verify the connection. Notice that this command usually doesn't stop unless you press Ctrl+C. Imagine what would happen if hundreds or thousands of pings were aimed at one Web site simultaneously. That much traffic would keep a Web site too busy to respond to any regular user.

One common way to start a DoS attack is with a script, written in a programming language such as Perl, that is set up to **ping** a Web site but doesn't actually allow a connection. Some DoS attacks set the return IP address to other computers inside the Web site's LAN. The Web site responds to the **ping**. The effect of the **ping** is multiplied by the number of computers on the LAN. This can easily crowd out any user who is really trying to reach that Web site.

Remember that a typical Denial of Service attack includes attempts to connect with commands such as **ping**. However, no actual network connection is ever made. The traffic caused by the attempts to connect keeps the attacked Web server so busy that regular users aren't able to access it.

Practice Questions

Question 1

> Which of the following utilities can be used to test a modem on any Linux distribution?
>
> ○ a. **modemconf**
>
> ○ b. **/dev/modem**
>
> ○ c. **modemcom**
>
> ○ d. **minicom**

Answer d is correct. The **minicom** utility is normally used in Linux to configure and troubleshoot a modem. The **modemconf** module is part of the Linuxconf configuration utility, most commonly associated with Red Hat Linux. Although it is possible to install Linuxconf on other Linux distributions, it doesn't normally come with many Linux distributions. Therefore, answer a is incorrect. The /dev/modem file is the device most commonly associated with a modem. Although it is usually linked to the actual modem device file, it is not related to configuring that or any other modem. Therefore, answer b is incorrect. No **modemcom** utility exists, so answer c is also incorrect.

Question 2

> Which of the following variables in the Apache configuration file, httpd.conf, points to the directory with the home page used for the Web server?
>
> ○ a. **DocumentRoot**
>
> ○ b. **Port**
>
> ○ c. **ScriptAlias**
>
> ○ d. **ServerRoot**

Answer a is correct. In the httpd.conf configuration file, the **DocumentRoot** variable is set to the directory with the Web site's home page. Other pages on that Web site can be in subdirectories of **DocumentRoot**. Since **Port** in httpd.conf is the TCP/IP port used to access Web sites on that Apache server, it is unrelated to the location of a directory. Therefore, answer b is incorrect. **ScriptAlias** is set to the directory with CGI or ASP scripts, which is usually different from the directory with the Web site home page. Therefore, answer c is also incorrect. **ServerRoot** specifies the directory with the Apache configuration file, which is usually different from the directory with the Web site home page, so answer d is also incorrect.

Question 3

Which of the following text commands would you use to dial the number of your ISP on a telephone that cannot handle touch-tone service? Assume that the local number you use to access your ISP is 87654321.

○ a. **AT 87654321**

○ b. **ATDP 87654321**

○ c. **ATDT**

○ d. **ATDT 87654321**

Answer b is correct. If your telephone does not have touch-tone service, your modem needs to dial using old-style pulses. This is accomplished with the **ATDP** command, which is short for ATtention, Dial Pulse. Answer a doesn't include any command such as **DT** or **DP** for dialing the number of your ISP, so it is incorrect. Answer c doesn't include the telephone number of your ISP, so the modem can't know what to dial. Therefore, it is also incorrect. Answer d uses touch-tone dialing. Because your telephone system cannot handle touch-tone service, it is also incorrect.

Question 4

Which of the following functions of the Squid server can be addressed by a command such as **ipchains** or **iptables**?

○ a. Caching service

○ b. Name service

○ c. IP addressing

○ d. Proxy service

Answer d is correct. Squid can be used as a proxy server, which means that it can represent other computers on its LAN for requests to other networks such as the Internet. Similarly, the **ipchains** or **iptables** commands can be used to allow the local computer to masquerade as any other computer on the LAN, which is effectively the same thing as a proxy server. Since neither **ipchains** nor **iptables** has any caching capabilities, answer a is incorrect. Name service is associated with the Domain Name Service (DNS). Since none of the services mentioned in the question include DNS functions, answer b is incorrect. Although the Dynamic Host Configuration Protocol (DHCP) is associated with assigning IP addresses, none of the services mentioned in the question include DHCP functionality. Therefore, answer c is also incorrect.

Question 5

You've just taken a job at the help desk of an Internet service provider. You've received a call from a user who is unable to log on to your system. Which of the following provides the most likely solution?

- ○ a. Reboot the modem server
- ○ b. Restart the Radius system
- ○ c. Use **minicom** to check problems with your modem server
- ○ d. Set up a proxy server to handle authentication

Answer b is correct. Radius is a common Linux modem and authentication server. Since some other modem servers might not include authentication, answer a is incorrect. **minicom** addresses modem configuration and hardware problems. Because this is unrelated to authentication (usernames and passwords), answer c is incorrect. Proxy servers don't handle authentication either, so answer d is also incorrect.

Question 6

Which of the following command utilities makes sure that an NIS client is properly associated with an NIS server on a LAN?

- ○ a. **ypconf**
- ○ b. **nisbind**
- ○ c. **ypbind**
- ○ d. **nfsd**

Answer c is correct. The **ypbind** daemon is the NIS client that also ensures that clients are properly bound to NIS servers. Remember, the Network Information System (NIS) provides a single database of users and passwords on a LAN. Protocols such as the Network File System (NFS) can use NIS for one set of permissions on shared directories on a LAN. There is no **ypconf** utility or daemon, so answer a is incorrect. And there is no **nisbind** utility or daemon, so answer b is incorrect. Although **nfsd** is the NFS daemon, it is not directly related to binding between clients and servers within the NIS. Therefore, answer d is also incorrect.

Question 7

Which of the following is required for a proper modern telephone modem connection?

○ a. pppd

○ b. COM1

○ c. /dev/modem

○ d. Squid

Answer a is correct. The Point-to-Point Protocol daemon (**pppd**) is required to use modern telephone modems on Linux. COM ports are required by many modems, though not all. In addition, not all modems use COM1. For both reasons, answer b is incorrect. While the /dev/modem file is commonly linked to the modem device, this file is only a convenience and is not used by all Linux distributions. Therefore, answer c is incorrect. Since Squid is a proxy server unrelated to modem connections, answer d is also incorrect.

Question 8

Which of the following is a typical directory location for **DocumentRoot** in an Apache server? [Check all correct answers]

☐ a. /usr/httpd

☐ b. /var/www

☐ c. /httpd

☐ d. /home/httpd

Answers b and d are correct. The /var/www and /home/httpd directories are typical locations for the **DocumentRoot** variable, which points to the location of the files associated with a Web site home page. Although you could create the directories in answers a and c, they are less commonly used; therefore, answers a and c are incorrect.

Question 9

Which of the following statements is most characteristic of a Denial of Service attack?

○ a. No traffic is allowed through to a Web site because of physical sabotage of the network connections.

○ b. A remote program sends a stream of messages to a Web site, overloading the network lines without ever creating a connection.

○ c. A cracker breaks into the files of an Internet service provider (ISP). The files with Radius authentication information are deleted, which keeps users from accessing the Internet through that ISP.

○ d. An inexperienced computer user downloads a Trojan horse with instructions on how to plant it on a business network.

Answer b is correct. A Denial of Service (DoS) attack is a fairly simple attack in which a large number of simultaneous attempts are made to verify the connection with commands such as **ping**. A full connection is never made; the result is that regular traffic attempting to connect to the targeted Web site is blocked. Although physical sabotage may deny service to the targeted Web server, it does not fit the common definition of a DoS attack. Therefore, answer a is incorrect. ISP authentication information is unrelated to DoS attacks, so answer c is incorrect. Although certain kinds of Trojan horse programs can help create a DoS attack, it is far from the only use of a Trojan horse program. Therefore, answer d is also incorrect.

Question 10

Which of the following is a common Linux newsreader?

○ a. trn

○ b. newsd

○ c. deb

○ d. listserv

Answer a is correct. The **trn** is the threaded Internet newsreader. Since there is no newsd newsreader or news daemon, answer b is incorrect. Since deb is a type of package common to the Debian and related Linux distributions, it also is not a newsreader. Therefore, answer c is also incorrect. Although listserv is a mailing list software package suitable for creating news-type messages, it is not a newsreader. Therefore, answer d is also incorrect.

Need to Know More?

 Hunt, Craig. *Linux Network Servers.* Alameda, CA: Sybex, 1999. ISBN 0-78212-506-9. An excellent book that describes the details of how to set up network services, with many substantive examples.

 Ziegler, Robert L. *Linux Firewalls.* Indianapolis, IN: New Riders Publishing, 2000. ISBN 0-73570-900-9. A fantastic, detailed guide to creating a firewall with the **ipchains** command utility. A second edition of this book is in progress at the time of this writing. I anticipate that it will cover **iptables**, virtual private networks, and secure shells equally well.

 Explore some of the free and commercial Radius-type servers for receiving modem connections to a Linux computer. You can review two of the more prominent efforts at **www.freeradius.org** and **www.gnu.org/software/radius/radius.html**.

 Review the documentation and download the software associated with the Apache Web server at **httpd.apache.org**. As of this writing, Apache is the market leader in Web servers. The details of Apache point to its flexibility, which is desired by Webmasters who want the flexibility to meet the needs of their customers.

 Explore the HOWTO for modems through the Linux Documentation Project at **www.linuxdoc.org/HOWTO/Modem-HOWTO.html**. This document includes a detailed discussion of modem configuration, partially in the context of the minicom utility.

 Explore the home page of the main Linux proxy server at **www.squid-cache.org**. This site includes documentation on how to set up Squid as both a proxy server, which can represent all of the computers on a LAN on external networks such as the Internet, and a caching server, which can store commonly viewed Web pages for faster service to its LAN.

Basic System Administration

Terms you'll need to understand:

- ✓ Virtual console
- ✓ Multitasking
- ✓ Multiuser
- ✓ Multiterminal
- ✓ User, group
- ✓ Account
- ✓ Password
- ✓ Shadow Password Suite
- ✓ **pwconv**
- ✓ **pwunconv**

- ✓ **gpconv**
- ✓ **gpunconv**
- ✓ /etc/shadow, /etc/gshadow
- ✓ **umask**
- ✓ **chown**, **chmod**, **chgrp**
- ✓ Permissions
- ✓ SUID, SGID
- ✓ **su**
- ✓ **sudo**, /etc/sudoers

Techniques you'll need to master:

- ✓ Using virtual consoles
- ✓ Understanding multitasking, multiterminal, and multiuser characteristics
- ✓ Administering users and groups
- ✓ Disabling user accounts

- ✓ Working with shadow passwords
- ✓ Setting file, directory, and superuser permissions
- ✓ Protecting critical files with the immutable flag
- ✓ Using superuser power responsibly

If you fit the target profile for the Linux+ exam, you have some of the skills associated with aspiring Linux system administrators. You want to demonstrate that you have some of the basic skills to administer a Linux system with users and groups.

Linux is a multitasking, multiuser, multiterminal system. When set up with appropriate accounts, users can log in with secure passwords. When files and directories are set up with appropriate permissions, they are secure; necessary applications and utilities are accessible to appropriate users. Although it is easy to get **root** user privileges with the **su** command, some additional skills and tools are required to administer a system responsibly as the **root** user.

The Multitasking, Multiuser, Multiterminal System

Although Linux can be the backbone of an excellent workstation, it also has all of the capabilities of a server. Because it can share resources among multiple programs, it is multitasking. Because it can handle simultaneous logons from multiple users, it is multiuser. And because there are multiple terminals available for one or more users, it is multiterminal. In other words, it is a multitasking, multiuser, multiterminal operating system.

Virtual Consoles

It is easy to log in more than once into a Linux computer. All you need to do is open up a new terminal, also known as a *virtual console*. Most Linux distributions are set up through the /etc/inittab file with four or more virtual consoles, accessible on the local computer. An example of this file is shown in Figure 11.1.

```
# getty-programs for the normal runlevels
# <id>:<runlevels>:<action>:<process>
# The "id" field MUST be the same as the last
# characters of the device (after "tty").
1:2345:respawn:/sbin/mingetty --noclear tty1
2:2345:respawn:/sbin/mingetty tty2
3:2345:respawn:/sbin/mingetty tty3
4:2345:respawn:/sbin/mingetty tty4
5:2345:respawn:/sbin/mingetty tty5
6:2345:respawn:/sbin/mingetty tty6
#S0:12345:respawn:/sbin/agetty -L 9600 ttyS0

# modem getty.
# mo:235:respawn:/usr/sbin/mgetty -s 38400 modem

# fax getty (hylafax)
# mo:35:respawn:/usr/lib/fax/faxgetty /dev/modem

# vbox (voice box) getty
# I6:35:respawn:/usr/sbin/vboxgetty -d /dev/ttyI6
# I7:35:respawn:/usr/sbin/vboxgetty -d /dev/ttyI7

# end of /etc/inittab
~
~
~
```

Figure 11.1   Console setup in /etc/inittab.

The command that starts different consoles is known as a *getty*. Based on the example, you could log into six different virtual consoles, each started by the **mingetty** commands shown in Figure 11.1. Just press Ctrl+Alt+F*n*, where *n* is typically one of the function keys between 1 and 6. Figure 11.1 illustrates consoles based on modem, fax, and even vbox, which is an answering machine for Linux. It's also possible to set up consoles on remote computers connected via serial cables or network cards.

The use of multiple virtual consoles allow you to run several programs simultaneously. Alternately, if a program gets out of control, you can open up a second virtual console to **kill** the associated PID (process identifier), as discussed in Chapter 8.

Multiple Logins

Linux is a true multiuser system. Multiple users can work on the same Linux computer, from different terminals, simultaneously. Individual users can also log in several times from the same account.

When logging in at a text console, one thing all users see is the message of the day (motd), stored in the /etc/motd file. You can edit this file with your text editor and add the message of your choice for your users. For example, if you were to add the message "There will be milk and cookies at 3 PM today in room 222" to /etc/motd, you would see something like Figure 11.2 when you log on. Just remember to change or delete the /etc/motd file when the current message expires.

> Be sure to remember that all users who log on at the command-line interface will see the message of the day from the /etc/motd file.

Users and Groups

Anyone who logs on to a Linux system needs a user account. Every user belongs to a group. Users and groups have rights and privileges that may differ by directory. Users have usernames, passwords, and home directories. You can create,

```
Welcome to SuSE Linux 7.2 (i386) - Kernel 2.4.4-4GB (tty4).

linux login: mj
Password:
Last login: Tue Aug 14 17:28:03 on tty4
There will be milk and cookies at 3 pm today in room 222.
mj@linux:~ > _
```

Figure 11.2   A logon with the message of the day (motd).

modify, disable, and delete users or groups. User and group information is stored in the /etc/passwd and /etc/group files.

Passwords

As discussed in Chapter 10, *authentication* enables you to verify usernames and passwords. Linux authentication is most closely associated with the /etc/passwd file, which includes data for every user on the Linux system. As you can see from Figure 11.3, the typical /etc/passwd file includes users associated with critical services, such as **mail, news, ftp,** and **apache.** Each line includes seven columns; each column is divided by a colon (:). Table 11.1 describes these columns based on the last entry in Figure 11.3, which includes information for user **tr.**

By default, the latest Linux distributions don't allow simple passwords such as dictionary words or simple patterns such as "abcd". There are readily available password-cracking programs that can decipher such passwords in minutes. In contrast, the best passwords are based on a combination of upper- and lowercase letters and numbers; such passwords can take weeks for the same programs to decipher. One easy way to set up such passwords is based on a favorite sentence; for example, "OJ6lh4hr" could stand for "On July 6, I hit 4 home runs."

Creating New Users

Several different ways exist for adding users. You can even add a new user by directly editing /etc/passwd. That is not necessary, however. The main command

```
root:$1$Bd7subP6$UpA51KeDj253VnSxRIBMR.:0:0:root:/root:/bin/bash
bin:*:1:1:bin:/bin:
daemon:*:2:2:daemon:/sbin:
adm:*:3:4:adm:/var/adm:
lp:*:4:7:lp:/var/spool/lpd:
sync:*:5:0:sync:/sbin:/bin/sync
shutdown:*:6:0:shutdown:/sbin:/sbin/shutdown
halt:*:7:0:halt:/sbin:/sbin/halt
mail:*:8:12:mail:/var/spool/mail:
news:*:9:13:news:/var/spool/news:
uucp:*:10:14:uucp:/var/spool/uucp:
operator:*:11:0:operator:/root:
games:*:12:100:games:/usr/games:
gopher:*:13:30:gopher:/usr/lib/gopher-data:
ftp:*:14:50:FTP User:/home/ftp:
nobody:*:99:99:Nobody:/█
nscd:!!:28:28:NSCD Daemon:/:/bin/false
mailnull:!!:47:47::/var/spool/mqueue:/dev/null
ident:!!:98:98:pident user:/:/bin/false
rpc:!!:32:32:Portmapper RPC user:/:/bin/false
rpcuser:!!:29:29:RPC Service User:/var/lib/nfs:/bin/false
xfs:!!:43:43:X Font Server:/etc/X11/fs:/bin/false
gdm:!!:42:42::/home/gdm:/bin/bash
apache:!!:48:48:Apache:/var/www:/bin/false
mj:$1$bExrfrAL#XuB9.adrxu51vlNuRbbb8.:500:500:Michael Jang:/home/mj:/bin/bash
tr:$1$gOLBGtL3$y2ScUF71kgq3iZwIScuFr1:501:501::/home/tr:/bin/bash
~
"/etc/passwd" 26L, 1044C
```

Figure 11.3   A typical /etc/passwd file.

Column	Example	Function
1	**tr**	Username
2	1EW5dr	Encrypted password
3	501	User ID
4	501	Group ID
5	Theodore Roosevelt	Information about the user
6	/home/tr	The user's home directory
7	**/bin/bash**	The user's login shell

Table 11.1   /etc/passwd columns.

in use today is **useradd**. The simplest way to create an account for user **tr** with this command is as follows:

```
useradd tr
```

This command adds a home directory for **tr** as well as an entry in the /etc/passwd file. By default, the contents of the new home directory are taken from the files in the /etc/skel directory. Compare the contents of /etc/skel with your own home directory. If your username is **tr,** make the comparison with the following commands:

```
ls -a /etc/skel
ls -a /home/tr
```

Note: This does not apply to S.uS.E., as of this writing.

If you haven't made many configuration changes, the hidden files that you see from both commands should be similar. Remember, hidden files start with a dot (.) and are shown when you run the **ls** command with the -**a** switch.

 Be sure to remember that when you create a new user, the default files for that user's home directory are copied from the /etc/skel directory.

Unfortunately, the **useradd tr** command isn't enough; before user **tr** can log in to his account, you need to add a password. The easiest way to do this is with the **passwd tr** command. You can then enter a password on behalf of **tr**. Next, tell **tr** to use the **passwd** command to change his password, keeping in mind the anticracking tips provided in the previous section.

Know that when you use the **useradd** command, the new account isn't usable until you've assigned a password.

You can review the **useradd** defaults with the **useradd -D** command. If you need to change these, a number of **useradd** switches are available. These are shown in Table 11.2.

Although there is a **-p** switch for assigning passwords, it doesn't work for most current Linux distributions, because passwords are encrypted by default.

Note: The **useradd** *command is the successor to* **adduser**. *Both were used in similar ways; the original* **adduser** *command created new users based on defaults in an /etc/adduser.conf configuration file.*

Modifying Existing Users

When you modify an existing user account, you're usually modifying one of three things: passwords, group membership, or personal information.

Modifying passwords is easy. If you're modifying your own password, just run the **passwd** command. You're prompted to enter your existing password, followed by your new password, twice. The **root** user can modify any user's password. For example, if user **tr** forgets his password, run the following command:

```
passwd tr
```

You're not even prompted for **tr**'s old password. Imagine the havoc someone could cause as the **root** user!

To modify group membership, open up the /etc/passwd file in a text editor. As shown previously in Table 11.1, the fourth column corresponds to the group ID

Table 11.2	useradd switches.
Switch	**Function**
-G *group_number*	Assign the new user to ***group_number***. The specified group should already exist.
-n	Negates Red Hat Linux group assignment behavior. Otherwise, Red Hat Linux assigns the same group ID (GID) and user ID (UID) numbers by default.
-u *user_id*	Assign the new user a specific UID number, ***user_id***.
-s *shell*	Specifies a different shell from the default. The absolute path should be listed to the shell executable file, for instance, /bin/ash.

(GID) number. Valid groups are documented in the /etc/group file, discussed later in this chapter in the section "Creating and Modifying Groups."

Modifying personal information is easier. Use your text editor to modify the fifth column for the desired user. Most user characteristics in other columns can be changed in the same way.

Disabling Accounts

Sometimes you temporarily want to keep a user from logging into your Linux computer. For example, you might not want to delete the account of an ISP user who hasn't paid his bill, at least not immediately. It is easy to disable accounts in Linux. Just open up the /etc/passwd file in a text editor and replace the second column (the password column) with an asterisk (*). For account **mj**, the line in /etc/passwd might look like the following:

```
mj:*:500:100:Michael Jang:/home/mj:/bin/bash
```

The account and home directory are still available; user **mj** just won't be able to log in to that account with any password.

 Know that two ways to disable an acount in the /etc/psswd file is to substitute an asterisk (*) for the encrypted password in the second column, or to substitute a script for the shell in the seventh column. The script can tell the user what he needs to do before you restore the account.

Deleting Users

It is easy to delete users from Linux with the **userdel** command. If user **tr** has left the company, you'll probably want to delete his account. After retrieving any files you may need from his home directory, the following command deletes **tr**'s information from /etc/passwd, as well as all files and subdirectories in the /home/tr directory:

```
userdel -r tr
```

Creating and Modifying Groups

It is easy to create a group. Just use the **groupadd** command. For example, if you want to add a group named **drafters**, the following command should work:

```
groupadd drafters
```

Except in Red Hat Linux, any new group automatically gets the first available group ID (GID) number above 99. In current versions of Red Hat Linux, the applicable number is 499. You can see this for yourself in the /etc/group file. For example, here is a typical line from this file for the **users** group:

```
users:x:100:mj,tr
```

This specifies a group with a GID of 100 and two users, **mj** and **tr**. The "x" tells you that the group password is encrypted in the /etc/gshadow file. If you open this file in a text editor, you can modify the name of the group, the GID, and the users who belong to this group.

You can delete a group with the **groupdel** command.

Using the Shadow Password Suite

The commands you've used so far to manage users and groups are part of the Shadow Password Suite. However, these are standard administrative commands. One way you can go further is by encrypting user and group passwords in the /etc/shadow and /etc/gshadow files, respectively.

Although any user can read the /etc/passwd and /etc/group files, only the **root** user has the permissions to read the /etc/shadow and /etc/gshadow files, which contain encrypted passwords.

 Keep in mind the fact that the user and group files created though the Shadow Password Suite (/etc/shadow, /etc/gshadow) have more restrictive permissions than their companion files (/etc/passwd, /etc/group). Only the **root** user is allowed to view these files.

The key commands in the Shadow Password Suite are as follows:

➤ pwconv—Converts an existing /etc/passwd file. Passwords that currently exist in /etc/passwd are replaced by an "x"; relevant information is transferred to the /etc/shadow file. If you've recently added new users by editing the /etc/passwd file in a text editor, you can run this command again to convert the passwords associated with any new users. This works even if other passwords are already encrypted.

➤ pwunconv—Reverses the process of the **pwconv** command.

➤ grpconv—Converts an existing /etc/group file; similar to **pwconv**. The relevant information is transferred to the /etc/gshadow file.

➤ grpunconv—Reverses the process of the **grpconv** command.

 Remember that the **pwconv** and **grpconv** commands are used to convert /etc/passwd and /etc/group to conform to the Shadow Password Suite.

Managing Permissions and Ownership

Everything in Linux is a file. Directories, drivers, and links are all just special kinds of files. What you can do with Linux depends on the permissions and ownership of each file. You can set default permissions with the **umask** command; you can change these permissions with the **chmod** command. The owner and group associated with each file can be modified with the **chown** and **chgrp** commands.

Permissions

First, you need to know how file permissions work in Linux. Start by trying out the **ls -l** command in your home directory. You'll see a series of lines such as the following associated with the bigshot file:

```
-rwxr-xr--   1   mj   users   4322   Aug   15   12:44   bigshot
```

The permissions for the bigshot file are shown in the 10 characters at the beginning of this line. Since the first character is a dash (-), this is a regular file. Among other things, it could represent a directory (**d**), a linked file (**l**), or a device (**c**). The remaining nine characters are grouped in threes; the first three are permissions for the file owner, the second three are permissions for the group owner, and the final three are permissions for all other users. In other words, the owner of this file (**mj**) can read (**r**), write (**w**), and/or execute (**x**) this file.

The middle three characters, in this case, **r-x**, allow all users in the **users** group to read (**r**) and/or execute (**x**) this file.

The last three characters, in this case, **r--**, allow all other users on this Linux computer to read this file. These other users are not allowed to write to this file, nor are they allowed to execute it if it is a script.

Note: To read the files in a directory, you need read (r) and execute (x) permissions.

chmod

You can change these permissions with the **chmod** command. For example, you might run the following command on the bigshot file:

```
chmod 761 bigshot
```

This revises the permissions associated with the bigshot file based on the three-number code described in Table 11.3. In this case, the first number (**7**) represents the new permissions for the owner; the second number (**6**) represents the new permissions for the group; and the third number (**1**) represents the new permissions for all other users.

Table 11.3	chmod permissions.	
Permission	**Number**	**Comment**
r	4	= r(4)
w	2	= w(2)
x	1	= x(1)
rx	5	= r(4) + x(1)
rw	6	= r(4) + w(2)
wx	3	= w(2) + x(1)
rwx	7	= r(4) + w(2) + x(1)

Observe how the number is based on the combined values of permissions; for example, the number associated with rx (5) is 4 (the value of r) + 1 (the value of x).

Reexamine the permissions associated with the bigshot file. Based on the chmod command, the owner (**7**) acquires read, write, and execute permissions. The users who are members of the **users** group (**6**) get read and write permissions. Finally, all other users are allowed only execute permission for the bigshot file.

umask

It would be best if you didn't have to use the **chmod** command to set file permissions all the time. The **umask** command sets the default permissions for all new files. When you type the **umask** command alone, you'll get an output like the following:

026

To understand this number, you need a clear understanding of the numeric value associated with permissions. Reread the previous section if necessary.

When the **umask** command is applied to a new file, you can get the default permissions by subtracting the **umask** value from 777. For the cited value of **umask**, 026, the default numeric permissions are 777–026=751.

Based on Table 11.3, this corresponds to read, write, and execute permissions for the file owner; read and execute permissions for other members of the same group as the file owner; and execute permission for all other users on that Linux computer.

Understand that default permissions for new files are based on the value of **umask**. For example, if **umask** returns 023, the numeric value of default permissions for newly created files is 754 (=777–023), which corresponds to read, write, and execute (**rwx**) permissions for the owner; read and execute (**rx**) permissions for the group; and read permission (**r**) for all other users.

chown

The **chown** command changes the owner of a file. If you assign a file to a new owner, that user gets all of the permissions associated with the owner of that file. To illustrate this, review the **ls -l** output for the bigshot file:

```
-rwxr-xr--  1  mj  users  4322  Aug  15  12:44  bigshot
```

The current owner of this file is user **mj**. If you were to run the **chown tr bigshot** command, user **tr** would take over ownership of bigshot, with read, write, and execute permissions on that file.

chgrp

The **chgrp** command changes the group owner of a file. The owner or the **root** user can change the group associated with a particular file.

In other words, if you were to run the **chgrp drafters bigshot** command, the new group owner would be **drafters**. The user **mj** does not have to be a member of the **drafters** group to make this work.

Every user who is a part of the **drafters** group would have read and execute permissions on the bigshot file.

Selective **Root** Permissions

The **root** user owns many of the executable files, utilities, and applications in Linux. Sometimes you want regular users to be able to run these files. You could give these users the **root** password, but that could cause trouble. The alternative is to selectively give users superuser power over these selected files, utilities, and applications.

As an example, examine **kppp**, which is the application for connecting to the Internet in the K Desktop Environment. The **ls -l** command on this file typically reveals the following:

```
-rwxr-xr-x  1 root  root  468313  June 22 10:13 /usr/sbin/kppp
```

Since individual users would want to configure their own ISPs on **kppp**, they need write access. That works for the **root** user and for other users if you set the SUID (set user ID) bit. To accomplish this on **kppp**, run the following command:

```
chmod u+s /usr/sbin/kppp
```

When you run the **ls -l** command again on **kppp**, you see the following:

```
-rwsr-xr-x  1 root  root  468313  June 22 10:13 /usr/sbin/kppp
```

Now all users get the same permissions as the **root** user. They can access **kppp** without knowing the **root** user password.

 Know how to use the **chmod u+s** *program* command to share access to a program owned by the **root** user. This command allows all users to run this *program*.

A similar scenario is when you're rolling out the installation of a new application to all users. You've just completed testing this new application to your local group of administrators. Call this application **helper**. Assume you get the following from the **ls -l** command:

```
-rwxrwx--x  1 root    root    643213  Aug 12 09:22 /usr/sbin/helper
```

To allow all users who are not in the same group as the **root** user to run this program, set the SGID (set group ID) bit. To accomplish this on the hypothetical **helper** application, run the following command:

```
chmod g+s /usr/sbin/helper
```

 Know how to use the **chmod g+s** *program* command to share a program owned by a specific group. This command allows all users to run this *program*.

A critical security issue is SUID and SGID files in users' home directories. If a file with a set ID bit exists in any user's home directory, it can provide a means for an outside user to gain **root** user access on your Linux system. This is a form of Trojan horse. For example, if you see something similar to the following file on any individual user's home directory, be afraid:

```
-r-xr-xrws  1 root    root    643213  Aug 12 09:22 ls
```

In this case, the set bit is associated with other's permissions. If the affected user's home directory is on the **$PATH** described in Chapter 7, then, when any user runs the **ls** command, he ends up running this command from this directory. This could send a file list from every user who tries to run **ls** to a cracker. Imagine the effect if there were a **su** command with similar permissions on someone's home directory. That script could send the **root** user's password to a cracker.

Remember to watch for files owned by the **root** user on individual users' directories. If any file has the SUID, SGID, or a similar bit specified, a cracker will be able to access this file from any account. This can also give that cracker **root** user privileges, which would allow him free reign over your Linux computer.

The SUID and SGID bits can also be critical security issues. Their use should be kept to an absolute minimum. Do not use SUID or SGID on a script unless absolutely necessary. However, one command where SUID is necessary is **passwd**, which allows users to set their own passwords.

Superuser Power

Even if you own the **root** user account for a Linux computer, don't use this account unless absolutely necessary. Many things can go wrong when you're the superuser. As suggested in earlier chapters, you can start as a regular user and invoke the **su** command to go into superuser mode when necessary. However, since you then would have to log out as the superuser, this entails risk as well. You can reduce the risk by setting the *immutable flag* on critical files. You can reduce the risk one step further by using the **sudo** or **su=c** command to limit the use of superuser power to specific situations.

Risky Business

As discussed in Chapter 7, the **rm** command can be risky when run as the **root** user. Just one misplaced space can result in the deletion of all files and directories on your Linux system. Among other things, mistakes when you're running as the **root** user or superuser can result in the following:

➤ Lost files and directories for individual users

➤ Damage to critical configuration files such as /etc/passwd, which can prevent logons by any user

➤ Security breaches associated with **root** user–owned files on individual user directories

Any of these conditions can be trouble. Imagine what would happen if a cracker got hold of the **root** user password even for just a short time.

Immutability

An *immutable* file cannot be changed or deleted, even by the **root** user. Although the **alias rm='rm -i'** setting prompts the user to confirm a deletion, the **rm -rf** command still overrides this alias. However, even this command can't delete an immutable file. You can set the immutable flag with the **chattr +i** command. For example, the following command protects the /etc/inittab file:

```
chattr +i /etc/inittab
```

Note: For more information on **rm** *and aliases, see Chapter 7.*

If you then tried to delete this file with the **rm -rf /etc/inittab** command, it would not work. The immutable flag causes **rm** to return the following message:

```
rm: cannot unlink '/etc/inittab': Operation not permitted
```

 Remember that when you set the immutable flag on a file with the **chattr +i** *filename* command, even the **root** user isn't allowed to delete that file.

If you want to revise the /etc/inittab file, you should first unset the immutable flag, in this case with the following command:

```
chattr -i /etc/inittab
```

Temporary Superusers

There are three major ways to run commands as the **root** user on a temporary basis. You could log in with the **su** command and the **root** password, but that involves risk until you log out of the **root** account. The other two ways are safer:

➤ **su -c** *"command"*—With the -c switch, **su** runs the command enclosed in double quotes for that one command only. You are prompted to verify the command with the **root** password. When the command is complete, Linux returns you to the regular account.

➤ **sudo**—With the **sudo** (superuser do) command, users specified in the /etc/sudoers file can run commands as the **root** user, within limits.

For example, the /etc/shadow file is normally accessible only to the **root** user. If you tried to open this as a regular user in the **vi** editor with the **vi /etc/shadow** command, you would get the following message:

```
"/etc/shadow" [Permission Denied]
```

However, the following command prompts you for the **root** password. If you enter the correct password, it works:

```
su -c "vi /etc/shadow"
```

Alternatively, if your username is properly configured in the /etc/sudoers file, you could run the following command (**sudo** doesn't require the double quotes):

```
sudo vi /etc/shadow
```

The first time you use **sudo**, you're prompted for a password. If your username is not properly configured in /etc/sudoers, it returns a message similar to the following:

```
mj is not in the sudoers file. This incident will be reported.
```

*Note: You can edit the /etc/sudoers file as the **root** user or superuser with the **visudo** command. The details of /etc/sudoers configuration are beyond the scope of this book and the Linux+ exam.*

 Remember how to use the **su -c** and **sudo** commands. They can be used to run commands or edit files normally accessible only to the **root** user or superuser.

Practice Questions

Question 1

As a new Linux system administrator, you have been asked by your supervisor to make sure all new users get a copy of the employee benefits policies in their home directories. These documents are several dozen pages in length. Where would you put these files?

- ○ a. /etc/motd
- ○ b. /home
- ○ c. /etc/passwd
- ○ d. /etc/skel

Answer d is correct. By default, new users get the files and directories contained in the /etc/skel directory. Since the /etc/motd file contains the message of the day, it can be used to share information with users. However, it is what all users see when they log on to Linux. Several dozen pages of documents in the logon message would not be the most productive use of your users' time. Therefore, answer a is incorrect. Although all users have access to the /home directory, that directory is not in the home directory for any specific user. (Specific user home directories have names such as /home/mj or /home/tr.) Therefore, answer b is incorrect. Since the /etc/passwd file is dedicated to storing user and password information, that is the wrong place for documents. Therefore, answer c is also incorrect.

Question 2

Which of the following statements best describes the differences between the /etc/passwd and /etc/shadow files? Hint: /etc/shadow is part of the Shadow Password Suite.

- ○ a. All users can read the /etc/passwd file; only the **root** user is allowed to read the /etc/shadow file.
- ○ b. All users can read the /etc/shadow file; only the **root** user is allowed to read the /etc/passwd file.
- ○ c. All users can read both the /etc/shadow and /etc/passwd files.
- ○ d. The immutable flag is set by default on /etc/shadow; until you remove this flag, no user can read this file.

Answer a is correct. By default, all users can read the /etc/passwd file. The Shadow Password Suite increases security by allowing only the **root** user to read the /etc/shadow file. Since only the **root** user can read /etc/shadow, answers b and c are both incorrect. While it's a good idea to set the immutable flag on /etc/shadow, it is not set by default. Even if this were the case, the **root** user can still read /etc/shadow. Therefore, answer d is also incorrect.

Question 3

One of your co-workers, A. Earhart, is starting a new project. She wants your help in setting up a directory, where she alone can create and modify files. Her home directory is /home/aearhart. Her project team includes users **owright**, **jyeagar**, and **jglenn**; all including **aearhart** are members of the **avion** group. They should have read and execute access to the project files. The files in the new directory should be invisible to other users on the Linux system. Which of the following actions would create the directory with the appropriate permissions?

- ○ a. Use **mkdir /home/aearhart/project** to set up the shared directory. Use the **chmod 770 /home/aearhart/project** command to set appropriate permissions.

- ○ b. Use **cd /home/aearhart/project** to set up the shared directory. Use the **chmod 750 /home/aearhart/project** command to set appropriate permissions.

- ○ c. Use **rmdir /home/aearhart/project** to set up the shared directory. Use the **umask 750 /home/aearhart/project** command to set appropriate permissions.

- ○ d. Use **mkdir /home/aearhart/project** to set up the shared directory. Use the **chmod 750 /home/aearhart/project** command to set appropriate permissions.

Answer d is correct. The **mkdir** command creates a directory, while the **chmod 750** command assigns full read, write, and execute (**rwx**) permissions to the owner and read and execute (**rx**) permissions to members of the owning group. Since **chmod 770** gives read, write, and execute permissions to all members of the group, answer a is not correct. Since the **cd** command does not create a directory (it only changes the current directory), answer b is not correct. Since the **umask** command sets default permissions for new files, it does not change the permissions on files (or directories) that already exist. Therefore, answer c is also incorrect.

Question 4

Based on the parameters of question 3, which commands may be used to make sure the proper user and group own the /home/aearhart/project directory?

- ○ a. **chmod 755 /home/aearhart/project; chgrp avion /home/ aearhart/project**
- ○ b. **chown avion /home/aearhart/project; chgrp aearhart /home/aearhart/project**
- ○ c. **chown aearhart /home/aearhart/project; chgrp avion /home/ aearhart/project**
- ○ d. **chusr aearhart /home/aearhart/project; chgrp aearhart /home/aearhart/project**

Answer c is correct. The objective is to give ownership of the /home/aearhart/ project directory to the user **aearhart** and the group **avion**. This is accomplished by the **chown** and **chgrp** commands, respectively. Although **chmod** changes the permissions associated with a file or directory, it does not affect ownership of that directory. Therefore, answer a is incorrect. You can't assign user ownership of the /home/aearhart/project directory to a group; therefore, answer b is incorrect. Since there is no **chusr** command, answer d is also incorrect.

Question 5

Andrew Jackson has asked for an account on your Linux system. You've created it with the following command:

```
useradd ajackson
```

Jackson has called you to complain that the account you created does not work. What else do you need to do?

- ○ a. Copy files and directories from /etc/skel to /home/ajackson.
- ○ b. Assign the bash shell (/bin/bash) to user **ajackson** in the /etc/passwd file.
- ○ c. Run the **passwd ajackson** command as the **root** user.
- ○ d. Run the **pwconv** command to make sure that the password on your Linux computer is encrypted.

Answer c is correct. By default, the **useradd** command doesn't assign a new password to a user. Linux doesn't allow anyone to log in to an account without a password. When you run **passwd ajackson** as root, you can then assign **ajackson** a password, which you can tell him to change with the **passwd** command as soon as he logs on for the first time. Since the **useradd** command already copies the files and directories from /etc/skel to the home directory of a new user, answer a is incorrect. Since the **useradd** command automatically assigns default shells to new users, answer b is incorrect. Since the **pwconv** program won't help if a password has not yet been assigned, answer d is also incorrect.

Question 6

You're having trouble deleting the bigbang file in your home directory. Your username is **hawk**, and you know the **root** user password. You use the **su** command to go into **root** user mode, but still you can't delete the bigbang file. What is the problem?

- ○ a. You need to log out and log back in as the **root** user.
- ○ b. The immutable flag is set. You should run the **chattr -i /home/hawk/bigbang** command to turn off the flag.
- ○ c. The immutable flag is set. You need to use the **chmod** command to give the **root** user write permissions on the /home/hawk/bigbang file.
- ○ d. The immutable flag is set. You need to use the **chmod** command to give user **hawk** read, write, and execute permissions on the /home/hawk/bigbang file.

Answer b is correct. When the immutable flag is set on a file, even the **root** user isn't allowed to delete that file. Since the **root** user can't delete the file without deactivating the immutable flag, answer a is incorrect. Since write permission does not allow any user to override the immutable flag to delete a file, answers c and d are both incorrect.

Question 7

> Marcie has temporarily left the company to return to school. You know that she will return to the company at the completion of her studies. You've given access to her files in /home/marcie to other trusted members of her group. Which of the following steps would disable Marcie's account?
>
> ○ a. **userdel -r marcie**
>
> ○ b. Edit the /etc/passwd file in a text editor. Navigate to the line associated with Marcie's account. Replace the entry in the second column with an x.
>
> ○ c. **chmod 700 /home/marcie**
>
> ○ d. Edit the /etc/passwd file in a text editor. Navigate to the line associated with Marcie's account. Replace the entry in the second column with an *.

Answer d is correct. In the /etc/passwd file, the second column associated with any user represents that user's password. When you replace it with an asterisk (*), you're effectively deleting that user's password. The result is as if passwords were never assigned to the **marcie** account; any attempt to log in to that account will fail. Since you're assuming Marcie is planning to return, you don't want to delete her account. Because the **userdel -r** command deletes accounts and associated home directories, answer a is incorrect. Because you're replacing the entry in the second column with an asterisk, not an x, answer b is incorrect. The **chmod 700 /home/marcie** command gives the owner of that directory (**marcie**) read, write, and execute permissions. Since that does not disable the account, answer c is also incorrect.

Question 8

> You have recently added some new users and groups by directly editing the /etc/passwd and /etc/group files. The old users and groups are associated with encrypted passwords in the /etc/shadow and /etc/gshadow files. Which of the following actions encrypts the passwords associated with the new users and groups?
>
> ○ a. **grpconv**; **pwconv**
>
> ○ b. First, you need to unencrypt all of the users and groups on the computer with the **grpunconv** and **pwunconv** commands. Then you can run the **grpconv** and **pwconv** commands.
>
> ○ c. **groupconv**; **userconv**
>
> ○ d. First, you need to unencrypt all of the users and groups on the computer with the **groupunconv** and **userunconv** commands. Then you can run the **groupconv** and **userconv** commands.

Answer a is correct. The **grpconv** command converts group passwords from the /etc/group file to the /etc/gshadow file. The **pwconv** command converts user passwords from the /etc/passwd file to the /etc/shadow file. Both commands work even if there is a mix of encrypted and unencrypted passwords in /etc/passwd and /etc/group. Since the **grpunconv** and **pwunconv** commands are unnecessary, answer b is incorrect. Since there is no **groupconv** or **userconv** command, answers c and d are both also incorrect.

Question 9

> As the system administrator for your group's Linux system, you've developed a script that automates some of the work for your users. Currently, the permissions on this script, /root/bighelp, are **-rwxrwxr--**. The owner and group are both **root**. Which of the following commands allows any user to run this script?
>
> ○ a. **chusr u+s /root/bighelp**
>
> ○ b. **sudo /root/bighelp**
>
> ○ c. **chmod u-s /root/bighelp**
>
> ○ d. **chmod u+s /root/bighelp**

Answer d is correct. The **chmod** command changes permissions. The **u+s** switch activates the SUID bit for owner permissions on this file, which now become

rws. Since there is no **chusr** command, answer a is incorrect. The **sudo** command requires the user to know the **root** password; that is something you do not want every user to know. Therefore, answer b is incorrect. The **u-s** switch deactivates any existing SUID bit for owner permissions on this file. Therefore, answer c is also incorrect.

Question 10

Which of the following commands would allow you to install the module for the 3COM Etherlink III card without staying in superuser mode after the command is complete? The correct module for this card is **3c589_cs.o**, and the kernel is version 2.4.2-4. Assume the directories shown contain the required driver module.

- O a. **insmod /lib/modules/2.4.2-4/3c589_cs.o**
- O b. **su insmod /lib/modules/2.4.2-4/3c589_cs.o**
- O c. **su -c insmod /lib/modules/2.4.2-4/3c589_cs.o**
- O d. **su -c "insmod /lib/modules/2.4.2-4/3c589_cs.o"**

Answer d is correct. The **su -c** command allows the use of a single command, in quotes, that could normally only be run by the **root** user or superuser. Since the **insmod** command can only be used by the **root** user, as discussed in Chapter 9, answer a is incorrect. The -c switch is required to pass another command along to **su**. Therefore, answer b is incorrect. Unless the command being passed is one word, it needs to be in double quotes so that **su** can see the whole command before it tries to process it. Therefore, answer c is incorrect.

Need to Know More?

 Mann, Scott, and Ellen L. Mitchell. *Linux System Security.* Upper Saddle River, NJ: Prentice-Hall, 2000. ISBN 0-13015-807-0. Subtitled "The Administrator's Guide to Open Source Security Tools," this book addresses the procedures behind files such as /etc/sudoers, appropriate procedures for changing permissions, and the pitfalls associated with SUID and SGID.

 Ward, Brian. *The Linux Problem Solver.* San Francisco, CA: No Starch Press, 2000. ISBN 0-88641-135-2. Ward provides solutions to 115 common problems in eight different areas, including printing, networking, and system crashes. It's a superb reference for finding elusive Linux administration answers quickly and easily.

 Explore the home page of the **sudo** command at **www.courtesan.com/ sudo/.** This Web site includes downloads for the latest version of **sudo** and documentation that allows you to use **sudo** and the companion file, /etc/sudoers, with minimal impact to the security of your Linux system.

 Remember the Linux System Administrators' Guide at **www.tml.hut.fi/ ~viu/linux/sag.** This guide includes important documentation related to all of the commands required to create and maintain user accounts. It includes a different method for disabling accounts. You can also find a copy of this guide through the Linux Documentation Project at **www.linuxdoc.org.**

More System Administration

Terms you'll need to understand:

✓ vi

✓ Command mode, insert mode, execute mode

✓ Shell scripts

✓ /etc/printcap

✓ Print filters

✓ Print spool

✓ Print queue

✓ lpr, lpq, lpc, lprm

✓ Remote access

✓ rlogin, rsh

✓ ftp, tftp

✓ ssh

✓ X Window

✓ $PATH, $DISPLAY, $TERM

Techniques you'll need to master:

✓ Using the **vi** editor in command, insert, and execute modes

✓ Listing various printer configuration tools

✓ Understanding the function of print filters

✓ Reading a typical printer configuration file (/etc/printcap)

✓ Working with various line printer commands

✓ Defining different ways to create a remote connection

✓ Modifying different command-line variables

This chapter continues coverage of the system administration requirements of the Linux+ exam, starting with a look at the **vi** editor. It continues with a detailed overview of printer commands and configuration. Network services can be used to administer Linux computers remotely. The **$PATH, $DISPLAY**, and **$TERM** variables allow you to control the environment of the command-line interface.

A Brief Review of vi

Linux relies on a large number of text files for configuration. Therefore, you need a text editor to configure Linux. Although Linux includes a number of generic text editors, the Linux+ exam requires that you know the basics of **vi**, the *VI*sual editor. The **vi** editor may seem old. The one- or two-letter commands are cryptic, but if you ever need to rescue your system with a boot disk, **vi** will be the only editor at your disposal.

It is easy to open a file with **vi**. For example, if you want to open the /etc/inittab file, use the following command:

```
vi /etc/inittab
```

There are three basic ways to work in **vi**. Command mode is the default; insert mode is how text is entered; and, with a few special characters, execute mode can be used to run regular shell commands.

Command Mode

When you open a file in **vi**, the first mode is command mode. This is what you use to scroll through text, search for different text strings, or delete specific characters, words, or lines.

One aid in **vi** is line numbers, which you can activate by typing the following in the editor:

```
:set nu
```

The result should look similar to Figure 12.1.

Remember that you can use the **:set nu** command to activate line numbers when editing a file in the **vi** text editor.

Getting Around

Although current versions of **vi** allow you to use the directional keys on your keyboard (arrows, Page Up, Page Down), this editor was designed for older

```
    25 12:2:wait:/etc/rc.d/rc 2
    26 13:3:wait:/etc/rc.d/rc 3
    27 14:4:wait:/etc/rc.d/rc 4
    28 15:5:wait:/etc/rc.d/rc 5
    29 16:6:wait:/etc/rc.d/rc 6
    30 ▌
    31 # Things to run in every runlevel.
    32 ud::once:/sbin/update
    33
    34 # Trap CTRL-ALT-DELETE
    35 ca::ctrlaltdel:/sbin/shutdown -t3 -r now
    36
    37 # When our UPS tells us power has failed, assume we have a few minutes
    38 # of power left.  Schedule a shutdown for 2 minutes from now.
    39 # This does, of course, assume you have powerd installed and your
    40 # UPS connected and working correctly.
    41 pf::powerfail:/sbin/shutdown -f -h +2 "Power Failure; System Shutting Down
       "
    42
    43 # If power was restored before the shutdown kicked in, cancel it.
    44 pr:12345:powerokwait:/sbin/shutdown -c "Power Restored; Shutdown Cancelled
       "
    45
    46
    47 # Run gettys in standard runlevels
    48 1:2345:respawn:/sbin/mingetty tty1
    49 2:2345:respawn:/sbin/mingetty tty2
```

Figure 12.1   Line numbers in **vi**.

keyboards that did not have these keys. Four lowercase letters take the place of the navigational arrows on the standard U.S. keyboard:

➤ **h**—Left Arrow

➤ **j**—Down Arrow

➤ **k**—Up Arrow

➤ **l**—Right Arrow

The alternatives to the Page Up and Page Down keys are **Ctrl+B** (back) and **Ctrl+F** (forward), respectively.

If you already know the line number you want, the **G** command can help. When used alone, it takes you to the last line in the file. When used with a line number, such as **20G**, it takes you to the desired line. As with Linux shells, capitalization makes a difference, so make sure you're using the uppercase **G** for this command.

 Remember how to use the **G** command to go to a specific line in a file in the **vi** editor.

Deleting Text

It is easy to delete text in **vi**. Three deletion commands are associated with the current location of the cursor:

➤ **x**—Deletes the current character, even if that character is a blank space or a tab

> **dw**—Deletes the current word

> **dd**—Deletes the current line

 If you accidentally delete something, the **u** command reverses the last command entered.

Searching

It is easy to search for words in **vi**. Just start with a forward slash. For example, if you want to search for the word "dollar" in a file, type the following:

```
/dollar
```

The cursor highlights the first place this word is found in the file. To proceed to the next copy of this word, type **n**. Just remember that capitalization matters in a search with **vi**. For example, the /**dollar** command would not find the word "Dollar" in the file.

Insert Mode

Insert mode is where you can insert text into the file. There are several ways to do this, relative to the current location of the cursor. The following list includes a few of those methods:

> **i**—Insert. Everything you type is inserted, starting at the current position of the cursor.

> **a**—Append. Everything you type is inserted, starting one character after the current position of the cursor. This is closely related to **A**, where everything you type is inserted, starting at the end of the line with the cursor.

> **o**—Open. Everything you type is inserted, starting one line below the current position of the cursor. Closely related is **O** (uppercase), where everything you type is inserted, starting one line above the current position of the cursor.

> **cw**—Change word. Deletes the word (or space) that corresponds to the current position of the cursor. You get to insert text starting with that word. Closely related is **cc**, which allows you to replace the current line.

Execute Mode

You can run regular shell commands from inside the **vi** editor. Just type :!, followed by the command. For example, if you were creating a script, you might need to know the directory location of a certain file. You could list the files in the /var/log directory with the following command:

```
:!ls /var/log
```

 Remember how to execute a regular shell command from inside the **vi** editor. Just type **:!** followed by the shell command.

Regular execute mode starts with the colon (:). Several file management commands are associated with execute mode, including **:q** to exit a file and **:w** to write the current text to the file. A number of basic commands for **vi** in all modes are shown in Table 12.1.

Table 12.1	Basic vi commands.
Command	**Description**
a	Starts insert mode after the current cursor position.
A	Starts insert mode by appending at the end of the current line.
cw	Deletes the current word and then enters insert mode to allow you to replace that word.
dd	Deletes the current line.
dw	Deletes the current word without entering insert mode.
G	Moves the cursor to the end of the line.
15G	Moves the cursor to the fifteenth line.
h	Moves the cursor left one space.
i	Enters insert mode.
o	Enters insert mode by opening a line directly below the current cursor.
O	Enters insert mode by opening a line directly above the current cursor.
:q	Exits from **vi**. If you have made changes and want to quit without saving, use **:q!**.
r	Replace; the next character that you type replaces the current character.
:set nu	Activates line numbers for the current file.
u	Undoes the last change.
:w	Writes the current file.
Esc	Exits from insert mode.
/*system*	Searches for the word *system* in the current file.

Shell Scripts

Shell scripting is one of the objectives of the Linux+ exam. However, the developers of the Linux+ exam understand that this is a skill associated with more advanced Linux system administrators; therefore, few if any shell script questions are expected. Nevertheless, even the newest Linux system administrators should understand the basics behind a shell script.

Linux shell scripts are similar to Microsoft batch files. They typically are used to automate otherwise tedious tasks such as backups at 3:00 A.M. As suggested by the name, they are based on the commands associated with a specific shell such as bash. They can include *filtered* commands such as **ps aux|grep httpd**, which can help you indentify specific issues.

 Know that scripts can include filtered commands.

When you create a script, keep the following principles in mind:

➤ *Comment the script*—Even a perfect script needs comments. If others are to understand the purpose behind a shell script, comments are essential. An example of a well-commented script is the Apache configuration file, httpd.conf.

➤ *Test the script*—As with any new application, scripts need to be tested before they are used in a production environment.

➤ *Organize your scripts*—Keep scripts together in one or more directories. Production and test scripts should be separated. Make it easy for others to find your scripts.

After a shell is specified, any legal command from that shell can be used in the script. Several common bash shell commands can be part of a shell script, as described in Table 12.2. With the appropriate permissions, shell scripts can be made executable like any other command. In fact, many Linux commands are just executable shell scripts.

Printers

One device generally not configured during Linux installation is the printer. Traditionally, printers are configured by directly editing the /etc/printcap file. However, the language associated with this file can be difficult to understand. Several Linux distributions include their own configuration tools. One useful generic configuration tool is known as Apsfilter.

Table 12.2 Some shell script commands.	
Command	**Description**
#!/bin/sh	Normally, any line that starts with a hash mark (**#**) is a comment. In this case, it specifies the shell language used in the file. The bash shell is usually associated with /bin/sh or /bin/bash; the Korn shell is associated with /bin/ksh; the enhanced C shell is associated with /bin/tcsh.
cut	Removes sections of text from a line.
find	Searches for a specific file.
grep	Searches for text within another file.
if	A conditional command that allows a choice. For example, the **if [$USER=mj]** command could specify special commands to be applied to user **mj**.

Linux uses print filters to translate print data in a file to a language that a printer can understand. These translated files are stored in printer spools until the printer is ready to take the data. Print files can be large; spools allow Linux to return to other tasks more quickly.

In this context, a number of commands are associated with administering printers on Linux.

/etc/printcap

The main Linux printer configuration file is printcap, normally located in the /etc directory. As you can see from Figure 12.2, a number of cryptic commands are associated with this file. For the Linux+ exam, just make a note of the two parameters discussed on the next page:

```
# /etc/printcap
#
lp|Printer1 auto:\
█   :lp=/dev/lp0:\
    :if=/etc/apsfilter/basedir/bin/apsfilter:\
    :sd=/var/spool/lpd/lp:\
    :lf=/var/spool/lpd/lp/log:\
    :af=/var/spool/lpd/lp/acct:\
    :mx#0:\
    :sh:
raw1|Printer1 raw:\
    :lp=/dev/lp0:\
    :if=/etc/apsfilter/basedir/bin/apsfilter:\
    :sd=/var/spool/lpd/raw1:\
    :lf=/var/spool/lpd/raw1/log:\
    :af=/var/spool/lpd/raw1/acct:\
    :mx#0:\
    :sf:\
    :sh:
~
~
~
~
~
~
```

Figure 12.2   A typical /etc/printcap file.

> **lp**—Line print, associated with a print device such as /dev/lp0. Normally, /dev/lp0 and /dev/lp1 correspond to the LPT1 and LPT2 printer ports that are more common in Microsoft operating systems.

> **sd**—Spool directory. When files are converted into a format for your printer, they are temporarily stored in the spool directory until the printer is ready to process the data. A typical spool directory is /var/spool/lpd/lp.

Configuration Tools

Because of the complexity of /etc/printcap, a number of printer configuration tools are available in Linux. With their menus, they can help you configure /etc/printcap based on options that are more easily understandable. Some of the tools are distribution specific:

> *printconf*—The latest Red Hat Linux GUI configuration utility.

> *YaST*—Yet another Setup Tool, the S.u.S.E. menu-driven configuration utility.

> *Webmin*—The Caldera Web browser–based configuration utility.

> *Apsfilter*—A distribution-neutral menu-based printer configuration utility.

Filters

The key to any printer configuration is the filter, which translates data from an application or editor to a language that a printer can understand. The two major printer graphic languages are Hewlett Packard's PCL (Printer Control Language) and Adobe's PostScript.

Print filters can be set up with one of the configuration utilities or directly edited into the /etc/printcap file. The major filters are as follows:

> *ghostscript*—An interpreter for PostScript files, which often have the .ps extension. Allows Linux to display .ps files in graphical user interfaces. Translates data for PostScript printers.

> *GNU enscript*—Translates data from ASCII files for PostScript printers. A GNU clone of the commercial enscript filter.

> *nenscript*—Also translates ASCII data for PostScript printers. Another GNU clone of the enscript filter.

> *magic*—A setting that detects the type of data inside a file and automatically calls up the right filter.

> *text*—A filter that reformats ASCII text to avoid "stair-stepping," in which printers add an extra line after every word.

Printing from a Spool

Print spools are typically located in the /var/spool/lpd directory. This corresponds to the **sd** setting in the /etc/printcap file, shown in Figure 12.2. There is a different spool subdirectory for each printer; in this case, /var/spool/lpd/lp contains regular print jobs and /var/spool/lpd/raw contains print jobs that have not been passed through a print filter.

Normally, print jobs are deleted with commands such as **lprm** and **lpc**, which are discussed in the following section. If these commands don't work, you can delete a print job by deleting the print file in the appropriate spool directory.

Line Printer Commands

Linux printers are managed by the line print daemon (**lpd**). A number of commands are associated with **lpd**, including the line printer request (**lpr**), the line printer query (**lpq**), the line printer control (**lpc**), and the line printer remove (**lprm**) programs.

lpr

The standard command for printing a file is **lpr**. In Linux, it's just another way of redirecting standard output, normally to a file on the spool directory. If you want to print the file named Chapter12, the command

```
lpr Chapter12
```

processes the contents of the Chapter12 file through the filter defined in the /etc/printcap file. The result is then sent to a file on the spool directory.

The spool is processed by the line print daemon (**lpd**), which acts as the print server. The server can be local or on a remote computer.

Alternatively, you can use **lpr** to send the print request to another printer. Assume there is a printer named "colors" in /etc/printcap. The following command sends the job to the colors printer by superseding default /etc/printcap settings:

```
lpr -Pcolors Chapter12
```

*Note: There is no space between the –P and the name of the printer for the **lpr** command. This is a quirk in Linux syntax that applies to a few commands and command switches.*

Other switches for the **lpr** command are shown in Table 12.3.

Table 12.3   Sample lpr commands.

Command	Description
lpr -h document	Prints document without a job control page, which normally includes the user account and the hostname of the source computer.
lpr -P*other* **document**	Prints document to the printer named "other", as defined in /etc/printcap. There is no space between the **-P** and the name of the printer.
lpr -s document	Prints document directly to the printer. No spool file is created. A shortcut if the partition with the spool directory is short on space.

lpq

The line printer query (**lpq**) command returns the current print queue. Unless you specify a printer, it gives you the print queue for the default printer, which is usually designated **lp** in the /etc/printcap file. Alternatively, if you want the print queue for a specific printer named "color", the following command should help:

```
lpq -Pcolor
```

As shown in Figure 12.3, the output includes a number of parameters about each print job:

➤ *Rank*—Current order in the print queue.

➤ *Owner*—The user requesting the print job.

➤ *Class*—Similar to *Rank*.

➤ *Job*—An arbitrary job number, which you can use with other commands such as **lpc** and **lprm**.

➤ *Files*—The file being printed.

➤ *Size*—The size of the file being printed.

➤ *Time*—The time of the print request.

lpc

The line printer control (**lpc**) command can help you manage printers and print spools and individual print jobs. For example, you can disable print requests to the printer named "color" with the following command:

```
lpc -Pcolor disable
```

```
[mj@laptop71 mj]$ lpq -Pcolor
Printer: color@localhost
Queue: 2 printable jobs
Server: pid 2654 active
Unspooler: pid 2656 active
Status: printing finished at 10:00:30.119
Rank    Owner/ID              Class Job Files              Size Time
active mj@localhost+653          A   653 basicdoc              904 10:00:19
2       tr@localhost+652         A   652 /etc/httpd/conf/http 41428 10:00:19
[mj@laptop71 mj]$ ▌
```

Figure 12.3   Current print queue.

Based on Figure 12.3, assume that user **tr** is some important person in your company. He wants his job to be printed immediately. The **lpc** command allows you to reorder print jobs. For example, the following command would place **tr**'s print job before the one started by user **mj**:

```
lpc topq 652
```

Just a few of the options associated with **lpc** are listed in Table 12.4.

lprm

There are times when you want to cancel a print job. If you're quick, you can stop the print job before it gets to the print queue, because binary word processors and graphics utilities take a little time to prepare files for the printer. Alternatively, you could use the **lprm** command to cancel a print job. For example, if you decide that user **tr**'s print job as shown in Figure 12.3 should be deleted, run the following command:

```
lprm 652
```

Table 12.4	lpc command switches.
Switch	**Description**
abort	Stops the print server.
disable	Temporarily stops new print jobs from entering the queue.
enable	Restores print access to the queue.
kill	Stops and restarts the print server.
-P	Specifies a printer. Use a name specified in /etc/printcap. Remember to avoid a space between this switch and the name of the printer.
status	Lists current status of all printers.
topq	Reorders jobs based on their job numbers as specified in the output from the **lpq** command.

The straightforward way to remove a print job is based on the job number, in this case, 652. However, you could use the **-P** or **-U** switch to specify all print jobs on a certain printer or those associated with a specific user ID (UID), respectively.

Remote Connections

Several applications take advantage of Linux network connections. Applications such as **telnet** allow you to log on through a remote terminal. File transfer applications such as **ftp** and **tftp** are more efficient for larger files. There is a series of other remote applications based on the "r" commands, including **rlogin** and **rsh**. However, most remote applications send critical messages such as passwords as unencrypted, clear text. Because of this, the "ssh" commands were developed to encrypt remote administrative messages.

Note: If you want to set up the "ssh" commands, you need to first remove the package associated with the "r" commands.

Because versions of many of these commands are available for other operating systems, it doesn't matter whether you're networking to or from another Linux computer.

telnet

The **telnet** command is the easy way to connect to a Linux computer. Once the network connection is made, it is just like any other Linux command-line interface. One advantage of **telnet** is that it is available on a variety of operating systems; Figure 12.4 shows an example of a **telnet** connection to a computer running Linux from a computer running the Windows 2000 operating system.

If you're having trouble with a **telnet** connection or terminal, your **telnet** client may be having a problem with the terminal messages sent from the Linux server that you're administering. One command that can help is the following:

```
TERM=vt100
```

This sets the messages to a terminal emulation program that has been in use since slave computers were moved from teletypes to computer screens.

Note: TERM is an environmental variable that does not change even when you change shells. These variables are covered in more detail later in the "Environmental Variables" section.

Know that if you're having trouble with a **telnet** connection, the **TERM=vt100** command can help by setting the terminal emulation program to a system that is more friendly to a remote connection.

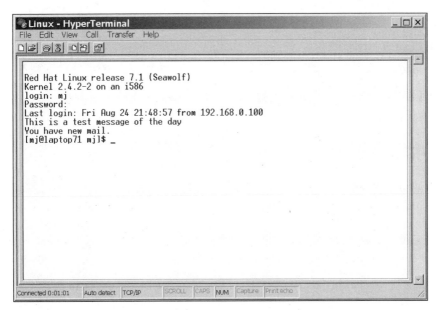

Figure 12.4 Remote access by **telnet**.

If you're administering a Linux computer that has a firewall, you'll probably need to activate the **telnet** port (23) first. The process depends on whether services are activated through the /etc/inetd.conf configuration file or various files in the /etc/xinetd.d directory. The details are beyond the scope of the Linux+ exam.

Remote Linux Login Access

Two other commands to access Linux computers remotely are **rsh** and **rlogin**. They are both functionally similar to **telnet**; the **rsh** command also allows access to a remote computer for a single command. Access depends on a configuration file named .rhosts in the appropriate user's home directory on the computer that you're trying to access. For example, if you want to check the file list in **tr**'s home directory on a computer named **linuxserver**, run the following command:

```
rsh -l tr linuxserver ls
```

Alternatively, you could just log in remotely from another Linux computer with the **rlogin** command. If you have the same account name on a remote computer named **linuxserver**, all you need is the **rlogin linuxserver** command. Alternatively, if you wanted to log into **tr**'s account, the following command might work:

```
rlogin -l tr linuxserver
```

In either case, you're prompted for a password by the remote computer.

The secure versions of **rsh** and **rlogin** are the **ssh** and **slogin** commands, respectively. They work in nearly the same manner, except messages are sent in encrypted format, and the authenticity of the target computer is also checked, as shown in Figure 12.5.

As with **telnet,** to use any of the remote Linux login commands you may need to activate the service and modify the firewall as required.

ftp and tftp

In Chapter 5, you learned about File Transfer Protocol (FTP) as an option for installing Linux. It and its cousin, Trivial File Transfer Protocol (TFTP), are the simplest ways to transfer files over a network. Like **telnet,** the **ftp** command allows you to connect to FTP servers on mixed networks. In other words, the client, server, or both can reside on a number of different operating systems, including Linux, Windows, Macintosh, and more.

TFTP provides no security and should not be enabled except for terminals or slave computers that require a separate level of authentication. You can access an FTP or TFTP server with the **ftp** or **tftp** command.

X Window

Remote connections even work with the Linux graphical user interface (GUI). The Linux GUI is sometimes known as the X Window. It is versatile; you can set up the X Window server and client applications on different computers. This makes it possible to have a graphical terminal without a hard drive.

The paradigm for X Window client/server relationships is not what you might expect; the server is on the local computer (with the graphics card), and the client is the graphical application such as **xterm,** Netscape, or The GIMP, which can reside on the hard drives of remote computers.

Command-Line Variables

Two types of variables set the stage for the command-line interface. These are known as local *shell* and *environment variables.* A shell variable stays with you

```
mj@linux:~ > slogin laptop71
The authenticity of host 'laptop71 (192.168.0.50)' can't be established.
RSA1 key fingerprint is ac:7d:89:31:a6:51:4f:4b:a9:fd:90:ed:b2:a8:1b:6d.
Are you sure you want to continue connecting (yes/no)? yes
Warning: Permanently added 'laptop71,192.168.0.50' (RSA1) to the list of known h
osts.
mj@laptop71's password:
Last login: Sat Aug 25 12:11:53 2001 from 192.168.0.100
This is a test message of the day
[mj@laptop71 mj]$ _
```

Figure 12.5 Remote access by **slogin.**

only as long as you use the same shell, such as bash or Korn. If you use more than one shell, the difference between shell and environment variables becomes important.

Shell Variables

A typical shell variable is **PATH**, which determines the commands you can use without the full directory path. Find your own **PATH** with the **echo $PATH** command. Shell variables are driven by profiles. The default configuration file for **PATH** is /etc/profile.

Other shell variables are taken from hidden files in a user's home directory. The actual files depend on your distribution. For example, you might customize your profile in the ~/.profile and/or ~/.bash_profile files. You might also add the **clear** command to a ~/.bash_logout or ~/.logout file to clear the screen of your last few commands when you exit from a shell or log out of your Linux computer.

 Remember that the tilde (~) is commonly used in Linux to represent any user's home directory. For example, any Linux user can check the files in his home directory with the **ls ~** command.

Environment Variables

To see your environment variables in the bash shell, type the **env** command. This gives you the current list of environmental variables. An example of this is shown in Figure 12.6.

```
PWD=/home/mj
LTDL_LIBRARY_PATH=/usr/lib
HOSTNAME=laptop71
LD_LIBRARY_PATH=/usr/lib
LESSOPEN=|/usr/bin/lesspipe.sh %s
KDE_DISPLAY=:0.0
KDEDIR=/usr
USER=mj
LS_COLORS=no=00:fi=00:di=01;34:ln=01;36:pi=40;33:so=01;35:bd=40;33;01:cd=40;33;01:
or=01;05;37;41:mi=01;05;37;41:ex=01;32:*.cmd=01;32:*.exe=01;32:*.com=01;32:*.btm=0
1;32:*.bat=01;32:*.sh=01;32:*.csh=01;32:*.tar=01;31:*.tgz=01;31:*.arj=01;31:*.taz=
01;31:*.lzh=01;31:*.zip=01;31:*.z=01;31:*.Z=01;31:*.gz=01;31:*.bz2=01;31:*.bz=01;3
1;*.tz=01;31:*.rpm=01;31:*.cpio=01;31:*.jpg=01;35:*.gif=01;35:*.bmp=01;35:*.xbm=01
;35:*.xpm=01;35:*.png=01;35:*.tif=01;35:
MACHTYPE=i386-redhat-linux-gnu
KDE_MULTIHEAD=false
MAIL=/var/spool/mail/mj
INPUTRC=/etc/inputrc
BASH_ENV=/home/mj/.bashrc
GTK_RC_FILES=/etc/gtk/gtkrc:/home/mj/.gtkrc:/home/mj/.gtkrc-kde
XMODIFIERS=@im=none
LANG=en_US
COLORTERM=
DISPLAY=:0.0
LOGNAME=mj
SHLVL=2
SESSION_MANAGER=local/laptop71:/tmp/.ICE-unix/921
:█
```

Figure 12.6 Typical environment variables.

Although environmental variables are the same when you change shells, they are different for each user. For example, in Figure 12.6, **HOME** is set to the home directory of the current user. **LOGNAME** is set to the user ID (UID). The directory with mail files (**MAIL**) is set to /var/spool/mail/mj. If your mail manager points to a different directory, such as /home/mj/mail, you can change that variable with the following command:

```
MAIL=/home/mj/mail
```

The command varies slightly according to the shell you are currently using. Further details are beyond the scope of the Linux+ exam.

Practice Questions

Question 1

> One of your colleagues has told you about the exciting new variables that she's added to the Apache configuration file. She tells you that they are somewhere around line 155. You've opened up the applicable /etc/httpd/conf/httpd.conf file in the **vi** text editor. Which of the following commands would take you to that line?
>
> ○ a. **:155G**
>
> ○ b. **155G**
>
> ○ c. **155**
>
> ○ d. **G155**

Answer b is correct. When you first open a file in **vi**, you're in command mode. The **G** command takes you to the last line of a file. The **1G** command takes you to the first line of a file. Therefore, the **155G** command takes you to line 155 of the applicable file. When you start a command with a colon (:), **vi** expects an editing command. Since **155G** is not an editing command, answer a is incorrect. A number by itself is not a command in **vi**; therefore, answer c is incorrect. The **G155** command just takes you to the end of the file; "155" is read as if it were a separate command. As explained for answer c, that is meaningless to **vi**. Therefore, answer d is also incorrect.

Question 2

> You want to administer a computer at a remote site. Which of the following commands can help you connect to that computer securely?
>
> ○ a. **rlogin**
>
> ○ b. **telnet**
>
> ○ c. **slogin**
>
> ○ d. **ftp**

Answer c is correct. The **slogin** command, like **ssh**, allows you to make a connection to the remote computer, with encrypted communications. Since the **rlogin** command does not encrypt communications, answer a is incorrect. Like **rlogin**, the **telnet** command normally does not allow for secure communications; in addition, access from other operating systems such as Microsoft Windows is more difficult to set up securely. Therefore, answer b is incorrect. The **ftp** command only allows you to transfer files to and from an FTP server. Therefore, answer d is also incorrect.

Question 3

Which of the following commands is most likely to create output similar to what you see in Figure 12.7?

```
Printer: lp@cash
 Queue: 3 printable jobs
 Server: pid 1323 active
 Unspooler: pid 1332 active
 Status: printing finished at 06:43:14
 Rank    Owner/ID    Class  Job  Files    Size Time
active mj@cash+121    A     121  dollar 232190 06:43:12
2        tr@cash+120   A     120  mark   583394 06:43:14
3        jb@cash+119   A     119  yen    120392 06:43:24
```

Figure 12.7 Question 3 output.

○ a. **lpc**

○ b. **lpr**

○ c. **lpd**

○ d. **lpq**

Answer d is correct. The line printer query command (**lpq**) queries the desired print server about current jobs in its queue. That is what is listed in Figure 12.7. Although it's possible to set up the line printer control (**lpc**) command with a switch to get the current queue, there is no switch shown with **lpc** in answer a, which is therefore incorrect. Since the line printer request (**lpr**) command prints files, it does not give the print queue. Therefore, answer b is also incorrect. Although the line print daemon (**lpd**) governs the print process through the queue, it is not normally used as a command. Therefore, answer c is also incorrect.

Question 4

You're in the middle of editing a large script file in the **vi** editor. You want to call on a special script, **bigfoot**, that was created by one of your users a few days ago, but you can't remember its directory location. Which of the following commands allows you to find the directory location without leaving the editor?

○ a. **!locate bigfoot**

○ b. **:find / -name bigfoot**

○ c. **!:find / -name bigfoot**

○ d. **:!locate bigfoot**

Answer d is correct. Under the circumstances, either the **find** or the **locate** command can serve the purpose. Each of the answers includes properly configured commands. The real question is how to get into execute mode in **vi**. The answer is that it can be done with the **:!** characters. The command that follows is executed in the default shell. Since there is no colon (:) to start command mode in **vi**, answer a is incorrect. Since there is no exclamation point (!) to start execute mode, answer b is also incorrect. And since the exclamation point and colon are in the wrong order, answer c is also incorrect.

Question 5

You've set up access from a Macintosh computer to administer a Linux server on the LAN through **telnet**. Unfortunately, when you run commands, the screen gets strange responses. You think there might be a problem with the terminal. Which of the following commands could solve the problem?

○ a. **TERM=xterm**

○ b. **TERM=vt100**

○ c. **TERMINAL=xterm**

○ d. **TERMINAL=VT100**

Answer b is correct. The VT100 terminal was developed for command-line communication between terminals and servers on a network. **xterm** is the terminal associated with the Linux X Window, which may not be appropriate for communication between a terminal and a server on a network. Therefore, answer a is incorrect. Since there is no **TERMINAL** environment variable, answers c and d are also incorrect. In addition, the Linux value associated with the VT100 terminal is **vt100**; you can't set **TERM=VT100**.

Question 6

Which of the following is not something you can do with the **lpc** command?

○ a. Disabling a printer

○ b. Reporting the status of a printer

○ c. Creating a print job

○ d. Revising the order of print jobs in the queue

Answer c is correct. The **lpc** command is versatile. Unlike **lpr**, however, it can't create a print job from a file. Since the **lpc** −P*laser* **disable** command disables the printer named *laser*, answer a is incorrect. Since the **lpc** −P*laser* **status** command returns the status of the printer named *laser*, answer b is also incorrect. Since the **lpc topq** *jobnumber* places the print job with *jobnumber* atop the printing queue, answer d is also incorrect.

Question 7

Which of the following is characteristic of an environment variable?

○ a. If you move from the bash shell to the Korn shell, new environment variables apply.

○ b. You can check your current environment variables with the **echo $ENV** command.

○ c. Your environment variables apply only to the bash shell.

○ d. You can check your current environment variables in the bash shell with the **env** command.

Answer d is correct. In the bash shell, the **env** command returns the list of currently set environment variables. Since environment variables do not change from shell to shell, answers a and c are both incorrect. Since **echo $ENV** returns the current value of the ENV variable, it is unrelated to environment variable characteristics; therefore, answer b is also incorrect.

Question 8

> Based on the output shown in Question 3 (see Figure 12.7), which of the following commands deletes user **jb**'s print job from the queue?
>
> ○ a. **lpq 119**
>
> ○ b. **lprm 119**
>
> ○ c. **lprm jb**
>
> ○ d. **lpc topq 119**

Answer b is correct. The **lprm** command removes a print job primarily by its job number, which is 119 in Figure 12.7. While the **lpq 119** command returns the status of job number 119, it does not stop or remove that job from the queue. Therefore, answer a is incorrect. Although you can use the **lprm** command to remove a job based on the name of the user, that requires the –U switch. Therefore, answer c is also incorrect. Since the **lpc topq 119** command sends job 119 to the top of the print queue, answer d is also incorrect.

Question 9

> You have just opened the Apache configuration file in the **vi** editor. Which of the following commands can you use to search for the **DocumentRoot** variable?
>
> ○ a. **/DocumentRoot**
>
> ○ b. **:SDocumentRoot**
>
> ○ c. **:iDocumentRoot**
>
> ○ d. **!DocumentRoot**

Answer a is correct. When in **vi** command mode, the forward slash (/) precedes any search term. Remember that Linux is case sensitive when you search for a term in an open **vi** file. Since there is no **S** command, answer b is not correct. Since the **:i** command would move **vi** to insert mode, the result would be adding **DocumentRoot** to the file starting with the current position of the cursor. Therefore, answer c is incorrect. Since there is no **!D** command, answer d is also incorrect.

Question 10

Which of the following passwords is most secure?

○ a. JimSmith

○ b. aa22BB44

○ c. 87654321

○ d. Hb8r0gk

Answer d is correct. The most secure passwords are based on a seemingly random combination of upper- and lowercase letters and numbers. For more information on this question, refer to Chapter 10. While JimSmith is not one specific word or name, the combination of two common names is a relatively easy password to crack. Therefore, answer a is incorrect. Although aa22BB44 is a combination of upper- and lowercase letters and numbers, the repeating pattern makes this password relatively easy to crack. Therefore, answer b is incorrect. The password 87654321 is probably the worst password in this list, because it is made up of one pattern of numbers. Therefore, answer c is also incorrect.

Need to Know More?

 Hontanon, Ramon J. *Linux Security.* Alameda, CA: Sybex, 2001. ISBN 0-78212-741-X. Includes detailed descriptions of Linux security settings.

 LeBlanc, Dee-Ann. *General Linux I.* Scottsdale, AZ: The Coriolis Group, 2000. ISBN 1-57610-567-9. Includes a good description of how to set up **telnet** securely.

 Muster, John. *Unix Made Easy.* Berkeley, CA: Osborne/McGraw-Hill, 1996. ISBN 0-07882-173-8. A solid textbook that includes many useful exercises on the **vi** editor.

 Pfaffenberger, Bryan. *Linux Command Instant Reference.* Alameda, CA: Sybex, 2000. ISBN 0-78212-748-7. A comprehensive guide to Linux commands, with switches and many examples. Commands are organized by function. Also includes a handy guide to several major text editors, including **vi**.

 Explore the home page for the Apsfilter applications at **www.apsfilter.org**, which can help configure printers on most any Linux distribution. It is one of the very few printer configuration programs that can be used on multiple Linux distributions.

 Once again, the Web site for the Linux Documentation Project is useful. For this chapter, useful HOWTO guides include the Printing and Printing Usage HOWTOs, available at **www.linuxdoc.org/HOWTO/ Printing-HOWTO/index.html** and **www.linuxdoc.org/HOWTO/ Printing-Usage-HOWTO.html**. Also important for remote administration is the Network Administrator's Guide, Second Edition, available online at **www.linuxdoc.org/LDP/nag2/index.html**.

Linux Maintenance

Terms you'll need to understand:

- ✓ **logrotate**
- ✓ **shutdown**
- ✓ **fsck, mkfs**
- ✓ **cron, crontab**
- ✓ **mount, umount**
- ✓ **df, du**
- ✓ Boot disk
- ✓ **dd**

- ✓ Backup
- ✓ XFree86 project
- ✓ X Window
- ✓ **xf86config**, XF86Config
- ✓ KDE, GNOME
- ✓ **xterm**
- ✓ **Xconfigurator, XF86Setup**

Techniques you'll need to master:

- ✓ Shutting down Linux gracefully
- ✓ Understanding log rotation
- ✓ Maintaining disks with **fsck**
- ✓ Formatting new partitions
- ✓ Using the **cron** command utility
- ✓ Working with **crontab** for troubleshooting
- ✓ Creating boot disks

- ✓ Checking disk allocations
- ✓ Mounting drives and directories
- ✓ Backing up according to a schedule
- ✓ Understanding basic X Window configuration files and utilities
- ✓ Opening a command-line interface inside the X Window

The essence of Linux administration is maintenance. Logs and backups are best rotated on a schedule. Graceful shutdowns help when you're using Linux partitions formatted to the ext2 file system. If all else fails, boot disks can help you recover your Linux system.

This chapter also addresses the basic tools for configuring the Linux graphical user interface (GUI), also known as the X Window. The only significant GUI command utility addressed in the Linux+ exam is **xterm**, however; this opens a command-line interface inside the X Window.

Monitoring Your System

You've already seen some of the files and commands associated with system monitoring, including **top, ps, dmesg,** and various log files in several previous chapters. Two other key tools addressed in this section are **logrotate** and **shutdown.** The **logrotate** command helps Linux keep order in your logs automatically. When used properly, **shutdown** (and related commands) makes sure your system stops and/or reboots gracefully.

*Note: Several other important system monitoring tools are not addressed by the Linux+ criteria, including **who**, **w**, and a whole host of network monitoring tools. For more information, see the items listed in the "Need to Know More?" section at the end of this chapter.*

logrotate

Log files can become quite large. One command utility that can keep them manageable is **logrotate.** It is normally run on a daily basis. You can set it up to compress, rotate, and even mail current log files. It can delete older log files. You'll see how it works in the next major section—on **cron** tools.

 Remember that the **logrotate** utility can be used to rotate and delete logs on a periodic basis, depending on the schedule in the /etc/crontab file.

shutdown

The standard way to reboot a Linux computer is with the **shutdown** command. Perhaps the most popular variation of this command starts the process of shutting down Linux immediately:

```
shutdown -h now
```

The -**h** switch halts the computer after shutdown is complete. By default, it starts **init** at run level 0. As discussed in Chapter 8, this halts your Linux computer. It first gracefully kills every currently running process before it unmounts all file systems and stops your computer. A number of variations on this command are shown in Table 13.1.

 Be sure to know how to use the **shutdown** command to halt or reboot Linux.

Don't Panic

Linux is a robust operating system. Required reboots are rare. When you install a new program or hardware component, you almost never have to reboot to activate the program or hardware driver. When you change the configuration, there are ways to restart the affected services without rebooting. If one program "freezes," you can use the **kill** command discussed in Chapter 8 to stop the program.

One thing that you should change on most Linux installations is the action associated with the Ctrl+Alt+Del keys. Open up /etc/inittab in a text editor, and add a hash mark (#) in front of the line so that it looks like the following (the actual code in your /etc/inittab file may be slightly different):

```
# ca::ctrlaltdel:/sbin/shutdown -t4 -r now
```

This action *comments out* the line that allows any user to restart Linux by pressing the Ctrl+Alt+Del keys. In other words, it is no longer part of your init configuration. This prevents frustrated users who are more familiar with Microsoft Windows from accidentally stopping the sessions of all users on a Linux computer. To make init read the revised file, run the **init q** command.

Table 13.1	Variations on shutdown.
Command	**Description**
shutdown -h now	Immediately starts the shutdown process via the **init 0** (halt) command.
shutdown -r now	Immediately starts the shutdown process via the **init 6** (reboot) command.
shutdown -h +10	Starts the shutdown process in 10 minutes.
halt	Functionally identical to **shutdown -h now**.
poweroff	Functionally identical to **shutdown -h now**.
reboot	Functionally identical to **shutdown -r now**.

Pressing the reset button or the On-Off switch when running Linux can be a dangerous thing. This action deletes all information on your RAM. Files you thought you had saved may still be on the RAM. For example, you may copy files to and from a floppy disk; the files are not actually written to the floppy until you unmount it from Linux with the **umount** command discussed later in the "**mount and umount**" section. If you press reset before unmounting the floppy, the files you thought were saved are actually lost.

 This is critical: If Linux freezes up, the reset button is the absolute last resort. When you save a file, it is often stored in RAM. That file is at risk until it is actually written to disk. The reset button wipes all data from the RAM.

Physical Security

Linux servers are set up for simultaneous access by many users. Some Linux distributions allow you to reset the **root** password just by rebooting in single user mode. For both reasons, physical security is important.

Any unauthorized users with physical access to your Linux server can end the sessions of all currently logged on users. All they need to do is turn off the computer. As will be discussed in Chapter 14, any user can reset the **root** user password to the code of his choice by typing **linux single** at the LILO **Boot:** prompt.

cron Tools

If you were a computer operating system and did not need sleep, you could back up users' files at night. You can rotate logs and delete temporary files while others are asleep.

The Linux daemon that performs these tasks on an automated basis is **crond**. When Linux boots, it starts **crond** as a process in the background. Every minute, it checks the appropriate configuration files to see if something needs to be run. These commands are governed by a global configuration file, /etc/crontab. Also, users can set up their own jobs with the **crontab** command.

/etc/crontab

The first configuration file examined by **cron** every minute is /etc/crontab. A typical setup for this file is shown in Figure 13.1.

The following is a line-by-line analysis of this file:

➤ *SHELL=/bin/bash*—The commands used in this file are based on the bash shell.

```
SHELL=/bin/bash
PATH=/sbin:/bin:/usr/sbin:/usr/bin
MAILTO=root
HOME=/
█
# run-parts
01 * * * * root run-parts /etc/cron.hourly
02 4 * * * root run-parts /etc/cron.daily
22 4 * * 0 root run-parts /etc/cron.weekly
42 4 1 * * root run-parts /etc/cron.monthly
~
~
~
~
~
~
~
~
~
~
~
~
~
~
~
~
```

Figure 13.1   A typical /etc/crontab configuration file.

➤ *PATH=/sbin:/bin:/usr/sbin:/usr/bin*—When the commands in this file are located in the noted directories, the full directory path is not required.

➤ *MAILTO=root*—Every time **cron** actually does something, notification is mailed to the user named **root**.

➤ *HOME=/*—The home directory associated with this /etc/crontab configuration file is the root (/) directory.

➤ *# run-parts*—A comment. The **run-parts** commands shown in the lines that follow this comment run every script file in the input directory. This allows you to organize the scripts you need to run periodically.

➤ *01 * * * * root run-parts /etc/cron.hourly*—This runs every script in the /etc/cron.hourly directory at one minute past every hour, every day.

➤ *02 4 * * * root run-parts /etc/cron.daily*—This runs every script in the /etc/cron.daily directory at 4:02 A.M., every day.

➤ *22 4 * * 0 root run-parts /etc/cron.weekly*—This runs every script in the /etc/cron.weekly directory at 4:22 A.M. every Sunday.

➤ *42 4 1 * * root run-parts /etc/cron.monthly*—This runs every script in the /etc/cron.monthly directory at 4:42 A.M. on the first day of every month.

The numbers and asterisks in the /etc/crontab file might seem cryptic. They are explained in the following section.

crontab Scheduling

The key to **cron** is understanding the time and date fields on the left side of each **cron** command. These five fields are, from left to right:

➤ *Minute*—Ranges from 0 through 59.

➤ *Hour*—Ranges from 0 through 23. For example, 0 hour is 12:00 A.M. (midnight), and 22 is 10:00 P.M.

➤ *Day*—Ranges from 1 through 31.

➤ *Month*—Ranges from 1 through 12.

➤ *Day of week*—Ranges from 0 through 7; 0 and 7 both represent Sunday.

If you want to specify a range such as every hour between 9:00 A.M and 5:00 P.M., set the second field to **9-17**. Alternatively, you can run a job every other day by setting the third field to ***/2**. As you can see, once you know each of the five fields (minute, hour, day, month, and day of week), there is nothing cryptic about any of the **cron** command fields.

 Know how to translate the time and date fields in /etc/crontab to determine when a specific job will be run. Memorize the function of each field.

Standard cron Jobs

As you can see from the /etc/crontab file in Figure 13.1, the jobs that are run are part of four directories. The most common **cron** jobs are run on a daily basis. Three common daily **cron** jobs are the following:

➤ **logrotate**—Rotates logs periodically. For example, Red Hat Linux rotates five weeks of logs, and the /var/log/messages entries from last week are kept in the /var/log/messages.1 file. Not all Linux distributions include **logrotate**. Some other Linux distributions include an /etc/logfiles configuration file for the **cron** daemon, which rotates various logs after they reach a certain size.

➤ **slocate.cron**—Refreshes the database associated with the **locate** command. Some Linux distributions perform this function in a cron file with *updatedb* in its name.

➤ **tmpwatch**—Deletes files in directories such as /tmp on a periodic basis.

Additional cron Jobs

You can add jobs to the list run by the **cron** daemon, **crond**, with the **crontab** command. As a user, you can use **cron** to back up files that you control. As the

Linux administrator with **root** privileges, you can back up other important Linux files and more. When you run the **crontab -e** command, you can edit your own settings in the **vi** editor.

Note: crontab uses vi by default. If for some reason you want to use another editor such as emacs, change the EDITOR environment variable with the export EDITOR=emacs command.

For example, assume that you've set up a script named **backmeup** in your home directory. This script is set up to back up all of the files in your home directory, /home/tr. You want to run **backmeup** every weekday evening at 11:36 P.M. Run **crontab -e** as a regular user. Type **i** to enter insert mode, and type in the following line:

```
36 23 * * 1-5    /home/tr/backmeup
```

Once you've saved the file, you can check the contents with the **crontab -1** command.

Note: The files created by crontab are typically stored in the /var/spool/cron directory or one of its subdirectories.

You can use **crontab** as a diagnostic tool. For example, if you're having problems every day at 10:12 P.M. with a specific daemon, you could set up a script to record the situation on your computer with commands such as **top** and **ps**. You could then set up a **crontab** job to run the script at desired times, such as 10:10 P.M., 10:11 P.M., and 10:12 P.M. The next day, you could check the results and hopefully diagnose the problem.

 Know how to set up a **crontab** job. While you don't need to know how to write a script, you should know how to use **crontab** to run that script on a schedule.

Disk Management

In Linux, partition management is the art of working with your disks. Sometimes, different commands and defaults apply to hard drives, floppy drives, and CD drives. Some drives and directories are mounted when Linux starts; others need to be mounted. Commands such as **du** and **df** allow you to monitor all mounted directories.

If you suspect trouble, **fsck** allows you to check and repair most Linux file systems. If you need to reformat, **mkfs** can handle most types of Linux file systems. If all else fails, you need to know how to make a boot disk, which can let you into a damaged Linux system; then you can use tools such as **fsck** to repair that file system.

mount and umount

When you install a floppy disk or CD on some of the latest Linux distributions, the files often appear in the assigned directories automatically. This service is courtesy of the auto mount daemon (**amd**). When properly configured, it also allows a computer to mount directories over a network.

As a Linux administrator, you need to know how to use the specific commands to mount and unmount floppies, CDs, and shared network directories. Fortunately, they are fairly straightforward. For example, to mount a CD on an existing /mnt/cdrom directory, run the following command:

```
mount /dev/cdrom /mnt/cdrom
```

This works in most cases because of the defaults set in the /etc/fstab configuration file, discussed in Chapter 6. Strictly speaking, the proper command for standard data CDs is this:

```
mount -t iso9660 /dev/cdrom /mnt/cdrom
```

The **iso9660** file type is the standard for data CDs. The **-t iso9660** switch isn't necessary if it's already in the format column in your /etc/fstab file. However, you can use the **-t** switch to temporarily supersede the default entry in this file.

You can mount a floppy disk with similar commands:

```
mount /dev/fd0 /mnt/floppy
mount /dev/fd1 /mnt/floppy
```

Generally, device fd0 applies to the first floppy drive on your computer. The fd1 device generally applies to the second floppy drive. If you want to supersede the file format assigned in /etc/fstab, the appropriate command is this:

```
mount -t ext2 /dev/fd0 /mnt/floppy
```

You may substitute vfat, ext3, or another appropriate file system for ext2. The file type you set can supersede the existing configuration in the /etc/fstab file.

 The default mount point for CDs and floppy drives on most Linux distributions is /mnt/cdrom and /mnt/floppy, respectively. This is consistent with the Filesystem Hierarchy Standard, discussed in Chapter 4. However, some Linux distributions use different mount directories such as /cdrom and /floppy. If in doubt, check the documentation associated with your distribution.

It's important to know how to use the **mount** command with a relative path. For example, if you're in the /home/tr directory and you've created an empty subdirectory named test, you can mount a CD on that directory with the **mount /dev/cdrom test** command. The corresponding command with the absolute path is **mount /dev/cdrom /home/tr/test**.

Unmounting a drive is easier. Just remember that the associated command is **umount** (not "unmount"). The following commands unmount a floppy and a CD drive:

```
umount /mnt/floppy
umount /mnt/cdrom
```

Remember that files may not actually be written to a drive until you unmount it. For example, if you save files to your floppy and physically eject it from your computer without running the appropriate **umount** command, the files won't be saved on your floppy.

As you read in Chapter 10, the process of mounting a shared network directory is similar, using commands such as **smbmount** and **smbumount**.

Current Allocations

There are two similar Linux commands for measuring allocated space on your computer: **df** and **du**. The free disk space command (**df**) lists the available space on each mounted volume. As you can see in Figure 13.2, the **df** command looks at the available space on each mounted volume, including mounted floppy, CD, and shared network directories. By default, the resulting partition sizes are shown in kilobytes. Alternatively, the **df -m** command would return a result with partition sizes defined in megabytes.

In contrast, the directory usage command (**du**) lists the amount of space used by each file in and below the current directory. A sample output is shown in Figure 13.3.

Take the following line from that output:

```
16     ./.gimp-1.2/gimpressionist
```

```
[mj@laptop71 mj]$ df
Filesystem           1k-blocks     Used Available Use% Mounted on
/dev/hda6            1123056     850420    215588  80% /
/dev/hda2              19519       3483     15028  19% /boot
/dev/hdb             652882     652882         0 100% /mnt/cdrom
//Experimental/LinuxPlus
                     2897280    1135552   1761728  40% /home/mj/test
/dev/fd0               1423       1150       274  81% /mnt/floppy
[mj@laptop71 mj]$ ▮
```

Figure 13.2   The **df** command shows available space on mounted volumes.

```
16        ./.gimp-1.2/gimpressionist
568       ./.gimp-1.2
264       ./.xvpics
4         ./%
8         ./.gphoto
4         ./.xmms/Skins
4         ./.xmms/Plugins
16        ./.xmms
20        ./.gnome/accels
4         ./.gnome/apps
44        ./.gnome/panel.d/default
48        ./.gnome/panel.d
4         ./.gnome/gnorpm.d/resources/distribs
8         ./.gnome/gnorpm.d/resources
12        ./.gnome/gnorpm.d
152       ./.gnome
8         ./.gnome_private
4         ./.gnome-desktop/Trash
20        ./.gnome-desktop
4         ./.netscape/cache
4         ./.netscape/archive
4         ./.netscape/xover-cache/host-news
8         ./.netscape/xover-cache
280       ./.netscape
4         ./.ssh
4         ./nsmail
51010     .
[mj@laptop71 mj]$ █
```

Figure 13.3   The **du** command shows space used by each file and directory.

The first dot refers to the current directory. The slash (/) navigates to a subdirectory, in this case, .gimp-1.2. The gimpressionist subdirectory (including files) takes up 16 kilobytes of disk space.

Disk Maintenance Commands

File systems everywhere are not perfect. If you experience a power failure, you can lose files in cache that have not been written to floppy or hard disks. Sometimes, the space is allocated, but the file is not there. These are some of the characteristics of a misaligned inode.

An *inode* is the identifier used on each Linux partition for a file. Every file gets its own inode. The inode includes the *metadata* about the file, which includes the permissions, size, linked files, access and modification times, and file locations on your drive (by disk block). If the inode is misaligned or corrupt, Linux can't find the associated file.

There are two key commands for maintaining a file system on a disk partition: **fsck** and **mkfs**. The file system check command (**fsck**) is used to check the integrity of a Linux file system. With the right switches, these commands can be used on any currently available Linux file system. If possible, misaligned inodes are repaired. The make file system command (**mkfs**) formats a partition; if all else fails, this command allows you to start from scratch.

Note: The fsck command is functionally similar to the MS-DOS chkdsk command.

The **fsck** command is fairly straightforward. As shown earlier in Figure 13.2, /dev/hda6 is formatted to the second extended file system (ext2). If you wanted to check the inodes associated with the hda6 partition, you would run the following command:

```
/sbin/fsck -t ext2 /dev/hda6
```

As noted in the previous section, mounted devices can be identified with the **df** command. By default, **fsck** is run on all default devices after a power failure or a fixed number of reboots (the number varies by Linux distribution). It is also a command that you can run from the standard Linux boot floppy.

Note: When you specify a file type for fsck, it calls another command customized for that file system. For example, e2fsck or fsck.ext2 is used to repair partitions formatted to the second extended file system (ext2); fsck.ext3 is used to repair partitions formatted to the third extended file system (ext3).

If Linux is currently running **fsck**, and the partition is formatted to a conventional Linux file system such as ext2, do not reset or turn off your computer. If you do, the inodes may be misaligned beyond repair. You could lose all of your data and have to reinstall Linux from scratch.

Keep in mind the fact that **fsck** can fix inodes that are misaligned. In other words, **fsck** makes sure that each inode is associated with the correct file. A common cause of misaligned inodes is a power failure.

The **mkfs** command is also straightforward. You can use it to format partitions. If you have an unformatted floppy, this command can be used to format it to the file system of your choice. For example, the following commands format a 1.44MB floppy associated with /dev/fd0 to the second extended (ext2) and VFAT file systems:

```
/sbin/mkfs -t ext2 /dev/fd0 1440
/sbin/mkfs -t vfat /dev/fd0 1440
```

Both **fsck** and **mkfs** are in the /sbin directory, so the full directory path (e.g., **/sbin/mkfs**) is required unless /sbin is in your path. As discussed in Chapter 7, the path can be checked with the **echo $PATH** command.

Disk Resizing

Two of the main file systems, ext2 and ReiserFS, are resizeable. In other words, you can change the amount of space on your hard drive allocated to a partition formatted to either of these file systems. The applicable commands are **resize2fs** and **resize_reiserfs**, respectively.

 Remember that you can use the **resize2fs** command to change the amount of space allocated to a partition formatted to the second extended file system (ext2).

Boot Disks

Linux boot disks are used to boot a computer. Some are customized to help you install a specific Linux distribution. Others are set up as rescue disks, which allow you to boot into Linux if the standard boot process does not work.

While you have a working Linux system, you should create a rescue disk customized for your computer with the **mkbootdisk** command. The command you use depends on the installed kernel, which you can check with the **uname -r** command.

For example, if the kernel number is 2.4.2-2, you can create a boot disk with the following command:

```
/sbin/mkbootdisk 2.4.2-2
```

*Note: The **mkbootdisk** command is currently available on Red Hat Linux and allied distributions.*

 Just as a reminder, many system administration commands won't work unless run as the **root** or superuser. As discussed in Chapter 11, you can use the **su -c "/sbin/mkbootdisk 2.4.2-2"** command to gain **root** privileges for that one command. Alternatively, if your username is properly configured in /etc/sudoers, the **sudo /sbin/mkbootdisk 2.4.2-2** command works equally well.

Normally, some free space is still available on the rescue disk. It's a good idea to store some other key files, such as /etc/inittab and /etc/passwd, in the free space.

Another way to create a rescue disk is with the **dd** command and the kernel in your /boot directory. For example, if your kernel file is named vmlinuz-2.4.2-2, use the following command:

```
dd if=/boot/vmlinuz-2.4.2-2 of=/dev/fd0 bs=8192
```

This command takes the image of the vmlinuz-2.4.2-2 kernel and transmits it to the floppy drive device fd0. The block size (**bs**) command is commonly used but is usually not required. One more command is required to make this work as a rescue disk: use the root device (**rdev**) command to imprint the normal mount point for the root directory (/). For example, in Figure 13.2, the **df** command shows the root directory mounted on /dev/hda6. In that case, run the following command:

```
/usr/sbin/rdev /dev/fd0 /dev/hda6
```

Boot disks will be used in Chapter 14 to rescue a damaged Linux system.

X Window

If you're thinking "Finally! We get to use the GUI in Linux," be prepared for a disappointment. The Linux+ exam barely covers the Linux GUI, also known as the X Window. What you do need to know is the configuration tools and files that you use to set up the X Window for others.

X Configuration Parameters

The standard X Window configuration file is XF86Config, located typically in the /etc/ directory or one of its subdirectories. With the introduction of XFree86 version 4.x in late 2000, the Linux X Window incorporated a unified X Server that could handle most graphics cards.

When you set up an X Window, a number of parameters are documented in XF86Config, including the following:

➤ *Input Devices*—Customizes the behavior of the keyboard and mouse that you use inside the X Window.

➤ *Monitor*—Sets the horizontal and vertical refresh rates associated with a monitor.

➤ *Modes*—Specifies different available screen sizes and densities.

➤ *Devices*—Customizes the settings associated with a graphics card.

➤ *Display*—Associates available video modes with a color depth. For example, 1 bit per pixel (bpp) is black and white, and 32 bpp is true color.

➤ *Server*—Since XFree86 version 3.x still supports more graphics cards, the server may also be specified in the XF86Config file.

 Remember that the X Window configuration file, XF86Config, includes settings for the mouse, keyboard, monitor, graphics card, screen sizes, and sometimes the X Server.

X Window Configuration Tools

You can use a number of command tools to configure the X Window. The work of the XFree86 project is used on all Linux distributions, as well as a number of Unix variants. Key X Window configuration tools include these:

➤ **XFree86**—The XFree86 **-configure** command can automatically configure some systems. The result is copied to a file such as XF86Config or XF86Config.new. Available only on distributions that include XFree86 version 4.

➤ **SuperProbe**—This command automatically probes your system. If successful, it specifies the graphics server and chipset associated with your setup. You can then use this information with a tool such as **xf86config** or **XF86Setup** to configure your system. Not available on all Linux distributions.

➤ **xf86config**—This standard configuration utility includes a series of menus in which you can specify the parameters for your keyboard, mouse, graphics card, and monitor.

➤ **XF86Setup**—This configuration tool is normally associated with XFree86 version 3. Because XFree86 version 4 does not support as many graphics cards, this configuration tool is still in use.

There are also some distribution-specific X Window configuration tools, including Red Hat's **Xconfigurator** and S.u.S.E.'s **SaX**. All of these tools configure the XFree86 configuration file associated with your Linux distribution.

 Know the names of the configuration tools that you can use to configure the X Window. Perhaps the most important of these tools is **xf86config**, because it configures all aspects of the XF86Config X Window configuration file associated with your Linux distribution. And remember that capitalization is important. For example, the **xf86config** tool modifies the XF86Config file.

X Window Applications

Because the Linux+ exam is essentially dedicated to the command-line interface, it is fitting that the only distribution-neutral graphical application explicitly addressed in the exam criteria is **xterm**. This is one of several applications that open a command-line interface inside the X Window. Figure 13.4 illustrates the simplicity of the interface.

As with most X Window applications, **xterm** can be called up through the menu associated with the window manager of your choice. Figure 13.5 illustrates the menu associated with Red Hat Linux 7.1 and KDE version 2.1.

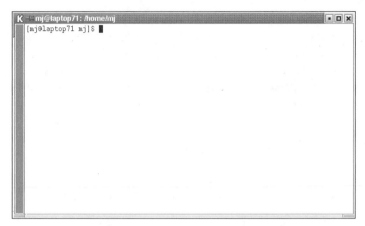

Figure 13.4   The **xterm** window provides a command-line interface inside the X Window.

 When in the X Window on a Linux workstation, you can log into a different virtual terminal. Press Ctrl+Alt+F*n*, where *n* is between 1 and 6. That should start a standard login screen. On most distributions, you can return to the X Window session by pressing Ctrl+Alt+F7.

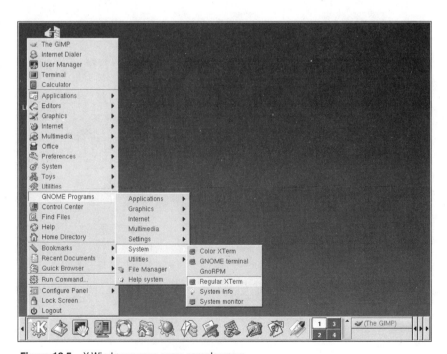

Figure 13.5   X Window menus seem complex now.

Note: There are a wide variety of Linux window managers, including KDE, GNOME, Enlightenment, FVWM95, Window Maker, AfterStep, Blackbox, and more. These window managers provide the look and feel for the X Window, including icons and menu interface. Generally, you'll select KDE or GNOME when you install Linux. See the "Need to Know More?" section at the end of this chapter for more information on these options.

Practice Questions

Question 1

> You're testing a new application in the X Window of a Linux test computer when the computer seems to freeze up. Which of the following actions should be used only as a last resort?
>
> ○ a. Press Ctrl+Alt+F2. Log in as the **root** user, and kill the PID associated with the new application.
>
> ○ b. Press Ctrl+Alt+Del to reboot the computer.
>
> ○ c. Use the **shutdown -h now** command.
>
> ○ d. Press the reset button.

Answer d is correct. Pressing the reset button is just like a sudden power failure on a Linux computer. Any files that have not yet been written to disk may be lost. Some files that you think you may have saved are also lost because they are still in RAM. The actions associated with answer a are what you should do first. If you can kill the PID associated with the new application, you do not need to reboot or reset Linux. Therefore, answer a is incorrect. Although you can use the Ctrl+Alt+Del keys to reboot Linux, that has the drawback of cutting off the sessions of any other users on that Linux system. Therefore, answer b is incorrect. Although the **shutdown -h now** command halts Linux, it has the same drawback as Ctrl+Alt+Del. Therefore, answer c is also incorrect.

Question 2

> If you wanted to change the configured resolution for your monitor, which of the following utilities would you use?
>
> ○ a. **XF86Config**
>
> ○ b. **xf86config**
>
> ○ c. **xf86setup**
>
> ○ d. **XFree86 -configure**

Answer b is correct. The **xf86config** command utility leads to a menu where you can configure every aspect of the X Window configuration on your Linux computer. It is also available on every current Linux distribution where the X Window is installed. Although you could directly edit the XF86Config file to change the resolution associated with your monitor, this file itself is not a command utility. Therefore, answer a is not correct. Although **XF86Setup** was a popular tool for XFree86 version 3.x X Window installations, it is not normally installed with the latest XFree86 version 4.x. And remember, Linux is case sensitive; for example, **xf86setup** is different from the actual tool, **XF86Setup**. Therefore, answer c is incorrect. While the **XFree86 -configure** command can be used to set up a generic configuration, it does not customize the configuration. Therefore, answer d is also incorrect.

Question 3

Which of the following commands creates a valid rescue floppy disk? Assume that the output from the **uname -r** command is "2.4.5-11".

○ a. **cp /boot/vmlinuz-2.4.5-11 /mnt/floppy**

○ b. **dd if=/boot/vmlinuz-2.4.5-11**

○ c. **/sbin/mkrescuedisk 2.4.5-11**

○ d. **/sbin/mkbootdisk 2.4.5-11**

Answer d is correct. While the Linux+ exam is distribution neutral, some questions require an understanding of Red Hat Linux–based commands. Assuming you're using Red Hat Linux, the **mkbootdisk** command in conjunction with the current version of the active version of the Linux kernel on your system can create a valid rescue disk. The **uname -r** command gives you the version number of the currently running Linux kernel. Although the **cp /boot/vmlinuz-2.4.5-11 /mnt/floppy** command would copy the Linux kernel to a floppy disk, it would not copy the other files needed to boot Linux from that disk. Therefore, answer a is not correct. Since the **dd** command needs an output file (**of**) such as your floppy drive (/dev/fd0), answer b is not correct. Since there is no **mkrescuedisk** command, answer c is also incorrect.

Question 4

Based on the following output from the **crontab -l** command, when will the backup script **/home/ichiro/backup** be run?

```
12 13 * * 6    /home/ichiro/backup
```

○ a. At 12:13 P.M. on the 6ᵗʰ day of each month

○ b. At 1:12 P.M. on the 6ᵗʰ day of each month

○ c. At 1:12 P.M. every Saturday

○ d. At 12:00 noon on June 13

Answer c is correct. The columns on a **cron** listing are, from left to right: minute, hour, day of month, month, day of week. Therefore, reading backwards, the code indicates that this program is run on Saturdays (6). The date and month are not specified, as illustrated by the asterisk (*). The time is the 13ᵗʰ hour and the 12ᵗʰ minute, which corresponds to 1:12 P.M. All other answers are incorrect.

Question 5

Which of the following statements best describes an inode?

○ a. A location on a hard drive

○ b. A listing of Linux file names and associated permissions

○ c. A block of data that locates a file on a partition and specifies its permissions

○ d. A command used to check the integrity of a partition

Answer c is correct. An inode includes information about characteristics of a Linux file, including permissions, the location of the file on the hard drive, the size of the file, and more. This is stored in a block of data at the beginning of a Linux partition. Although an inode does locate a file on a partition, it is not by itself a location. Therefore, answer a is incorrect. Every file has its own unique inode. One inode does not contain information on multiple files. Therefore, answer b is incorrect. Although the integrity of an inode is important to the integrity of a partition, there is no Linux inode command. Therefore, answer d is also incorrect.

Question 6

> Which of the following is the configuration file associated with the Linux X Window?
>
> ○ a. xf86config
>
> ○ b. XF86Config
>
> ○ c. XF86.conf
>
> ○ d. X.conf

Answer b is correct. XF86Config is the standard configuration file associated with the Linux X Window. Remember that it contains configuration data for the keyboard, mouse, graphics card, and monitor. The **xf86config** command utility is not the X Window configuration file. Therefore, answer a is incorrect. Nevertheless, it is still an important script to remember because it can help you set up the XF86Config file. Since there is no XF86.conf or X.conf file associated with the Linux X Window, answers c and d are also incorrect.

Question 7

> Which of the following commands would not help you realign the inodes to help you save the data on a partition?
>
> ○ a. **fsck**
>
> ○ b. **fsck.ext2**
>
> ○ c. **e2fsck**
>
> ○ d. **mkfs**

Answer d is correct. The **mkfs** command formats a partition, which does not help you save data. The **fsck, fsck.ext2,** and **e2fsck** commands are all tools that can help you realign the inodes on a partition. Therefore, answers a, b, and c are all incorrect. The **fsck.ext2** and **e2fsck** commands apply specifically to the partition that is formatted to the second extended file system (ext2).

Question 8

You're currently in **tr**'s home directory. It includes an empty directory named cdrom. Which of the following commands would mount the CD that you just inserted in **tr**'s cdrom directory?

○ a.   **mount -t iso9660 /dev/cdrom /mnt/cdrom**

○ b.   **mount /mnt/cdrom /dev/cdrom**

○ c.   **mount /dev/cdrom cdrom**

○ d.   **mount -t iso9660 /mnt/cdrom /home/tr/cdrom**

Answer c is correct. The desired mount point is the cdrom subdirectory of the current working directory. The absolute path (/home/tr/cdrom) is not required; in addition, specifying the file type for a CD is generally not required. Although answer a correctly mounts the CD on the /mnt/cdrom directory, that is not the directory specified in the question. Therefore, answer a is incorrect. Since answers b and d do not mount the CD-ROM device (/dev/cdrom has to come first), both answers also are incorrect.

Question 9

Three of the following commands essentially perform the same function. Which of the following commands does not belong with the others?

○ a.   **halt**

○ b.   **init 6**

○ c.   **shutdown -h now**

○ d.   **poweroff**

Answer b is correct. The **init 6** command reboots your system. You can verify this in the /etc/inittab configuration file. Since **halt, shutdown -h now,** and **poweroff** all shut down and halt the Linux computer, answers a, c, and d all are incorrect.

Question 10

You're testing a new application, **monet**, that monitors network activity. For some reason, the computer where the new application is installed seems to crash at 3:47 A.M. every Thursday. You want to check the CPU load associated with this application one minute before the crash. Which of the following lines should you add to your **crontab**?

- ○ a. **Thurs * * 3 46   ps aux I grep monet**
- ○ b. **3 46 * * 4   ps aux I grep monet**
- ○ c. **46 3 * * 5   ps aux I grep monet**
- ○ d. **46 3 * * 4   ps aux I grep monet**

Answer d is correct. In a **crontab** entry, the first number corresponds to the minute the specified command should be run, 46 in this case. The second number corresponds to the hour. The third number corresponds to the numeric day, in this case, 3. The fourth number corresponds to the month. The fifth number corresponds to the day of the week, where 0 is Sunday, 1 is Monday, and so on. Therefore, Thursday corresponds to the number 4. All other answers are incorrect.

Need to Know More?

 Mann, Scott, and Ellen L. Mitchell. *Linux System Security.* Upper Saddle River, NJ: Prentice Hall, 2000. ISBN 0-13015-807-0. This book includes excellent information on security and network monitoring tools.

 Welsh, Matt, Lar Kaufman, and Matthias Kalle Dalheimer. *Running Linux.* Sebastapol, CA: O'Reilly & Associates, 1999. ISBN 1-56592-469-X. Possibly the key resource text on the Linux operating system. Although much of the information in this book is based on older versions of Linux, the basic data is concise, well written, and applicable today. For example, it provides excellent explanations of **crontab** and general disk management.

 Everyone who relies on a Linux computer should know what to do if there is a crash. An introduction to boot disks and crash rescue is available in the LILO, Linux Crash Rescue HOWTO from the Linux Documentation Project. This is available online at **www.linuxdoc.org/ HOWTO/LILO-crash-rescue-HOWTO.html**. Of particular interest is the list of Linux distributions that you can fit on a 1.44MB floppy disk.

 A substantial number of window managers are available for Linux. The two most popular ones, KDE and GNOME, are fully featured. They include a number of applications such as office suites. The work of the K Desktop Environment (KDE) can be found online at **www.kde.org**. The work of the GNU Network Object Model Environment (GNOME) can be found online at **www.gnome.org**.

 Good explanations of inodes are difficult to find. The best that I've seen is based on an article that describes inodes on the Berkeley Standard Distribution (BSD). Since BSD is also a Unix clone, inodes on Linux follow the same principles. This article can be found online at **www.onlamp.com/pub/a/bsd/2001/03/07/FreeBSD_Basics.html**.

Troubleshooting

Terms you'll need to understand:

✓ Data collection

✓ Problem isolation

✓ Linux Documentation Project

✓ Scientific method

✓ Boot disk, rescue disk

✓ Core dump

✓ Linux Loader (LILO)

✓ Single user mode

✓ **route**

✓ **netstat**

✓ **ping**

✓ **traceroute**

Techniques you'll need to master:

✓ Collecting data from users

✓ Isolating problems

✓ Using the scientific method

✓ Getting help online

✓ Understanding core dumps

✓ Using rescue disks

✓ Replacing a lost **root** password

✓ Restoring LILO

✓ Bypassing an unworkable graphical login screen

✓ Diagnosing common errors

✓ Using network troubleshooting utilities

✓ Identifying network server failures

Troubleshooting is the art of solving problems. When you have a problem, experience or good documentation sometimes allows for a quick solution. Otherwise, good troubleshooting practices require a systematic analysis. You have already used basic troubleshooting techniques in a number of previous chapters to install hardware, software, Linux application packages, and more. This chapter uses what you've already learned to help you manage a Linux system, limited to the topics addressed on the CompTIA Linux+ exam.

Linux includes extensive log files that can help you with the troubleshooting process. Some of these files were addressed in Chapter 6. If you're not able to boot Linux, however, you can't get to the log files to help diagnose the problem. There are several ways to get around boot problems with Linux boot and rescue floppy disks.

Basic Philosophy

Once you've collected the data you need, most Linux problems have "simple" solutions, but the ability to find these solutions often takes years of experience. Sometimes this experience is available online. If you don't know what to do and can't find resources that identify your problem, you need to think about the situation systematically with the basic scientific method.

Data Collection

When you're trying to help a user, you need to listen for the facts you can use. As a Linux administrator, you should be able to check the situation on the applicable server. You can collect data by prompting users to enter commands at their own workstations. Alternatively, you can use **telnet** to check your user's computer remotely. The goal of data collection is to classify the basic problem into one of the following categories:

➤ *User*—User-related issues fall into all categories. Your users may need instructions on how to work with their hardware, applications, or Linux configurations.

➤ *Hardware*—Physical installation and Linux-related hardware configuration issues were addressed in Chapters 3 and 9.

➤ *Linux configuration*—This includes nonphysical network-configuration issues. Several chapters address basic configuration issues; many configuration files, such as for Samba and NFS, are beyond the scope of the Linux+ exam.

➤ *Application software*—While detailed application configuration is beyond the scope of the Linux+ exam, the data you collect by checking applications on your test computers is a starting point for troubleshooting.

Problem Isolation

Before you can identify a problem, you should categorize it. When you become more experienced with handling user problems, you may notice that they fall into different categories. Six major categories of Linux problems are as follows:

➤ *Login*—A user can't log into the Linux system. In Chapter 11, you learned that, as the **root** user, you could assign a new password to a user. For example, if the username is **ez**, run the **passwd ez** command.

➤ *Rights*—A user is unable to access a file, utility, or application. In Chapter 11, you learned to manage the permissions associated with files, directories, utilities, applications, and more. Essential commands include **chmod, chown**, and **chgrp**.

➤ *Printing*—A user can't print a desired file. In Chapter 12, you learned to manage printers on a Linux print server. Essential commands include **lpr, lpc, lpq**, and **lprm**.

➤ *LAN access*—A user is having trouble accessing shared directories or applications over a network. You learned about some of the basic services, including Samba, NFS, and NIS, in several previous chapters. Detailed configuration of these services (and therefore troubleshooting them as well) is beyond the scope of the Linux+ exam.

➤ *WAN access*—External network access is also a problem for a modern network. Email and Internet access services are now perceived as critical in the corporate world. One WAN troubleshooting command in this chapter is **traceroute**, addressed in the "Bottoms Up" section.

➤ *Configuration*—To some extent, everything is a configuration issue. This category covers basic issues such as incompatible drivers, software packages, and backup/restore issues. These are addressed in the "Common Errors" section.

You've learned about all of these problems, to some extent, in previous chapters.

Quick Results

Computers have become ubiquitous in the modern organization. When a computer breaks down, people notice. Most organizations still use a Microsoft operating system, and the management in many of those organizations is comforted that it can lean on Microsoft when it has a question about software. However, the delays associated with relying on any third party, including Microsoft, are not good for productivity.

When a Linux computer breaks down, however, people become concerned. Organizations can't rely on Microsoft to support Linux. Unless they have purchased a support contract from a company such as Linuxcare, they need to rely on Linux experts such as yourself to solve the problem. If you do not have the answer, you need to know where you can go to get help quickly. Although you can contract with a company such as Linuxcare for support, you can also use the three main public sources of help on Linux:

➤ *Linux Documentation Project*—This is a comprehensive source of Linux solutions, which includes HOWTOs, man pages, frequently asked question (FAQ) lists, and book-length guides. It's available online at **www.linuxdoc.org**.

➤ *Newsgroups*—There are several dozen Internet newsgroups. Many Linux newsgroup contributors want to demonstrate their knowledge by solving any problem you may have. Most newsgroups are collected in the Usenet database, searchable as of this writing through the **groups.google.com** Web site. The mailing lists affiliated with many Linux distributions offer a similar service.

➤ *Distribution archives*—Many distributions keep a database of problems and solutions on their Web sites. These are known on some Web sites as *knowledge bases*.

For best results, be prepared before asking a question on a newsgroup. In your messages, include details of what you have already done to try to solve the problem. In addition, include relevant sections of configuration files, as well as the resources (books, HOWTOs, etc.) you consulted to try to solve the problem.

Scientific Method

If all else fails, there is the basic scientific method: observe, theorize, and test. Observe the problem and related configuration. Theorize by making your best educated guess about the cause of the problem. And test your guess by attempting to reproduce the problem.

When you observe a problem, collect the appropriate configuration data. For example, if a user is having trouble connecting to your Web server, look at your Apache configuration file (httpd.conf). Alternatively, if a user is having trouble connecting to an outside Web site, check your firewall and proxy setup. The trouble could be based on the **ipchains** or **iptables** commands in your firewalls or the setup related to any proxy server you have configured, such as Squid.

To make an educated guess, you need to draw upon the resources at your disposal. For example, you know from Chapter 10 that the **DocumentRoot** variable in httpd.conf is set to the default directory that should contain home pages on an Apache server. Alternatively, if users on your LAN can't access the Internet, service may be disabled in the firewall setup related to the settings in the /etc/services file or the /etc/xinetd.d directory.

One way to test your assumption is to copy the suspect configuration files to a test computer. For example, if you believe a problem with your firewall is blocking the users on your LAN from accessing the Internet, copy that file to the test computer. If the test computer has the same problem, you know that it is related to the copied configuration file. Otherwise, the problem lies elsewhere.

Boot Issues

In the ideal world, you've created a rescue disk customized for your Linux configuration during the installation process. You'll never lose your **root** password. And the Linux Loader (LILO) never gets overwritten.

In the real world, however, you'll encounter all of these problems. You need to know what to do in each of these situations.

Rescue Disk Options

If you ever have a problem booting Linux, you can use a boot disk or a rescue disk. These terms are often used interchangeably; nevertheless, there are specific functions associated with boot and rescue disks:

➤ *Boot disk*—A floppy used to start a Linux system, often used for installing Linux. Some boot disks can be used to rescue a currently installed Linux system. Boot disks were addressed in Chapter 5.

➤ *Rescue disk*—A floppy used to rescue or boot a currently installed Linux system. Rescue disks were addressed in Chapter 13.

Generally, it's best if you have a rescue disk customized for your specific Linux installation. A customized rescue disk automatically installs the correct kernel and drivers on the correct partitions. Alternatively, with a bit of configuration, you can use many Linux boot disks as rescue disks. For example, Figure 14.1 illustrates the use of a Red Hat Linux 7.1 boot disk to start a S.u.S.E. Linux 7.2 system.

Note that kernel version number 2.4.2-2 corresponds to the default Red Hat 7.1 kernel. (The S.u.S.E. 7.2 default kernel is 2.4.4-4.) Since the root directory partition is different on each system, the following was entered at the LILO boot: prompt:

```
linux root=/dev/hda3
```

In this case, /dev/hda3 represents the location of the root directory on the S.u.S.E. system. The Red Hat boot disk can then find Linux on the S.u.S.E. computer. Since the kernels are different, errors such as those shown in Figure 14.1 are to be

```
modprobe: modprobe: Can't open dependencies file /lib/modules/2.4.2-2/modules.de
p (No such file or directory)
Starting syslog services                                           done
Starting lpd                                                       done
Starting service at daemon:                                        done
Loading keymap qwerty/us.map.gz                                    done
Loading compose table winkeys shiftctrl latin1.add                done
Loading console font lat1-16.psfu                                  done
Setting up console ttys                                            done
Starting CRON daemon                                               done
Starting Name Service Cache Daemon                                 done
Starting personal-firewall (final) [not active]                   unused
Starting console mouse support (gpm):                             done
modprobe: Can't open dependencies file /lib/modules/2.4.2-2/modules.dep (No such
 file or directory)
Starting httpd [ ]                                                 done
Master Resource Control: runlevel 3 has been                   reached
Failed services in runlevel 3:                                 network
Skipped services in runlevel 3:  personal-firewall.initial pcmcia personal-firew
all.final

Welcome to SuSE Linux 7.2 (i386) - Kernel 2.4.2-2 (tty1).

linux login:
```

Figure 14.1   Booting a S.u.S.E. system with a Red Hat boot disk.

expected. Nevertheless, this is an alternate way to access a Linux system that is
sufficient to allow you to restore and/or reconfigure the appropriate configuration files.

Most distributions allow you to create a boot disk with some form of the
dd if=/boot/*imagefile***of=/dev/fd0** command. The image file that you
use is of a kernel; for most Linux distributions, the name of the file is
vmlinux or *vmlinuz*, sometimes with the version number of the kernel
at the end of the file name. Many distributions have their own specific
methods for creating rescue disks, such as Debian's **mkboot** or Red
Hat's **mkbootdisk** command. The **mkbootdisk** command is covered in
Chapter 13. Check the documentation for your distribution for more
details.

Lost **Root** Password

Recovery from a lost **root** password may be too easy in Linux. All you need to do
is to start Linux in single user mode. Reboot your computer. When you see the
LILO **Boot:** prompt, enter the following:

```
linux single
```

Break this command into two parts. Entering **linux** starts the Linux operating
system. The following word (**single**) is read as a Linux command after Linux
boots. You can enter many commands at this prompt, such as **append** and **init**.

The **linux single** command at the LILO boot: prompt starts Linux in single user mode. This is a fairly simple setup, with no networking, one terminal, and one logged-on user: **root**. As the **root** user, you can then change the **root** password with the **passwd** command. As **root**, you're not prompted for the old password; just enter the desired password, subject to the limitations discussed in Chapter 11, and you're ready to go.

Since there is no networking associated with single user mode, remote administrators can't help you with this process.

*Note: The ability to run Linux in single user mode is a security hole. Anyone who has physical access to your computer and can reboot your system can change your **root** password using this technique. Some distributions have closed this security hole; when you reboot those distributions in single user mode, you are prompted for the forgotten **root** password.*

If you forget the **root** password while logged in as the **root** user, the process is even easier. Just run the **passwd** command. Since you're already the **root** user, Linux doesn't prompt you for the current **root** password.

Remember that you can reset the **root** password by starting Linux in single user mode. Just enter **linux single** at the LILO boot: prompt. When Linux boots, run the **passwd** command. You're not even prompted for the current **root** password. Since single user mode does not include networking, you cannot reset the **root** password remotely.

No Operating System Found

The title of this section looks like a nightmare scenario for the Linux administrator. Either Linux has been deleted from your computer, or your computer just can't find Linux on the right hard drive partition. Restoring Linux from a backup is beyond the scope of the Linux+ exam, but there is a fairly simple solution if your computer just can't find Linux on the right partition.

The Linux Loader (LILO), as discussed in earlier chapters, helps your computer find installed operating systems on your hard drives. Three of the possible LILO problems are the following:

➤ *Deleted LILO*—It's possible to delete LILO on your computer accidentally. For example, if you boot your computer with a Microsoft boot disk, you can delete LILO from the MBR with the **fdisk /MBR** command.

➤ *Incorrect partition*—If the **root** variable in your /etc/lilo.conf file does not point to the correct partition, LILO can't boot Linux on your computer.

➤ *Missing boot image*—If all you see of the LILO **Boot**: promt is "LI," the secondary boot loader file, /boot/boot.b, may be missing. You can restore this file from a rescue disk.

Generally, the solution is to reinstall LILO on the primary master IDE hard drive with the following command:

```
/sbin/lilo
```

But how can you run a Linux command if you can't start Linux? Just use a Linux boot or rescue disk.

It is important to know that you can use a Linux boot or rescue disk to restore the Linux boot loader, LILO, to the master boot record (MBR) of your hard drive. Once Linux boots, you can do this with the **/sbin/lilo** command.

X Login

As discussed in Chapter 6, you can set up the **id** variable in etc/inittab for a graphical user interface (GUI) login screen. If there is a problem while starting the X Window login screen, you can alternatively access a command-line interface, also known as *console mode*. There are two possible ways to access console mode in this situation:

➤ **Ctrl+Alt+F***n*—This command key combination normally starts a console mode login screen; the variable *n* is a number between 1 and 6.

➤ **Ctrl+Alt+Backspace**—This command key combination normally exits out of the X Window. If the **id** variable is set to the run level associated with a GUI login screen, it restarts the X Server to try to access the X Window login screen again. Otherwise, it returns you to the command-line interface.

Know the command key combinations such as **Ctrl+Alt+F1** that you can use to access a command-line interface console mode if Linux gets stuck and is set up for an X Window login.

Common Errors

You've already examined many common errors throughout this book. You've collected and installed appropriate drivers in Chapters 3 and 9. You've learned when to reconfigure the Linux kernel in Chapters 2 and 9. In this section, you'll extend this knowledge by learning about package compatibility, more backup and restore issues, and what to do with a core dump.

Incompatible Packages

In Chapter 6, you learned about some of the commands you can use to install **rpm** and .tar.gz packages. Problems fall into three different categories:

➤ *Package dependencies*—As discussed in Chapter 6, the **rpm** command checks for any prerequisite packages before installation. If you install a .tar.gz package with an unsatisfied prerequisite, however, you may not get a package dependency error message.

➤ *Library errors*—These errors are a result of problems with a shared program, such as a C language compiler.

➤ *Version conflicts*—When you use a different version of a Linux kernel, not all related software will work. For example, the boot of a S.u.S.E. Linux 7.2 operating system with a Red Hat Linux 7.1 boot disk, as shown in Figure 14.1, includes a problem with the network card. This is because of a version conflict in the associated driver.

The quickest way to find the solution is to consult with others who have had the same problem. This is best done through the Web site home page for the package, applicable newsgroups, mailing lists, or knowledge bases.

Problem Restoring Files

Three basic reasons exist for restoring files from a backup. First, you may want just the old versions of a file. Second, critical hardware such as a hard drive may have failed. Third, a cracker may have broken into your system.

In the first case, no special precautions are required unless you don't want to overwrite all of your current files from the backup archive. In the latter two cases, you're probably restoring your system from scratch. In other words, you're reinstalling Linux and then restoring key files from a backup.

For example, assume you're trying to restore the files associated with an Apache server. You restore the files, but users still can't access your Web site. There are several possible issues:

➤ *Archived using relative path*—As discussed in Chapter 6, the right way to archive files with the **tar** command is through an absolute path. For example, if you're archiving the Web pages on an Apache server, use a command such as **tar xzvf /var/www/html**. Otherwise, you need to navigate to the directory from where you made the backup when you use **tar** to restore an archive.

➤ *Service configuration*—The files you backed up may not be all the files used by the service. For example, the Apache configuration file, httpd.conf, is usually located in a different directory from the actual Web pages. If your default

DocumentRoot is different from the standard Apache configuration, users will probably get only the default Apache server page on their browsers.

➤ *Basic configuration*—Alternatively, the appropriate network configuration files such as /etc/services may not allow traffic to your Web server. This and other configuration issues that may keep Apache and other network services from running are covered in the "Network Troubleshooting" section.

Especially if your system has been cracked or infected, it's often best to reinstall Linux. This ensures that *Trojan horses,* which may be masquerading as common commands such as **ls**, are eliminated. Then you can restore data specific to your computer from archives dated before the infection.

Core Dump

A *core dump* is a snapshot of your RAM when a service or application crashes on your computer. The typical core dump file has a simple name: core. It's usually placed in the home directory of the person who was using the application when it crashed. Unless needed by the developers to help troubleshoot the application, you can usually safely delete these large files from your system.

Network Troubleshooting

Troubleshooting a network is no different from troubleshooting a single computer. You collect data, identify and isolate the problem, use your resources to look for quick results, and—if that doesn't work—apply the scientific method.

Once you've checked the physical connections, network data collection is based on commands such as **netstat** and **route**. Isolating the problem requires different commands, such as **ping** and **traceroute**.

 The commands in this section are important. Try them out on a Linux computer, preferably one on a LAN connected to another network such as the Internet. If you're using a Linux computer at home with a direct connection to the Internet, use the Default Gateway IP address as defined by your ISP as the address for the router computer. Alternatively, the **netstat**, **route**, and **ping** commands also work on a Microsoft Windows computer in MS-DOS mode. The Microsoft version of **traceroute** is the **tracert** command.

Network Status

The basic command to check the status of a Linux network has a straightforward name: **netstat**. This command can be used to show routing tables, proxy connec-

```
[root@laptop71 mod]# netstat -a | more
Active Internet connections (servers and established)
Proto Recv-Q Send-Q Local Address            Foreign Address        State
tcp       0      0 *:exec                    *:*                    LISTEN
tcp       0      0 *:1024                    *:*                    LISTEN
tcp       0      0 *:login                   *:*                    LISTEN
tcp       0      0 *:shell                   *:*                    LISTEN
tcp       0      0 *:printer                 *:*                    LISTEN
tcp       0      0 *:rsync                   *:*                    LISTEN
tcp       0      0 *:finger                  *:*                    LISTEN
tcp       0      0 *:sunrpc                  *:*                    LISTEN
tcp       0      0 *:http                    *:*                    LISTEN
tcp       0      0 *:x11                     *:*                    LISTEN
tcp       0      0 *:ftp                     *:*                    LISTEN
tcp       0      0 *:ssh                     *:*                    LISTEN
tcp       0      0 *:telnet                  *:*                    LISTEN
tcp       0      0 laptop71:smtp             *:*                    LISTEN
tcp       0      0 192.168.0.50:ftp          Experimental:1875      ESTABLISHED
tcp       0      0 192.168.0.50:telnet       Experimental:1876      ESTABLISHED
tcp       0      0 192.168.0.50:1027         Experimental:netbios-ssn ESTABLISHED
udp       0      0 *:1024                    *:*
udp       0      0 *:tftp                    *:*
udp       0      0 *:623                     *:*
udp       0      0 *:sunrpc                  *:*
Active UNIX domain sockets (servers and established)
Proto RefCnt Flags      Type      State     I-Node Path
unix  2      [ ACC ]    STREAM    LISTENING 2499   /tmp/.ICE-unix/1090
--More--
```

Figure 14.2   Available connections found by the **netstat -a** command.

tions to outside networks, interface statistics, and more. For example, the **netstat** -a command displays all available connections. As shown in Figure 14.2, the Local Address column displays names and numbers, which correspond to TCP/IP ports described in earlier chapters. In the Foreign Address column, you can see **ftp, telnet,** and Samba connections that are established between the local computer and the computer named **Experimental**.

A variation of this command can be used to find routing tables:

```
netstat -nr
```

A routing table lists currently configured paths from your computer to another computer on or outside your network. Linux uses these paths to find the computers to which you want to connect. A few other significant **netstat** commands are shown in Table 14.1.

Table 14.1	netstat commands.
Command	**Function**
netstat -a	Display all available connection ports, also known as *sockets*.
netstat -n	Display routing table in numeric format, which uses IP addresses by default. Does not require access to DNS.
netstat -r	Display routing table.
netstat -M	Display masqueraded connections, which connect computers on your LAN to external networks.

The **route -n** or **netstat -n** commands return IP addresses. You need to know that, since they do not require access to a DNS server, they do not send or receive information on a network.

The **netstat -nr** command is functionally equivalent to the **route** command. The difference is that, with **route**, you can manually add an address to a routing table. For example, if you've added more computers to your LAN with a network IP address of **192.168.33.0**, you can add the route to these computers with the following command:

```
route add -net 192.168.33.0 netmask 255.255.255.0 dev eth0
```

Don't be too concerned if you do not fully understand the **netstat -r** command. It is shown simply to illustrate that **route** can add another entry to your routing table.

Remember that while the **netstat -nr** command is functionally equivalent to **route**, you can modify routing tables only with the **route** command. Also, the **netstat -nr** command displays the actual working routing table for your computer. Both commands display routing information through your LAN while your network card, such as eth0, is active.

Bottoms Up

If you have a specific problem on your network, such as a user who is complaining about not having Web or email access, the first thing to do is quiz the user. Based on your knowledge of browsers and email managers, make sure the user knows how to access the desired service. If you're on a connected network, log onto that user's computer through **telnet**. This data collection process also helps you to identify and isolate the problem.

If you establish that the problem does not reside with the user or his computer, check your resources. You may be able to find the solution from your own experience or that of others or through online resources.

If you still don't have a solution, it's time to use the scientific method: observe the problem, theorize about the cause, and test a solution. The principle is to look at your system from the bottom up; in other words, hardware is much more likely to be the problem than the user application. Network hardware diagnostic tools such as **ifconfig** are discussed in Chapter 9.

Linux includes a number of tools that allow you to work from the most basic network connection all the way to the connections required for the application.

These command tools are based on the **ping** and **traceroute** commands. When diagnosing network connections, run the following commands in this order:

➤ **ping 127.0.0.1**—If you see a continuous response such as "64 bytes from 127.0.0.1...," TCP/IP is properly installed on your computer. Press Ctrl+C to stop the response.

➤ **ping** *your_ip_address*—Substitute the IP address defined for your network card for *your_ip_address*, based on the output from the **ifconfig** command. If you see a similar continuous response, your network card is properly configured. Don't forget to press Ctrl+C when you're ready to move on.

➤ **ping** *your_host_name*—Substitute the hostname for your computer, which usually can be found in the /etc/HOSTNAME or /etc/hosts file. If you see the same response as with the previous command, hostnames are properly configured on your computer. Don't forget to press Ctrl+C when you're ready to move on.

➤ **ping** *another_ip_address*—Substitute the IP address of another computer on your LAN for *another_ip_address*. You can use the **ifconfig** command on Linux and Microsoft Windows computers to find their IP addresses. If you see a similar continuous response, communication is working on your LAN. One useful IP address to check is that owned by the router or gateway that connects your LAN to other networks. Don't forget to press Ctrl+C when you're ready to move on.

➤ **ping** *another_host_name*—Substitute the name of a computer on a connected network for *another_host_name*. If you're connected to the Internet, one example is **ping www.coriolis.com**. If this works, your LAN's gateway or router computer is properly configured, and communication is possible to and from your LAN. Don't forget to press Ctrl+C when you're ready to move on.

➤ **traceroute** *another_host_name*—Use another name on a connected network. If you're connected to the Internet, a **traceroute www.coriolis.com** command returns the addresses of the path your messages take to the Coriolis Web site. If you're diagnosing a problem on interconnected networks, this command stops either at the destination or at the router or gateway that is having a problem.

For example, if you're having trouble with the **ping** command for the IP address of the router or gateway on your LAN, check the IP address of some other computer on your network. If you cannot connect to other computers on your LAN, there may be a problem with the cables or connections. Otherwise, there may be trouble with the hardware on the router computer.

Remember how to check the connections between your computer and the router or gateway computer that connects your LAN to other networks. These connections are physical (are the cables connected snugly?) and logical (based on the results of various **ping** and **traceroute** commands).

Specific Services

Now you can apply this knowledge and what you learned in previous chapters to specific services. Assume one of the users on your LAN tells you that he cannot access some service such as Internet Web pages, email on external network servers, FTP download sites, or **telnet** connections. If none of these services are working, use the techniques described in the previous section. Check each service against the configuration shown in the /etc/inetd.conf file or the files in the /etc/xinetd.d directory (the file varies by distribution). Check the active services in /etc/services, as discussed in Chapter 6.

For example, assume a user is able to access email but not the Internet connection from a computer on your LAN. If the email server is outside your network, you can assume that the connection to outside networks through the router is working. Then you should check anything that may be blocking the Web connection, such as a firewall based on **ipchains** or **iptables**, information in the /etc/hosts.allow, /etc/hosts.deny, and/or the /etc/services files on the router computer. Another possible firewall is based on the configuration of a proxy server such as Squid. These services and commands were discussed in several previous chapters.

 If one network service works and another does not, check the firewall and /etc/hosts.allow and /etc/hosts.deny files on the router computer. Check the configuration of the proxy server on the router computer. Check the available services as defined in the /etc/inetd.conf file or the /etc/xinetd.d directory.

Practice Questions

Question 1

Company policy dictates that you change your **root** password every seven days. You aren't allowed to alternate between two different passwords. You've forgotten the password you're using this week. Assume your Linux distribution does not require a password when you boot Linux in run level 1. Which of the following actions is most appropriate?

- ○ a. Run the **init 1** command.
- ○ b. Reboot Linux and enter the **linux single** command at the LILO **Boot**: prompt.
- ○ c. Reboot Linux with a rescue disk and enter the **linux init 1** command at the LILO boot: prompt.
- ○ d. Reinstall Linux.

Answer b is correct. Entering **linux single** at the LILO **Boot**: prompt starts Linux in single user mode. You can then use the **passwd** command to reset your **root** user password. The **init** command can be run only by the **root** or superuser. Since you've forgotten the **root** password, you can't run **init**, at least not without rebooting. Therefore, answer a is incorrect. Run level 1 corresponds to single user mode. If you can reboot Linux, there is no need for a rescue disk. Therefore, although using a rescue disk and entering **linux init 1** at the LILO boot: prompt works, it is less efficient. Therefore, answer c is also not correct. Although you can reinstall Linux and set a new **root** password, that would destroy the current files saved on that Linux system by you and your users. Therefore, answer d is also not correct.

Question 2

> You've created a rescue disk with the following command:
>
> ```
> dd if=/boot/vmlinuz of=/dev/fd0
> ```
>
> You're now having trouble booting Linux on your computer. When you boot your computer from the rescue disk, which of the following actions should you take?
>
> ○ a. Nothing. Rescue disks automatically boot the installed version of Linux on your computer.
>
> ○ b. Enter the **linux single** command at the LILO **Boot**: prompt.
>
> ○ c. Enter **linux root=/dev/*hda2***, where ***hda2*** corresponds to the location of the Linux operating system root directory on your computer.
>
> ○ d. Enter **linux append root=/dev/*hda2***, where ***hda2*** corresponds to the location of the Linux operating system root directory on your computer.

Answer c is correct. Until you identify the partition with your root (/) directory, Linux does not know from where to boot your computer. Unless you used the **rdev** command to identify the partition with your root directory, rescue disks created with commands such as **dd** do not contain enough information. Therefore, answer a is incorrect. While the **linux single** command tries to start Linux in single user mode, it does not work if it cannot find the partition with your root directory. Therefore, answer b is also incorrect. Since the **append** command is used to pass information about hardware such as RAM and network cards, it does not apply to defining partitions. Therefore, answer d is also incorrect.

Question 3

> One of the users on your LAN is having trouble accessing email. You use an email service that is on an outside network. The networks all use TCP/IP. There is no trouble accessing Web pages through the Internet. All of the following items might cause the email problem except:
>
> ○ a. Squid
>
> ○ b. Firewall
>
> ○ c. Proxy service
>
> ○ d. Router hardware

Answer d is correct. If you have access to outside networks, you know there is a solid physical connection between your LAN and the outside network through the router. Also, since you can access Web pages through the Internet, you know that at least part of the Linux configuration is working. Since Squid is the basic Linux proxy server, which can regulate traffic coming in from the Internet, it could be blocking email messages. Therefore, answer a is not correct. Since the **ipchains** or **iptables** command in a firewall can selectively block Web or email access, answer b is not correct. Since Squid is also a type of proxy service, answer c is also incorrect.

Question 4

You've set up Linux with a login screen at an X Window interface. For some reason, the GUI login screen does not appear. Which of the following command key combinations allows access to a console interface?

○ a. **Ctrl+Alt+F1**

○ b. **F1**

○ c. **Ctrl+Alt+Backspace**

○ d. **Ctrl+F1**

Answer a is correct. The **Ctrl+Alt+F1** key combination allows access to a command-line interface console, also known as a *getty*, as discussed in Chapter 11. There is no effect associated with pressing just the **F1** key; therefore, answer b is not correct. While the **Ctrl+Alt+Backspace** key combination can restart an X Window login interface, it may not start a command-line interface console, depending on the settings in your /etc/inittab file. Therefore, answer c is incorrect. Since the **Ctrl+F1** key combination has no effect from the X Window, answer d is also incorrect.

Question 5

Which of the following commands can you use to find the current routing table on your computer, without connecting to a DNS server?

○ a. **netstat**

○ b. **netstat -nr**

○ c. **netroute**

○ d. **netstat -ar**

Answer b is correct. The **netstat -nr** command uses numeric IP addresses and therefore does not require access to a DNS server to find associated hostnames. Since the **netstat** command alone defines a number of network parameters other than routing table information, answer a is not correct. Since there is no **netroute** command, answer c is also incorrect. As defined earlier in Table 14.1, the **netstat -ar** command defines the active routing table. Since it does not use numeric IP addresses, however, it requires access to a DNS server; therefore, answer d is also incorrect.

Question 6

Which of the following commands or sets of commands can you use to create a rescue disk for your Linux computer? Assume that your root partition is on the second logical partition of your primary master IDE hard drive and the Linux kernel is available in the /boot/vmlinuz file, and that it is version 2.4.2-2.

○ a. **mkbootdisk**

○ b. **dd if=/boot/vmlinuz of=/dev/fd0; rdev=/dev/hda2**

○ c. **dd if=/boot/vmlinuz of=/dev/fd0; rdev=/dev/hda6**

○ d. **mkrescuedisk 2.4.2-2**

Answer c is correct. The first command in this answer creates a generic Linux boot disk for this kernel from the appropriate kernel file. It sends this file as output to the first floppy disk drive on your computer. The second logical partition is hda6. Since the root directory is not mounted on hda2, answer b is incorrect. While the **mkbootdisk 2.4.2-2** command would work in Red Hat Linux, the command shown does not include the kernel number, as discussed in Chapter 13. Therefore, answer a is also incorrect. Since there is no **mkrescuedisk** command, answer d is also incorrect.

Question 7

> You have a dual-boot computer with one hard drive that contains both the Linux and Windows ME operating systems. One day, you start your computer and do not see any LILO boot: prompt. All you see is the Windows ME operating system. Your colleague at the next desk tells you that he thought your computer was broken and ran the **fdisk /MBR** command on your computer from a Microsoft Windows boot disk. Which of the following actions will restore your current system?
>
> ○ a. Start your computer from a Linux rescue disk. After logging in, run the **/sbin/lilo** command.
>
> ○ b. Start your computer from a Microsoft boot disk. After your computer boots, run the **fdisk /lilo** command.
>
> ○ c. Start your computer from a Linux rescue disk. After logging in, run the **/sbin/fdisk /etc/lilo.conf** command.
>
> ○ d. Start your computer from a Microsoft boot disk. After your computer boots, run the **lilo /MBR** command.

Answer a is correct. The **/sbin/lilo** command loads the information from the /etc/lilo.conf file into the master boot record (MBR) of your hard drive. There is no /lilo switch associated with the Microsoft **fdisk** command; no known command associated with **fdisk** loads LILO from a Microsoft operating system. Therefore, answer b is incorrect. Since the Linux **fdisk** command is not used to load any configuration files to an MBR, answer c is incorrect. Since there is no **lilo** command on current Microsoft boot disks, answer d is also incorrect.

Question 8

> Which of the following statements best describes a core dump?
>
> ○ a. It is a copy of all data from the Linux swap partition when you run the **halt** or **reboot** command in Linux.
>
> ○ b. It is a copy of all data from your RAM when an application crashes on Linux.
>
> ○ c. It contains the error messages associated with booting Linux.
>
> ○ d. It contains all of the code from a crashed application.

Answer b is correct. By definition, a core dump contains the data from your RAM when an application crashes on Linux. Since there is no crash associated with running the **halt** or **reboot** command, answer a is incorrect. As discussed in

Chapter 5, error logs associated with booting Linux are defined in the /etc/syslog.conf file, which does not include a file named core. Therefore, answer c is incorrect. Since applications can crash before all of the applicable code is loaded into RAM, a core dump may not contain all of the code from a crashed application. Therefore, answer d is also incorrect.

Question 9

There seems to be a problem with networking on your LAN. You're able to connect to shared directories on other computers on your LAN, but you are unable to access Internet Web pages or the mail servers at your ISP. Which of the following commands can tell you if the problem is with your router's network card? Assume your IP address is **10.12.66.223** and the IP address of the router on your LAN is **10.12.66.231**.

- ○ a. **ping 127.0.0.1**
- ○ b. **ping 10.12.66.223**
- ○ c. **ping 10.12.66.255**
- ○ d. **ping 10.12.66.231**

Answer d is correct. If you get a response when you **ping** the router's IP address, the network card on the router is working. Although answer a can confirm that TCP/IP is properly installed on your computer, it does not address the question. Therefore, answer a is incorrect. Although answer b can confirm that IP addresses are properly configured for your network card, it also does not address the question. Therefore, answer b is also incorrect. Answer c creates a "broadcast" call to all computers associated with network address **10.12.66.0**, but it also does not answer the question. Therefore, answer c is also incorrect.

Question 10

You need a quick solution to a problem you're having on a Linux computer. You've collected all the information you can about the problem. Which of the following sources may contain an answer to your problem? [Check all correct answers]

- ❑ a. The Linux Documentation Project
- ❑ b. Usenet groups
- ❑ c. Knowledge bases associated with individual Linux distributions
- ❑ d. man pages

Answers a, b, c, and d are all correct. The Linux Documentation Project at **www.linuxdoc.org** includes HOWTOs, book-length guides, and more on various Linux topics. Usenet groups, searchable through **groups.google.com**, are a database of online Linux questions and answers. Many Linux distributions include knowledge bases from support questions and answers associated with users of their distributions. The man pages associated with various files and commands are manuals that also might address any problems you have.

Need to Know More?

Danesh, Arman, and Michael Jang. *Mastering Linux, Second Edition.* Alameda, CA: Sybex, 1999. ISBN 0-78212-915-3. A substantial guide to Linux, geared for novice users.

Frampton, Steve. *Linux Administration Made Easy.* Lincoln, NE: iUniverse, 2000. ISBN 0-59515-482-4. A basic guide to administering Linux, also available online at **www.linuxdoc.org/LDP/lame/ LAME/linux-admin-made-easy/index.html**.

Pfaffenberger, Bryan. *Linux Clearly Explained.* San Francisco, CA: Morgan-Kaufmann, 1999. ISBN 0-12553-169-9. A basic guide to Linux, also geared for novice users.

A useful guide to getting help from Linux gurus online is available from the founder of the Open Source Initiative, Eric Raymond, at **www.tuxedo.org/~esr/faqs/smart-questions.html**.

Many mailing lists are associated with Linux and some of the specific distributions. Access and subscription information is available online at **oslab.snu.ac.kr/~djshin/linux/mail-list**.

Several dozen Usenet newsgroups online are dedicated to Linux. These messages are archived and can be searched through the Google portal at **groups.google.com**.

Sample Test

At the beginning of this chapter, I provide pointers to help you develop a successful test-taking strategy, including how to choose proper answers, how to decode ambiguity, how to work within the CompTIA testing framework, how to decide what you need to memorize, and how to prepare for the test. Then, in the rest of this chapter, I include 94 questions on subject matter pertinent to the CompTIA Linux+ Exam XK0-001. In Chapter 16, you'll find the answer key to this test. Good luck!

Questions, Questions, Questions

There should be no doubt in your mind that you are facing a test full of specific and pointed questions. Each exam includes 95 questions, and you will be allotted 120 minutes to complete the exam.

Note: The 95th question on every Linux+ exam requests permission to use your name in the CompTIA database of certified Linux+ professionals. You can decline this question without penalty. Grading is based on the first 94 questions.

Each question on the exam is multiple choice with a single answer.

You should always take the time to read a question at least twice before selecting an answer. Read each question carefully, and look for additional hints or instructions when selecting answers.

Picking Proper Answers

Obviously, the only way to pass any exam is to select enough of the right answers to obtain a passing score. However, CompTIA's exams are not standardized like the SAT and GRE exams; they are far more diabolical and convoluted. In some cases, questions are strangely worded, and deciphering them can be a real challenge. In those cases, you may need to rely on answer-elimination skills. Almost always, at least one answer out of the possible choices for a question can be eliminated immediately because it matches one of these conditions:

➤ The answer does not apply to the situation.

➤ The answer describes a nonexistent issue, an invalid option, or an imaginary state.

➤ The answer may be eliminated because of information in the question itself.

After you eliminate all answers that are obviously wrong, you can apply your retained knowledge to eliminate further answers. Look for items that sound correct but refer to actions, commands, or features that are not present or not available in the situation that the question describes.

If you're still faced with a blind guess among two or more potentially correct answers, reread the question. Try to picture how each of the possible remaining answers would alter the situation. *Be especially sensitive to terminology*; sometimes the choice of words ("remove" instead of "disable") can make the difference between a right answer and a wrong one.

Only when you've exhausted your ability to eliminate answers but remain unclear about which of the remaining possibilities is correct should you guess at an answer. An unanswered question offers you no points, but guessing gives you at least some chance of getting a question right; just don't be too hasty when making a blind guess.

 Since this is a fixed-length test, you can wait until the last round of reviewing marked questions (just as you're about to run out of time or out of unanswered questions) before you start making guesses. Although guessing should be a last resort, you should answer every question. You don't lose any credit if you answer a question incorrectly.

Decoding Ambiguity

CompTIA exams have a reputation for including questions that can be difficult to interpret, confusing, or ambiguous. In my experience with numerous exams, I consider this reputation to be completely justified. The CompTIA exams are tough, and they're deliberately made that way.

The only way to beat CompTIA at its own game is to be prepared. You'll discover that many exam questions test your knowledge of things that are not directly related to the issue raised by a question. This means that the answers you must choose from, even incorrect ones, are just as much a part of the skill assessment as the question itself. For example, if you don't know something about most aspects of the **vi** editor, you may not be able to eliminate answers that are wrong because they relate to an area of **vi** commands other than the one that's addressed by the question at hand. In other words, the more you know about the software, the easier it will be for you to tell right from wrong.

Questions often give away their answers, but you have to be Sherlock Holmes to see the clues. Often, subtle hints appear in the question text in such a way that they seem almost irrelevant to the situation. You must realize that each question is a test unto itself and that you need to inspect and successfully navigate each question to pass the exam. Look for small clues, such as the mention of times, permissions, usernames, and configuration settings. Little things such as these can point to the right answer if they're properly understood; if missed, they can leave you facing a blind guess.

Another common difficulty with certification exams is vocabulary. CompTIA has an uncanny knack for naming some utilities and features entirely obviously in some cases and completely inanely in other instances. Be sure to brush up on the key terms presented at the beginning of each chapter of this book. You may also want to read the Glossary at the end of this book the day before you take the test.

Working within the Framework

The test questions appear in random order, and many elements or issues that are mentioned in one question may also crop up in other questions. It's not uncommon to find that an incorrect answer to one question is the correct answer to another question, or vice versa. Take the time to read every answer to each question, even if you recognize the correct answer to a question immediately. That extra reading may spark a memory or remind you about a Linux feature or function that helps you on another question elsewhere in the exam.

Since you're taking a fixed-length test, you can revisit any question as many times as you like. If you're uncertain of the answer to a question, check the box that's provided to mark it for easy return later on. You should also mark questions that you think may offer information you can use to answer other questions. On fixed-length tests, I usually mark somewhere between 25 and 50 percent of the questions. The testing software is designed to let you mark every question if you choose; use this framework to your advantage. Everything you'll want to see again should be marked; the testing software can then help you return to marked questions quickly and easily.

 I strongly recommend that you first read the entire test quickly, before getting caught up in answering individual questions. Doing this will help to jog your memory as you review the potential answers and can help you identify questions that you want to mark for easy access to their contents. You can also identify and mark the tricky questions for easy return. The key is to make a quick pass over the 94 substantive questions to begin with—so that you know what you're up against—and then survey the questions more thoroughly on a second pass, when you can begin to answer all questions systematically and consistently.

Deciding What to Memorize

The amount of memorization you must undertake for an exam depends on how well you remember what you've read and how well you know the software by heart. If you're a visual thinker and can see the switches associated with different commands in your head, you won't need to memorize as much as someone who's less visually oriented. However, the exam will stretch your ability to memorize product features and functions, commands, utilities, and daemons, as well as how they all relate to Linux as a whole.

At a minimum, you'll want to memorize the following kinds of information:

➤ Hardware configuration

➤ Linux drives and partitions

➤ Package configuration management

➤ Basic networking commands

➤ Network services

➤ Command-line interface commands

➤ Administrative utilities

If you work your way through this book while sitting at a machine with Linux installed and work with the files and commands as they're discussed throughout, you should have little or no difficulty mastering this material. Also, don't forget that the Cram Sheet at the front of the book is designed to capture the material that's most important to memorize; use this to guide your studies as well.

Preparing for the Test

The best way to prepare for the test—after you've studied—is to take at least one practice exam. I've included one here in this chapter for that reason; the test questions are located in the pages that follow. (Unlike the questions in the preceding chapters in this book, the answers don't follow the questions immediately; you'll have to flip to Chapter 16 to review the answers separately.)

Give yourself 105 minutes to take the exam (so you'll have time to review marked questions at the end), and keep yourself on the honor system—don't look at earlier text in the book or jump ahead to the answer key. After all, you won't have these resources in your hands when you take the actual exam. When your time is up or you've finished the questions, you can check your work in Chapter 16. Pay special attention to the explanations for the incorrect answers; these can also help to reinforce your knowledge of the material. Knowing how to recognize correct answers is good, but understanding why incorrect answers are wrong can be equally valuable.

Taking the Test

Relax. Once you're sitting in front of the testing computer, there's nothing more you can do to increase your knowledge or preparation. Take a deep breath, stretch, and start reading that first question.

You don't need to rush, either. You have plenty of time to complete each question and to return to the questions that you skipped or marked for return. If you read a question twice and you remain clueless, you can mark it. Both easy and difficult questions are intermixed throughout the test in random order. If you're taking a fixed-length test, don't cheat yourself by spending too much time on a hard question early in the test, thereby depriving yourself of the time you need to answer the questions at the end of the test.

One strategy is to read through the entire test and, before returning to marked questions for a second visit, figure out how much time you've got per question. As you answer each question, remove its mark. Continue to review the remaining marked questions until you run out of time or complete the test.

That's it for pointers. Good luck!

Sample Test

Question 1

Which of the following commands will take you to your home directory?

- ○ a. **cd /home/mj**
- ○ b. **cd ~**
- ○ c. **cd /home/tr**
- ○ d. **cd ../..**

Question 2

You've installed a new application on a test computer. During testing, you've run into a number of problems that you are unable to troubleshoot. Where should you look first for help?

- ○ a. Newsgroups where other users discuss the application.
- ○ b. The log files associated with the application.
- ○ c. Before doing anything else, install the application on a production computer and see if you still have the same problems.
- ○ d. The Web site home page for the application.

Question 3

You've run into some difficulty with your Apache server configuration file, /etc/httpd/httpd.conf. You've backed up a copy of this file in your home directory, /home/jkp/httpd.bak. Which of the following commands compares these two files and returns each line that was changed?

- ○ a. **change /etc/httpd/httpd.conf /home/jkp/httpd.bak**
- ○ b. **diff /etc/httpd/httpd.conf /home/jkp/httpd.bak**
- ○ c. **mv /etc/httpd/httpd.conf /home/jkp/httpd.bak**
- ○ d. **grep /etc/httpd/httpd.conf /home/jkp/httpd.bak**

Question 4

Take a look at the following excerpt from the /home/rn directory:

```
-r--r--rws 1 root root 264313 May 23 10:36 who
```

What should you do?

- ○ a. Delete the file named "who" just in the /home/rn directory.
- ○ b. Delete all instances of files with the name "who".
- ○ c. Investigate the purpose of this file. If you can't track it down to the user or another administrator, consider reinstalling Linux.
- ○ d. Test this command by running the /home/rn command yourself. Observe the result. Consult the /var/log/messages file for additional data and then take action.

Question 5

You have a growing LAN, and you no longer want to maintain or assign IP addresses. You set up a DHCP server on your LAN that will also assign IP addresses on an adjacent network. Which of the following commands would you use to test the DHCP server?

- ○ a. **dhcpcd**
- ○ b. **pumpd**
- ○ c. **bootp**
- ○ d. **dhcpd**

Question 6

Based on the figure below, an excerpt from the **ps aux** command, which of the following commands stops every instance of program **abcd** most grace-fully and efficiently?

```
USER       PID %CPU %MEM   VSZ  RSS TTY    STAT START  TIME COMMAND
root       384  0.0  1.0  1436  668 ?      S     06:00  0:00 /usr/sbin/cron
root       414  0.0  1.2 11760  776 ?      S     06:00  0:00 /usr/sbin/abcd
root       416  0.0  1.2 11760  776 ?      S     06:00  0:00 /usr/sbin/abcd
root       417  0.0  1.2 11760  776 ?      S     06:00  0:00 /usr/sbin/abcd
root       418  0.0  1.2 11760  776 ?      S     06:00  0:00 /usr/sbin/abcd
root       420  0.0  1.2 11760  776 ?      S     06:00  0:00 /usr/sbin/abcd
root       421  0.0  1.2 11760  776 ?      S     06:00  0:00 /usr/sbin/abcd
root       422  0.0  1.2 11760  776 ?      S_    06:00  0:00 /usr/sbin/abcd
mj         498  1.0  2.4  2596 1480 tty1   S     06:04  0:00 -bash
mj         511  0.0  2.4  2436 1500 tty1   R     06:05  0:00 ps aux
```

- ○ a. **kill abcd**

- ○ b. **killall [384-422]**

- ○ c. **kill -9 abcd**

- ○ d. **killall abcd**

Question 7

Assume that you have just logged on as a regular user. Which of the following commands allows you to edit the file with user passwords associated with the Shadow Password Suite?

- ○ a. **vi /etc/shadow**

- ○ b. **visu vi /etc/passwd**

- ○ c. **sudo -c "vi /etc/shadow"**

- ○ d. **su -c "vi /etc/shadow"**

Question 8

Which of the following commands corresponds to read, write, and execute permissions on the next file you create for all users? Hint: This corresponds to -rwxrwxrwx permissions.

- ○ a. **umask 000**

- ○ b. **umask 777**

- ○ c. **chmod 777**

- ○ d. **chmod 000**

Question 9

Your colleague has given you a data file on an MS-DOS–formatted floppy disk. Based on the following excerpt from the /etc/fstab file, which of the following commands would you use to **mount** that disk on your Linux system?

```
/dev/fd0  /floppy  ext3  noauto,owner  0 0
```

○ a. **mount -t ext2 /dev/fd0 /floppy**

○ b. **mount -t vfat /dev/fd0 /mnt/floppy**

○ c. **mount -t vfat /dev/fd0 /floppy**

○ d. **mount /dev/fd0 /floppy**

Question 10

When you look through the /var/log directory you see a new file, httpd.crit. Assume that it is a legitimate file, created for legitimate reasons. Which of the following statements is the best possible description of this file?

○ a. It contains critical information related to your Web access.

○ b. It includes critical messages about the actions taken by your Apache Web server.

○ c. It contains error messages related to access to your Apache Web server.

○ d. It includes critical notices related to access through your router.

Question 11

Your manager has told you to see if you can set up Linux on an older computer. It includes a 386 CPU, 16MB of RAM, and a 100MB hard drive. Which of the following statements represents a viable option?

○ a. You can't install Linux on this computer; you need at least a 486 CPU.

○ b. You can set this up as a graphical workstation, with all of the software associated with the typical current Linux distribution.

○ c. You can set up a DNS server on this computer, including associated data files.

○ d. You can set up an Apache server on this computer, including associated log files.

Question 12

> Which of the following commands can you use to change the amount of
> space allocated to a second extended file system partition?
>
> ○ a. **resize**
>
> ○ b. **resize2fs**
>
> ○ c. **ext2resize**
>
> ○ d. **resizext2fs**

Question 13

> Which of the following commands gives you the current routing table with-
> out requiring network activity to access a DNS server?
>
> ○ a. **route**
>
> ○ b. **netstat -r**
>
> ○ c. **route -n**
>
> ○ d. **netstat**

Question 14

> You're trying to replace a second Ethernet network card in a PCMCIA slot on
> your computer. You've read on the network card manufacturer's Web site
> that the Linux pcnet32.o driver supports this network card. You know this
> driver is available in the /lib/modules/2.4.4-4/kernel/drivers/net directory.
> Which of the following commands should you try first to install the driver for
> this card?
>
> ○ a. **modprobe**
>
> ○ b. **insmod /lib/modules/2.4.4-4/kernel/drivers/net/pcnet32.o**
>
> ○ c. **lsmod /lib/modules/2.4.4-4/kernel/drivers/net/pcnet32.o**
>
> ○ d. **SuperProbe**

Question 15

You're configuring Linux for the second time on one of the computers in your organization. You had trouble with the first network card, but you finally configured Linux in a way that it recognized the card using IRQ 12 and I/O 0x330. You just installed the network card in the second Linux computer. It is the only network card on that computer. Note the following excerpt from the /etc/lilo.conf file.

```
images=/boot/vmlinuz-2.4.2-2
    label=linux
```

When you boot that computer, what should you enter at the LILO **Boot:** prompt?

○ a. **append="ether=12,0x330,eth1"**

○ b. **append="ether=12,0x330,eth0"**

○ c. **linux ether=12,0x330,eth1**

○ d. **linux ether=12,0x330,eth0**

Question 16

You're having trouble with a Linux computer. It does not boot normally. You do not have a rescue disk for your system, but you have a printout of the output from the **mount** command in the figure below.

Which of the following commands should you enter at the LILO **Boot:** prompt? Assume **linux** boots Linux on your computer.

```
/dev/hda3 on / type ext2 (rw)
proc on /proc type proc (rw)
devpts on /dev/pts type devpts (rw,mode=0620,gid=5)
/dev/hda1 on /boot type ext2 (rw)
shmfs on /dev/shm type shm (rw)
//Experimental/LinuxPlus on /home/mj/tmp type smbfs (0)
```

○ a. **linux single**

○ b. **linux root=/dev/hda3**

○ c. **linux /=/dev/hda3**

○ d. **linux /boot=/dev/hda1**

Question 17

Your serial mouse, installed on COM3, no longer works reliably. You want to check the associated IRQ port and I/O address against other hardware. What is the standard IRQ port and I/O address associated with COM3?

○ a. IRQ 4, I/O 02e8

○ b. IRQ 4, I/O 03e8

○ c. IRQ 3, I/O 02f8

○ d. IRQ 3, I/O 03f8

Question 18

Which of the following commands is required to create and format a Linux partition?

○ a. **fips**

○ b. **fdisk**, **format**

○ c. **fdisk**, **mkfs**

○ d. **lilo**, **fdisk**

Question 19

You are working with some older computers, hoping to create a computer suitable for use as a router or a DNS server. One computer has a good motherboard that is designed to handle non-parity RAM. From another computer, you have some RAM with parity. If you install the RAM on the motherboard, what is the most likely result?

○ a. When you try booting, you'll hear multiple beeps. Then the computer will stop before it can access the BIOS or an operating system.

○ b. The computer boots successfully. However, after a period of time, the RAM overheats, which causes an intermittent crash.

○ c. The parity RAM is added to the available video memory of the computer.

○ d. The computer boots successfully. The parity bit on the RAM is ignored.

Question 20

Assume you have forgotten the current superuser password for your Linux computer. On several Linux distributions, which of the following commands allows you to reset the **root** user password?

○ a. Restart your computer. When Linux reboots, log in again, then enter the **init 1** command. When you see the command-line interface prompt, run the **passwd** command.

○ b. Restart your computer. When your computer reboots, wait until you see the LILO **Boot**: prompt. At that prompt, enter the **init 1** command. When you see the command-line interface prompt, run the **passwd** command.

○ c. Restart your computer. When your computer reboots, wait until you see the LILO **Boot**: prompt. At that prompt, enter the **linux single** command. When you see the command-line interface prompt, run the **passwd** command.

○ d. Run the **shutdown -r now** command, wait until your computer reboots, then at the LILO **Boot**: prompt enter the **linux single** command. When you see the prompt, run the **passwd** command.

Question 21

Which of the following corresponds to an ATA device?

○ a. eth0

○ b. hdd

○ c. sdc

○ d. ttyS1

Question 22

What is the purpose of the **lpc** command?

○ a. It allows you to delete a specific print job from a specific printer.

○ b. It allows you to enable or disable a printer or reorder the print jobs associated with a specific print queue.

○ c. It allows you to configure a printer with an appropriate filter such as Apsfilter for PCL or PostScript printers.

○ d. It allows you to find the job number associated with each entry in a specific print queue.

Question 23

You're assembling a new computer. It includes a hard drive on position hda and a CD drive on position hdb. There are no drives on position hdc or hdd. What can you expect about the performance of the hard drive on this computer?

- ○ a. The hard drive will perform well.
- ○ b. The hard drive will be limited by the speed of the CPU.
- ○ c. The hard drive will be limited by the speed of transfer to the CD drive.
- ○ d. The hard drive will not work at all.

Question 24

You're experimenting with creating a number of partitions for mounting different directories. You want to set up the /var directory as a resizable area on the hda7 partition. Which of the following file systems should you use?

- ○ a. ext2
- ○ b. ext3
- ○ c. VFAT
- ○ d. XFS

Question 25

One of the users on your LAN is having trouble connecting to an FTP server on the Internet. She has no problems with access to Web or email servers outside your network. You've established that she is using the correct commands to access FTP. Which of the following things should you check?

- ○ a. Whether your company has paid its ISP bill.
- ○ b. The settings on Squid.
- ○ c. The configuration of the user's network card.
- ○ d. The DNS server for your network.

Question 26

You've just set up Linux and are having trouble connecting to your ISP. When you run the **ls -l /dev/modem** command, you see that it is properly linked to the /dev/ttyS0 device. Assume that the modem speaker works and your telephone uses a rotary dialer. The number for your ISP is 987654321. Which of the following commands in **minicom** tests whether your modem can connect to your ISP?

○ a. **AT987654321**

○ b. **ATDT987654321**

○ c. **ATDP987654321**

○ d. **ATA0987654321**

Question 27

When assembling your new computer, you're not sure what to do when you get to the floppy drive controller cable. At the end, it has a rectangular connector, with 2 rows and 17 holes on each row. There is no guide tooth on the floppy drive to align the cable. There is no way to know the correct orientation for this cable. What would happen if you accidentally installed the controller cable upside down?

○ a. The crossed power lines for the floppy drive would destroy the circuits on the drive.

○ b. The crossed power lines for the floppy drive would destroy circuits on your motherboard.

○ c. There would be no crossed power lines for the floppy drive; the power connector is separate, and the floppy drive would still work fine.

○ d. The crossed power lines for the floppy drive would keep it from working; the floppy drive power light would stay on as long as power was available through the floppy power connector.

Question 28

After installing Linux, which of the following log files can help you decipher the successes and failures of your new operating system?

- ○ a. /var/log/wtmp
- ○ b. /proc/messages
- ○ c. /var/log/messages
- ○ d. /var/log/maillog

Question 29

You have installed a Linux distribution with kernel 2.4.18. Loadable modules are enabled. You have just installed a new USB mouse on your computer. What do you need to do to get Linux to recognize the mouse?

- ○ a. Nothing.
- ○ b. Reboot Linux.
- ○ c. Disable loadable modules in the kernel.
- ○ d. Linux does not recognize a USB mouse.

Question 30

Which of the following practices is the most useful physical security requirement for a Linux server?

- ○ a. Maintain a password-protected screensaver on the Linux server.
- ○ b. Never leave the Linux computer unattended while it is running.
- ○ c. Keep passwords stored in a locked file cabinet.
- ○ d. Keep the Linux server in a locked room.

Question 31

No matter what you do, it seems like your Linux computer always boots in single user mode. Which of the following parameters should you check?

- ○ a. The number associated with **initdefault** in /etc/inittab.
- ○ b. The values associated with **append** in /etc/lilo.conf.
- ○ c. The partition with the root (/) directory in /etc/fstab.
- ○ d. The parameters for the bash shell in /etc/profile.

Question 32

Wide SCSI, Ultra Wide SCSI, and Ultra2 Wide SCSI devices share all of the following characteristics except:

- ○ a. A 16-bit bus
- ○ b. 68 pins on each cable
- ○ c. 16 Logical Unit Numbers
- ○ d. Data transfer speed

Question 33

You're planning the setup of a Linux computer as a server on your organization's network. Which of the following is consistent with best practices for documentation?

- ○ a. Keep a copy of key configuration files on a different partition on the same computer.
- ○ b. Record the hardware configuration details in a binder in the same room as the Linux server.
- ○ c. Keep a copy of each user's password in a locked filing cabinet in the same room as the Linux server.
- ○ d. Record the inode number of every file in a binder in the same room as the Linux server.

Question 34

Based on the following output from the **ifconfig** command, you can find a number of parameters assigned to your network card. All of the following parameters are available in the figure below, except:

```
mj@linux:~ > /sbin/ifconfig
eth0      Link encap:Ethernet  HWaddr 00:50:56:A7:00:23
          inet addr:192.168.0.100  Bcast:192.168.0.255  Mask:255.255.255.0
          inet6 addr: fe80::250:56ff:fea7:23/10 Scope:Link
          inet6 addr: fe80::50:56a7:23/10 Scope:Link
          UP BROADCAST RUNNING MULTICAST  MTU:1500  Metric:1
          RX packets:453 errors:0 dropped:0 overruns:0 frame:0
          TX packets:16 errors:0 dropped:0 overruns:0 carrier:0
          collisions:0 txqueuelen:100
          RX bytes:48856 (47.7 Kb)  TX bytes:1558 (1.5 Kb)
          Interrupt:9 Base address:0x1000

lo        Link encap:Local Loopback
          inet addr:127.0.0.1  Mask:255.0.0.0
          inet6 addr: ::1/128 Scope:Host
          UP LOOPBACK RUNNING  MTU:16436  Metric:1
          RX packets:0 errors:0 dropped:0 overruns:0 frame:0
          TX packets:0 errors:0 dropped:0 overruns:0 carrier:0
          collisions:0 txqueuelen:0
          RX bytes:0 (0.0 b)  TX bytes:0 (0.0 b)

mj@linux:~ > _
```

- ○ a. IP address
- ○ b. MAC address
- ○ c. Loopback address
- ○ d. Gateway address

Question 35

If the internal battery in your computer loses power, all of the following information may be lost except:

- ○ a. Current time on the internal computer clock
- ○ b. BIOS menu
- ○ c. CMOS settings
- ○ d. BIOS password

Question 36

You're using a communications protocol that cannot handle encrypted passwords. You need to disable the Shadow Password Suite. Which of the following pairs of commands restores the original clear-text passwords that you had encrypted into the /etc/shadow and /etc/gshadow files?

○ a. **gconv; passunconv**

○ b. **grpunconv; passunconv**

○ c. **gconv; pwunconv**

○ d. **grpunconv; pwunconv**

Question 37

When you downloaded a kernel patch from the Internet, the name you clicked on was kernel-patch-2.4.4-66.i386.tar.gz. The file that was downloaded is kernel-patch-2.4.4-66.i386.tgz. Which of the following commands will unarchive this patch from the /tmp directory?

○ a. **tar xvf /tmp/kernel-patch-2.4.4-66.i386.tgz**

○ b. **tar xzf /tmp/kernel-patch-2.4.4-66.i386.tgz**

○ c. **tar cvf /tmp/kernel-patch-2.4.4-66.i386.tgz**

○ d. **tar czf /tmp/kernel-patch-2.4.4-66.i386.tgz**

Question 38

Which of the following daemons is associated with communication through a telephone modem connection?

○ a. **smbd**

○ b. **lpd**

○ c. **nfsd**

○ d. **pppd**

Question 39

You're in the middle of editing a long script using the **vi** editor. You want to use a specific data file, and you know it's in your home directory (/home/tr) but have forgotten the name. How do you look up the file without exiting from **vi**?

- O a. Press the Esc key to return to command mode, then type the **ls /home/tr** command.
- O b. Type !: to start execute mode, then type the **ls /home/tr** command.
- O c. Type Ctrl+x to start execute mode, then type the **ls /home/tr** command.
- O d. Press F1 to start command mode, then type the **ls /home/tr** command.

Question 40

You have three hard drives, each of which has an operating system. One is an IDE hard drive on position hda. The other two are SCSI drives, with SCSI or LUN numbers of 3 and 6. Which hard drive's operating system does your computer boot?

- O a. The hda drive
- O b. The SCSI 3 drive
- O c. The SCSI 6 drive
- O d. It depends on your CMOS settings

Question 41

You've created a new command called **manage** in your home directory. You originally set it so only you would have permission to do anything with it. You've tested it, and now you want others to try it out. You don't want others to delete this file accidentally, however. You copy it to the /bin directory. Which of the following commands sets up the right permissions?

- O a. **chmod 777 /bin/manage**
- O b. **chown 755 /bin/manage**
- O c. **chgrp 711 /bin/manage**
- O d. **chmod 755 /bin/manage**

Question 42

You have a computer with shared memory. In other words, part of the RAM can be used by the graphics card. You've just increased the amount of RAM allocated to your graphics card and want to increase the color depth from 8bpp to 32bpp. Which of the following tools would you use?

- ○ a. **xf86setup**
- ○ b. **SuperProbe**
- ○ c. **xfree86**
- ○ d. **xf86config**

Question 43

You're in the process of moving the files for your Web site from another type of Web server to Apache. Some people tell you to put the files in the /var/www directory. Others suggest that the files should be copied to the /home/httpd directory. How do you know where you should put these files?

- ○ a. Look for the **DocumentRoot** variable in the httpd.conf configuration file.
- ○ b. Apache automatically checks both directories for the basic files for your Web site.
- ○ c. Look for the **HomeRoot** variable in the httpd.conf configuration file.
- ○ d. You have to set this directory when you first log in as the **apache** user.

Question 44

You're having trouble accessing the router from your local computer. You've checked this by running the **ping** command to the IP address of the router. Until you set up access, you cannot connect to the Internet. Which of the following things should you do?

- ○ a. Run the **/sbin/ifconfig** command. If you do not see an eth0 entry, run the **/sbin/ifconfig eth0 up** command.
- ○ b. Run the **/sbin/lsconfig** command. If you do not see an eth0 entry, run the **/sbin/ifup eth0** command.
- ○ c. Run the **/sbin/ifconfig** command. If you see an eth0 entry, run the **/sbin/ifdown eth0** command.
- ○ d. Run the **/sbin/lsconfig** command. If you see an eth0 entry, run the **/sbin/ifconfig eth0 up** command.

Question 45

One of your users, **chirac**, has called to tell you that he is no longer able to log on to the Linux server. Based on the following excerpt from /etc/passwd, what is the reason for this?

```
chirac:*:543:100:wine:/home/chirac:/bin/ash
```

- ○ a. The wrong shell is configured for user **chirac**.
- ○ b. No password is configured.
- ○ c. The user is not named wine.
- ○ d. The group ID number, 100, should match the user ID number, 543.

Question 46

One of your colleagues is showing you the output from a *protocol analyzer*, which can detect the types of messages that are being transmitted over a network. The protocol analyzer shows a large number of **ping** commands being sent to your Web server. Others on the Internet are having trouble accessing your Web server. What kind of problem are you having?

- ○ a. There is no problem; this is normal traffic from DNS servers and Internet routers checking connectivity to your Web site.
- ○ b. Someone is using your Web site to test their connectivity to the Internet.
- ○ c. There is insufficient capacity on the Internet connection to your Web site.
- ○ d. Someone is using a DoS attack on your Web site.

Question 47

Which of the following commands can install and remove the modules associated with a newly installed or recently uninstalled hardware device?

- ○ a. **insmod**
- ○ b. **rmmod**
- ○ c. **lsprobe**
- ○ d. **modprobe**

Question 48

You're setting up a Sendmail server for the first time and want to install the latest version on your Linux server. Assume you've downloaded the sendmail-8.12.0-1.3.i386.rpm package to the /tmp directory. Which of the following commands installs this package?

○ a. **tar xzvf /tmp/sendmail-8.12.0-1.3.i386.rpm**

○ b. **rpm -Uvh /tmp/sendmail-8.12.0-1.3.i386.rpm**

○ c. **tar -Uvh /tmp/sendmail-8.12.0-1.3.i386.rpm**

○ d. **rpm xzvf /tmp/sendmail-8.12.0-1.3.i386.rpm**

Question 49

You've just added more information to the file that governs automated jobs on your computer, /etc/crontab. Which of the following commands forces the **cron** daemon to reread this configuration file with your changes?

○ a. **killall cron**

○ b. **kill -HUP `cat /var/run/cron.pid`**

○ c. **kill -HUP cron**

○ d. **killall -HUP `cat /var/run/cron.pid`**

Question 50

You're planning to set up a new Internet Web site and have just installed Apache on your Linux computer. You have acquired the rights to the **Ilovelinuxmorethanjohnlovesgolf.com** domain name. The name of your computer is **webserver**. What name should you assign to the **ServerName** variable in the Apache configuration file, httpd.conf?

○ a. /home/httpd or /var/www

○ b. **www.ilovelinuxmorethanjohnlovesgolf.com**

○ c. **webserver**

○ d. **ScriptAlias**

Question 51

Your supervisor tells you that she wants a crime database program, **/opt/bin/anticrime** run at the highest priority. From the **ps aux I grep anticrime** command, you find that **anticrime** is currently being run by user **jb** (your supervisor), with a PID of 1539. Which of the following commands gives the currently running **anticrime** program a higher priority on your system?

- ○ a. **nice -n -10 anticrime**
- ○ b. **renice 10 1539**
- ○ c. **nice -n 10 anticrime**
- ○ d. **renice -10 1539**

Question 52

If you want to install Linux on a computer with a dedicated mail server, and you have a network with Microsoft and Linux computers, which of the following services do you need?

- ○ a. Mail and Samba
- ○ b. NFS and Sendmail
- ○ c. Common Internet File System and Sendmail
- ○ d. Apache and Samba

Question 53

As the developers in your company work on the newest security software, Antiterror, different versions of the beta are being released weekly. The current version, **antiterror-7**, is located in the /opt/bin/antiterror-7 directory. Later versions will be released in parallel directories; for example, the next version will be located in the /opt/bin/antiterror-8 directory. Everyone who is testing this software is running the **/opt/test/antiterror** command. Which of the following actions would ensure that the testers get the latest version of the software next week?

- ○ a. **ln /opt/test/antiterror /opt/bin/antiterror-7/antiterror-7**
- ○ b. **ln /opt/test/antiterror.lnk /opt/bin/antiterror-8/antiterror-8**
- ○ c. **ln /opt/test/antiterror /opt/bin/antiterror-8/antiterror-8**
- ○ d. **ln antiterror /opt/bin/antiterror-8/antiterror-8**

Question 54

You're trying to upgrade your **telnet** package with the newest RPM file. However, when you run the **rpm -Uvh telnet-0.19-21.i386.rpm** command, you get the following message:

```
failed to open /var/lib/rpm/packages.rpm:
    Permission denied
error: cannot open /var/lib/rpm/packages.rpm
```

What steps do you need to take?

○ a. Rerun the command as the superuser.

○ b. Run the **chmod u+s /var/lib/rpm/packages.rpm** command.

○ c. Download the newest version of /var/lib/rpm/packages.rpm from your Linux distribution's Web site.

○ d. Run the **chmod 777 /var/lib/rpm/packages.rpm** command.

Question 55

The head Linux administrator has taken a vacation and has given you the **root** password that is being used this week. Her supervisor has told you to install the newest version of the **pppd** package, pppd-2.4.1-12.i386.rpm, which is already installed in the /tmp directory. You are logged in as a regular user. Your username is not included in /etc/sudoers. Which of the following commands installs this package?

○ a. **rpm -Uvh /tmp/pppd-2.4.1-12.i386.rpm**

○ b. **sudo rpm -Uvh /tmp/pppd-2.4.1-12.i386.rpm**

○ c. **su -c "rpm -Uvh /tmp/pppd-2.4.1-12.i386.rpm"**

○ d. **tar xzvf /tmp/pppd-2.4.1-12.i386.rpm**

Question 56

Based on the following output from the **crontab -l** command, when will the program **/home/nws/hurricane** be run?

```
36 5 12 6 *    /home/nws/hurricane
```

○ a. At 5:12:36 A.M. on the 6th day of each month

○ b. At 5:36 A.M. on June 12

○ c. At 12:36 A.M. on May 5

○ d. At 5:36 A.M. every Friday and Saturday

Question 57

Which of the following commands allows you to connect to a remote computer with a password that is encrypted over your network connection?

○ a. **rsh**

○ b. **slogin**

○ c. **telnet**

○ d. **securesh**

Question 58

You're setting up an older computer for Linux that includes a mix of legacy and plug-and-play hardware components. What should you do to keep the plug-and-play hardware from taking the channels needed by the legacy components?

○ a. In the computer CMOS settings, reserve the serial and printer ports required by the legacy hardware.

○ b. In the computer CMOS settings, reserve the IRQ ports, I/O addresses, and DMA channels required by the plug-and-play hardware.

○ c. In the computer CMOS settings, reserve the IRQ ports, I/O addresses, and DMA channels required by the legacy hardware.

○ d. Replace the legacy hardware with plug-and-play hardware.

Question 59

You've added a new user with the **useradd jkp** command. Why can't user **jkp** log on immediately?

○ a. You need to set up the default files in /home/jkp.

○ b. You need to assign a default shell such as /bin/bash to **jkp** in the /etc/passwd file.

○ c. You need to assign a password.

○ d. You need to change the default permissions of the /etc/passwd file to allow **jkp** to log on.

Question 60

You have just installed a modem. You've tried configuring it, and you've tried testing it with **minicom**. It does not work. On the box, it states that modem operation is integrated with your operating system. Which of the following statements describes the most likely problem?

○ a. You need to enable loadable modules in the Linux kernel.

○ b. This modem is designed to work with a non-Linux operating system.

○ c. You should try disconnecting your printer before testing the modem.

○ d. This modem is designed to work with a different Linux kernel.

Question 61

Which of the following packages allows you to restrict incoming traffic through appropriate commands in the /etc/hosts.allow and /etc/hosts.deny files?

○ a. **ipchains**

○ b. **iptables**

○ c. **ALL:ALL**

○ d. **tcp_wrappers**

Question 62

> You have several SCSI devices attached to a Wide SCSI controller. They are all operating properly on your Linux system. You install a new SCSI device that has worked for you before on other computers. After installing this device, suddenly none of your SCSI devices work. Which of the following statements describes the most likely problem?
>
> ○ a. The device has sent an electrical charge through the SCSI cable that has damaged the Wide SCSI controller.
>
> ○ b. The new device is not properly configured in the SCSI BIOS.
>
> ○ c. You've assigned the new device a SCSI LUN of 7.
>
> ○ d. The new device is a SCSI hard drive that causes problems with the Linux Loader.

Question 63

> You've had a hard drive failure. Fortunately, you previously saved everyone's home directory in an archive with the **tar czvf backup-home.tgz /home** command. You've reinstalled Linux on a new hard drive. After navigating to the root (/) directory, you want to reinstall everyone's home directory. You've logged on as user **tr** and have copied the archive to the /tmp directory. What happens when you run the following command?
>
> ```
> [tr@linuxserver /tmp]$ tar xzvf backup-home.tgz
> ```
>
> ○ a. The home directory of each user is restored to the original location.
>
> ○ b. The home directory of each user is restored to the /tmp/home directory.
>
> ○ c. Home directories are not restored.
>
> ○ d. Home directories are restored to the root (/) directory.

Question 64

You do not see the LILO boot: prompt or any other prompt that allows you to install Linux. You suspect that the Linux Loader was somehow deleted from your computer's MBR. What should you do?

○ a. Start Linux with an MS-DOS boot disk and run the **fdisk /MBR** command.

○ b. Start Linux with a rescue disk and run the **/sbin/lilo** command.

○ c. Start Linux with a rescue disk and run the **/sbin/lilo -MBR** command.

○ d. Start Linux in single user mode with the **linux single** command.

Question 65

Based on the following excerpt from the /etc/fstab file, all of the following statements are true except:

```
/dev/hda8   /root   ext3   defaults   1 3
```

○ a. The home directory of the superuser is mounted on the fourth logical partition of the primary master IDE hard drive.

○ b. The top-level directory in Linux is mounted on the fourth extended partition of the primary master IDE hard drive.

○ c. The /root directory is formatted to the third extended file system.

○ d. The /root directory is the third one mounted when you boot Linux.

Question 66

If you run the following command to **mount** your CD drive, which of the following commands would access files on that drive? Assume the required directories already exist.

```
mount -t iso9660 /dev/hdc mnt/cdrom
```

Note: The output from the **pwd** command is /root.

○ a. **ls /mnt/cdrom**

○ b. **ls mnt**

○ c. **ls /root/mnt/cdrom**

○ d. **ls /cdrom**

Question 67

The amount of data related to hurricanes is huge; they often require the use of supercomputers. You have set up a Linux supercomputer to process data from the newest hurricane over the Atlantic. This data is collected in the /home/tr/hurr-data file. You've also set up a program to process the data, **windy**, in the /opt/bin directory. Which of the following commands processes the data into the /home/tr/hurr-output file for later analysis?

○ a. **/opt/bin/windy | /home/tr/hurr-data < /home/tr/hurr-output**

○ b. **/opt/bin/windy < /home/tr/hurr-data | /home/tr/hurr-output**

○ c. **/opt/bin/windy < /home/tr/hurr-data > /home/tr/hurr-output**

○ d. **/opt/bin/windy > /home/tr/hurr-data > /home/tr/hurr-output**

Question 68

All of the following items are related to authentication except:

○ a. Radius modem server

○ b. /etc/passwd

○ c. NIS

○ d. /etc/inittab

Question 69

Based on the excerpt from /etc/inittab shown in the figure below, what command would you use from the command-line interface to restart Linux with a graphical user interface login screen? Assume that the comment lines in this file, which start with a hash mark (#), are accurate.

```
# default runlevel
id:3:initdefault:

# check system on startup
# first script to be executed if not booting in emergency (-b) mode
si:I:bootwait:/etc/init.d/boot

# /etc/init.d/rc takes care of runlevel handling
#
# runlevel 0  is  System halt   (Do never use this for initdefault)
# runlevel 1  is  Single user mode
# runlevel 2  is  Local multiuser without remote network (e.g. NFS)
# runlevel 3  is  Full multiuser with network
# runlevel 4  is  Not used
# runlevel 5  is  Full multiuser with network and xdm
# runlevel 6  is  System reboot (Do never use this for initdefault)
#
l0:0:wait:/etc/init.d/rc 0
l1:1:wait:/etc/init.d/rc 1
l2:2:wait:/etc/init.d/rc 2
l3:3:wait:/etc/init.d/rc 3
#l4:4:wait:/etc/init.d/rc 4
l5:5:wait:/etc/init.d/rc 5
l6:6:wait:/etc/init.d/rc 6
                                                        32,1          20%
```

- ○ a. Change the 3 to a 5 in the line with the **id** and **initdefault** commands.
- ○ b. **init 5**.
- ○ c. **shutdown -r now**.
- ○ d. **init 3**.

Question 70

In the **vi** editor, which of the following commands allows you to navigate to the top of the file?

- ○ a. **G**
- ○ b. **0G**
- ○ c. **1G**
- ○ d. **i**

Question 71

Which of the following commands creates a Linux boot disk for your computer? Assume that the version number associated with your kernel is 2.4.5-13, the kernel in your /boot directory is named vmlinuz, and there is only one floppy drive on your computer.

- ○ a. **mkdisk 2.4.5-13**
- ○ b. **dd if=/boot/vmlinuz of=/dev/fd0 bs=8192**
- ○ c. **mount /dev/fd0 /mnt/floppy; dd if=/boot/vmlinuz of=/dev/fd0 bs=4096**
- ○ d. **mkrescuedisk 2.4.5-13**

Question 72

The second printer on your print server isn't working. You believe that the root cause is an IRQ conflict between the printer and another device. The printer was working before, and you haven't added any new hardware. You suspect that another administrator accidentally changed the IRQ port associated with LPT2:, the previously assigned port for that printer. What is the standard IRQ port associated with LPT2:?

- ○ a. 5
- ○ b. 6
- ○ c. 7
- ○ d. 8

Question 73

Which of the following passwords is most secure?

- ○ a. ponmlkji
- ○ b. AA33bb88
- ○ c. MikeJang
- ○ d. Ta6Lcotn

Question 74

You've just configured a connection to a new ISP. They've told you the IP address of their DNS server, **24.1.80.33**. Which of the following files is the most appropriate place for this information?

○ a. /etc/hosts

○ b. /etc/host.conf

○ c. /etc/resolv.conf

○ d. /etc/nslookup.conf

Question 75

Which of the following provides detailed and organized information on the use of many Linux applications and services?

○ a. man pages

○ b. **www.linuxdoc.org**

○ c. **httpd.apache.org**

○ d. Linux newsgroups

Question 76

User **jb** calls you up and tells you that, for security reasons, she doesn't want to see her latest print job on the **cash** print queue processed at this time. She wants you to cancel that job. Based on the output from **lpq -Pcash** shown in the figure below, which of the following commands do you want to use?

```
Printer: cash@sash
 Queue: 3 printable jobs
 Server: pid 1323 active
 Unspooler: pid 1332 active
 Status: printing finished at 06:43:14
 Rank   Owner/ID     Class  Job  Files      Size Time
active mj@cash+121    A      121  dollar 232190 06:43:12
2       tr@cash+120    A      120  mark   583394 06:43:14
3       jb@cash+119    A      119  yen    120392 06:43:24
```

○ a. **lpq -Pcash 121**

○ b. **lprm -Pcash 121**

○ c. **lpc -Pcash 121**

○ d. **lpd -Pcash disable**

Question 77

You've just been asked to look for errors on a Linux computer. You're not familiar with the distribution. Where do you look to find the location of the log files?

○ a. /var/log/messages

○ b. /proc

○ c. /etc/inittab

○ d. /etc/syslog.conf

Question 78

Every night at about 3 A.M., your Linux server stops working. Assume that you are user **tr**. Others access this server for their files from other countries, so this is probably not an attack by a cracker. Which of the following actions should you take to try to identify the problem?

○ a. Check your /var/log/messages file to see what happened when Linux locked up.

○ b. Open up your crontab configuration file with a **crontab** command. Insert a **ps aux >> /home/tr/stopproblem** command in the file that opens. Enter this command several times in your crontab file for the minutes before 3 A.M.

○ c. Open up your crontab configuration file with a **crontab** command. Insert a **dmesg >> /home/tr/stopproblem** command in the file that opens. Enter this command several times for the minutes before 3 A.M.

○ d. Upgrade your Linux kernel. This is indicative of a problem with an older driver or a missing security update.

Question 79

> When you try deleting the bigstick file as the superuser from **tr**'s home directory, you get the following message:
>
> ```
> rm: cannot unlink '/home/tr/bigstick': Operation
>     not permitted
> ```
>
> Which of the following statements best describes the problem?
>
> ○ a. As the superuser, you do not have full **root** user privileges.
>
> ○ b. You need to log in as user **tr** to delete this file.
>
> ○ c. The immutable flag was set on this file.
>
> ○ d. The alias associated with the **rm** command does not allow immediate deletion of any file.

Question 80

> Someone has told you that you could configure the third Ethernet network card on your computer by typing **linux ether=11,0x320,eth2** at the LILO boot: prompt. This computer is the main Internet Web server for your business, however, so you do not want to reboot the computer. Which of the following commands would also assign the noted items to the specified network card?
>
> ○ a. **ifconfig eth2 irq 0x320 io_addr 11**
>
> ○ b. **ifconfig eth2 io_addr 11 irq 0x320**
>
> ○ c. **ifconfig eth2 irq 11 io_addr 0x320**
>
> ○ d. **ifconfig irq 11 io_addr 0x320 eth2**

Question 81

You've been asked to solve a problem with one of the 500MHz CPU test computers in the office, which seems to work intermittently. Based on the information in /proc/cpuinfo, shown in the figure below, what is the problem?

```
processor       : 0
vendor_id       : AuthenticAMD
cpu family      : 5
model           : 8
model name      : AMD-K6(tm) 3D processor
stepping        : 12
cpu MHz         : 611.042
cache size      : 64 KB
fdiv_bug        : no
hlt_bug         : no
f00f_bug        : no
coma_bug        : no
fpu             : yes
fpu_exception   : yes
cpuid level     : 1
wp              : yes
flags           : fpu vme de pse tsc msr mce cx8 pge mmx syscall 3dnow k6_mtrr
bogomips        : 697.95
```

○ a. The wrong CPU is installed.

○ b. Other components on the computer cannot handle the productivity of the CPU.

○ c. Excess heat builds up in the CPU.

○ d. /proc/cpuinfo provides no information to solve this problem.

Question 82

You have hard drives with a lot more space than you need. Which of the following directories or types of swap areas should not be installed on a separate partition?

○ a. Swap space

○ b. /sbin

○ c. /home

○ d. /var

Question 83

The **ps aux** command typically lists dozens or even hundreds of processes that are currently running on a Linux computer. Searching through this list can be a difficult process. Which of the following commands is the best way to filter the output for currently running Apache processes?

- ○ a. **ps aux | grep apached**
- ○ b. **ps aux | grep httpd**
- ○ c. **ps aux | less**
- ○ d. **ps aux | more httpd**

Question 84

Where will you find most configuration files in the Filesystem Hierarchy Standard?

- ○ a. /bin
- ○ b. /sbin
- ○ c. /home
- ○ d. /etc

Question 85

On a USB-enabled laptop computer, you have Linux installed with kernel version 2.4.1. You install a PCMCIA network card and wonder why it isn't automatically installed. What is the problem?

- ○ a. Loadable modules are not enabled.
- ○ b. Only USB plug-and-play support is enabled in this kernel.
- ○ c. USB support is not enabled until kernel version 2.4.2.
- ○ d. Linux does not support USB hot-plugging.

Question 86

Which of the following commands can give you the relationship between a MAC address and an IP address?

- ○ a. **nslookup**
- ○ b. **arp**
- ○ c. **ipconfig**
- ○ d. **macd**

Question 87

Assume your Information Technology director has asked you whether you should upgrade your computers from Linux kernel version 2.2.16 to version 2.4.2. All of the following statements are appropriate reasons to upgrade a kernel except:

- ○ a. You want your users to be able to install driver modules on their own computers.
- ○ b. You want to address a security issue that directly affects the configuration of your computers.
- ○ c. You want to set up the ReiserFS journaling file system on one of your partitions.
- ○ d. You want to incorporate the latest support for USB hardware.

Question 88

What type of hardware device can you connect to the cable shown in the figure below?

- ○ a. A floppy drive
- ○ b. An IDE hard drive
- ○ c. A regular SCSI hard drive
- ○ d. A Wide SCSI hard drive

Question 89

Which of the following actions is most likely to lose data that you thought you had already saved on a Linux computer?

○ a. Pressing Ctrl+Alt+Del

○ b. Running the **shutdown -h now** command

○ c. Running the **umount /mnt/floppy** command after saving a file to your floppy drive

○ d. Pressing the On-Off switch on your computer

Question 90

You're trying to set up a network of Linux computers with a single database of usernames and passwords. You've used **ypbind** to connect to this service. What is the name of the service?

○ a. NFS

○ b. **ypd**

○ c. NIS

○ d. Samba

Question 91

You've set up a script in the /usr/sbin directory to help employees submit their timecards, which contain the hours worked on each project, to your payroll department. The name of the script is **hours**. It currently is set up to execute only for user **tr**. Which of the following commands allows all users on your system to run **hours**?

○ a. **chmod u+s hours**

○ b. **chmod u-s /usr/sbin/hours**

○ c. **chmod u+s /usr/sbin/hours**

○ d. **chmod g+s /usr/sbin/hours**

Question 92

You have had a power failure on your Linux system, and you had forgotten to activate the uninterruptible power supply. When you start your computer again, Linux has trouble booting. You're able to restart your computer with a rescue disk. Based on the following excerpt from /etc/fstab, what should you do once you've logged on?

```
/dev/hda3   /       ext3   defaults   1 1
/dev/hda6   /boot   ext3   defaults   1 2
```

○ a. **fsck -t ext2 /dev/hda3; fsck -t ext2 /dev/hda6**

○ b. **fsck -t ext3 /dev/hda3; fsck -t ext2 /dev/hda6**

○ c. **fsck -t ext3 /dev/hda3; fsck -t ext3 /dev/hda6**

○ d. **fsck -t auto /dev/hda3; fsck -t /dev/hda6**

Question 93

You're planning to install Linux on 10 computers in your office. Assume these computers are set up with identical hardware. Which of the following protocols is best suited to install Linux simultaneously on all 10 computers?

○ a. HTTP

○ b. NFS

○ c. NIS

○ d. FTP

Question 94

Which of the following processes has a PID with a lower number than any other process?

○ a. Single user mode

○ b. init

○ c. vmlinuz

○ d. lilo

16

Answer Key

1. b	20. c	39. b	58. c	77. d
2. d	21. b	40. d	59. c	78. b
3. b	22. b	41. d	60. b	79. c
4. c	23. c	42. d	61. d	80. c
5. a	24. a	43. a	62. c	81. c
6. d	25. b	44. a	63. a	82. b
7. d	26. c	45. b	64. b	83. b
8. a	27. d	46. d	65. b	84. d
9. c	28. c	47. d	66. c	85. a
10. b	29. a	48. b	67. c	86. b
11. c	30. d	49. b	68. d	87. a
12. b	31. a	50. b	69. b	88. c
13. c	32. d	51. d	70. c	89. d
14. a	33. b	52. c	71. b	90. c
15. d	34. d	53. c	72. a	91. c
16. b	35. b	54. a	73. d	92. c
17. b	36. d	55. c	74. c	93. b
18. c	37. b	56. b	75. b	94. b
19. d	38. d	57. b	76. b	

Explanations

In this chapter, I have included explanations for every question in Chapter 15. I urge you to analyze each explanation and to think about each question again. A subtle change in the question often makes a difference in the answer.

Many of the wrong answers deserve analysis as well. If you understand why the wrong answers are not correct, you'll understand more of the concepts; this gives you a better chance at getting the answers right on the actual Linux+ exam. If you need more information, a pointer is provided at the end of each explanation to the relevant chapter(s) where the concepts are discussed.

Question 1

Answer b is correct. All users can use the **cd ~** command to return to their home directories. The **cd /home/mj** and **cd /home/tr** commands bring any user to the specified home directories. If these usernames do not belong to you, these commands won't bring you to your home directory. Therefore, answers a and c are both incorrect. The **cd ../..** command brings the user up two directory levels. For example, if you're in the /home/mj directory, this command brings you to the root (/) directory. For more information on basic commands as well as on the significance of the tilde (~) and the double-dots (..), refer to Chapter 7.

Question 2

Answer d is most likely to help you find a solution. The developers of most applications collect problems and solutions in a repository. This is usually collected and documented on the Web site associated with the application. Although other users on a newsgroup can be helpful, they usually don't have the same level of knowledge of the application as the developers. Therefore, answer a is not correct. Although log files can help identify problems, they can also be difficult to find. When you do find them, they can be difficult to understand. Therefore, answer b is also not correct. The idea behind using a test computer is to identify and solve problems before they can harm your users on a production computer. Therefore, answer c is also not correct. For more information on testing applications prior to installation on production computers, refer to Chapters 5 and 6.

Question 3

Answer b is correct. The **diff** command compares two text files, line by line, and returns each line that has changed. Since there is no **change** command, answer a is incorrect. The **mv** command would move the /etc/httpd/httpd.conf to /home/jkp/httpd.bak, overwriting any file that is there. Since this is not a comparison, answer c is also not correct. The **grep** command takes the next phrase, in this case /etc/httpd/httpd.conf, as a search term in the file that follows, /home/jkp/httpd.bak. Since this does not define the differences between the two files, answer d is also incorrect. For more information on these commands, refer to Chapter 8.

Question 4

Answer c is correct. A file like the one shown includes the execute bit associated with the permissions of most other users (which does not include the owner or members of the owning group). In other words, a cracker who logs into this Linux system could run this command as just about any user. The **who** command is commonly used to find currently logged-on users. To have a file of the same name in someone's home directory—with the other's execute bit specified—is dangerous. This is probably a Trojan horse program that sends information to the cracker who created it. You may not know what other Trojan horses have been planted on this computer. If you can't identify the cause, the safest approach is to start from scratch, restoring key files from secure backups. Since you do not know if there are other Trojan horse files on this system, answer a is not correct. Since you need the **who** command as a system administration tool, answer b is also not correct. Since this is probably a Trojan horse, you should not run the command yourself. Therefore, answer d is also incorrect. For more information on the related SUID and SGID bits, refer to Chapter 11.

Question 5

Answer a is correct. When you run the **dhcpcd** command, you're starting the daemon that requests an IP address from the DHCP server. This is sometimes run as **dhcpcd -r** on older Linux distributions. Although the **pump -r** command is commonly used for the same purpose on Red Hat Linux distributions, there is no corresponding **pumpd** command. Therefore, answer b is incorrect. Although the BOOTP protocol is required on a router to allow a DHCP server to assign addresses on adjacent networks, there is no corresponding **bootp** command for regular DHCP client computers. Therefore, answer c is also incorrect. Answer d is a little tricky, since most daemons include only a "d" at the end of the associated protocol or service. DHCP is one exception to this rule. Therefore, answer d is also incorrect. For more information on the commands used to test DHCP servers, see Chapter 4.

Question 6

Answer d is correct. The **killall** command can be used with the name of the program or process to be killed, even if it is running several times simultaneously. Since the **kill** command requries a PID (process identifier), answer a is not correct. The **killall** command doesn't work with PIDs; even if it did, you could not specify multiple PIDs in the manner shown. Therefore, answer b is also not correct. The -9 switch terminates any running process immediately, which can leave temporary files clogging up your system. Since this is not "graceful," answer c is also incorrect. For more information on the **kill** and **killall** commands, refer to Chapter 8.

Question 7

Answer d is correct. The **su -c** command allows you to run commands or open files normally accessible only to the **root** user. The specified command and file generally must be enclosed in double quotes. Before the command is executed, the bash shell prompts you for the **root** password. The /etc/shadow file is the Shadow Password Suite file that contains the encrypted passwords. By default, the permissions on this file allow access only to the **root** user. Since /etc/shadow is accessible only to the **root** user and regular users do not have **root** privileges, answer a is not correct. Answer b would work if it started with the **sudo** command. Since there is no **visu** command, answer b is also incorrect. Since there is no -c switch associated with the **sudo** command, answer c is also incorrect. For more information on these commands, see Chapter 11.

Question 8

Answer a is correct. The **umask** command sets numeric criteria for permissions. If the value of **umask**=000, the default permissions given to a new file are based on the numbers that correspond to full read (**r**), write (**w**), and execute (**x**) permissions for all users, which correspond to a numeric value of 777. The actual permissions are based on this numeric value minus the value of **umask**. If you have a **umask** value of 000, this means any new files you create get (777–000=) 777 permissions. Since a **umask** of 777 leads to files with no permissions (777–777=) 000 for any user, answer b is not correct. Although you could apply the **chmod** 777 command to give **rwx** permissions to all users for a specific file, it does not change the default permissions on newly created files. Therefore, answer c is also incorrect. Although the **chmod 000** command has an opposite effect to **chmod** 777, it still doesn't change the default permissions on a newly created file. Therefore, answer d is also incorrect. For more information on **umask** and permissions, refer to Chapter 11.

Question 9

Answer c is correct. Since the default file system for the floppy drive is the third extended file system (ext3), you need to specify the file system type on your floppy with the -t vfat switch. The specified location for mounting a floppy is the /floppy directory and assumes that your distribution is configured with this directory. Since the second extended file system (ext2) does not support an MS-DOS floppy disk, answer a is not correct. Since the specified mount directory is /floppy—and not /mnt/floppy—answer b is not correct. Since you do need to specify the MS-DOS VFAT file system, answer d is also incorrect. (If the default file format in the /etc/fstab entry was *auto* and not ext3, answer d would work.) For more information on file systems, /etc/fstab, and the **mount** command, refer to Chapters 6 and 11.

Question 10

Answer b is correct. There is a hierarchy of system logs that corresponds to log file extensions. For example, .crit log files are related to critical messages for the service. The service is **httpd**, the Apache daemon, which is run by the Apache Web server. Since Web access corresponds to using a browser such as Netscape or Konqueror on a client, this is not an Apache server problem. Therefore, answer a is not correct. Since there is a .err category available for error messages, answer c is also not correct. Since the Apache server does not run routers, answer d is also incorrect. For more information on log file categories and the governing /etc/syslog.conf configuration file, see Chapter 5.

Question 11

Answer c is correct. You can set up Linux on the specified computer for a limited purpose such as a DNS server. Remember, Linus Torvalds developed the Linux kernel in 1991 for his computer with a 386 CPU. Some Linux distributions can be installed on computers with a 386 CPU; therefore, answer a is incorrect. Graphical Linux workstations should be installed on the latest hardware with at least 32MB of RAM. And Linux distributions are now typically distributed on one or more CDs, each of which contains over 600MB of data. That is considerably larger than the specified 100MB hard drive. Therefore, answer b is also incorrect. Since Apache servers are often associated with large log files, the hard drive is not suitable for installing this type of service. Therefore, answer d is also incorrect. For more information on Linux minimum hardware requirements and appropriate services, see Chapter 2.

Question 12

Answer b is correct. The **resize2fs** command allows you to change the amount of space allocated to a partition that is formatted to the second extended file system (ext2). The **resize_reiserfs** command allows you to change the amount of space allocated to a partition formatted to the Reiser file system (ReiserFS). Since there is no **resize, ext2resize,** or **resizext2fs** command, answers a, c, and d are all incorrect. For more information on these file systems, refer to Chapter 5. For more information on these commands, see Chapter 13.

Question 13

Answer c is correct. The **route -n** command uses the IP addresses in the current routing table. Without the -n switch, **route** gives the hostnames of the computers in the routing table, which requires DNS access to find the associated IP addresses. Although the database of hostnames and IP addresses may be stored in /etc/hosts on a small network, it is usually located on a DNS server, which is often located on a remote network. A similar explanation applies to the **netstat** command; the **netstat -n** command would use IP addresses instead of hostnames. Since there is no -n switch associated with answers a, b, and d, these answers are all not correct. For more information on these commands, refer to Chapter 14.

Question 14

Answer a is correct. Assuming loadable modules are installed, which is the default for Linux kernel 2.4 and higher, the **modprobe** command can install and remove many driver modules associated with installing and removing hardware. Since you've installed and removed a network card, there are drivers to install and remove as well. Since the **insmod** command only installs a driver module, answer b is not correct. Since the **lsmod** command only lists currently installed driver modules, answer c is not correct. Since the **SuperProbe** command checks only the settings associated with your graphics hardware, answer d is also incorrect. For more information on **modprobe, insmod, lsmod,** and module management, please refer to Chapter 9.

Question 15

Answer d is correct. The **linux** command at the LILO boot: prompt starts Linux on the local computer. The information that follows assigns IRQ 12 and I/O 0x330 to eth0, which is the first Ethernet card on this computer. Although the **append** command is appropriate inside the /etc/lilo.conf configuration file, it does not work at the LILO **Boot:** prompt. Therefore, answers a and b are both incorrect. Since eth1 represents the *second* Ethernet network card on the computer, answer c is also incorrect. For more information on using **append** or options at the LILO **Boot:** prompt, please refer to Chapter 6.

Question 16

Answer b is correct. Since you're using a boot disk from another computer, it is not likely that the partition with your root (/) directory matches the partition with the other computer's root (/) directory. Therefore, you need to specify the correct partition for your computer at the LILO boot: prompt. Since the **linux single** command still needs to access your root (/) directory before it can start your computer in single user mode, answer a is not correct. By convention, the variable that represents the **root** directory at the LILO boot: prompt is **root**, not /. Therefore, answer c is also not correct. Since the Linux kernel is already available by default on any Linux boot or rescue disk, you do not need to specify the partition with the /boot directory on your system. And the boot process still needs to know the location of your root (/) directory. Therefore, answer d is also incorrect. For more information, see Chapters 13 and 14.

Question 17

Answer b is correct. COM3 is associated with IRQ_4 and I/O 03e8. This is a detail to be memorized. COM1 and COM3 always correspond to IRQ_4. COM2 and COM4 always correspond to IRQ_3. The "f" in an I/O address corresponds to COM1 or COM2; the "e" in an I/O address corresponds to COM3 or COM4. For more information on COM ports and their associated settings, refer to Chapter 3.

Question 18

Answer c is correct. The **fdisk** command allows you to configure and size a partition. The **mkfs** command allows you to format that partition. Although you can split a partition into two parts with **fips**, you still need to format the second partition. Therefore, answer a is incorrect. Since the **format** command in Linux is not related to formatting a partition, answer b is incorrect. Since the **lilo** command does not create or format a partition, answer d is also incorrect. For more information on creating and formatting partitions, refer to Chapter 5.

Question 19

Answer d is correct. Normally, parity RAM works on a motherboard that expects non-parity RAM. The parity bit is simply ignored. However, if you tried to install non-parity RAM on a motherboard that expects parity RAM, the motherboard does not find the parity bit that it expects, and it cannot recognize the RAM. This is expressed in multiple beeps through your computer's speaker. But since you're using parity RAM on a non-parity motherboard, there is no problem, and therefore answer a is not correct. Since the parity bit is ignored, there is no extra information being sent through the RAM. No extra data means no overheating, and therefore answer b is also incorrect. Even on a motherboard that shares memory between the video system and the rest of the computer, the parity or non-parity characteristics of the RAM do not change the allocation of memory. Therefore, answer c is also incorrect. For more information on the RAM that you can use in different motherboards, refer to Chapter 9.

Question 20

Answer c is correct. Since access to the **shutdown** and **reboot** commands is limited to the **root** user on many Linux distributions, you may have to use the physical On-Off switch on your computer. (Do not use the On-Off switch while Linux is running the **fsck** command!) The **linux single** command starts Linux in single user mode, which includes superuser privileges. You can then use the **passwd** command to reset the **root** password without having to know the current **root** password. Although this technique does not work in every Linux distribution, it is one major reason why physical access to a Linux server should be limited. Since access to the **init 1** command is limited to the **root** user, and since the question assumes that you do not have the **root** password, answer a is not correct. Since you need to specify an operating system to start at the LILO boot: prompt, answer b is not correct. Since access to the **shutdown** command is normally limited to the **root** user, answer d is also not correct. For more information on this process, see Chapter 14.

Question 21

Answer b is correct. ATAPI or ATA devices are the mass storage devices that correspond to the AT Attachment Packet Interface. The standard IDE drives on most PCs are ATA devices. The hdd device corresponds to the slave drive attached to the second ATAPI controller. The eth0 device corresponds to the first Ethernet card on a PC. Since that is not related to ATA standards, answer a is not correct. The sdc device corresponds to the third SCSI hard drive. Since that is based on a different standard from ATA, answer c is also not correct. The ttyS1 device corresponds to COM2, which is commonly used for a telephone modem. Since that is based on a different standard from ATA, answer d is also not correct. For more information on basic PC hardware standards, refer to Chapter 3.

Question 22

Answer b is correct. The **lpc** command allows you to status, enable, or disable a printer. It also allows you to reorder the current jobs on a printer, based on their job numbers. You can find the current job numbers with the **lpq** command. The **lpc** command does not allow you to remove a specific job. That is the province of the **lprm** command. Therefore, answer a is not correct. Since the **lpc** command is not related to the configuration of a printer, answer c is also incorrect. Since you need the **lpq** command to find the job numbers of print jobs in a specific print queue, answer d is also incorrect. For more information on commands related to the line print daemon (**lpd**), please refer to Chapter 12.

Question 23

Answer c is correct. A hard drive on position hda and a CD drive on position hdb indicate that both drives are connected to the same IDE hard drive controller cable. When the CD is operating, data transfer speed to the hard drive is limited to the capacity of the CD drive. Since CD drives are much slower than hard drives, it is not correct to characterize this as good performance. Therefore, answer a is not correct. Since the CPU is generally much faster than a hard drive, it is not a limiting factor on the speed of a hard drive. Therefore, answer b is also not correct. Yet, as long as the hard drive is correctly configured in the computer's CMOS settings, it will work. Therefore, answer d is also incorrect. For more information on IDE hard drive and CD drive positions and interactions, refer to Chapter 3.

Question 24

Answer a is correct. Of the available choices, only the ext2 file system is resizable. The ext3 and XFS file systems are journaling file systems that are associated with a fixed amount of space. Therefore, answers b and d are both incorrect. The Microsoft VFAT file system is also limited to a fixed amount of space. Therefore, answer c is also not correct. If you want the best of both worlds, ext3 may be a viable option, since it is easily convertible to and from the ext2 file system. As discussed in Chapter 13, ReiserFS is also a resizable journaling file system. For more information on your options for file systems, refer to Chapter 5.

Question 25

Answer b is correct. Squid is the proxy server for Linux. The settings on Squid can affect communication on any of the ports defined in /etc/services, which includes Web access though http port 80, email receipt access through pop3 port 110 or imap port 143, as well as FTP access through port 21. Since there is communication between your LAN and the Internet in Web and email service, FTP service probably hasn't been interrupted by your ISP due to nonpayment of any bills. Therefore, answer a is not correct. Since standard network cards do not differentiate by type of traffic, the configuration of the user's network card does not make a difference. Therefore, answer c is also incorrect. Since there is Web access, the DNS server is successfully translating addresses such as **www.mommabears.com** to IP addresses such as **199.70.68.2**. DNS servers do not discriminate between types of services. Therefore, answer d is also incorrect.

Question 26

Answer c is correct. The **ATDP** command in **minicom** sends a message to your modem to dial the following numbers in pulse dialing mode. A pulse system is associated with telephones with rotary dialers. The **AT** command by itself is a request for attention from your modem. If you see an "OK" output from this command, you've confirmed that **minicom** can communicate with your modem. Nevertheless, it does not tell a modem how to dial a number; therefore, answer a is not correct. Since the **ATDT** command is used for touch-tone dialing, the signals it creates may not be understood by a telephone system that expects pulses. Therefore, answer b is not correct. Since the **ATAO** command sets up your modem to answer an incoming call, it does not connect your modem to your ISP. Therefore, answer d is also incorrect. For more informtion on **minicom**, see Chapter 10.

Question 27

Answer d is correct. Although the main power line is separate, there is still a small amount of power sent through each active wire in the floppy controller cable. The crossed power lines would lead to the power light staying on for as long as power is available to your computer. Since the small amount of power that is sent through the floppy controller cable does not burn out circuits, the floppy drive and motherboard are both safe. Therefore, answers a and b are both incorrect. Each wire in the floppy controller cable has a function. If you installed the cable upside down, each wire would not match its intended connector. Therefore, answer c is also incorrect. For more information on controller cables, refer to Chapter 9.

Question 28

Answer c is correct. The /var/log/messages file is the typical location for the log file that lists successes and failures associated with detected hardware and initiated daemons on your computer. The /var/log/wtmp file is associated with login successes and failures and is therefore not related to hardware detection or daemons. Therefore, answer a is incorrect. Since there is normally no /proc/messages file in current Linux distributions, answer b is also incorrect. Although /var/log/maillog lists messages associated with mail access on a Red Hat Linux computer, that is also not related to hardware detection or daemons. Therefore, answer d is also incorrect. For more information on post-boot log files, refer to Chapter 5.

Question 29

Answer a is correct. Later Linux kernels starting with version 2.4.0 recognize the most common USB components, using the USB hot-swappable features, if loadable modules are enabled in the kernel. No action is required. Since you do not need to reboot Linux to get Linux to recognize common USB devices, answer b is not correct. Since loadable modules are required to automatically install a device associated with a USB component, answer c is also incorrect. Since Linux distributions with the given kernel do recognize and support at least the most common USB devices, answer d is also incorrect. For more information on USB support, refer to Chapter 3.

Question 30

Answer d is correct. You don't want unauthorized users to have physical access to the Linux server computer. On many Linux distributions, an unauthorized user can reboot that computer in single user mode to gain access to that computer without a password. Once in single user mode, that person can reset the **root** password to the password of his or her choice. A password-protected screensaver does not prevent an unauthorized user from rebooting the computer by turning it off and on. Therefore, answer a is not correct. It is impractical in most organizations to keep watch over a Linux server 24 hours every day. Although answer b can work, it is less practical than answer d. Therefore, answer b is incorrect. Good security practices mean that all users, especially the **root** user, change their passwords on a regular basis. It is therefore impractical to keep such passwords written down and stored. And it is unnecessary because the **root** user can reset the password of any user. Therefore, answer c is also incorrect. For more information on best practices in security and documentation, see Chapters 2, 11, and 13.

Question 31

Answer a is correct. The initial run level when you boot is determined by the number associated with the **id** and **initdefault** parameters in /etc/inittab. In fact, this is symptomatic of the following line in /etc/inittab: **id:1:initdefault**, where 1 represents single user mode in the given distribution. The **append** parameter is used to set IRQ ports, I/O channels, and DMA addresses for a specific hardware component in /etc/lilo.conf. Since that is unrelated to the run level in which Linux starts, answer b is not correct. If the partition associated with the root (/) directory is incorrectly configured, your computer wouldn't even finish booting, much less find single user mode. Therefore, answer c is also incorrect. Since the parameters for the bash shell in any configuration file, including /etc/profile, do not determine the initial run level, answer d is also incorrect. For more information on troubleshooting, see Chapter 14. For more information on /etc/inittab and various run levels, see Chapter 6.

Question 32

Answer d is correct. These standards are designed to transfer data at different speeds. Wide SCSI allows data transfer at speeds up to 20MBps. Ultra Wide SCSI allows data transfer at speeds up to 40MBps. Ultra2 Wide SCSI allows data transfer at speeds up to 80MBps. Since all three standards are based on a 16-bit bus, answer a is not correct. Since 16-bit buses are associated with 68-pin data cables, usually organized in two rows of 34 wires each, answer b is also incorrect. Since 16-bit buses are also associated with 16 SCSI numbers, or Logical Unit Numbers (LUNs), each of which can be assigned to a different SCSI device, answer c is also incorrect. Remember, the hierarchy of SCSI numbers is, from highest to lowest: 7, 6, 5, 4, 3, 2, 1, 0, 15, 14, 13, 12, 11, 10, 9, 8. SCSI number 7 is reserved for the SCSI host adapter. For more information on SCSI devices, refer to Chapter 3.

Question 33

Answer b is correct. If you ever need to reconfigure or replace hardware, it helps to have configuration details such as IRQ port, I/O address, and DMA channels readily available. Since computer hard drives sometimes fail, you may not be able to access configuration files on a failed hard drive. Therefore, answer a is incorrect. It is best to have all users change their passwords on a regular basis, and it is best to not keep any record of such passwords to help promote the confidentiality of user data. Besides, if you accidentally left the file with user passwords outside the cabinet, unauthorized persons could gain access to your files. Therefore, answer c is also incorrect. Since the **mkfs** command automatically restores inode numbers, it is not necessary to record the inode number for every file on your Linux computer. Besides, most systems include many thousands of files. Therefore, answer d is also incorrect. For more information on best documentation practices, see Chapter 2. For more information on hardware concepts such as IRQ, I/O, and DMA, see Chapter 3. For more information on the **mkfs** command, see Chapter 13.

Question 34

Answer d is correct. The gateway address is not shown in the **ifconfig** output in the figure. The IP address of the Ethernet card is **192.168.0.100**; the IP address of the loopback device is **127.0.0.1**. The IPv6 address is also shown for eth0. Therefore, answer a is not correct. The MAC address corresponds to the hardware address of the Ethernet card, which is **00:50:56:A7:00:23**. Therefore, answer b is also not correct. The IP address of the loopback device is also known as the *loopback address.* Therefore, answer c is also not correct. For more information on **ifconfig**, see Chapter 9. For more information on IP and MAC addresses, see Chapter 4.

Question 35

Answer b is correct. The BIOS menu is permanently stored in a read-only memory (ROM) chip that does not depend on power. Since the current time on the internal computer clock does depend on the power from the battery, answer a is not correct. Since CMOS settings are not stored in ROM, these settings do depend on power from the computer battery. Therefore, answer c is also not correct. One of the standard ways to reset the password associated with a BIOS menu is to remove the computer battery for some period of time. Therefore, answer d is also not correct. (Some newer motherboards do not keep the BIOS password in CMOS. Battery removal in this case does not reset the password; instead, an adjustment to a BIOS jumper is required to remove the password. This is still the exception, however.) For more information on BIOS, CMOS, and the effect of the computer battery, see Chapter 3.

Question 36

Answer d is correct. The commands that unconvert encrypted passwords from the /etc/shadow and /etc/gshadow files are **pwunconv** and **grpunconv**, respectively. Since the **gconv** and **passunconv** commands do not exist, answers a, b, and c are all incorrect. The commands that encrypt passwords are **pwconv** and **grpconv**. For more information on these commands and the Shadow Password Suite, refer to Chapter 11.

Question 37

Answer b is correct. A file in .tgz format is equivalent to a file in .tar.gz format. It is archived and compressed. The **tar** command's **z** switch uncompresses, and the **x** switch extracts the archive from the file. Since the **tar xvf** command does not uncompress the file, answer a is not correct. Since the **tar cvf** command does not extract files from the archive, answer c is also incorrect. Since **tar czf** also does not extract files from the archive, answer d is also incorrect. The **c** switch in fact attempts to collect files into an archive. For more information on the **tar** command and associated switches, refer to Chapter 6.

Question 38

Answer d is correct. The Point-to-Point Protocol daemon (**pppd**) governs current TCP/IP connections through a telephone modem. Since **smbd**, the Samba daemon, is associated with communications on a regular LAN between Linux/Unix and Microsoft Windows and/or IBM computers, answer a is not correct. Since the line print daemon (**lpd**) is not closely related to any networking protocol such as **pppd**, answer b is also incorrect. Since **nfsd**, the Network File System daemon, is associated with communications on a regular LAN between Linux/Unix computers, answer c is also not correct. For more information on **pppd**, see Chapter 10.

Question 39

Answer b is correct. The !: command in the **vi** editor is required to start execute mode, which allows you to run regular shell commands. Pressing the Esc key does return you to **vi** command mode. This allows you to run regular **vi** commands. However, you cannot run regular shell commands in **vi** command mode. Therefore, answer a is not correct. Since the **Ctrl+X** command in **vi** does not do anything, answer c is incorrect. Since pressing the F1 key starts a help screen in **vi**, it does not allow you to run shell commands. Therefore, answer d is also incorrect. For more information on the **vi** editor, read Chapter 12.

Question 40

Answer d is correct. The choice that your computer makes between IDE and SCSI hard drives depends on the settings saved in your CMOS. Since you do not know if these settings point to the IDE hard drive first, answer a is not correct. Since SCSI drive 6 has a higher priority than SCSI drive 3, answer b is also not correct. Since you do not know if your CMOS settings point to the SCSI drives first, answer c is also incorrect. For more information on CMOS, IDE, and SCSI drives, see Chapter 3.

Question 41

Answer d is correct. The **chmod** command can be used to adjust permission levels for the file owner, members of the file owner's group, and all other users on that Linux computer. As the owner, you should generally have full read (**r**), write (**w**), and execute (**x**) permissions. As discussed in Chapter 11, this corresponds to a permission level of 4 (**r**) + 2 (**w**) + 1 (**x**) = 7. Other users, including members of your group, need a minimum of read (**r**) and execute (**x**) permissions to actually run a command. As discussed in Chapter 11, this corresponds to a permission level of 4 (**r**) + 1 (**x**) = 5. The **chmod 777** command gives full permissions to all users. You do not want to do this for users other than yourself. Therefore, answer a is not correct. The **chown** command changes ownership of a given file from one user to another. Since **chown 755** does not affect file permissions, answer b is also not correct. The **chgrp** command changes ownership of a given file from one group to another. Since **chgrp 711** does not affect file permissions, answer c is also not correct. For more information on these commands and permissions, see Chapter 11.

Question 42

Answer d is correct. The **xf86config** tool can be used to configure your graphics card, monitor, mouse, and keyboard. Although there is an **XF86Setup** tool, there is no **xf86setup** tool. Remember, the choice of upper- or lowercase letters matters in Linux. Therefore, answer a is incorrect. Although the **SuperProbe** command utility can be used to find the characteristics of your graphics card and monitor, it does not set the color depth. Therefore, answer b is also incorrect. Although the **XFree86 -configure** command can set up some basic configurations, there is no **xfree86** command. Therefore, answer c is also incorrect. For more information on Linux X Window or graphical user interface command utilities, refer to Chapter 13.

Question 43

Answer a is correct. The default location for Web site files for an Apache server is determined by the directory associated with the **DocumentRoot** variable in the httpd.conf configuration file. Although this directory is usually either /var/www or /home/httpd by default, Apache does not automatically search both directories. Therefore, answer b is not correct. Since there is no **HomeRoot** variable in httpd.conf, answer c is also not correct. Since you do not log in as the user **apache** when configuring this service, answer d is also not correct. For more information about basic Apache configuration parameters, refer to Chapter 10.

Question 44

Answer a is correct. If you do not see an eth0 entry in the output from /sbin/ifconfig, then your computer's network card is not active. Either the /sbin/ifconfig eth0 up or the /sbin/ifup eth0 command can activate a properly configured Ethernet network card. Since there is no **lsconfig** command, answers b and d are both incorrect. An inactive network card can keep you from accessing the router on your LAN. Thus, you do not want to deactivate your network card. The **ifdown eth0** command deactivates the eth0 network card. Therefore, answer c is also incorrect. For more information on configuring and activating network cards, see Chapter 9.

Question 45

Answer b is correct. An asterisk (*) in the password position is associated with a disabled user. To solve this problem, run the **passwd chirac** command as the **root** or superuser. The configured shell is indicated by the last entry, **/bin/ash**. Since the ash shell is a valid shell in Linux, answer a is not correct. The entry in the fifth column, **wine**, does not affect anything about the user. In fact, you could leave this blank. Therefore, answer c is incorrect. Although the default GID (group ID) number matches the UID (user ID) number in Red Hat Linux installations, this is not a requirement. Therefore, answer d is also incorrect. In fact, different sets of numbers for GID and UID can help you set up groups independent of any specific user. For more information on the configuration of the /etc/passwd file, refer to Chapter 11.

Question 46

Answer d is correct. The conditions described in the question, which include a large number of **ping** messages and trouble accessing your Web server, are characteristic of a Denial of Service (DoS) attack. Connectivity checks from a DNS server or an Internet router are not frequent and generally do not affect access to a Web site. Therefore, answer a is not correct. Occasional testing by individual users with the **ping** command does not create enough traffic to affect access to a Web site. Therefore, answer b is also not correct. Although you could try to address a DoS attack by increasing the amount of traffic that you can handle, DoS attacks can be easily increased beyond the capacity of even the largest Web sites. Therefore, answer c is also incorrect. For more information on DoS attacks, see Chapter 10. For more information on the use of the **ping** command, see Chapter 14.

Question 47

Answer d is correct. The **modprobe** command detects currently installed hardware. If hardware without drivers are detected, **modprobe** attempts to install the appropriate drivers. If previously installed hardware is removed, **modprobe** removes the hardware drivers, as well as any other driver that may have depended on this hardware in the *autoclean* process. Since the **insmod** command only installs drivers, answer a is not correct. Since the **rmmod** command only removes installed drivers, answer b is also not correct. Since there is no **lsprobe** command, answer c is also not correct. For more information on these commands and associated capabilities, refer to Chapter 9.

Question 48

Answer b is correct. The **rpm** command is used to install packages with the .rpm extension. The -Uvh switches allow this package to be used as an upgrade to other Sendmail packages (-U), verifies the installed files (-v), and adds hashmarks to signify the progress of the installation (-h). Although the **tar xzvf** command can extract a binary package from a file such as sendmail-8-12.0.tar.gz, it does not unarchive or decompress a package in an .rpm file. Therefore, answer a is not correct. Since the -Uvh switches do not unarchive a package with the **tar** command, answer c is also incorrect. Since there are no **x, z,** or **f** switches associated with the **rpm** command, answer d is also incorrect. For more information on these commands and package management, refer to Chapter 6.

Question 49

Answer b is correct. The -**HUP** switch restarts the specified process. The **kill** command requires a PID (process identifier) number. These numbers are stored in the /var/run directory, in files with the .pid extension. The back quotes around the **cat /var/run/cron.pid** command input the appropriate PID number to the **kill -HUP** command. Since the **killall** command by itself doesn't restart a process, answer a is not correct. Since the **kill** command requires a PID number, answer c is also incorrect. Since the **killall** command works only with the name of a process, answer d is also incorrect. For more information on the **kill** and **killall** commands, see Chapter 8.

Question 50

Answer b is correct. The **ServerName** variable should be set to what you want users to enter in their browsers to access your Web site. The /home/httpd or /var/www directory is normally associated with the **DocumentRoot** variable, which is the location of the files for your Web site. Since this is unrelated to the name people use to access your Web site, answer a is incorrect. If the Web site is accessible only on your LAN, you could assign the hostname of your computer, **webserver**, to the **ServerName** variable. But since this is to be a public Web site on the Internet, the hostname alone doesn't work. Therefore, answer c is also incorrect. The **ScriptAlias** variable is normally set to the directory on your computer with script files for your Web pages. Since this is unrelated to the name people use to access your Web site, answer d is also incorrect. For more information on Apache configuration, see Chapter 10.

Question 51

Answer d is correct. The **renice** command is used to reprioritize a currently running process. Negative numbers are used to raise the priority associated with a process. Since the **nice** command only affects the priority of new processes, answers a and c are both incorrect. Since the **renice** command in answer b uses a positive number, it lowers the priority of the **anticrime** program on your system. Therefore, that answer is also incorrect. For more information on these commands, refer to Chapter 8.

Question 52

Answer c is correct. The Common Internet File System (CIFS) is more commonly known as Samba. This system is used to allow computers with Unix-type operating systems such as Linux and FreeBSD to communicate with computers with Microsoft- and/or IBM-type operating systems. Sendmail is the most common mail server installed on Linux computers. Since there is no "Mail" service for Linux, answer a is incorrect. Since the Network File System (NFS) connects only Unix-type operating systems such as Linux, answer b is incorrect. Since Apache is the most common Web server for Linux, it does not fulfill the needs of standard mail service. Therefore, answer d is also incorrect. For more information on these topics, see Chapter 2.

Question 53

Answer c is correct. The **ln** command links one command to another. When you run the first file listed, it runs the linked file, which is the second file listed in the command. Since **antiterror-7** is the program from this week, it does not meet the requirements of the question. Therefore, answer a is not correct. Since there is no standard .lnk file in Linux, answer b is also not correct. Since the **ln antiterror** command does not specify the absolute path to the **antiterror** file, the effect depends on the current working directory, which is not specified. Therefore, answer d is also incorrect. For more information on the **ln** command, refer to Chapter 7.

Question 54

Answer a is correct. The message shown is not direct, but it is the standard message that you see if you try to run the **rpm** command to install or upgrade a package as a regular user. Changing the permissions associated with the /var/lib/rpm/packages.rpm file does not affect the result. Therefore, answers b and d are both incorrect. There is no error in the /var/lib/rpm/packages.rpm file. Downloading a new version of this file does not affect the result. Therefore, answer c is also incorrect. For more information on the **rpm** command and package installation, refer to Chapter 6.

Question 55

Answer c is correct. Although regular users are not prohibited from running the **rpm** command, it does not work for installing packages unless you're working with **root** or superuser privileges. Among the available choices, the **su -c** command allows you to gain superuser privileges for the one command, assuming that you know the **root** password. Since you are logged in as a regular user, the **rpm** command won't work for you; therefore, answer a is not correct. Since your username is not in /etc/sudoers, the **sudo** command won't allow you to run commands such as **rpm**; therefore, answer b is also incorrect. Since the **tar** command won't work with an RPM file, answer d is also incorrect. For more information on the **su** and **sudo** commands, refer to Chapter 11. For more information on the **tar** and **rpm** commands, refer to Chapter 6.

Question 56

Answer b is correct. The columns in a **cron** listing are, from left to right: minute, hour, day of month, month, and day of week. Therefore, the code in the question indicates this program is run on the 36th minute of the 5th hour of the 12th day of the 6th month (June). Since **cron** uses a 24-hour clock, the 5th hour is in the morning. Answers a, c, and d do not cite the time or date in the correct fashion, and all are therefore not correct. When reviewing a **crontab** entry, remember that the last number corresponds to dates from Sunday through Saturday, where 0 and 7 correspond to Sunday. For more information on **cron** and **crontab** entries, refer to Chapter 13.

Question 57

Answer b is correct. The **slogin** command allows you to set up a remote connection using communication protocols that are encrypted over a network. The **rsh** command does allow you to set up a remote connection; however, passwords are sent through the network in clear text. Therefore, answer a is not correct. The **telnet** command also allows you to set up a remote connection. It shares the same weakness as **rsh**, in that it also sends passwords in clear text. Therefore, answer c is also incorrect. Since there is no **securesh** command, answer d is also incorrect. For more information on the "r" and "ssh" sets of commands as well as **telnet**, refer to Chapter 12.

Question 58

Answer c is correct. You want to reserve the IRQ ports, I/O addresses, and DMA channels required by the legacy hardware in your computer's CMOS settings, so they are unavailable when the plug-and-play hardware looks for an open setting. Since serial and printer ports are external physical ports, they use the same settings whether or not you install a plug-and-play or legacy device in either type of port. Therefore, answer a is not correct. Since you do not know what channels will be taken by plug-and-play hardware, you cannot know what settings to reserve for your legacy hardware in CMOS. Therefore, answer b is also not correct. Although you could replace the legacy hardware with plug-and-play hardware, that is not cost effective and defeats the purpose of setting up an older computer for Linux. Therefore, answer d is also not correct. For more information on this topic, refer to Chapter 9.

Question 59

Answer c is correct. The **useradd** command that is shown does not assign passwords. If your Linux computer is set up with encrypted passwords through the Shadow Password Suite, it is not possible to assign passwords with **useradd**. You can add a new password for user **jkp** as the superuser with the **passwd jkp** command. Since the **useradd** command automatically adds the necessary files to /home/jkp from the /etc/skel directory, answer a is not correct. Since a default shell is automatically assigned in /etc/passwd for all new users, answer b is also not correct. The default permissions of /etc/passwd allow users to log on to a Linux computer. The same permissions apply on /etc/passwd to all users. Therefore, answer d is also incorrect. For more information on adding and deleting users, refer to Chapter 11.

Question 60

Answer b is correct. The most common problem with Linux modem configuration is the use of Winmodems, which are software modems that use Microsoft Windows driver libraries to support some of their systems. Loadable modules relate to the ability of Linux to install a new driver automatically. They do not determine whether there is an appropriate driver for a modem. Therefore, answer a is not correct. There are no potential IRQ or I/O conflicts between a printer on a standard LPT1 or LPT2 port and a modem on a COM1, COM2, COM3, or COM4 port. Therefore, answer c is also not correct. Although an upgraded Linux kernel can handle additional modems, the available kernels as addressed in the Linux+ criteria do not address the most common Linux modem issue, the Winmodem. Therefore, answer d is also not correct. For more information on Winmodems, refer to Chapter 9.

Question 61

Answer d is correct. The **tcp_wrappers** package allows you to limit or regulate inbound traffic on a TCP/IP network. Although this package may be set up with **ipchains** or **iptables** commands in the /etc/hosts.allow and /etc/hosts.deny files, these are commands and not packages. Therefore, answers a and b are both incorrect. Although the **ALL:ALL** command in a /etc/hosts.deny file stops all traffic from coming into a computer, it is not a Linux package. Therefore, answer c is also incorrect. For more information on firewalls, the **tcp_wrappers** package, and these commands, refer to Chapter 4.

Question 62

Answer c is correct. You should never assign SCSI Logical Unit Number (LUN) 7 to any SCSI device, because that is assigned to the SCSI controller by default. If you did assign LUN 7 to a SCSI device, that would lead to a conflict, and neither device would work. Although electrostatic charges are a risk whenever you work with electronic equipment, the configuration issue described in answer c is a definite cause of the problem. Therefore, answer a is not correct. Although improper configuration in a SCSI BIOS can prevent any single SCSI device from working, it should not cause a problem with all SCSI devices. Therefore, answer b is also not correct. The installation of a new SCSI device does not change any of the assignments in the Linux Loader. Therefore, answer d is also not correct. For more information on SCSI hardware and LUN numbers, refer to Chapter 3.

Question 63

Answer a is correct. First, remember that a file with a .tgz extension is archived and compressed by default. Remember, if you see a forward slash in front of the directory or file name, you're using the absolute and not the relative path.. Since the command in this question used the absolute path to archive home directories, it doesn't matter what directory you're using when you restore from the archive. The home directory of each user is restored to the original location. If you had archived with the relative path, the given command would restore home directories to /tmp/home. But since you used the absolute path, answer b is not correct. Since the archive exists in the current directory (/tmp), it is restored by the given command. Therefore, answer c is not correct. Since the archive was created using the absolute path (/home), it is restored using the absolute path, which leads to the /home directory. Since this is a subdirectory of root (/), answer d is also not correct. For more information on the **tar** command, refer to Chapter 6. For more information on how absolute and relative paths affect the **tar** command, refer to Chapter 7.

Question 64

Answer b is correct. The **/sbin/lilo** command restores the information from /etc/lilo.conf to the Master Boot Record (MBR) of your computer's hard drive. The MS-DOS **fdisk /MBR** command is one way to overwrite an existing Linux Loader on your MBR. Therefore, answer a is not correct. No switch is required for the **/sbin/lilo** command. In fact, the -**MBR** switch keeps this command from working. Therefore, answer c is also incorrect. Starting Linux in single user mode does not restore your Linux Loader to the MBR. Therefore, answer d is also incorrect. For more information on restoring the Linux Loader to the MBR, refer to Chapter 14.

Question 65

Answer b is correct. There is only one available extended partition on any hard drive. The top-level directory in Linux is root (/), not /root. In addition, you can neither format an extended partition nor mount a directory on that partition. The /root directory is the home directory of the **root** or superuser. The /dev/hda8 device does correspond to the fourth logical partition on the primary master IDE hard drive. Therefore, answer a is incorrect. The third extended file system does correspond to ext3; therefore, answer c is also incorrect. The last number in the cited /etc/fstab line (3) does correspond to the order in which it is mounted when you boot Linux. Therefore, answer d is also incorrect. For more information on the /etc/fstab configuration file, see Chapter 6.

Question 66

Answer c is correct. The directory specified by the **mount** command is mnt/cdrom. Since that is a relative path, that specifies a subdirectory of the current directory, /root. Therefore, the **ls /root/mnt/cdrom** command should list some of the files on the CD. Since the relative path was used and the current directory is /root, not root (/), answer a is not correct. Although the **ls mnt** command would list the name of the cdrom subdirectory, it would not list any of the files on the CD. Therefore, answer b is also not correct. Since there is no reference to the /cdrom directory in the command, answer d is also not correct. For more information on the **mount** command, see Chapter 13. For more information on absolute and relative directory paths, see Chapter 7.

Question 67

Answer c is correct. The left-facing redirection arrow (<) sends data from the /home/tr/hurr-data file for processing by the **/opt/bin/windy** program. The right-facing redirection arrow (>) sends the result to the /home/tr/hurr-output file. Since there is no input data to the **/opt/bin/windy** program, there is no output from this program. Therefore, answer a is not correct. With respect to answer b, although there is output from the **/opt/bin/windy < /home/tr/hurr-data** command, when you pipe (|) it, you're telling the bash shell to have it processed by another program. Since the output isn't entered into the /home/tr/hurr-output file, answer b is also incorrect. If there were output from the **/opt/bin/windy** program alone, it would overwrite the data in the /home/tr/hurr-data file. Since this is not your objective, answer d is also incorrect. For more information on pipes (|) and redirection arrows, refer to Chapter 7.

Question 68

Answer d is correct. Although the /etc/inittab file is the configuration of how the first Linux process, **init**, starts on your computer, it does not ask for nor does it confirm your rights as a user to access this Linux system. Since the Radius modem server is an authentication server for users who connect by modem, answer a is not correct. Since the /etc/passwd file is the standard Linux file with usernames and passwords, answer b is also incorrect. Since the Network Information Service (NIS) provides a single database of usernames and passwords on a Unix/Linux local area network, answer c is also incorrect. For more information on authentication services, see Chapter 10. For more information on /etc/inittab, see Chapter 6. For more information on passwords, see Chapter 11.

Question 69

Answer b is correct. As the **root** or superuser, you can run the **init** command. When you run **init 5**, this restarts Linux services based on the information from /etc/inittab shown in the question. Although changing the 3 to a 5 in the **id:3:initdefault** line would lead to a graphical login the next time you boot Linux, it does not start a graphical login screen from the current command-line interface. Therefore, answer a is not correct. The **shutdown -r now** command reboots Linux immediately. Since the /etc/inittab file still points to run level 3, Linux will still boot in command-line mode. Therefore, answer c is also incorrect. Running the **init 3** command restarts Linux services in command-line mode. Therefore, answer d is also incorrect. For more information on the /etc/inittab configuration file and Linux run levels, see Chapter 6.

Question 70

Answer c is correct. The **1G** command in **vi** navigates to the top of a file. Since the **G** command with no line number navigates to the bottom of a file, answer a is not correct. Since the **0G** command can't find a line 0 in the file, no action is taken. Therefore, answer b is also not correct. Since the **i** command starts input mode from the current position of the cursor, answer d is also incorrect. For more information on the **vi** editor, see Chapter 12.

Question 71

Answer b is correct. The **dd** command sets up files on another drive such as a floppy based on an image such as a Linux kernel. The first floppy drive on a Linux computer corresponds to device fd0, or /dev/fd0. The **bs** switch, which determines the amount of data copied in each block, isn't always required. Although either the **mkbootdisk** command in Red Hat Linux or the **mkboot** command in Debian Linux can create customized boot disks, there is no **mkdisk** command. Therefore, answer a is not correct. Since the **dd** command does not work on a mounted floppy drive, answer c is also not correct. Since there is no **mkrescuedisk** command, answer d is also incorrect. For more information on creating boot and rescue disks, refer to Chapter 14.

Question 72

Answer a is correct. IRQ 5 is the standard IRQ port assigned to LPT2:. Sound cards are often also assigned to IRQ 5, which may cause problems for a second printer. Since IRQ 6 is typically assigned to the floppy disk controller, answer b is incorrect. Since IRQ 7 is typically assigned to the first printer port (LPT1), answer c is also incorrect. Since IRQ 8 is typically assigned to the CMOS realtime clock, answer d is also incorrect. For more information on IRQ assignments, see Chapter 3.

Question 73

Answer d is correct. A seemingly random mixture of numbers and upper- and lowercase letters is much more difficult to crack than a set of letters that follows a pattern or includes actual words. Such passwords need not be difficult to remember; Ta6Lcotn could stand for "There are 6 Linux computers on this network." Since ponmlkji corresponds to a pattern, eight consecutive letters of the alphabet (backwards), answer a is not correct. Although AA33bb88 is somewhat random, the repeating letters and numbers do make it easier to crack. Therefore, answer b is also not correct. Although MikeJang seems like a good password, it consists of two words fused together. It is relatively easy for a "good" password cracking program to decipher this kind of password. Therefore, answer c is also not correct. For more information on good passwords, refer to Chapter 11.

Question 74

Answer c is correct. Information related to DNS servers should be stored in the /etc/resolv.conf configuration file. A typical line in this file is **nameserver 24.1.80.33**; in Linux, DNS servers are often known as nameservers, which are based on the Berkeley Internet Name Domain (BIND). Since the /etc/hosts file is designed as a static database of names and IP addresses, it fulfills a function similar to a DNS server. It is a common practice to store names and IP addresses in this file. However, since it does not normally contain the IP address locations of a DNS server, answer a is incorrect. The /etc/host.conf file determines how your computer looks for an IP address. If the main entry in this file is **order bind, hosts,** your computer looks first to the DNS server as defined in /etc/resolv.conf to find the IP address of a desired computer. But since /etc/host.conf does not itself contain the location of a DNS server, answer b is also incorrect. The **nslookup** command is commonly used to test a connection to a DNS server. But since there is no /etc/nslookup.conf configuration file, answer d is also incorrect. For more information on DNS and related files, refer to Chapter 4.

Question 75

Answer b is correct. The Linux Documentation Project keeps an online repository of HOWTOs and Linux guides available online at **www.linuxdoc.org**. Although the man pages provide considerable information on commands and even a number of configuration files, they do not provide detailed instructions on Linux applications and services in the way done through the Linux Documentation Project. Therefore, answer a is not correct. Although Apache is covered in detail on the Apache home page at **httpd.apache.org**, this site does not address many other Linux services in appreciable detail. Therefore, answer c is also incorrect. Although the Linux newsgroups are a repository of helpful people, they are not the starting point in any research. Rarely are complete instructions provided on Linux newsgroups. Therefore, answer d is also incorrect. For more information on Linux resources and how they can help you troubleshoot a problem, refer to Chapter 14.

Question 76

Answer b is correct. The **lprm** command deletes print jobs from a queue based on the name of the printer and the print job number. Since the **lpq** command only finds the queue of print jobs, answer a is not correct. Although the **lpc** command can reorder print jobs in a queue based on their job numbers, it cannot delete any specific print job. Therefore, answer c is also incorrect. Since the **lpd** command starts the line print daemon that enables queues and other commands, it is a prerequisite to printing. However, this command cannot remove any specific print job. Therefore, answer d is also incorrect. For more information on the commands associated with **lpd**, refer to Chapter 12.

Question 77

Answer d is correct. The standard configuration file that locates standard Linux log files is /etc/syslog.conf. Although startup messages are stored in the /var/log/messages file, there are usually a number of other log files on every Linux computer. Therefore, answer a is incorrect. Hardware configuration information is organized in the /proc directory. Since this is not a Linux log file, at least not in the standard sense, answer b is also incorrect. The /etc/inittab file configures Linux at various run levels. It is not related to log files. Therefore, answer c is also incorrect. For more information on basic log files, see Chapter 5.

Question 78

Answer b is correct. For problems where a server stops working, you're interested in the load from each process. The **ps aux** command includes the percentage of available RAM and CPU used by each process. Chances are good that the offending process is using some large percentage of either your RAM or CPU. The double right arrow (>>) appends data from the command on its left to the file on its right. Since /var/log/messages relate to boot messages, this file doesn't record what happens when a Linux server stops working. Therefore, answer a is not correct. The **dmesg** command includes messages similar to what you can already find from /var/log/messages. Therefore, answer c is also not correct. A problem like the one in the question is most probably not a problem with the kernel. If it is a problem with the kernel, the recorded output from the **ps aux** command would provide clues. Therefore, answer d is also not correct. For more information on setting up jobs with **crontab**, refer to Chapter 13.

Question 79

Answer c is correct. The immutable flag prevents the deletion of a file by any user, even the **root** or superuser. You can set the immutable flag with the **chattr +i** *filename* command. Since the superuser has full **root** user privileges, answer a is not correct. Since the **root** user cannot delete a file where the immutable flag is set, user **tr** cannot delete this file either. Therefore, answer b is also incorrect. Although it is a common practice in many Linux distributions to set an alias of **rm**='rm -i', that action simply prompts the user to confirm deletion of a given file. Since it does not prevent the superuser from deleting that file, answer d is also incorrect. For more information on immutable files, see Chapter 11.

Question 80

Answer c is correct. When you use the **ifconfig** command to assign an IRQ port and I/O address to a network card, the order of information is important. The first item is the card name, eth2, which corresponds to the third Ethernet card on this computer. The next item is the IRQ port, followed by the I/O address. Since IRQ numbers on a standard PC are between 0 and 15, answer a is not correct. Since the order of information in answer b is also reversed, that answer is also incorrect. Since the name of the network card (eth2) is in the wrong location, answer d is also incorrect. For more information on using **ifconfig** to assign IRQ ports and I/O addresses to a network card, see Chapter 9.

Question 81

Answer c is correct. The data in the figure indicates that the CPU is overclocked, or made to run beyond its rated capacity. When a CPU is overclocked, it means additional power is sent through the CPU, which increases heat. If a CPU becomes hot enough, it stops working, which leads to a system crash. After the CPU has a chance to cool down, the computer can start working again, which matches the criteria of the question. An overclocked CPU need not be the wrong CPU. In fact, moderate overclocking does not have to exceed the capabilities of this particular motherboard. Therefore, answer a is not correct. The only listed component running above rated capacity is the CPU. There is no information in this regard on other components on this computer. Therefore, you do not know if the other components are overloaded. Therefore, answer b is also incorrect. Since the /proc/cpuinfo file lists a CPU speed about 20 percent above the rated capacity, you have confirmation that this does provide information to help solve the listed problem. Therefore, answer d is also not correct. For more information on CPU and related hardware issues, refer to Chapter 9.

Question 82

Answer b is correct. The /sbin directory contains many system administration commands and should not be configured on a separate partition. Although Linux swap space can be configured in a file, it is best to set it up in its own partition. Therefore, answer a is incorrect. Since you may want to limit the space allocated to individual users' home directories, it is appropriate to configure /home on a separate partition. Therefore, answer c is also incorrect. Since you may want to limit the space allocated to potentially huge log files, it is appropriate to configure /var on a separate partition. Therefore, answer d is also incorrect. For more information on these directories and their relationship to the Filesystem Hierarchy Standard, see Chapter 4.

Question 83

Answer b is most correct. When you pipe (|) the output from **ps aux** to **grep httpd**, the **grep** command *filters* the **ps aux** output for any occurrence of the text string "httpd", then returns each line with this string as output. Since the daemon associated with Apache is **httpd**, not **apached**, answer a is not correct. Although the **ps aux | less** command would allow you to use the Page Up and Page Down keys, or even **vi** commands to search through the output, that is not as efficient as having the lines with "httpd" directly available in the output. Therefore, answer c is also incorrect. The **ps aux | more httpd** command does not eyen do as well as **ps aux | less**. The output is piped (|) to the **more** command. After the output is complete, the shell tries to execute the **httpd** command. Since that does not help you search for the process lines associated with "httpd", answer d is also incorrect. For more information on **ps** and **grep**, see Chapter 8.

Question 84

Answer d is correct. The /etc directory contains most Linux configuration files, including those related to passwords (/etc/passwd), startup configuration (/etc/inittab), mounted directories (/etc/fstab), and more. Since the /bin directory contains basic command-line utilities such as **chown, echo, gzip, ping,** and **tar,** it is not an appropriate location for configuration files. Therefore, answer a is not correct. Since the /sbin directory contains administrative commands such as **fdisk, fsck, init, lilo,** and **modprobe,** it is also not a suitable location for configuration files. Therefore, answer b is also not correct. The /home directory contains the home directory for each user. As these directories are usually not accessible to others, they are generally not a suitable location for configuration files. Therefore, answer c is also not correct. For more information on commands, directories, and how they fit in the Filesystem Hierarchy Standard, refer to Chapter 4.

Question 85

Answer a is correct. Linux can install the driver modules associated with a PCMCIA network card if loadable modules are enabled. Since PCMCIA cards are not USB cards, answers b, c, and d do not address the question and are therefore all incorrect. For more information on loadable modules, refer to Chapter 9.

Question 86

Answer b is correct. The **arp** command, which uses the TCP/IP Address Resolution Protocol, matches the MAC address of a specific hardware card with an IP address. Since the **nslookup** command looks to a DNS server for the IP address of a specific Web site, it does not give you information on the MAC address associated with that Web site. Therefore, answer a is not correct. Although the **ifconfig** command does give you the MAC and IP addresses of a specific network card, answer c lists **ipconfig,** which is not a real command. Therefore, answer c is incorrect. Since there is no **macd** command, answer d is also incorrect. For more information on these commands, see Chapters 4 and 9.

Question 87

Answer a is correct. One reason to upgrade from a version 2.2 kernel to a version 2.4 kernel is to enable loadable modules, which automatically install the appropriate drivers for many hardware components. Users can install their own driver modules with the **insmod** command on either type of kernel. Since it is appropriate to upgrade or patch a kernel to address a security issue, answer b is incorrect.

Since it is appropriate to upgrade or patch a kernel to enable support for journaling file systems such as ReiserFS, ext3, or XFS, answer c is also incorrect. Since nearly full USB support was introduced with kernel version 2.4, it is appropriate to upgrade the kernel for this purpose. Therefore, answer d is also incorrect. For more information on when to upgrade or patch a kernel, refer to Chapter 2.

Question 88

Answer c is correct. The 50 sockets or pins shown on the connector correspond to a regular SCSI connector. Since floppy controller cables include 34 wires, answer a is not correct. Since IDE controller cables include 40 wires, answer b is also not correct. Since Wide SCSI controller cables include 68 wires, answer d is also not correct. For more information on controller cables, see Chapter 3.

Question 89

Answer d is correct. Linux keeps a significant amount of data in RAM. Even after saving a file to a disk, that file isn't written to that disk until your computer is less busy processing other data. When you press the On-Off switch on your computer, that wipes the data currently in RAM. Depending on the configuration in your /etc/inittab file, the **Ctrl+Alt+Del** command typically reboots your computer. Although you should generally deactivate this command in /etc/inittab, that file normally shows a link between that command and a **shutdown** command. The **shutdown** command first writes data currently in RAM to your disks. Therefore, answers a and b are both incorrect. The **umount /mnt/floppy** command first writes any data from RAM that is earmarked for your floppy and then unmounts the floppy drive from Linux. No data is lost as a result of this command; therefore, answer c is also not correct. For more information on these commands and their effects, refer to Chapter 13.

Question 90

Answer c is correct. The Network Information Service (NIS) is used to create a single database of usernames and passwords on a network with Linux computers. It also works if the network includes computers that are running other Unix-style operating systems such as Solaris or FreeBSD. Although the Network File System (NFS) is required to support NIS, NFS does not itself affect the database of usernames and passwords for the network. Therefore, answer a is not correct. Although NIS was originally known as the "yellow pages," there is no associated **ypd** daemon, at least in later versions of Linux. Therefore, answer b is also incorrect. Samba is the service that allows network communication between Linux and Microsoft Windows and/or IBM computers. Although it can affect the database of usernames and passwords for the network, it does not use **ypbind**. Therefore, answer d is also incorrect. For more information about the Network Information Service, refer to Chapter 5.

Question 91

Answer c is correct. You want to set the user ID bit, also known as the SUID bit, to allow other users on your system to execute the **/usr/sbin/hours** program. The **u+s** switch is required to make this happen. Even though the /usr/sbin directory is in the **PATH** for most users, you still need to specify the full path when changing permissions with commands such as **chmod**. Therefore, answer a is not correct. Since the **u-s** switch removes any existing SUID bit, answer b is also incorrect. The **g+s** switch sets the SGID bit, which gives all users permissions equal to those of the group owner of the **/usr/sbin/hours** program. Since this program is set up to execute only for user **tr**, this command does not provide access for other users; therefore, answer d is also incorrect. For more information on SUID and SGID bits, see Chapter 11.

Question 92

Answer c is correct. The **fsck** command checks and realigns the inodes that allow Linux to find each of your files. As shown in the excerpt from /etc/fstab, both systems are formatted to the third extended file system (ext3). The best way to set up **fsck** is by checking the devices associated with a specific partition. Since ext2 is the wrong file system for both partitions, answers a and b are both incorrect. Since the -t switch requires you to specify a file system, answer d is also incorrect. For more information on the use of the **fsck** command, refer to Chapter 13.

Question 93

Answer b is correct. The network communication service most well-suited to Linux and Unix computers is NFS, which is the Network File System. Although it is possible to install Linux from files on a Web server, it is less efficient than NFS on Linux computers. In addition, HTTP installation is an option available only on some Linux distributions; even when available, it won't install Linux simultaneously on multiple computers. Therefore, answer a is incorrect. NIS, which is the Network Information System, is not a protocol for transferring files. Therefore, answer c is not correct. Although it is possible to install Linux from files on an FTP server, it is less efficient than NFS on Linux computers and also won't install Linux simultaneously on multiple computers. Therefore, answer d is also incorrect. For more information on these services, refer to Chapter 5.

Question 94

Answer b is correct. The first process on a Linux computer is **init**, which has a PID number, or process identifier, of 1. Although single user mode corresponds to run level 1 on most Linux distributions, this is different from the first process. Therefore, answer a is not correct. The vmlinuz file in the boot directory usually corresponds to the Linux kernel that is loaded. Although this is loaded before **init** is run, it comes before any processes are started. Therefore, answer c is also incorrect. Although the first thing your computer sees from Linux when it boots is information from /etc/lilo.conf in the Master Boot Record (MBR), that is not the first process in the Linux operating system either. Therefore, answer d is also incorrect. For more information on **init** and associated processes, refer to Chapter 8.

Appendix
GNU General Public License

Version 2, June 1991

Copyright (C) 1989, 1991 Free Software Foundation, Inc.

59 Temple Place, Suite 330, Boston, MA 02111-1307 USA

Everyone is permitted to copy and distribute verbatim copies of this license document, but changing it is not allowed.

Preamble

The licenses for most software are designed to take away your freedom to share and change it. By contrast, the GNU General Public License is intended to guarantee your freedom to share and change free software—to make sure the software is free for all its users. This General Public License applies to most of the Free Software Foundation's software, and to any other program whose authors commit to using it. (Some other Free Software Foundation software is covered by the GNU Library General Public License instead.) You can apply it to your programs, too.

When we speak of free software, we are referring to freedom, not price. Our General Public Licenses are designed to make sure that you have the freedom to distribute copies of free software (and charge for this service if you wish), that you receive source code or can get it if you want it, that you can change the software or use pieces of it in new free programs; and that you know you can do these things.

To protect your rights, we need to make restrictions that forbid anyone to deny you these rights or to ask you to surrender the rights. These restrictions translate to certain responsibilities for you if you distribute copies of the software, or if you modify it.

For example, if you distribute copies of such a program, whether gratis or for a fee, you must give the recipients all the rights that you have. You must make sure that they, too, receive or can get the source code. And you must show them these terms so they know their rights.

We protect your rights with two steps: (1) copyright the software, and (2) offer you this license which gives you legal permission to copy, distribute and/or modify the software.

Also, for each author's protection and ours, we want to make certain that everyone understands that there is no warranty for this free software. If the software is modified by someone else and passed on, we want its recipients to know that what they have is not the original, so that any problems introduced by others will not reflect on the original authors' reputations.

Finally, any free program is threatened constantly by software patents. We wish to avoid the danger that redistributors of a free program will individually obtain patent licenses, in effect making the program proprietary. To prevent this, we have made it clear that any patent must be licensed for everyone's free use or not licensed at all.

The precise terms and conditions for copying, distribution and modification follow.

Terms and Conditions for Copying, Distribution, and Modification

This License applies to any program or other work, which contains a notice placed by the copyright holder saying it may be distributed under the terms of this General Public License. The "Program," below, refers to any such program or work, and a "work based on the Program" means either the Program or any derivative work under copyright law: that is to say, a work containing the Program or a portion of it, either verbatim or with modifications and/or translated into another language. (Hereinafter, translation is included without limitation in the term "modification".) Each licensee is addressed as "you."

Activities other than copying, distribution and modification are not covered by this License; they are outside its scope. The act of running the Program is not restricted, and the output from the Program is covered only if its contents constitute a work based on the Program (independent of having been made by running the Program). Whether that is true depends on what the Program does.

1. You may copy and distribute verbatim copies of the Program's source code as you receive it, in any medium, provided that you conspicuously and appropriately publish on each copy an appropriate copyright notice and disclaimer of warranty; keep intact all the notices that refer to this License and to the absence of any warranty; and give any other recipients of the Program a copy of this License along with the Program.

   You may charge a fee for the physical act of transferring a copy, and you may at your option offer warranty protection in exchange for a fee.

2. You may modify your copy or copies of the Program or any portion of it, thus forming a work based on the Program, and copy and distribute such modifications or work under the terms of Section 1 above, provided that you also meet all of these conditions:

   (a) You must cause the modified files to carry prominent notices stating that you changed the files and the date of any change.

   (b) You must cause any work that you distribute or publish, that in whole or in part contains or is derived from the Program or any part thereof, to be licensed as a whole at no charge to all third parties under the terms of this License.

   (c) If the modified program normally reads commands interactively when run, you must cause it, when started running for such interactive use in the most ordinary way, to print or display an announcement including an appropriate copyright notice and a notice that there is no warranty (or else, saying that you provide a warranty) and that users may redistribute the program under these conditions, and telling the user how to view a copy of this License. (Exception: if the Program itself is interactive but does not normally print such an announcement, your work based on the Program is not required to print an announcement.)

   These requirements apply to the modified work as a whole. If identifiable sections of that work are not derived from the Program, and can be reasonably considered independent and separate works in themselves, then this License, and its terms, do not apply to those sections when you distribute them as separate works. But when you distribute the same sections as part of a whole which is a work based on the Program, the distribution of the whole must be on the terms of this License, whose permissions for other licensees extend to the entire whole, and thus to each and every part regardless of who wrote it.

   Thus, it is not the intent of this section to claim rights or contest your rights to work written entirely by you; rather, the intent is to exercise the right to control the distribution of derivative or collective works based on the Program.

In addition, mere aggregation of another work not based on the Program with the Program (or with a work based on the Program) on a volume of a storage or distribution medium does not bring the other work under the scope of this License.

3. You may copy and distribute the Program (or a work based on it, under Section 2) in object code or executable form under the terms of Sections 1 and 2 above provided that you also do one of the following:

(a) Accompany it with the complete corresponding machine-readable source code, which must be distributed under the terms of Sections 1 and 2 above on a medium customarily used for software interchange; or,

(b) Accompany it with a written offer, valid for at least three years, to give any third party, for a charge no more than your cost of physically per- forming source distribution, a complete machine-readable copy of the corresponding source code, to be distributed under the terms of Sections 1 and 2 above on a medium customarily used for software interchange; or,

(c) Accompany it with the information you received as to the offer to dis- tribute corresponding source code. (This alternative is allowed only for noncommercial distribution and only if you received the program in ob- ject code or executable form with such an offer, in accord with Subsec- tion b above.)

The source code for a work means the preferred form of the work for making modifications to it. For an executable work, complete source code means all the source code for all modules it contains, plus any associated interface defi- nition files, plus the scripts used to control compilation and installation of the executable. However, as a special exception, the source code distributed need not include anything that is normally distributed (in either source or binary form) with the major components (compiler, kernel, and so on) of the operating system on which the executable runs, unless that component itself accompanies the executable.

If distribution of executable or object code is made by offering access to copy from a designated place, then offering equivalent access to copy the source code from the same place counts as distribution of the source code, even though third parties are not compelled to copy the source along with the object code.

4. You may not copy, modify, sublicense, or distribute the Program except as expressly provided under this License. Any attempt otherwise to copy, modify, sublicense or distribute the Program is void, and will automatically terminate your rights under this License. However, parties who have received copies, or rights, from you under this License will not have their licenses terminated so long as such parties remain in full compliance.

5. You are not required to accept this License, since you have not signed it. However, nothing else grants you permission to modify or distribute the Program or its derivative works. These actions are prohibited by law if you do not accept this License. Therefore, by modifying or distributing the Program (or any work based on the Program), you indicate your acceptance of this License to do so, and all its terms and conditions for copying, distributing or modifying the Program or works based on it.

6. Each time you redistribute the Program (or any work based on the Program), the recipient automatically receives a license from the original licensor to copy, distribute or modify the Program subject to these terms and conditions. You may not impose any further restrictions on the recipients' exercise of the rights granted herein. You are not responsible for enforcing compliance by third parties to this License.

7. If, as a consequence of a court judgment or allegation of patent infringement or for any other reason (not limited to patent issues), conditions are imposed on you (whether by court order, agreement or otherwise) that contradict the conditions of this License, they do not excuse you from the conditions of this License. If you cannot distribute so as to satisfy simultaneously your obligations under this License and any other pertinent obligations, then as a consequence you may not distribute the Program at all. For example, if a patent license would not permit royalty-free redistribution of the Program by all those who receive copies directly or indirectly through you, then the only way you could satisfy both it and this License would be to refrain entirely from distribution of the Program.

If any portion of this section is held invalid or unenforceable under any particular circumstance, the balance of the section is intended to apply and the section as a whole is intended to apply in other circumstances.

It is not the purpose of this section to induce you to infringe any patents or other property right claims or to contest validity of any such claims; this section has the sole purpose of protecting the integrity of the free software distribution system, which is implemented by public license practices. Many people have made generous contributions to the wide range of software distributed through that system in reliance on consistent application of that system; it is up to the author/donor to decide if he or she is willing to distribute software through any other system and a licensee cannot impose that choice.

This section is intended to make thoroughly clear what is believed to be a consequence of the rest of this License.

8. If the distribution and/or use of the Program is restricted in certain countries either by patents or by copyrighted interfaces, the original copyright holder who places the Program under this License may add an explicit geographical distribution limitation excluding those countries, so that distribution is permitted only in or among countries not thus excluded. In such case, this License incorporates the limitation as if written in the body of this License.

9. The Free Software Foundation may publish revised and/or new versions of the General Public License from time to time. Such new versions will be similar in spirit to the present version, but may differ in detail to address new problems or concerns.

Each version is given a distinguishing version number. If the Program specifies a version number of this License which applies to it and "any later version", you have the option of following the terms and conditions either of that version or of any later version published by the Free Software Foundation. If the Program does not specify a version number of this License, you may choose any version ever published by the Free Software Foundation.

10. If you wish to incorporate parts of the Program into other free programs whose distribution conditions are different, write to the author to ask for permission. For software, which is copyrighted by the Free Software Foundation, write to the Free Software Foundation; we sometimes make exceptions for this. Our decision will be guided by the two goals of preserving the free status of all derivatives of our free software and of promoting the sharing and reuse of software generally.

No Warranty

11. BECAUSE THE PROGRAM IS LICENSED FREE OF CHARGE, THERE IS NO WARRANTY FOR THE PROGRAM, TO THE EXTENT PERMITTED BY APPLICABLE LAW. EXCEPT WHEN OTHERWISE STATED IN WRITING THE COPYRIGHT HOLDERS AND/OR OTHER PARTIES PROVIDE THE PROGRAM "AS IS" WITHOUT WARRANTY OF ANY KIND, EITHER EXPRESSED OR IMPLIED, INCLUDING, BUT NOT LIMITED TO, THE IMPLIED WARRANTIES OF MERCHANTABILITY AND FITNESS FOR A PARTICULAR PURPOSE. THE ENTIRE RISK AS TO THE QUALITY AND PERFORMANCE OF THE PROGRAM IS WITH

YOU. SHOULD THE PROGRAM PROVE DEFECTIVE, YOU AS-
SUME THE COST OF ALL NECESSARY SERVICING, REPAIR OR
CORRECTION.

12. IN NO EVENT UNLESS REQUIRED BY APPLICABLE LAW OR
AGREED TO IN WRITING WILL ANY COPYRIGHT HOLDER,
OR ANY OTHER PARTY WHO MAY MODIFY AND/OR REDIS-
TRIBUTE THE PROGRAM AS PERMITTED ABOVE, BE LIABLE
TO YOU FOR DAMAGES, INCLUDING ANY GENERAL, SPE-
CIAL, INCIDENTAL OR CONSEQUENTIAL DAMAGES ARISING
OUT OF THE USE OR INABILITY TO USE THE PROGRAM (IN-
CLUDING BUT NOT LIMITED TO LOSS OF DATA OR DATA
BEING RENDERED INACCURATE OR LOSSES SUSTAINED BY
YOU OR THIRD PARTIES OR A FAILURE OF THE PROGRAM
TO OPERATE WITH ANY OTHER PROGRAMS), EVEN IF SUCH
HOLDER OR OTHER PARTY HAS BEEN ADVISED OF THE POS-
SIBILITY OF SUCH DAMAGES.

How to Apply These Terms to Your New Programs

If you develop a new program, and you want it to be of the greatest possible use
to the public, the best way to achieve this is to make it free software which everyone can redistribute and change under these terms.

To do so, attach the following notices to the program. It is safest to attach them
to the start of each source file to most effectively convey the exclusion of warranty; and each file should have at least the "copyright" line and a pointer to
where the full notice is found.

```
<one line to give the program's name and
a brief idea of what it does.>
Copyright (C) 19yy  <name of author>

This program is free software; you can
redistribute it and/or modify it under the
terms of the GNU General Public License as
published by the Free Software Foundation;
either version 2 of the License, or
(at your option) any later version.

This program is distributed in the hope that
it will be useful, but WITHOUT ANY WARRANTY;
without even the implied warranty of
```

Also add information on how to contact you by electronic and paper mail.

If the program is interactive, make it output a short notice like this when it starts in an interactive mode:

```
Gnomovision version 69, Copyright (C) 19yy
name of author Gnomovision comes with
ABSOLUTELY NO WARRANTY; for details type
'show w'. This is free software, and you are
welcome to redistribute it under certain
conditions; type 'show c' for details.
```

The hypothetical commands 'show w' and 'show c' should show the appropriate parts of the General Public License. Of course, the commands you use may be called something other than 'show w' and 'show c'; they could even be mouse-clicks or menu items—whatever suits your program.

You should also get your employer (if you work as a programmer) or your school, if any, to sign a "copyright disclaimer" for the program, if necessary. Here is a sample; alter the names:

```
Yoyodyne, Inc., hereby disclaims all copyright
interest in the program 'Gnomovision'
(which makes passes at compilers) written
by James Hacker.

<signature of Ty Coon>, 1 April 1989
Ty Coon, President of Vice
```

This General Public License does not permit incorporating your program into proprietary programs. If your program is a subroutine library, you may consider it more useful to permit linking proprietary applications with the library. If this is what you want to do, use the GNU Library General Public License instead of this License.

Glossary

*

A wildcard character that represents zero or more alphanumeric characters. For example, if you were to run the **ls a*** command, you would see all files starting with the letter *a*. If you have a file named a, you would see this file in the listing as well.

.

Also known as the *dot*, this represents the current directory.

..

The double dot represents the parent of the current directory.

<

A redirection. The content from the term to the right of this arrow is redirected as standard input (stdin) to the file to the left of the arrow. Commonly used to input several terms or data from a file to a program.

>

A redirection. Standard output (stdout) from the term to the left of this arrow is redirected to the file to the right of the arrow. If the file already exists, it is overwritten.

>>

Redirect and append. Standard output (stdout) from the term to the left of this arrow is redirected to the end of the file listed to the right of the arrow. Does not overwrite the file to the right of the arrow.

&

When used after a program name, the ampersand (**&**) instructs your shell to run that program in the background.

?

A wildcard character that represents one alphanumeric character. For example, if you were to run the **ls a?** command, you would see all files with two characters starting with the letter *a*, such as a1, ab, a6, ax, and so on.

[]

Brackets. Used to define a range of search terms.

|

A pipe. Standard output (stdout) from the term or command to the left of the pipe is redirected as standard input to the term or command to the right of the pipe.

2>

Redirect standard error. Standard error (stderr) from the term to the left of the arrow is redirected to the file to the right of the arrow. If the file already exists, it is overwritten.

/

The root directory. This is the top directory in any Linux system.

/bin

The Linux directory with basic command-line utilities.

/boot

The Linux directory with startup utilities, often including the Linux kernel.

/dev

The Linux directory with device drivers.

/etc

The Linux directory with most basic configuration files.

/etc/crontab

The configuration file for the **cron** daemon.

/etc/fstab

The configuration file that lists volumes to be mounted during Linux boot and those that can be mounted after boot.

/etc/group

The file that lists all groups set up on your Linux computer. Passwords are either encrypted in this file or are marked with an *x*. In the latter case, passwords are encrypted in the /etc/gshadow configuration file.

/etc/hosts

The configuration file where you can associate computer names and IP addresses on your local network. This file is an alternative to DNS on smaller networks.

/etc/hosts.allow

The file where you can list the computers or the IP addresses allowed to send information through the local computer, usually for delivery on the connected local area network. *See also* **tcp wrappers**.

/etc/hosts.deny

The file where you can list the computers or the IP addresses not allowed to send information through the local computer, usually for the connected local area network. *See also* **tcp wrappers**.

/etc/inittab

The configuration file that specifies run levels as well as local and remote virtual consoles.

/etc/motd

The configuration file associated with the message of the day. The content is shown to all users when they log in.

/etc/passwd

The file that lists all users that are set up on your Linux computer. Passwords are either encrypted in this file or are marked with an *x*. In the latter case, passwords are encrypted in the /etc/shadow configuration file.

/etc/printcap
The configuration file for printers. Includes many print daemon parameters, including the print filter and print spool directory.

/etc/profile
A configuration file with variables for all users. Whether the variables are environment-wide or specific to one shell depends on your Linux distribution.

/etc/resolv.conf
The configuration file with the fully qualified domain names or IP addresses of your DNS servers.

/etc/skel
The directory with default configuration files for individual users. If you want to create a new user, you can copy the files from this directory to your new user's home directory.

/etc/sudoers
The configuration file that grants **root** permissions to specific users.

/etc/syslog.conf
The configuration file that specifies the location of various log files.

/etc/XF86Config
The main configuration file for the Linux X Window. Sometimes located at /etc/X11/XF86Config.

/home
The Linux directory that contains home directories for regular individual users.

/lib
The Linux directory that contains program libraries referenced by the Linux kernel and command-line utilities.

/mnt
The Linux directory that contains the directory used as a mount point for removable media, such as floppy or CD-ROM drives.

/opt
The Linux directory that is commonly used for third-party applications, such as WordPerfect or Applixware.

/proc
The virtual Linux directory that contains currently running kernel-related processes.

/root
The home directory for the **root** user for the local system. A subdirectory of the top-level root (/) directory.

/sbin
The Linux directory that contains many system administration commands.

/sbin/lilo
The command that incorporates information from the /etc/lilo.conf file in the Master Boot Record.

/tmp
The Linux directory commonly used for temporary files, such as downloads from the Internet.

/usr
A Linux directory with a number of smaller programs and applications.

/var
The Linux directory for variable data, such as print spools and log files.

A+
The CompTIA exam on hardware and operating system technologies. Many of the Linux+ hardware objectives are based on the A+ exam.

absolute path
The fully defined path to a file or directory in Linux, starting with the root directory.

Accelerated Graphics Port (AGP)
A specialized PCI port customized for fast transfer of data to and from a graphics card.

Address Resolution Protocol (ARP)
The TCP/IP protocol that associates hardware and IP addresses on a network card.

adduser
A command that partially automates the process of adding users in Linux.

alias
A Linux command used to designate a word that is equivalent to a Linux command. Commonly used to help MS-DOS users make the transition to Linux; one common alias command is **alias dir="ls -l"**. It also can be used to simplify access to longer commands, such as **alias pser="ps aux | grep httpd"**.

amd
The auto mount daemon, which automatically mounts configured devices such as floppy and CD drives.

Apache
The Linux Web server, also known as **httpd**.

append
A LILO configuration command used to assign IRQs and I/O addresses to peripherals, such as network cards.

application server
A centralized location, such as a Linux server, from which users can call up different applications, such as word processors and spreadsheets.

apsfilter
A package that includes all filters necessary to configure most printers on Linux.

arp
The command associated with the Address Resolution Protocol (ARP).

artistic license
Allows the original copyright holder to control public modifications by other developers. Similar to the GPL.

AT
The attention command for a modem. Used in several modem terminal utilities, including **minicom**.

ATA
AT Attachment. Related to ATAPI.

ATAPI
AT Attachment Packet Interface. The most common interface for CD-ROM drives. Also known as ATA.

authentication
Refers to any server or application that checks usernames and passwords.

bash

Bourne Again SHell. Possibly the most common shell in use in Linux.

basic input/output system (BIOS)

The first program that runs when you start your computer. It initializes your hardware and starts the process of booting. You can customize this process in the BIOS menu. The custom settings are saved in the CMOS.

bg

A command that resumes suspended programs in the background of the command-line interface. You can suspend a program with the **Ctrl+Z** command and then resume it in the background with the **bg** command. After you run this command, you get a command-line interface that allows you to run another program.

binary

The compiled form of a package is known as a *binary* because it is in binary code, the 1s and 0s of computer communication.

BIND

A computer with a database of names and IP addresses. Also known as the *Domain Name Service (DNS) server* or a *nameserver*.

BIOS

See basic input/output system.

BNC

The connector for the coaxial cables most closely associated with Thinnet.

boot disk

Generally used to refer to a floppy disk that helps you boot Linux. A boot disk may not contain the location of your root directory. In that case, use the **linux root=/dev/hda**x command at the LILO **Boot:** prompt where *x* is a number that identifies the partition with the root (/) directory. Some boot disks are specially configured to start the Linux installation process.

broadcast address

The network address used to send messages to every computer on a LAN. On a TCP/IP network, the broadcast address is the last address in the range for the LAN. For example, if the network address is **192.168.12.0** and the network mask is **255.255.255.0**, the broadcast address for that network is **192.168.12.255**.

bus

A communications channel inside a computer. PC buses are dedicated to PCI cards and ISA cards as well as RAM.

cache

Information stored locally for faster retrieval.

cat

The concatenate command sends the contents of a file to your standard output, usually the screen. Similar to the MS-DOS **type** command.

cd

The Linux change directory command.

chap-secrets

A file with authentication information for connecting to servers that verifies passwords using the Challenge Handshake Authentication Protocol (CHAP).

chat
The utility that allows Linux to communicate with a modem through **pppd**.

chattr
The command that allows you to set or unset the *immutable* flag. **chattr +i** *filename* sets the flag; **chattr -i** *filename* unsets the flag.

chgrp
The command to reassign the group associated with a file or directory.

chmod
The command to change the permissions associated with a file or directory.

chown
The command to reassign the ownership of a file or directory.

CLI
See command-line interface.

client/server
A relationship between computers on a LAN, where client computers have their own independent CPUs and hard drives. Client computers get services such as files, print access, and Web service from one or more server computers.

closed source
Any software for which the source code is not available to the general public.

CMOS Settings
See Complementary Metal Oxide Semiconductor (CMOS) settings.

COM
Serial communications port. The four standard COM ports are COM1, COM2, COM3, and COM4.

command completion
In a Linux shell, this is the ability to complete partial commands with the Tab key.

command-line interface (CLI)
The operating system interface that you control with text-based commands.

command mode
The mode in the **vi** editor in which you can enter normal navigation and editing commands.

Common Internet File System (CIFS)
See Samba.

Complementary Metal Oxide Semiconductor (CMOS) settings
The settings associated with the BIOS. Although the BIOS memory is always available, if there is no power from the computer battery, CMOS settings are lost.

core dump
A snapshot of your RAM when an application crashes. Used by developers to help diagnose problems.

cp
The Linux copy command.

CPU
Central processing unit. The main processing engine in a personal computer.

cracker
A user who tries to break into computer systems for malicious reasons.

cron

The command that runs scheduled jobs. In some Linux distributions, this is also the daemon.

crond

The **cron** daemon for some Linux distributions.

crontab

The command that allows you to edit your own **cron** files. *See* /etc/crontab for a typical **cron** file.

daemon

Any program resident in your RAM that watches for signals to go into action. For example, a network daemon such as **httpd** (Apache) watches for a request for a Web page before it moves into action.

dd

Device dump. This command is used to unpack images to other directories and is especially suited for floppy disks.

Denial of Service (DoS)

An attack in which a flood of messages such as a **ping** is sent to a server such as an Apache Web server. The number or size of the messages is so high that it stops access to the associated Web site. One common DoS attack is associated with a Perl-based script that sends messages to a Web server without completing the connection.

df

The disk free space command, which summarizes used and free disk space on each mounted volume.

DHCP

Dynamic Host Configuration Protocol. You can use a DHCP server to ration or assign IP addresses on your network.

dhcpcd

The command used to test a DHCP server. *See also* **pump**.

diff

A command that lists the differences between two text files, line by line.

Disk Druid

The Red Hat Linux partition-management utility.

diskless workstation

A network computer without independent storage such as a hard disk. Older computers can be set up as Linux diskless workstations for use as terminals or routers.

distribution

A Linux distribution is an integrated collection of software packages, which usually includes a customized installation program.

DMA

direct memory address. For peripherals with independent processing capability that can bypass your CPU.

dmesg

The Linux command that recites the messages associated with booting Linux on your computer, including installed hardware and daemons.

DNS

See Domain Name Service.

DocumentRoot

An Apache variable that is set to the root directory for Apache HTML files.

domain

A group of computers administered as a single unit. The computers in a local area network are commonly organized in a domain.

domain name

The name associated with a specific network. Examples of domain names on the Internet are **CompTIA.org**, **Linux.net, Coriolis.com**, and **mommabears.com**.

Domain Name Service (DNS)

A system that translates domain names such as **Coriolis.com** to IP addresses such as **38.187.128.10**. Usually set up as a database on a server. Sometimes also known as the Domain Name System.

driver

A Linux file that allows hardware to communicate with the kernel.

du

The disk usage command. Lists the files used in your current directory and subdirectories as well as their sizes.

dual boot

A configuration in which you have two accessible operating systems when you boot on one computer.

emacs

Also known as *GNU/emacs*. A text editor based on the LISP programming language.

enscript

A print filter that translates ASCII files for PostScript printers.

environment variable

A variable that remains constant when you move from shell to shell. You can find your environment variables with the **env** command.

Ethernet

A standard type of local area network with a maximum data transmission speed of 10Mbps. Variations on Ethernet are available for faster speeds: Fast Ethernet has a maximum data transmission speed of 100Mbps; Gigabit Ethernet has a maximum data transmission speed of 1,000Mbps.

execute mode

The mode in the **vi** editor in which you can execute shell commands. Start execute mode with the :! command.

export

When this command is applied to a shell variable, it makes that variable work for all shells.

ext2

The Linux second extended file system.

ext3

The Linux third extended file system.

extended partition

A partition designed to contain multiple logical drives. When you need more than four partitions, you can set up an extended partition, which can then be subdivided into multiple logical partitions.

Fast SCSI
A SCSI-2 standard with an 8-bit controlling bus, 50-pin cables, and a maximum data transfer speed of 10MBps.

Fast Wide SCSI
A SCSI-2 standard with a 16-bit controlling bus, 68-pin cables, and a maximum data transfer speed of 20MBps.

fdisk
A utility that sets up primary and extended partitions as well as logical drives on a hard disk. Different versions of fdisk are available for MS-DOS and Linux. The **fdisk /MBR** command overwrites your Master Boot Record for MS-DOS or Microsoft Windows operating systems.

FHS
See Filesystem Hierarchy Standard.

file
A Linux command that allows you to view the type of any specific file.

file server
A centralized location for sharing files, such as a Linux server.

File Transfer Protocol (FTP)
A protocol used to transfer files between two computers in a TCP/IP network.

Filesystem Hierarchy Standard (FHS)
The standard way to store files on different directories on Linux, Unix, and related operating systems.

find
A command that allows you to search through different directories for a specific file.

fips
See First Interactive Partition Splitter (fips).

firewall
A computer between your network and another network such as the Internet. A firewall is designed to protect a network from the ravages of crackers who might try to break into your network.

First Interactive Partition Splitter (fips)
The Linux utility that you run in MS-DOS to divide active partitions without deleting data.

free software
Any software that is distributed without charge. Both GPL and open-source software are free software in accordance with the limits as stated in the respective licenses. Both GPL and open-source software are subsets of free software; in other words, not all free software is governed by the GPL or the Open Source Initiative.

Free Software Foundation (FSF)
The Free Software Foundation (FSF) is the group behind the GNU components of Linux. According to its Web site, the FSF is "dedicated to eliminating restrictions on copying, redistribution, understanding, and modification of computer programs." Because the FSF's work makes up most of the Linux operating system, it refers to the operating system discussed in this book as "GNU/Linux."

freeware

A software license that does not allow modification. More restrictive than the GPL.

fsck

A command used to check and repair a Linux file system.

FTP

See File Transfer Protocol (FTP).

fully qualified domain name (FQDN)

A name that uniquely identifies your computer, consisting of its hostname and the domain name of your network. For example, if your computer's hostname is **linux** and the domain name of your network is **mommabears.com**, your fully qualified domain name is **linux.mommabears.com**.

gateway

The name given to a computer or device that transfers messages between networks. To reach other networks, you need to configure your computer with the IP address of your gateway, which is also known as the *gateway address*.

gateway address

The IP address of a computer on a LAN that is also directly connected to another network.

General Public License (GPL)

A copyright for free software, which requires a release with source code and prevents others from modifying or re-releasing the software under any license other than the GPL.

getty

Another name for a console or a login port.

ghostscript

A print filter for PostScript files.

GNOME

The GNU Network Object Model Environment (GNOME) is one of the two most popular Linux GUI desktop environments.

GNU

GNU's Not Unix. Symbolizes the work of the FSF for programs and applications that clone the functionality of Unix.

GNU enscript

A GNU clone of the commercial enscript filter.

Gopher

An older system for displaying files over the Internet.

graphical user interface (GUI)

An interface that uses the graphical capabilities of your computer and monitor to create a visual interface for your programs.

graphics mode

The graphical resolution that you set on your video card for display on your monitor.

grep

A command to search through a file for a text string. Outputs any matching line.

group

Every user in Linux belongs to one or more groups. You can assign common permissions on a file or directory to the members of a specific group.

grpconv
The command that encrypts passwords from /etc/group to /etc/gshadow. Part of the Shadow Password Suite.

grpunconv
The command that unencrypts passwords from /etc/gshadow to /etc/group. Part of the Shadow Password Suite.

GUI
See graphical user interface (GUI).

gunzip
A command that uncompresses a compressed file.

gzip
A command that compresses a file.

hacker
In the Linux world, hackers are good people who make, or *hack*, improvements for software.

halt
A command that shuts down Linux and stops your computer. Commonly associated with run level 0.

hardware address
The address assigned to a specific network card. Every network card created today is supposed to be built with a unique hardware address, which you can identify with the /sbin/ifconfig command. Hardware addresses are normally shown in hexadecimal notation. Also known as a *MAC address*.

Hardware Compatibility List (HCL)
A list of hardware components that work seamlessly with an application or one or more Linux distributions.

head
A command that gives you a view of the first few lines of a file.

help
A switch that you can use to find more information about the switches associated with a specific command. For example, if you want more information on the **ls** command, type **ls --help**.

history
A command that gives you a list of more recent previously used commands, in order.

home directory
The starting directory for every Linux user. For standard users, the home directory is /home/*username* (substitute the actual username for *username*). For the **root** user, the home directory is /root. Sometimes represented by the tilde (~); for example, users can run the **cd ~** command to navigate to their home directories.

hostname
A name given to a computer. In a TCP/IP network, each computer needs a unique hostname on that network. *See* fully qualified domain name.

hot-swappable hardware
Hardware that can be installed or removed while the computer is on. The hardware is often automatically

detected, and the appropriate drivers are installed or removed. Commonly associated with PCMCIA, USB, and IEEE 1394 hardware.

HOWTOs
Manuals associated with the Linux Documentation Project. HOWTOs for many Linux topics are available on the **www.linuxdoc.org** Web site.

HTML
HyperText Markup Language. The commands embedded in text files most commonly used to create Web pages.

httpd.conf
The main Apache configuration file.

hub
A device that connects the computers on a local area network (LAN).

I/O
Input/output address. Dedicated locations in your RAM for peripherals to store information while waiting for service from your CPU.

IDE
Integrated Drive Electronics. The most common standard for PC internal hard drives and CD drives in use today. *See also* ATA or ATAPI.

IEEE 1394
A type of peripheral. Also known by the trade names FireWire and iLink. Support for IEEE 1394 devices was incorporated into Linux starting with kernel 2.4.

ifconfig
A Linux command used to configure or check the status of network cards.

ifdown
A script that can deactivate a specified network card.

ifup
A script that can activate a specified network card.

immutable
A characteristic of a file that cannot be deleted, even by the **root** user. Can be set with the **chattr +i** *filename* command.

info
A utility that provides a structured way to look through different man pages.

init
The first program that starts when you start Linux. As a daemon, init starts other programs like your shell. It also watches for signals that might shut down your computer, such as a power failure signal from an Uninterruptible Power Supply (UPS).

initdefault
A command in the /etc/inittab file that specifies the default run level when you start Linux.

inode
An identifier associated with each Linux file.

input device
Used in the XF86Config configuration file for keyboard and mouse settings.

insert mode
The mode in the **vi** editor where you can insert text.

insmod
The Linux command that adds drivers to your system after Linux boots on your computer.

interactivity
In a Linux shell, this is the ability to reference the **HISTORY** of previously used commands.

internet
Two or more LANs connected together.

Internet
The worldwide group of networks, sometimes known (not quite accurately) as the World Wide Web.

IP address
A numeric address used for computers on a TCP/IP network. IP addresses are typically formatted as four numbers between 0 and 255 divided by dots.

ipchains
A firewall utility command commonly associated with Linux kernel 2.2. Can also be used on Linux systems with kernel 2.4.

iptables
A firewall utility command introduced with Linux kernel 2.4.

IPv4
IP version 4. The standard method of IP addressing used since the development of TCP/IP in the 1970s. An IPv4 address has 32 bits.

IPv6
IP version 6. The method of IP addressing that is being incorporated into the Internet today. IPv4 addresses work seamlessly in IPv6. An IPv6 address has 128 bits.

IRQ
Interrupt Request. There are typically 16 IRQ channels in a PC for different peripherals and devices to ask for service from your CPU.

ISA
Industry Standard Association. Also the name of a standard for peripherals that you install inside a computer.

iso9660
The standard format for CDs.

journaling file system
A file system that constantly updates data on the file structure. Although this occasionally reduces performance during regular operation, it minimizes the risks and recovery time after a disk crash.

KDE
The K Desktop Environment (KDE) is one of the two main available Linux GUI desktop environments.

kernel
The part of your operating system that translates commands from your programs to your hardware.

kickstart
The Red Hat utility associated with automated Linux installations on multiple computers.

kill
A command you can use to end a currently running program or process. You need the PID of the program or process in question.

killall

A command you can use to end a currently running program or process. You need to know the command that starts the program or process in question.

kppp

The KDE-based service for modem connections.

LAN

See local area network.

legacy hardware

Generally used to refer to hardware that does not have plug-and-play characteristics.

less

A command that allows you to view the contents of a file, one screen at a time. You can use the Page Up and Page Down keys on your keyboard to scroll through the subject file in either direction.

LILO

See Linux Loader.

lilo.conf

The LILO configuration file.

Linux Documentation Project

The project that maintains the main library of Linux information, including HOWTOs, book-length guides, manual (man) pages, and lists of FAQs (Frequently Asked Questions). You can find these documents on the **www.linuxdoc.org** Web site.

Linux Loader (LILO)

Used to boot the Linux kernel. The Linux Loader is normally stored in your hard disk's Master Boot Record (MBR).

LinuxConf

Red Hat's graphical administration utility.

ln

The link command. Creates a second file that is linked to the first. When you edit one linked file, the changes are also seen in the other file. When you run a file linked to a script or a program, Linux runs that script or program.

loadable modules

The drivers associated with Linux kernel 2.4 that automatically load and remove the drivers for some "hot-swappable" devices.

local area network (LAN)

A group of two or more computers connected together for data exchange.

locate

A command that searches through a database of files on your computer. This database may not reflect the latest changes that you've made to your system.

logical partition

A division of an extended partition set up as a volume. You can set up a Linux directory to mount on a logical partition.

Logical Unit Number (LUN)

See SCSI number.

login

A category of user mode programs. Associates a user's ID with a shell and other personalized settings.

login shell
The shell or command-line interpreter that starts by default when a user logs into a Linux account.

logrotate
The command that rotates the most recent log to another file name and then starts a new log. Usually included in a **cron** schedule.

lpc
The line printer control command allows you to manage communication between Linux and your printer.

lpd
The line printer daemon is an application resident in memory that awaits print-related commands.

lpq
The line printer query command returns your current print queue or the jobs that are currently waiting for other jobs to be completed on your printer.

lpr
The line printer request command is a print client that requests print service from the line printer daemon.

lprm
The line printer remove command allows you to remove jobs currently stored in your print queue.

LPT
Line print terminal, the 25-pin port most commonly associated with printers. Standard printer ports are LPT1 and LPT2.

ls
The command used to list the contents of a directory.

lsmod
The command that lists drivers currently loaded on your system.

lsof
A command that lists the files open by processes that are currently running in Linux.

MAC address
Also known as a Media Access Control address. *See* hardware address.

magic
A filter commonly used to detect different types of files and convert them for use by configured printers.

major.minor.patch
The standard format for Linux kernel release version numbers. Currently, Linux is on its second major release. "Minor" releases are also significant. An odd-numbered minor release of a kernel is beta software and is not suitable for production. The patch number reflects minor changes to the kernel.

man
The command that calls up manual pages. For example, if you want to see the manual page for the **cd** command, type **man cd**.

masquerading
The system by which a computer such as a router or proxy server represents another computer on a LAN.

Master Boot Record (MBR)

The first area read on your hard disk; it locates operating systems on your hard disk by their primary partition or logical drive.

master-slave

A relationship between computers on a network. A slave computer has little or no independent processing power and might not even have a hard drive. It gets access to the operating system and almost all applications through the master computer.

mkboot

A Debian Linux command that creates a rescue floppy disk.

mkbootdisk

A Red Hat Linux command that creates a rescue floppy disk.

mkdir

The Linux make directory command.

mkfs

A command used to build a Linux file system.

mkswap

The Linux command to build a swap partition.

modem

A device that allows you to connect to another computer or a network through a standard analog telephone line. Short for *mod*ulator-*dem*odulator, for the actions required to translate the 1s and 0s of computer communication to the sine waves of sound transmitted by regular telephones.

modprobe

The command that checks the status of current devices and drivers. If there are additional hardware devices associated with loadable modules, this command installs the associated drivers. If there are installed drivers that are no longer required because of the removal of some hardware, this command removes those drivers.

modules

Drivers that can be dynamically loaded to install a hardware device on Linux. *Loadable modules* were introduced in Linux kernel 2.4.

more

A command that allows you to view the contents of a file, one screen or page at a time.

mount

The Linux command that's required before you can access any storage device. For example, you can mount a CD-ROM on some Linux distributions with the **mount -t iso9660 /dev/cdrom /mnt/cdrom** command.

mount point

The directory where a certain partition or logical drive is to be mounted.

multitasking

The ability to run more than one program or process simultaneously.

multiterminal

The ability to access a single Linux computer from more than one terminal. The multiterminal characteristic of Linux enables multiple users to log on simultaneously.

multiuser
A run level at which more than one user can run programs in Linux at the same time.

mv
The Linux move command that effectively changes the name and possibly the location of a file.

nameserver
See BIND.

nenscript
A GNU clone of the commercial enscript filter.

netstat
A command that allows you to show the routing table or the status of current network connections.

Network+
The CompTIA exam on networking technologies. Some Network+ concepts are covered on the Linux+ exam.

network address
An IP address that defines the group of available IP addresses on a local area network.

Network File System (NFS)
The Network File System is the standard protocol to connect two or more Linux or Unix computers in a network.

Network Information System (NIS)
A central database for users and passwords on a Unix/Linux network.

network interface card (NIC)
A device that allows your computer to communicate directly on a network.

A NIC is different from a modem because it does not have to translate the 1s and 0s of computer communication to sound waves.

network mask
An IP address that helps you define a range of IP addresses on a single local area network. Also known as a *subnet mask* or a *netmask*.

NFS
See Network File System (NFS).

nfsd
The network file system daemon.

NIS
See Network Information System (NIS).

nslookup
A command used to check information from a DNS server.

open source
A method and a license for releasing software. Open source software is freely redistributed and includes the source code. Modifications to open source software must be made by "patch" to preserve the integrity of the original software. The open source license is not specific to any product.

Open Source Initiative (OSI)
A group started by Eric Raymond in 1998 to defend "free software." The OSI has its own license that is slightly less restrictive than the GPL. *See also* open source.

overclocking
The practice of running a CPU faster than the normal rated speed.

pap-secrets

A file that stores logon information for servers that verify passwords with the Password Authentication Protocol (PAP).

parity bit

A data bit that allows for error checking and sometimes error correction. Some types of RAM and some modem communication systems include a parity bit.

partition

A logical part of a hard drive.

password

The combination of letters and numbers that you use for a specific username. Passwords that consist of a random combination of numbers, uppercase letters, and lowercase letters are strongly encouraged.

patch

A unit of code, or programming instructions, that can be added to a command, program, or application to repair or upgrade its capabilities. A common means of upgrading a Linux kernel.

$PATH

A Linux variable that specifies the directories where Linux automatically looks for a command. If a directory is not located in your **$PATH** variable, you need to specify the absolute path to run a program or script from that directory.

PC card

See PCMCIA.

PCI

Peripheral Component Interconnect. A standard for peripherals that you can install inside your computer.

PCL

See Printer Control Language (PCL).

PCMCIA

Credit card–sized peripherals for PCMCIA standard slots. Developed by the Personal Computer Memory Card International Association. Also known as a *PC card*.

PID

Process identifier. If you want to kill a program, you need its PID. You can find PIDs with the appropriate **ps** command.

ping

The command that checks a network connection. Based on the packet internet groper.

pipe

A Linux command construct that uses the | (pipe) character, in which the standard output from one command is directed as standard input to a second command.

plug-and-play

The capability of a computer BIOS and/or operating system to automatically assign or configure communication channels with various components and peripherals.

port

A physical interface for connecting a hardware device, such as a printer, keyboard, or mouse. In Apache configuration, the TCP/IP channel used for communication with the Web site. The typical port for Apache is 80. To adapt a program or application for a different operating system. For example, XFS was ported from IRIX to Linux.

PostScript
The printer language developed by Adobe for communication with printers.

power-on self test (POST)
A series of hardware tests performed by your computer when you power it on.

PPID
Parent process identifier. You can sometimes kill a stubborn process by killing its parent, based on the PPID number, which you can find though the **ps l** command.

ppp-on
A standard script that can start a PPP connection through your modem.

primary partition
A partition that can include a Master Boot Record. You can set up a Linux directory to mount on a primary partition. Each hard disk can be configured with up to four primary partitions.

print queue
A list of current print jobs that includes their status and the order in which they will be processed.

print server
A computer directly connected to a printer that processes print requests from all computers on a network.

print spool
The directory associated with the files processed for a specific printer.

printconf
A Red Hat Linux printer configuration utility, introduced in Red Hat 7.1.

Printer Control Language (PCL)
The language developed by Hewlett-Packard for communication with printers.

ps
The process status command that shows currently running programs and utilities. Commands such as **ps aux** return all programs and daemons currently running on your Linux computer. It also outputs PIDs, which you can use to identify and kill programs of your choice.

PS/2
A port developed by IBM commonly used to connect a mouse or a keyboard to a PC.

pump
The Red Hat Linux command used to test a DHCP server. *See also* **dhcpcd**.

pwconv
The command that encrypts passwords from /etc/passwd to /etc/shadow. Part of the Shadow Password Suite.

pwd
The Linux command that returns your present working directory.

pwunconv
The command that unencrypts passwords from /etc/shadow to /etc/passwd. Part of the Shadow Password Suite.

Radius Modem Server

A server that receives and authenticates users who connect to a Linux server through a modem.

RAM

See random access memory.

random access memory (RAM)

The main dynamic memory inside your computer.

rawrite

An MS-DOS–based Linux utility. The **rawrite** utility is primarily used to unpack the files from Linux images, such as boot.img to a floppy disk.

Raymond, Eric

The founder of the Open Source Initiative, which is the group behind the open source license.

reboot

The **reboot** command halts current programs before rebooting your computer. Commonly associated with run level 6. When you run the **reboot** command, Linux initializes the halt run level (0) before restarting your computer.

recompile

The process associated with changing the settings on an existing kernel. The kernel is then reprocessed into binary format. For example, if you want to enable loadable modules in a Linux kernel, you recompile it.

redirection

Used in reference to standard input, standard output, or standard error. Any of these data streams can be redirected with various directional commands: >, >>, 2>, <.

ReiserFS

A fast journaling file system.

relative path

The path to a Linux file or directory that is relative to your current working directory.

rescue disk

A disk, usually a 1.44MB floppy, that you can use to boot your computer into Linux. When customized for a particular computer, a rescue disk specifies the partition with the root (/) directory.

RJ-45

The type of connector associated with a standard twisted-pair Ethernet cable. This is similar to a standard telephone jack (RJ-11), except it includes eight wires per cable.

rlogin

The "r" command that supports remote logins using clear-text authentication.

rm

The Linux remove command that deletes files. Depending on the switch you use, this command can also delete directories.

rmdir

The remove directory command. This command does not work if the directory you are trying to delete is not empty.

rmmod

The command that removes drivers currently loaded on your system.

route
A command that allows you to show or revise the routing table.

router
See gateway.

rp3
The GNOME-based service for telephone modem connections.

run level
A parameter defined in the /etc/inittab file that defines different processes and daemons. Different run levels are associated with different conditions in Linux, such as single or multiuser mode.

Samba
The network program that allows computers running Linux to communicate with computers running Microsoft or IBM operating systems. Uses the Server Message Block (SMB) protocol. Also known as the Common Internet File System (CIFS).

SaX
The S.u.S.E. X configuration tool.

ScriptAlias
The Apache variable associated with the directory with scripts, usually written as a CGI or an ASP script.

SCSI
Small Computer Systems Interface. A type of connector for disk drives and other peripherals.

SCSI-1
The first SCSI standard, with an 8-bit controlling bus, 50-pin cables, and a maximum data transfer speed of 5MBps.

SCSI-2
The second SCSI standard. For details, *see* Fast SCSI, Wide SCSI, and Fast Wide SCSI.

SCSI-3
The third SCSI standard. For details, *see* Ultra SCSI, Ultra Wide SCSI, and Ultra2 Wide SCSI.

SCSI number
The designator given to a SCSI device attached to a PC. Depending on whether there is an 8-bit or 16-bit SCSI bus, there are 8 or 16 SCSI numbers on a system. SCSI devices have a priority depending on their number: 7, 6, 5, 4, 3, 2, 1, 0, 15, 14, 13, 12, 11, 10, 9, 8. Sometimes also known as a *Logical Unit Number (LUN)*.

sendmail
The Linux-based mail transport agent, which allows you to set up mail servers.

serial device
Any hardware device that uses a serial port such as COM1 or COM2.

Server Message Block (SMB)
See Samba.

ServerName
The Apache variable associated with the name of a Web site such as **mommabears.com**.

services
Linux services are the applications that add functionality for other users, such as Apache, Squid, BIND, and Sendmail.

setserial

A command to find the serial port information associated with a device.

SGID

Set group ID bit. Associated with the **chmod g+s** *filename* command. Grants other users the same permissions as the group owner of the file.

shadow

The /etc/shadow file is the encrypted password file.

Shadow Password Suite

The set of files and commands associated with encrypted passwords in Linux, including **pwconv**, **pwunconv**, **grpconv**, **grpunconv**, /etc/shadow, and /etc/gshadow.

shareware

A limited version of freeware. Anyone who uses shareware for more than a limited period of time is required to pay a fee.

shell

A command interpreter. The most commonly known Linux shell is *bash*, which was developed from the original Unix Bourne shell.

shell script

A group of shell commands collected into a file. Scripts, like programs, are executable.

shell variable

A variable that may change from shell to shell.

shutdown

A command that shuts down Linux. Depending on the switch you use, this command can halt or reboot your computer.

single user mode

A run level at which only one user can run programs in Linux. Commonly associated with run level 1 or S. If you boot into single user mode, no login is required, and you have root privileges.

source code

The programming instructions and commands associated with a command, utility, or application.

Squid

A service with two purposes: It can work as a proxy for other computers on a LAN, or it can store commonly used information in a local cache for faster retrieval.

ssh

Secure shell. The set of commands that allow you to log in remotely, using encrypted authentication.

Stallman, Richard

The founder of the Free Software Foundation and the GNU General Public License (also known as *copyleft*).

standard error (stderr)

Error output from a Linux shell, usually to the monitor.

standard input (stdin)

Input to a Linux shell, usually from the keyboard.

standard output (stdout)

Output from a Linux shell, usually to the monitor.

Structured Query Language (SQL)

A database language.

subnet mask

See network mask.

sudo

The command associated with asserting root privileges based on information in the /etc/sudoers file.

SUID

Set user ID bit. Associated with the **chmod u+s** *filename* command. Grants other users the same permissions as the owner of the file.

SuperProbe

A command that detects key parts of your video controller.

superuser

When a regular user wants **root** privileges on a Linux computer, he can log on as a superuser with the **root** user's password. Also known as *sudo*.

swap partition

A volume on your hard disk that is set up for overflow from RAM. If the RAM in your computer is not sufficient, less-used information is moved to the swap partition.

system message logging

The process of collecting messages about one or more daemons.

tail

A command that gives you a view of the final few lines of a file.

tar

A command that collects (or extracts) a series of files into a one-file archive.

TCP/IP

A suite of protocols for network communication most commonly associated with the Internet.

tcp_wrappers

The package associated with regulating traffic to and from a network through a firewall through the /etc/hosts.allow and /etc/hosts.deny files.

tcpd

The TCP daemon.

telnet

An application available on many operating systems, including Linux and Microsoft Windows, that allows you to log in remotely to a Linux server.

TERM

An environment variable that determines the type of terminal communication. Common choices are **xterm**, for the GUI command-line interface window, and vt100, for the remote text connection.

terminator

A device that you install at the end of a chain of SCSI devices.

tftp

The command that starts a connection using the trivial file transfer protocol.

Thinnet

A type of Ethernet network that uses coaxial cables, which are physically similar to cable TV cables.

tin

The Internet newsreader.

token ring

A type of local area network in which only the computer with the "token" is allowed to communicate. Token ring–style networks are available at 10Mbps and 100Mbps.

top
This command lists the programs and utilities in order of their load on your system resources, especially CPU and RAM.

Torvalds, Linus
The main developer of the kernel at the core of the Linux operating system.

traceroute
A command that tracks the path taken by a message from your computer to the specified destination computer.

trn
The threaded read news Internet newsreader.

Trojan horse
A malicious program that is usually set up to look like a regular program or command.

twisted-pair
A reference to wires that are twisted together to minimize electromagnetic effects. Also the most common form of Ethernet networking.

Ultra SCSI
A SCSI-3 standard with an 8-bit controlling bus, 50-pin cables, and a maximum data transfer speed of 20MBps.

Ultra Wide SCSI
A SCSI-3 standard with a 16-bit controlling bus, 68-pin cables, and a maximum data transfer speed of 40MBps.

Ultra2 Wide SCSI
A SCSI-3 standard with a 16-bit controlling bus, 68-pin cables, and a maximum data transfer speed of 80MBps.

umask
The command used to set up default permissions for any files and directories that you subsequently create.

umount
This command unmounts any directory that you may have previously mounted.

Universal Serial Bus (USB)
A type of peripheral. Support for many USB devices, including the ability to "hot-swap," is included in Linux kernel 2.4.

Unix
The operating system developed in the late 1960s and early 1970s at AT&T's Bell Labs. The functional ancestor to Linux.

USB
See Universal Serial Bus (USB).

useradd
A command that automates the creation of users in Linux based on the defaults shown when you run the **useradd -D** command.

userdel
A command that deletes a specific user, including his home directory and entry in the /etc/passwd configuration file.

username
The name that you use at the login: prompt to access an account.

utilities

Commands used inside a shell.

vertical resolution

The number of horizontal lines shown on a monitor.

VFAT

Virtual File Allocation Table. A system used to format volumes to be read by Microsoft operating systems.

vi

A basic Linux text editor.

video controller

A computer card with independent processing capability that manages graphics for display on your monitor.

video memory

The memory on your computer that is dedicated to graphics. Usually resident on a video controller.

video RAM

See video memory.

video server

The type of video controller resident on your computer.

virtual console

See virtual terminal.

virtual display

Hidden GUI screens where you can open and store other applications.

virtual terminal

Every console where a user can log on to Linux, locally or remotely, is a virtual terminal.

vmlinuz

A common file name for the Linux kernel.

WAN

See wide area network.

Webmin

The Caldera all-in-one configuration tool.

wide area network (WAN)

Two or more geographically separate networks connected together.

Wide SCSI

A SCSI-2 standard with a 16-bit controlling bus, 68-pin cables, and a maximum data transfer speed of 10MBps.

wildcard

A character such as * or ? that can represent other characters.

winmodem

A modem that substitutes Microsoft Windows driver libraries for some modem hardware controllers.

X Login

A login at a GUI screen.

X Window

The Linux graphical user interface (GUI).

X11

Another name for the X Window.

Xconfigurator

The Red Hat GUI configuration tool.

xdm

The command that starts a GUI login screen.

xf86config

A text-based GUI configuration tool.

XF86Setup

The main GUI configuration tool from the XFree86 project.

XFree86

The group that creates Linux drivers for video adapters. It also creates and maintains the XF86Setup program, which is the main utility for configuring the Linux graphical user interface (GUI). Also, a command. When used with the -**config** switch, it can be used to configure some graphics systems.

XFS

A fast journaling file system, developed by Silicon Graphics originally for the 64-bit IRIX operating system. The largest allowable XFS file is 8,192 *petabytes*, or about 8,192,000,000GB. It is now available for Linux.

xterm

The standard command-line interface window inside the Linux GUI.

YaST

The S.u.S.E. Linux all-in-one configuration tool.

ypbind

The daemon that ensures NIS clients are properly connected to an NIS server on a LAN.

Index